ON SHATTERED GROUND

During the years of 1861–1865, Americans bore eloquent witness to a wrenching war that tore a nation apart. Through a selection of primary documents ranging from the familiar and essential to lesser-known accounts, *On Shattered Ground* places the reader on the bloody battlefields and anxious home fronts, and peels away the layers of romantic sentimentality and hardened views that have evolved in our national consciousness, giving a more immediate experience of a country in crisis.

In their own words, statesmen like Abraham Lincoln and Frederick Douglass; generals like Grant and Lee; artists such as Walt Whitman, Mark Twain, Herman Melville, Louisa May Alcott, and Ambrose Bierce; and ordinary citizens, slaves, and soldiers articulate the reality of an unfolding war in all its dread, uncertainty, horror, and hope.

The documents in this collection offer a moving mosaic in the hope that readers may form their own narrative of the American Civil War.

Roger Panetta is a Visiting Professor of History at Fordham University.

Eileen Panetta is an Associate Professor of English and American Literature at Iona College.

ON SHATTERED GROUND

A Civil War Mosiac
1861–1865

EDITED AND WITH AN INTRODUCTION BY

Roger Panetta & Eileen Panetta

SIGNET CLASSICS

SIGNET CLASSICS
Published by New American Library, a division of
Penguin Group (USA) Inc., 375 Hudson Street,
New York, New York 10014, USA
Penguin Group (Canada), 90 Eglinton Avenue East, Suite 700, Toronto,
Ontario M4P 2Y3, Canada (a division of Pearson Penguin Canada Inc.)
Penguin Books Ltd., 80 Strand, London WC2R 0RL, England
Penguin Ireland, 25 St. Stephen's Green, Dublin 2,
Ireland (a division of Penguin Books Ltd.)
Penguin Group (Australia), 250 Camberwell Road, Camberwell, Victoria 3124,
Australia (a division of Pearson Australia Group Pty. Ltd.)
Penguin Books India Pvt. Ltd., 11 Community Centre, Panchsheel Park,
New Delhi - 110 017, India
Penguin Group (NZ), 67 Apollo Drive, Rosedale, Auckland 0632,
New Zealand (a division of Pearson New Zealand Ltd.)
Penguin Books (South Africa) (Pty.) Ltd., 24 Sturdee Avenue,
Rosebank, Johannesburg 2196, South Africa

Penguin Books Ltd., Registered Offices:
80 Strand, London WC2R 0RL, England

Published by Signet Classics, an imprint of New American Library,
a division of Penguin Group (USA) Inc.

First Signet Classics Printing, November 2012
10 9 8 7 6 5 4 3 2 1

Printed in the United States of America

For our children,
Roger and Jeanine
Jane and Claire

Acknowledgments

We would like to express our appreciation to Tracy Bernstein for her support, patience, and guidance in completing this work, as well as to her assistant, Talia Platz, cover designer Mary Ellen O'Boyle, and the entire team at New American Library and Signet Classics.

We are also grateful to the Fordham University Library staff for graciously helping us locate, and for providing, Civil War materials.

Contents

1863

1864

1865

ON SHATTERED GROUND

INTRODUCTION

When Ulysses S. Grant accepted Robert E. Lee's surrender at Appomattox Courthouse in April of 1865, the bloody four-year Civil War effectively ended. At least the shooting and the dying stopped. Few could imagine that the end of hostility would not close the book on the War but serve as an ironic preamble to a long and contentious battle over its memory and meaning.

The Civil War has deep roots in American history; indeed some locate the War's origins in the founding moments of the nation, when the equality and freedom promised by the Declaration of Independence were challenged by the Constitution's equivocation on slavery and its delicate balancing of state and federal power. Over time the volatile issue of slavery would become entangled with the tension between local and national authority.

The Missouri Compromise of 1820 placed the slavery question in the national spotlight, allowing as it did the admission of one slave and one free state at a time and drawing a dividing line at latitude 36'30". These stopgap measures provided a fragile political design that forestalled the day of reckoning. Jefferson's apprehension, shared by many, that the Union was now in danger was vividly expressed in his claim that "we have the wolf by the ear, and we can neither hold him, nor safely let him go. Justice is in one scale, and self-preservation in the other"—a predicament that would haunt the politics of the antebellum period. The nineteenth-century American drive to fill the continent kept slavery entangled with politics and fostered organized efforts by abolitionists and apologists to attack and defend slavery, feeding the idea that we were divided into sections reflecting two distinct ways of life—Cavalier and Yankee.

The incendiary combination of slavery and territorial expansion inserted itself into the Mexican War and emerged as a full-blown national crisis in 1850. The political hangover from the war provoked new anxieties about the Union, which were resolved by a series of congressional actions known as the Compromise of 1850. The admission of California as a free state, which upset the slave state–free state equilibrium, was offset by the Fugitive Slave Act federally protecting the return of runaway slaves, a concession that opened the door to a passionate debate about the definitions of freedom and property. Other acts abolished the slave trade in the nation's capital and called for the status of slavery in the territories of Utah and New Mexico to be decided by popular sovereignty, a scheme that promised to attract the embattled forces of pro- and antislavery in an open public confrontation.

The political atmosphere was so charged that even these 1850 compromises, which drew on the political skills of Henry Clay, Daniel Webster, and John C. Calhoun and the residual affection for the Union, only served to exacerbate the situation. The Fugitive Slave Law convinced Northerners that there was a federal conspiracy to protect slavery, while Southerners rushed to Kansas to defend the territory against the influx of Northern antislavers. The issue was dramatized by Harriet Beecher Stowe's *Uncle Tom's Cabin* (1852), which framed the debate in vivid moral and religious terms. This bestselling novel transformed the political debate into a crusade using, as it did, Christian images and language understood by all Americans. Its visceral impact moved Northerners and Southerners to harden their positions and deepen their resolve.

The radical provisions of the 1850 Compromise began to fray as national attention turned to Kansas and Nebraska, both territories north of the 1820 Missouri divide at 36'30". On the heels of Stephen Douglass's 1854 enabling legislation, which provided for the self-determination of these two territories using the mechanism of popular sovereignty, communities north and south were galvanized and Kansas received an influx of money and settlers, Bibles and guns, expressing widespread suspicions of any political process.

Blood was in the air. Competing territorial governments in Lecompton and Topeka triggered proslavery violence in Lawrence and were in turn met by John Brown's murders at Pottawatomie Creek. Few doubted that lines were being drawn and fiercely defended. In May 1856, South Carolina congressman Preston Brooks, acting to uphold Southern honor, caned Massachusetts Senator Charles Sumner unconscious, spilling Northern blood on the floor of the Senate chamber. United States senators now began to arm themselves. The old political alignments broke down in this highly contentious and volatile atmosphere.

The last chance to allay the growing uncertainties through the law and the political process came with the Dred Scott case in 1857. Chief Justice Taney and the majority of the Court ruled that Scott, a slave, did not gain freedom by residing in a free state or territory; indeed he was not a citizen and had no legal standing. Not surprisingly, the Taney opinion placated the South and provoked the North. The decision and the sectional response exposed the intractability of the slavery issue, the polarization of the political parties, and, most tellingly, the loss of any middle ground friendly to debate and compromise. Lincoln's ominous conclusion in 1858 warned of what lay ahead:

> If we could first know where we are and whither we are tending, we could better judge what to do and how to do it. We are now far into the fifth year since a policy was initiated with the avowed object and confident promise of putting an end to slavery agitation. Under the operation of that policy, that agitation has not only not ceased but has constantly augmented. In my opinion, it will not cease until a crisis shall have been reached and passed. "A house divided against itself cannot stand." I believe this government cannot endure, permanently, half slave and half free.

If any public action were needed to demonstrate the loss of political will, John Brown's raid at Harpers Ferry in May of 1859 made that abundantly clear. The messianic Brown led an armed band of blacks and whites in an effort to capture and distribute federal arms to slaves and instigate a general uprising. His capture by Robert E. Lee, subsequent trial, and hanging provided the warring camps with a martyred hero and an Anti-Christ. The growing sense of plots and conspiracies north and south changed the political vocabulary of the day in which the words of political discourse were replaced by the language of suspicion and paranoia.

All now waited on the 1860 election.

Nothing better epitomizes the deep divisions within the country over the causes and meaning of the War than the lengthy list of terms used by the North and the South to name it. While the consensus term "Civil War" is most widely adopted in classrooms, in governmental organizations, and even among the general public, this neutral term may simply mask a quiet but persistent historical debate about the War. The list is wide ranging:

The War for Southern Independence
The Second American Revolution
The War for States' Rights
Mr. Lincoln's War
The Confederate War
The War of Secession
The Great Rebellion
The War Against Slavery
The War Between the States
The War of Northern Aggression
The War to Preserve the Union
The War for Southern Freedom
The War of the North and South
The Lost Cause

Over the years, each of these terms enjoyed a distinct moment of popularity when it was favored by historians, educators, and politicians as an expression of their interpretation of the War. While the meaning of each term is self-evident, their breadth and variety are a testament to the enduring contentiousness about the War.

For over one hundred fifty years, historians and citizens have debated the causes and consequences of the War. Anniversaries intensify these questions and generate new historical debates. From the fifty-year anniversary to the centennial and the sesquicentennial, we have imagined very different narratives. Nor have the spaces between these exercises in memory been fallow. Indeed the sixty thousand publications about the War testify to a primal fascination with and the enduring power of the event. However it's not just the scale of this outpouring; each generation takes its turn looking with new eyes and crafting a history that mirrors its own values and ways of thinking.

So in this period of the sesquicentennial, we look again, filled with all the concerns of our own time. We now see a wrenching and traumatic War, which tore asunder the national fabric. This present volume, *On Shattered Ground*, aims, through a selection of primary documents, to place the reader on the field of battle and on the anxious home front. Our goal is to help the reader peel away the layers of romantic overlay and hardened views; to feel and see the unfolding War in all its dread and uncertainty as well as high expectation. The Civil War shattered the ground on which the nation was built and not only severed the ties between North and South but, in the scope of its destruction, upended families, communities, racial assumptions, and even notions of life and death. Americans of the time were profoundly shocked by the War's length and deadliness; they suffered a trauma so wide ranging that it affected the conduct of the War and so deeply imbedded itself in the national psyche that we continue to struggle with healing and meaning.

Embattled Americans displayed a remarkable self-consciousness about the events of 1861–1865. They wrote letters, kept diaries, published journals, sang songs, composed poems, and read countless newspaper stories. The progress of the War was also widely documented in photographs and illustrations. This outpouring was not limited by age, gender, rank, or class. Americans intuited the historical significance of the moment and the importance of creating a durable memory. In addition to personal and journalistic accounts, there were countless biographies, histories, and specialized journals.

In compiling this anthology, we have tried for a balance of familiar and less well-known works, for perspectives both central to the flow of events and those peripheral or "off to the side," inviting the reader to take a second look at the Emancipation Proclamation or consider the impact of Willie Lincoln's death in the midst of national tragedy.

In the interest of breadth, collections like this run the risk of becoming encyclopedic. This volume includes fewer documents, some of which are of considerable length, inviting readers to immerse themselves more fully in a single experience, to feel the ground, whether Brokenburn plantation or Gettysburg village or Libby prison, under their feet.

Frederick Jackson Turner, the historian of the American frontier, believed that "each age writes the history of the past anew with reference to the conditions uppermost in its own time." To understand the truth of Jackson's observation, we need only compare the 1960 centennial and its vision of the causes and meaning of the War with the sesquicentennial's consensus, at least among historians, that slavery was the central, instigating and driving force. While this correction is welcome, the views of the general public are more varied and susceptible to the workings of the memory industry, whose outpouring of films, novels, documentaries, pageants, battle reenactments, memorials and historic sites have covered the War in a sentimental shroud.

Perhaps the most powerful contribution to the making of the popular War memory since *Gone With the Wind* is Ken Burns' nine-part PBS Civil War series, which was viewed by forty million Americans over five nights in September of 1990. No published history or film had commandeered such a large national audience or left such a powerful imprint on the public imagination. Critics rushed in with praise while many historians pointed to its intellectual flaws and limitations. Defenders applauded the emotional power and evocative images that brought the dark side of the War and the horrors of slavery to the forefront. The unmistakable beauty of the series and the smooth and easy-flowing narrative created a sense of fullness and completeness that was quickly challenged by academic historians. Did Burns eschew problematic analysis for the certainty of storytelling? Where were the voices of women and African-Americans? Did Burns do enough to dismantle the sentimentalist perspective of the glorious Lost Cause? Did he sufficiently probe the economic, political, and social impact of the War?

Perhaps of necessity, an approach like that of Burns is essential for a mass television audience. We hope to give the reader of this volume a chance to hear the voices of those who felt the impact of the War, to consider the words they spoke, and stand in the places where they stood. The documents in this collection constitute the pieces, large and small, major and minor, in a mosaic that when assembled by readers may create their own narrative of that time.

1861

The year 1861 really begins on November 6, 1860, with the election of the Republican candidate, Abraham Lincoln. A fractured political system with four sectional parties called into question the legitimacy of the results and made it possible for a candidate with a minority of the popular vote to win the presidency. While Lincoln's 1.8 million votes represented almost 40 percent of the votes cast, it made him a minority president with only a sectional constituency. In many ways the four-way election foreshadowed the shattering of the Union. In this limbo of the postelection period, secessionists labeled Lincoln the "black republican," an advocate of the end of slavery; they emphasized the immediacy of the danger, compelling them to act quickly and decisively. This shadow time provided a cover for innumerable rumors to gain public credence and deepened the politics of paranoia.

Lincoln's watchful waiting, a by-product of his political sensitivity and his recognition of the dangers of the moment, coincided with his powerlessness as president-elect. Within six weeks of the election, South Carolina had seceded. Six other states followed, and at a February meeting in Montgomery, Alabama, drafted a constitution that, while it shared much in common with the Federal Constitution, contained key restraints that would limit the powers of the new Confederacy, with eventual dire consequences. In March, ratification was greeted by Southerners with jubilation and a sense of liberation; everywhere in the region fire-eaters enjoyed an ecstatic moment. The North felt the sense of momentum was shifting and, while many politicians and newspaper writers considered the move mere puffery and bluff, a fearful inevitability was beginning to grip their imaginations.

In a final effort to contain the secessionist fallout, the Senate cobbled together the Crittenden Compromise, designed to placate the South and provide a cooling-off period. This last attempt at a political solution drew on a long history of compromise that had steered the Union through some of its most dangerous waters. The history of sectional disaffection was tethered to the workings of political bargaining, which always seemed to provide the gift of time, even convincing the nation that we had a special national talent for such negotiations. We debated and we compromised and the Union endured. The Senate rejected the Crittenden proposals in mid-January. This vote marked the end of national politics as it had been practiced for over half a century and reminded Americans of the tentative nature and uncertainty of the republican experiment. Debate, give-and-take, philosophical sparring provided no remedies. The differences between North and South had solidified and altered the capacity of American politics.

Lincoln appreciated the historical gravity of the moment. In his Inaugural Address on March 4, he recognized that it might be his last chance to stem the tide of secession. He reiterated his limited political objectives about slavery where it existed. He defended the perpetual character of the Union, thereby undercutting any expectation of peaceful separation. These reassurances were intended to counter Southern fears about the threat to the existing social order, but they would have a hard time getting a hearing in the midst of the secessionist din.

Lincoln probably recognized the futility of his reassurances; indeed, he understood that on the eve of war, all he could hope to do was to distinguish his position from that of the opposition and begin to set the historic record straight. War was coming, and he gave voice to the reasons for separation as he saw it.

In other words, the Inaugural Address aimed to place the responsibility for war on the South. Lincoln wanted the South to act first and feel the full weight of the deeply rooted mystic chords of memory that bound the nation. A respite might open the door for Union sentiment in the South to collect itself and contest the hold of the secessionists on Southern thinking.

Fort Sumter, a federal outpost in Charleston Harbor, became the center of the war of nerves. In the game of brinkmanship, Lincoln demonstrated the political acumen that would become the hallmark of his presidency. The debate within the cabinet on whether to reinforce or abandon Fort Sumter was an immediate test of his power and capabilities. He won support for a proposal to reprovision the garrison in a way that secured his primacy.

The South would be compelled to fire the first shot. That they did on April 12, 1861.

The attack on Sumter and its surrender on April 14, 1861, was greeted with euphoria in the South and a sense of inevitability in the North. Lincoln moved quickly and called for seventy-five thousand men, provoking the immediate secession of Virginia, Arkansas, North Carolina, and Tennessee. He then established a naval blockade of the Confederacy, skirting the legal implications of recognition implied in such an action and underlining the significance not only of the navy but of trade and commerce to the Southern economy. This action was not unrelated to the issue of international recognition, thus expanding the War to the high seas and laying the seeds for the Trent Affair, in which two Confederate diplomats were removed from a British vessel.

Control of the seas and especially the coastal waters of the Confederacy was part of General Winfield Scott's Anaconda Plan, which recognized the geographical breadth of the War and planned to squeeze the Confederacy from the East and West. For Scott the control of the Mississippi was decisive. But this would take time.

All expected a short and decisive war with little bloodshed, contained to local battlefields with no civil disruption. It was that hopeful if not fanciful premise that drew Washingtonians to Manassas, Virginia, to witness what they assumed would be a short military engagement worthy of an afternoon picnic. Early Union advances were quickly reversed and the Federals retreated to Washington in disarray, creating a panic in the capital. When the Confederates moved their capital from Montgomery to Richmond, they became a preoccupation for military planners and politicians who were now fixated on the strategic importance and symbolic value of the capital cities.

As the year ended, the hopes for a short war receded; now lack of preparation on both sides was evident. Lincoln warned of the danger of slipping into a remorseless revolutionary struggle. He now turned to General George McClellan—Little Mac—to organize the Army of the Potomac and take the War to the Confederacy.

South Carolina Ordinance of Secession

(1860)

After the election of Abraham Lincoln, South Carolina became the first state to secede from the Union. In Charleston on December 20, 1860, a convention unanimously passed the ordinance of secession, declaring South Carolina a free and independent country. South Carolina also adopted the Declaration of the Immediate Causes Which Induce and Justify the Secession of South Carolina from the Federal Union. All of the violations of Southern states' rights mentioned in the documents were about slavery. The people of Charleston went wild with joy amid fireworks, booming cannons, and ringing bells. Within six weeks, six other states in the Deep South followed South Carolina out of the Union. Although President Buchanan protested, no military response followed except a failed attempt to resupply Fort Sumter using the ship *Star of the West*, which was fired upon by South Carolina forces and turned back before it reached the fort.

An ordinance to dissolve the union between the State of South Carolina and other States united with her under the compact entitled "The Constitution of the United States of America."

We, the people of the State of South Carolina, in convention assembled, do declare and ordain, and it is hereby declared and ordained, That the ordinance adopted by us in convention on the twenty-third day of May, in the year of our Lord one thousand seven hundred and eighty-eight, whereby the Constitution of the United States of America was ratified, and also all acts and parts of acts of the General Assembly of this State ratifying amendments of the said Constitution, are hereby repealed; and that the union now subsisting between South Carolina and other States, under the name of the "United States of America," is hereby dissolved.

Done at Charleston the twentieth day of December, in the year of our Lord one thousand eight hundred and sixty.

Declaration of the Immediate Causes Which Induce and Justify the Secession of South Carolina from the Federal Union

The people of the State of South Carolina, in Convention assembled, on the 26th day of April, A.D., 1852, declared that the frequent violations of the Constitution of the United States, by the Federal Government, and its encroachments upon the reserved rights of the States, fully justified this State in then withdrawing from the Federal Union; but in deference to the opinions and wishes of the other slaveholding States, she forbore at that time to exercise this right. Since that time, these encroachments have continued to increase, and further forbearance ceases to be a virtue.

And now the State of South Carolina having resumed her separate and equal place among nations, deems it due to herself, to the remaining United States of America, and to the nations of the world, that she should declare the immediate causes which have led to this act. In the year 1765, that portion of the British Empire embracing Great Britain, undertook to make laws for the government of that portion composed of the thirteen American Colonies. A struggle for the right of self-government ensued, which resulted, on the 4th of July, 1776, in a Declaration, by the Colonies, that they are, and of right ought to be, FREE AND INDEPENDENT STATES; and that, as free and independent States, they have full power to levy war, conclude peace, contract alliances, establish commerce, and to do all other acts and things which independent States may of right do.

They further solemnly declared that whenever any form of government becomes destructive of the ends for which it was established, it is the right of the people to alter or abolish it, and to institute a new government. Deeming the Government of Great Britain to have become destructive of these ends, they declared that the Colonies are absolved from all allegiance to the British Crown, and that all political connection between them and the State of Great Britain is, and ought to be, totally dissolved.

In pursuance of this Declaration of Independence, each of the thirteen States proceeded to exercise its separate sovereignty; adopted for itself a Constitution, and appointed officers for the administration of government in all its departments—Legislative, Executive and Judicial. For purposes of defense, they united their arms and their counsels; and, in 1778, they entered into a League known as the Articles of Confederation, whereby they agreed to entrust the administration of their external relations to a common agent, known as the Congress of the United States, expressly declaring, in the first Article that each State retains its sovereignty, freedom and independence, and every power, jurisdiction and right which is not, by this Confederation, expressly delegated to the United States in Congress assembled. Under this Confederation the war of the Revolution was carried on, and on the 3rd of September, 1783, the contest ended, and a definite Treaty was signed by Great Britain, in which she acknowledged the independence of the Colonies in the following terms:

ARTICLE 1—His Britannic Majesty acknowledges the said United States, viz: New Hampshire, Massachusetts Bay, Rhode Island and Providence Plantations, Connecticut, New York, New Jersey, Pennsylvania, Delaware, Maryland, Virginia, North Carolina, South Carolina and Georgia, to be FREE, SOVEREIGN AND INDEPENDENT STATES; that he treats with them as such; and for himself, his heirs and successors, relinquishes all claims to the government, propriety and territorial rights of the same and every part thereof.

Thus were established the two great principles asserted by the Colonies, namely: the right of a State to govern itself; and the right of a people to abolish a Government when it becomes destructive of the ends for which it was instituted. And concurrent with the establishment of these principles, was the fact, that each Colony became and was recognized by the mother Country a FREE, SOVEREIGN AND INDEPENDENT STATE.

In 1787, Deputies were appointed by the States to revise the Articles of Confederation, and on 17th September, 1787, these Deputies recommended for the adoption of the States, the Articles of Union, known as the Constitution of the United States.

The parties to whom this Constitution was submitted, were the several sovereign States; they were to agree or disagree, and when nine of them agreed the compact was to take effect among those concurring; and the General Government, as the common agent, was then invested with their authority.

If only nine of the thirteen States had concurred, the other four would have remained as they then were—separate, sovereign States, independent of any of the provisions of the Constitution. In fact, two of the States did not accede to the Constitution until long after it had gone into operation among the other eleven; and during that interval, they each exercised the functions of an independent nation.

By this Constitution, certain duties were imposed upon the several States, and the exercise of certain of their powers was restrained, which necessarily implied their continued existence as sovereign States. But to remove all doubt, an amendment was added, which declared that the powers not delegated to the United States by the Constitution, nor prohibited by it to the States, are reserved to the States, respectively, or to the people. On the 23d May, 1788, South Carolina, by a Convention of her People, passed an Ordinance assenting to this Constitution, and afterwards altered her own Constitution, to conform herself to the obligations she had undertaken.

Thus was established, by compact between the States, a Government with definite objects and powers, limited to the express words of the grant. This limitation left the whole remaining mass of power subject to the clause reserving it to the States or to the people, and rendered unnecessary any specification of reserved rights.

We hold that the Government thus established is subject to the two great principles asserted in the Declaration of Independence; and we hold further, that the mode of its formation subjects it to a third fundamental principle, namely: the law of compact. We maintain that in every compact between two or more parties, the obligation is mutual; that the failure of one of the contracting parties to perform a material part of the agreement, entirely releases the obligation of the other; and that where no arbiter is provided, each party is remitted to his own judgment to determine the fact of failure, with all its consequences. In the present case, that fact is established with certainty. We assert that fourteen of the States have deliberately refused, for years past, to fulfill their constitutional obligations, and we refer to their own Statutes for the proof.

The Constitution of the United States, in its fourth Article, provides as follows: No person held to service or labor in one State, under the laws thereof, escaping into another, shall, in consequence of any law or regulation therein, be discharged from such service or labor, but shall be delivered up, on claim of the party to whom such service or labor may be due.

This stipulation was so material to the compact, that without it that compact would not have been made. The greater number of the contracting parties held slaves, and they had previously evinced their estimate of the value of such a stipulation by making it a condition in the Ordinance for the government of the territory ceded by Virginia, which now composes the States north of the Ohio River.

The same article of the Constitution stipulates also for rendition by the several States of fugitives from justice from the other States. The General Government, as the common agent, passed laws to carry into effect these stipulations of the States. For many years these laws were executed. But an increasing hostility on the part of the non-slaveholding States to the institution of slavery, has led to a disregard of their obligations, and the laws of the General Government have ceased to effect the objects of the Constitution. The States of Maine, New Hampshire, Vermont, Massachusetts, Connecticut, Rhode Island, New York, Pennsylvania, Illinois, Indiana, Michigan, Wisconsin and Iowa, have enacted laws which either nullify the Acts of Congress or render useless any attempt to execute them. In many of these States the fugitive is discharged from service or labor claimed, and in none of them has the State Government complied with the stipulation made in the Constitution. The State of New Jersey, at an early day, passed a law in conformity with her constitutional obligation; but the current of anti-slavery feeling has led her more recently to enact laws which render inoperative the remedies provided by her own law and by the laws of Congress. In the State of New York even the right of transit for a slave has been denied by her tribunals; and the States of Ohio and Iowa have refused to surrender to justice fugitives charged with murder, and with inciting servile insurrection in the State of Virginia. Thus the constituted compact has been deliberately broken and disregarded by the non-slaveholding States, and the consequence follows that South Carolina is released from her obligation.

The ends for which the Constitution was framed are declared

by itself to be to form a more perfect union, establish justice, insure domestic tranquility, provide for the common defence, promote the general welfare, and secure the blessings of liberty to ourselves and our posterity.

These ends it endeavored to accomplish by a Federal Government, in which each State was recognized as an equal, and had separate control over its own institutions. The right of property in slaves was recognized by giving to free persons distinct political rights, by giving them the right to represent, and burthening them with direct taxes for three-fifths of their slaves; by authorizing the importation of slaves for twenty years; and by stipulating for the rendition of fugitives from labor.

We affirm that these ends for which this Government was instituted have been defeated, and the Government itself has been made destructive of them by the action of the non-slaveholding States. Those States have assumed the right of deciding upon the propriety of our domestic institutions; and have denied the rights of property established in fifteen of the States and recognized by the Constitution; they have denounced as sinful the institution of slavery; they have permitted open establishment among them of societies, whose avowed object is to disturb the peace and to eloign the property of the citizens of other States. They have encouraged and assisted thousands of our slaves to leave their homes; and those who remain, have been incited by emissaries, books and pictures to servile insurrection.

For twenty-five years this agitation has been steadily increasing, until it has now secured to its aid the power of the common Government. Observing the forms of the Constitution, a sectional party has found within that Article establishing the Executive Department, the means of subverting the Constitution itself. A geographical line has been drawn across the Union, and all the States north of that line have united in the election of a man to the high office of President of the United States, whose opinions and purposes are hostile to slavery. He is to be entrusted with the administration of the common Government, because he has declared that that Government cannot endure permanently half slave, half free, and that the public mind must rest in the belief that slavery is in the course of ultimate extinction.

This sectional combination for the submersion of the Constitution, has been aided in some of the States by elevating to citizenship, persons who, by the supreme law of the land, are incapable of becoming citizens; and their votes have been used to inaugurate a new policy, hostile to the South, and destructive of its beliefs and safety.

On the 4th day of March next, this party will take possession of the Government. It has announced that the South shall be excluded from the common territory, that the judicial tribunals shall be made sectional, and that a war must be waged against slavery until it shall cease throughout the United States.

The guaranties of the Constitution will then no longer exist; the equal rights of the States will be lost. The slaveholding States will no longer have the power of self-government, or self-protection, and the Federal Government will have become their enemy.

Sectional interest and animosity will deepen the irritation, and all hope of remedy is rendered vain, by the fact that public opinion at the North has invested a great political error with the sanction of more erroneous religious belief.

We, therefore, the People of South Carolina, by our delegates in Convention assembled, appealing to the Supreme Judge of the world for the rectitude of our intentions, have solemnly declared that the Union heretofore existing between this State and the other States of North America, is dissolved, and that the State of South Carolina has resumed her position among the nations of the world, as a separate and independent State; with full power to levy war, conclude peace, contract alliances, establish commerce, and to do all other acts and things which independent States may of right do.

Adopted December 24, 1860

The Crittenden Compromise

The Crittenden Compromise was a series of four congressional proposals and six amendments to the U.S. Constitution formulated in late 1860 by Senator John Crittenden of Kentucky. The Compromise was a last-ditch effort to maintain the Union by offering certain reassurances to the slaveholding states. Among other things, it ratified the boundary (latitude 36'30") between the slave and free states established by the Missouri Compromise of 1820 and extended that line to California. It endorsed the continuation of slavery in all areas where it already existed. Unsupported by President-elect Lincoln, the Compromise was rejected in the Senate by a vote of 20 to 19 and in the House of Representatives by a vote of 113 to 80. Its defeat sounded a death knell to efforts to avert war.

Whereas serious and alarming dissensions have arisen between the northern and southern states, concerning the rights and security of the rights of the slaveholding States, and especially their rights in the common territory of the United States; and whereas it is eminently desirable and proper that these dissensions, which now threaten the very existence of this Union, should be permanently quieted and settled by constitutional provisions, which shall do equal justice to all sections, and thereby restore to all the people that peace and good-will which ought to prevail between all the citizens of the United States: Therefore,

Resolved by the Senate and House of Representatives of the United States of America in Congress assembled, (two thirds of both Houses concurring,) That the following articles be, and are hereby, proposed and submitted as amendments to the Constitution of the United States, which shall be valid to all intents and purposes, as part of said Constitution, when ratified by conventions of three-fourths of the several States:

Article 1: In all the territory of the United States now held, or hereafter acquired, situate north of 36 degrees 30 minutes, slavery or involuntary servitude, except as a punishment for crime, is prohibited while such territory shall remain under territorial government. In all the territory south of said line of latitude, slavery of the African race is hereby recognized as existing, and shall not be interfered with by Congress, but shall be protected as property by all the departments of the territorial government during its continuance. And when any territory, north or south of said line, within such boundaries as Congress may prescribe, shall contain the population requisite for a member of Congress according to the then Federal ratio of representation of the people of the United States, it shall, if its form of government be republican, be admitted into the Union, on an equal footing with the original States, with or without slavery, as the constitution of such new State may provide.

Article 2: Congress shall have no power to abolish slavery in places under its exclusive jurisdiction, and situate within the limits of States that permit the holding of slaves.

Article 3: Congress shall have no power to abolish slavery within the District of Columbia, so long as it exists in the adjoining States of Virginia and Maryland, or either, nor without the consent of the inhabitants, nor without just compensation first made to such owners of slaves as do not consent to such abolishment. Nor shall Congress at any time prohibit officers of the Federal Government, or members of Congress, whose duties require them to be in said District, from bringing with them their slaves, and holding them as such during the time their duties may require them to remain there, and afterwards taking them from the District.

Article 4: Congress shall have no power to prohibit or hinder the transportation of slaves from one State to another, or to a Territory, in which slaves are by law permitted to be held, whether that transportation be by land, navigable river, or by the sea.

Article 5: That in addition to the provisions of the third paragraph of the second section of the fourth article of the Constitution of the United States, Congress shall have power to provide by law, and it shall be its duty so to provide, that the United States shall pay to the owner who shall apply for it, the full value of his fugitive slave in all cases where the marshal or other officer whose duty it was to arrest said fugitive was prevented from so doing by violence or intimidation, or when, after arrest, said fugitive was rescued by force, and the owner thereby prevented and obstructed in the pursuit of his remedy for the recovery of his fugitive slave under the said clause of the Constitution and the laws made in pursuance thereof. And in all such cases, when the United States shall pay for such fugitive, they shall have the right, in their own name, to sue the county in which said violence, intimidation, or rescue was committed, and to recover from it, with interest and damages, the amount paid by them for said fugitive slave. And the said county, after it has paid said amount to the United States, may, for its indemnity, sue and recover from the wrong-doers or rescuers by whom the owner was prevented from the recovery of his fugitive slave, in like manner as the owner himself might have sued and recovered.

Article 6: No future amendment of the Constitution shall affect the five preceding articles; nor the third paragraph of the second section of the first article of the Constitution; nor the third paragraph of the second section of the fourth article of said Constitution; and no amendment will be made to the Constitution which shall authorize or give to Congress any power to abolish or interfere with slavery in any of the States by whose laws it is, or may be, allowed or permitted.

And whereas, also, besides those causes of dissension embraced in the foregoing amendments proposed to the Constitution of the United States, there are others which come within the jurisdiction of Congress, and may be remedied by its legislative power; and whereas it is the desire of Congress, so far as its power will extend, to remove all just cause for the popular discontent and agitation which now disturb the peace of the country, and threaten the stability of its institutions; Therefore,

1. Resolved by the Senate and House of Representatives of the United States of America, in Congress assembled, That the laws now in force for the recovery of fugitive slaves are in strict pursuance of the plain and mandatory provisions of the Constitution, and have been sanctioned as valid and constitutional by the judgement of the Supreme Court of the United States; that

the slaveholding States are entitled to the faithful observance and execution of those laws, and that they ought not to be repealed, or so modified or changed as to impair their efficiency; and that laws ought to be made for the punishment of those who attempt by rescue of the slave, or other illegal means, to hinder or defeat the due execution of said laws.

2. That all State laws which conflict with the fugitive slave acts of Congress, or any other constitutional acts of Congress, or which, in their operation, impede, hinder, or delay the free course and due execution of any of said acts, are null and void by the plain provisions of the Constitution of the United States; yet those State laws, void as they are, have given color to practices, and led to consequences, which have obstructed the due administration and execution of acts of Congress, and especially the acts for the delivery of fugitive slaves, and have thereby contributed much to the discord and commotion now prevailing. Congress, therefore, in the present perilous juncture, does not deem it improper, respectfully and earnestly to recommend the repeal of those laws to the several States which have enacted them, or such legislative corrections or explanations of them as may prevent their being used or perverted to such mischievous purposes.

3. That the act of the 18th of September, 1850, commonly called the fugitive slave law, ought to be so amended as to make the fee of the commissioner, mentioned in the eighth section of the act, equal in amount in the cases decided by him, whether his decision be in favor of or against the claimant. And to avoid misconstruction, the last clause of the fifth section of said act, which authorizes the person holding a warrant for the arrest or detention of a fugitive slave, to summon to his aid the posse comitatus, and which declares it to be the duty of all good citizens to assist him in its execution, ought to be so amended as to expressly limit the authority and duty to cases in which there shall be resistance or danger of resistance or rescue.

4. That the laws for the suppression of the African slave trade, and especially those prohibiting the importation of slaves in the United States, ought to be made effectual, and ought to be thoroughly executed; and all further enactments necessary to those ends ought to be promptly made.

Abraham Lincoln: First Inaugural Address
(March 4, 1861)

On February 18, two weeks before Lincoln's inauguration, Jefferson Davis had been inaugurated in Mobile, Alabama, as president of the Confederacy. Secession was already a fact. Lincoln, who traveled from Springfield with family and friends, was forced, because of assassination fears, to approach Washington by a clandestine route and under heavy surveillance, though he insisted on riding to the Capitol in an open carriage with President Buchanan. Chief Justice Roger B. Taney administered the executive oath on the east portico of the Capitol.

Fellow-Citizens of the United States:

In compliance with a custom as old as the Government itself, I appear before you to address you briefly and to take in your presence the oath prescribed by the Constitution of the United States to be taken by the President before he enters on the execution of this office.

I do not consider it necessary at present for me to discuss those matters of administration about which there is no special anxiety or excitement.

Apprehension seems to exist among the people of the Southern States that by the accession of a Republican Administration their property and their peace and personal security are to be endangered. There has never been any reasonable cause for such apprehension. Indeed, the most ample evidence to the contrary has all the while existed and been open to their inspection. It is found in nearly all the published speeches of him who now addresses you. I do but quote from one of those speeches when I declare that—

I have no purpose, directly or indirectly, to interfere with the institution of slavery in the States where it exists. I believe I have no lawful right to do so, and I have no inclination to do so.

Those who nominated and elected me did so with full knowledge that I had made this and many similar declarations and had never recanted them; and more than this, they placed in the platform for my acceptance, and as a law to themselves and to me, the clear and emphatic resolution which I now read:

> Resolved, That the maintenance inviolate of the rights of the States, and especially the right of each State to order and control its own domestic institutions according to its own judgment exclusively, is essential to that balance of power on which the perfection and endurance of our political fabric depend; and we denounce the lawless invasion by armed force of the soil of any State or Territory, no matter what pretext, as among the gravest of crimes.

I now reiterate these sentiments, and in doing so I only press upon the public attention the most conclusive evidence of which the case is susceptible that the property, peace, and security of no section are to be in any wise endangered by the now incoming Administration. I add, too, that all the protection which, consistently with the Constitution and the laws, can be given will be cheerfully given to all the States when lawfully demanded, for whatever cause—as cheerfully to one section as to another.

There is much controversy about the delivering up of fugitives from service or labor. The clause I now read is as plainly written in the Constitution as any other of its provisions:

> No person held to service or labor in one State, under the laws thereof, escaping into another, shall in consequence of any law or regulation therein be discharged from such service or labor, but shall be delivered up on claim of the party to whom such service or labor may be due.

It is scarcely questioned that this provision was intended by those who made it for the reclaiming of what we call fugitive slaves; and the intention of the lawgiver is the law. All members of Congress swear their support to the whole Constitution—to this provision as much as to any other. To the proposition, then, that slaves whose cases come within the terms of this clause "shall be delivered up" their oaths are unanimous. Now, if they would make the effort in good temper, could they not with nearly equal unanimity frame and pass a law by means of which to keep good that unanimous oath?

There is some difference of opinion whether this clause should be enforced by national or by State authority, but surely that difference is not a very material one. If the slave is to be surrendered, it can be of but little consequence to him or to others by which authority it is done. And should anyone in any case be content that his oath shall go unkept on a merely unsubstantial controversy as to how it shall be kept?

Again: In any law upon this subject ought not all the safeguards of liberty known in civilized and humane jurisprudence to be introduced, so that a free man be not in any case surrendered as a slave? And might it not be well at the same time to provide by law for the enforcement of that clause in the Constitution which guarantees that "the citizens of each State shall be entitled to all privileges and immunities of citizens in the several States"?

I take the official oath today with no mental reservations and with no purpose to construe the Constitution or laws by any hypercritical rules; and while I do not choose now to specify particular acts of Congress as proper to be enforced, I do suggest that it will be much safer for all, both in official and private stations, to conform to and abide by all those acts which stand unrepealed than to violate any of them trusting to find impunity in having them held to be unconstitutional.

It is seventy-two years since the first inauguration of a President under our National Constitution. During that period fifteen different and greatly distinguished citizens have in succession administered the executive branch of the Government. They have conducted it through many perils, and generally with great success. Yet, with all this scope of precedent, I now enter upon the same task for the brief constitutional term of four years under great and peculiar difficulty. A disruption of the Federal Union, heretofore only menaced, is now formidably attempted.

I hold that in contemplation of universal law and of the Constitution the Union of these States is perpetual. Perpetuity is implied, if not expressed, in the fundamental law of all national governments. It is safe to assert that no government proper ever had a provision in its organic law for its own termination. Continue to execute all the express provisions of our National Constitution, and the Union will endure forever, it being impossible to destroy it except by some action not provided for in the instrument itself.

Again: If the United States be not a government proper, but an association of States in the nature of contract merely, can it, as a contract, be peaceably unmade by less than all the parties who made it? One party to a contract may violate it—break it, so to speak—but does it not require all to lawfully rescind it?

Descending from these general principles, we find the proposition that in legal contemplation the Union is perpetual confirmed by the history of the Union itself. The Union is much older than the Constitution. It was formed, in fact, by the Articles of Association in 1774. It was matured and continued by the Declaration of Independence in 1776. It was further matured, and the faith of all the then thirteen States expressly plighted and engaged that it should be perpetual, by the Articles of Confederation in 1778. And finally, in 1787, one of the declared objects for ordaining and establishing the Constitution was "to form a more perfect Union."

But if destruction of the Union by one or by a part only of the States be lawfully possible, the Union is less perfect than before the Constitution, having lost the vital element of perpetuity.

It follows from these views that no State upon its own mere motion can lawfully get out of the Union; that resolves and ordinances to that effect are legally void, and that acts of violence within any State or States against the authority of the United States are insurrectionary or revolutionary, according to circumstances.

I therefore consider that in view of the Constitution and the laws the Union is unbroken, and to the extent of my ability, I shall take care, as the Constitution itself expressly enjoins upon me, that the laws of the Union be faithfully executed in all the States. Doing this I deem to be only a simple duty on my part, and I shall perform it so far as practicable unless my rightful masters, the American people, shall withhold the requisite means or in some authoritative manner direct the contrary. I trust this will not be regarded as a menace, but only as the declared purpose of the Union that it will constitutionally defend and maintain itself.

In doing this there needs to be no bloodshed or violence, and there shall be none unless it be forced upon the national authority. The power confided to me will be used to hold, occupy, and possess the property and places belonging to the Government and to collect the duties and imposts; but beyond what may be necessary for these objects, there will be no invasion, no using of force against or among the people anywhere. Where hostility to the United States in any interior locality shall be so great and universal as to prevent competent resident citizens from holding the Federal offices, there will be no attempt to force obnoxious strangers among the people for that object. While the strict legal right may exist in the Government to enforce the exercise of these offices, the attempt to do so would be so irritating and so nearly impracticable withal that I deem it better to forego for the time the uses of such offices.

The mails, unless repelled, will continue to be furnished in all parts of the Union. So far as possible the people everywhere shall have that sense of perfect security which is most favorable to calm thought and reflection. The course here indicated will be followed unless current events and experience shall show a modification or change to be proper, and in every case and exigency my best discretion will be exercised, according to circumstances actually existing and with a view and a hope of a peaceful solution of the national troubles and the restoration of fraternal sympathies and affections.

That there are persons in one section or another who seek to destroy the Union at all events and are glad of any pretext to do it I will neither affirm nor deny; but if there be such, I need address no word to them. To those, however, who really love the Union may I not speak?

Before entering upon so grave a matter as the destruction of our national fabric, with all its benefits, its memories, and its hopes, would it not be wise to ascertain precisely why we do it? Will you hazard so desperate a step while there is any possibility that any portion of the ills you fly from has no real existence? Will you, while the certain ills you fly to are greater than all the real ones you fly from, will you risk the commission of so fearful a mistake?

All profess to be content in the Union if all constitutional rights can be maintained. Is it true, then, that any right plainly written in the Constitution has been denied? I think not. Happily, the human mind is so constituted that no party can reach to the audacity of doing this. Think, if you can, of a single instance in which a plainly written provision of the Constitution has ever been denied. If by the mere force of numbers a majority should deprive a minority of any clearly written constitutional right, it might in a moral point of view justify revolution; certainly would if such right were a vital one. But such is not our case. All the vital rights of minorities and of individuals are so plainly assured to them by affirmations and negations, guaranties and prohibitions, in the Constitution that controversies never arise concerning them. But no organic law can ever be framed with a provision specifically applicable to every question which may occur in practical administration. No foresight can anticipate nor any document of reasonable length contain express provisions for all possible questions. Shall fugitives from labor be surrendered by national or by State authority? The Constitution does not expressly say. May Congress prohibit slavery in the Territories? The Constitution does not expressly say. Must Congress protect slavery in the Territories? The Constitution does not expressly say.

From questions of this class spring all our constitutional controversies, and we divide upon them into majorities and minorities. If the minority will not acquiesce, the majority must, or the Government must cease. There is no other alternative, for continuing the Government is acquiescence on one side or the other. If a minority in such case will secede rather than acquiesce, they make a precedent which in turn will divide and ruin them, for a minority of their own will secede from them whenever a majority refuses to be controlled by such minority. For instance, why may not any portion of a new confederacy a year or two hence arbitrarily secede again, precisely as portions of the present Union now claim to secede from it? All who cherish disunion sentiments are now being educated to the exact temper of doing this.

Is there such perfect identity of interests among the States to compose a new union as to produce harmony only and prevent renewed secession?

Plainly the central idea of secession is the essence of anarchy. A majority held in restraint by constitutional checks and limitations, and always changing easily with deliberate changes of popular opinions and sentiments, is the only true sovereign of a free people. Whoever rejects it does of necessity fly to anarchy or to despotism. Unanimity is impossible. The rule of a minority, as a permanent arrangement, is wholly inadmissible; so that, rejecting the majority principle, anarchy or despotism in some form is all that is left.

I do not forget the position assumed by some that constitutional questions are to be decided by the Supreme Court, nor do I deny that such decisions must be binding in any case upon the parties to a suit as to the object of that suit, while they are also entitled to very high respect and consideration in all parallel cases by all other departments of the Government. And while it is obviously possible that such decision may be erroneous in any given case, still the evil effect following it, being limited to that particular case, with the chance that it may be overruled and never become a precedent for other cases, can better be borne than could the evils of a different practice. At the same time, the candid citizen must confess that if the policy of the Government upon vital questions affecting the whole people is to be irrevocably fixed by decisions of the Supreme Court, the instant they are made in ordinary litigation between parties in personal actions the people will have ceased to be their own rulers, having to that extent practically resigned their Government into the hands of that eminent tribunal. Nor is there in this view any assault upon the court or the judges. It is a duty from which they may not shrink to decide cases properly brought before them, and it is no fault of theirs if others seek to turn their decisions to political purposes.

One section of our country believes slavery is right and ought to be extended, while the other believes it is wrong and ought not to be extended. This is the only substantial dispute. The fugitive-slave clause of the Constitution and the law for the suppression of the foreign slave trade are each as well enforced, perhaps, as any law can ever be in a community where the moral sense of the people imperfectly supports the law itself. The great body of the people abide by the dry legal obligation in both cases, and a few break over in each. This, I think, can not be perfectly cured, and it would be worse in both cases after the separation of the sections than before. The foreign slave trade, now imperfectly suppressed, would be ultimately revived without restriction in one section, while fugitive slaves, now only partially surrendered, would not be surrendered at all by the other.

Physically speaking, we can not separate. We can not remove our respective sections from each other nor build an impassable wall between them. A husband and wife may be divorced and go out of the presence and beyond the reach of each other, but the different parts of our country can not do this. They can not but remain face to face, and intercourse, either amicable or hostile, must continue between them. Is it possible, then, to make that intercourse more advantageous or more satisfactory after separation than before? Can aliens make treaties easier than friends can make laws? Can treaties be more faithfully enforced between aliens than laws can among friends? Suppose you go to war, you can not fight always; and when, after much loss on both sides and no gain on either, you cease fighting, the identical old questions, as to terms of intercourse, are again upon you.

This country, with its institutions, belongs to the people who inhabit it. Whenever they shall grow weary of the existing Government, they can exercise their constitutional right of amending it or their revolutionary right to dismember or overthrow it. I can not be ignorant of the fact that many worthy and patriotic citizens are desirous of having the National Constitution amended. While I make no recommendation of amendments, I fully recognize the rightful authority of the people over the whole subject, to be exercised in either of the modes prescribed in the instrument itself; and I should, under existing circumstances, favor rather than oppose a fair opportunity being afforded the people to act upon it. I will venture to add that to me the convention mode seems preferable, in that it allows amendments to originate with the people themselves, instead of only permitting them to take or reject propositions originated by others, not especially chosen for the purpose, and which might not be precisely such as they would wish to either accept or refuse. I understand a proposed amendment to the Constitution—which amendment, however, I have not seen—has passed Congress, to the effect that the Federal Government shall never interfere with the domestic institutions of the States, including that of persons held to service. To avoid misconstruction of what I have said, I depart from my purpose not to speak of particular amendments so far as to say that, holding such a provision to now be implied constitutional law, I have no objection to its being made express and irrevocable.

The Chief Magistrate derives all his authority from the people, and they have referred none upon him to fix terms for the separation of the States. The people themselves can do this if also they choose, but the Executive as such has nothing to do with it. His duty is to administer the present Government as it came to his hands and to transmit it unimpaired by him to his successor.

Why should there not be a patient confidence in the ultimate justice of the people? Is there any better or equal hope in the world? In our present differences, is either party without faith of being in the right? If the Almighty Ruler of Nations, with His eternal truth and justice, be on your side of the North, or on yours of the South, that truth and that justice will surely prevail by the judgment of this great tribunal of the American people.

By the frame of the Government under which we live this same people have wisely given their public servants but little power for mischief, and have with equal wisdom provided for the return of that little to their own hands at very short intervals. While the people retain their virtue and vigilance no Administration by any extreme of wickedness or folly can very seriously injure the Government in the short space of four years.

My countrymen, one and all, think calmly and well upon this whole subject. Nothing valuable can be lost by taking time. If there be an object to hurry any of you in hot haste to a step which you would never take deliberately, that object will be frustrated by taking time; but no good object can be frustrated by it. Such of you as are now dissatisfied still have the old Constitution unimpaired, and, on the sensitive point, the laws of your own framing under it; while the new Administration will have no immediate power, if it would, to change either. If it were admitted that you who are dissatisfied hold the right side in the dispute, there still is no single good reason for precipitate action. Intelligence, patriotism, Christianity, and a firm reliance on Him who has never yet forsaken this favored land are still competent to adjust in the best way all our present difficulty.

In your hands, my dissatisfied fellow-countrymen, and not in mine, is the momentous issue of civil war. The Government will not assail you. You can have no conflict without being yourselves the aggressors. You have no oath registered in heaven to destroy the Government, while I shall have the most solemn one to "preserve, protect, and defend it."

I am loath to close. We are not enemies, but friends. We must not be enemies. Though passion may have strained it must not break our bonds of affection. The mystic chords of memory, stretching from every battlefield and patriot grave to every living heart and hearthstone all over this broad land, will yet swell the chorus of the Union, when again touched, as surely they will be, by the better angels of our nature.

THE DEBATE OVER FORT SUMTER

From the Diary of Gideon Welles (1802–1878)

Sometimes referred to as "Father Neptune" because of his white whiskers and his position in Lincoln's cabinet as Secretary of the Navy, Welles, as his first act in office, dispatched the warship *Powhattan* to reinforce Fort Sumter just before its fall in April of 1861. Although he had no knowledge of naval matters when he took office, he rapidly doubled the size of the navy, supported the development of ironclad ships, and implemented the naval blockade that was part of Scott's Anaconda Plan. His diary is often cited as singularly valuable in providing insight into the complex struggles within the Lincoln war cabinet. He himself vigorously guarded his own authority and that of President Lincoln against the encroachments of Secretary of State William Seward. An advocate of propriety and procedure, he was described by a journalist of the time as "slightly fossiliferous."

Among other matters, and that for which he had especially requested our attendance that morning, was certain intelligence of a distressing character from Major Anderson at Fort Sumter, stating that his supplies were almost exhausted, that he could get no provisions in Charleston, and that he with his small command would be wholly destitute in about six weeks. Under these circumstances it became a question what action should be taken, and for that purpose, as well as to advise us of the condition of affairs, he had convened the gentlemen present.

The information was to most of us unexpected and astounding, and there was, on the part of such of us as had no previous intimation of the condition of things at Sumter, an earnest determination to take immediate and efficient measures to relieve and reinforce the garrison. But General Scott, without opposing this spontaneous resolution, related the difficulties which had already taken place, and stated the formidable obstacles which were to be encountered from the numerous and well-manned batteries that were erected in Charleston Harbor. Any successful attempt to reinforce or relieve the garrison by sea he supposed impracticable. An attempt had already been made and failed. The question was, however, one for naval authorities to decide, for the army could do nothing. Commander Ward, a gallant officer, had tendered his services on a former occasion when the subject was considered, and was ready at any time to take command of an expedition, if one were ordered. General Scott said he did not expect any conclusion would be arrived at, at this meeting. He had called the gentlemen together by direction of the President to communicate what information he had, and was glad to have his mind relieved of overburthened care and responsibility with which it had been loaded for months. He especially requested me to consult with naval men, and had thought it advisable that Commander Ward, then on the receiving-ship at Brooklyn, should come to Washington, as he had already been made somewhat familiar with the subject.

The meeting adjourned with an understanding that we would come together on the following day at the Executive Mansion. In the mean time the gentlemen were to give the subject earnest consideration.

When we met on the succeeding day, the same gentlemen, with the exception of Judge Holt, were present, and there were two or three others, beside the President.

Many of the naval officers then in Washington and about the Navy Department were of questionable fidelity. A number had already resigned and most of those who were tainted with secession soon left the service; but some of them, on a further consideration of the subject, aided perhaps by adventitious circumstances, determined to abide by the flag and the Union. Whilst there were doubts and uncertainty on every hand as to who could be trusted, I knew Commodore Stringham to be faithful, and therefore had, with the concurrence of the President, selected him to assist me in matters of detail. With him I communicated freely and fully in regard to the condition of Sumter and the ability of the Navy to throw in supplies for its relief. Both he and Commander Ward were confident that the Navy could reinforce the garrison and furnish it with men and provisions. The President had been apprised of the condition of things at Sumter, on the 4th of March, and had referred the subject to General Scott for advice, with directions to consult the Secretaries of War and Navy. Some, but not a very lengthened, discussion took place at this first interview at the Executive Mansion. There was a very general and very determined opinion expressed that Fort Sumter ought to be and should be reinforced. Major Anderson and all the officers of the garrison expressed in a measure the professional opinion that reinforcements could not be thrown into the fort in time for their relief with a force of less than twenty thousand good and well-disciplined men. Generals Scott and Totten declared it was impracticable, and Mr. Seward, who made many suggestions and inquiries, had doubts, and was evidently wholly opposed to any attempt at relief.

No conclusion was required or expected at this interview. The President then, and until decisive steps were finally taken, was averse to offensive measures, and anxious to avoid them. In council, and in personal interviews with myself and others, he enjoined upon each and all to forbear giving any cause of offense; and as regarded party changes consequent upon a change of administration, while they would necessarily be made elsewhere, he wished no removal for political causes to be made in the Southern States, and especially not in Virginia. Although disturbed by the fact that the supplies of the garrison at Sumter were so limited, he was disinclined to hasty action, and wished time for the Administration to get in working order and its policy to be understood. He desired, I think on the suggestion of Mr. Seward, that General Scott should prepare a statement of the position of Sumter, and of the other batteries, and of preparations in Charleston and Charleston Harbor,—the strength of each, how far and long could the garrison maintain itself and repel an attack if made, what force would be necessary to overcome any rebel force or organized military of the State of South Carolina, should she bid defiance to and resist the Federal authorities.

No regular Cabinet-meetings were held in these days, nor for several weeks subsequently, but the heads of Departments were frequently convened, always by special summons through the Secretary of State. Sometimes there was not a full attendance, but on such occasions when there was an omission to invite any members, the absentees were considered not particularly interested in the questions submitted, or the questions did not affect the unrepresented Departments.

The Secretary of State was, of course, apprised of every meeting and never failed in his attendance, whatever was the subject-matter, and though entirely out of his official province. He was vigilantly attentive to every measure and movement in other Departments, however trivial,—as much so as to his own,—watched and scrutinized every appointment that was made or proposed to be made, but was not communicative in regard to the transactions of the State Department. Other members began to interchange views on these proceedings by which one of the heads of Departments was exclusively apprised on all measures, and at length Mr. Chase, as the second in rank and by request of his associates, inquired at one of the special meetings, whether it had not been usual in past administrations to have regular Cabinet-meetings on stated days of each week, and if it would not be conducive to unity and efficiency were the Administration to conform to past usage in that respect.

Mr. Seward very promptly replied that it was not advisable to consume the time of all the gentlemen on stated days and when perhaps it would be unnecessary. The President had only to send word to the State Department, at any time, day or night, when he wanted to call his Cabinet together, or any portion of them, and he, Seward, would take upon himself to have every member notified whose attendance was required. The times were such, he remarked, that the President might find it necessary to call them, or portions of them, frequently, perhaps daily, and even oftener, together, for consultation.

It was said on the other hand, by all the members except Mr. Seward, that the stated meetings need not prevent special calls whenever the President deemed proper, and that it was advisable, for the sake of unity and efficacy, that all the members should attend these meetings and share in the responsibility, instead of having partial gatherings.

The President concurred in these views of the majority, and it was decided that thereafter the Cabinet should assemble at meridian on Tuesdays and Fridays.

Commander Ward, who was summoned to Washington, expressed his readiness to receive orders and to carry supplies to

Sumter. He had volunteered to perform this service to the late administration, but his offer was then declined. There was a belief at that time that the garrison could not be reinforced by the Navy, and to attempt it would, President Buchanan feared, bring on hostilities. This in substance was the report of Commander Ward to me. I called with him on General Scott, who I then perceived was now decidedly opposed to any attempt to relieve Major Anderson. The Navy he was confident could not do it, and an army of at least twenty thousand men would be necessary, he said, to effect it. We had no such army, and the Government could not collect and arm one, to say nothing of the discipline and training, before the garrison would starve. Commander Ward and also Commodore Stringham at first thought that a supply of provisions and a small number of men might be thrown into the fort by means of two small fast tugs, which could run in in the night. Even if one of the tugs was lost, which they did not believe would be the case, the other could relieve the garrison. Of course, the tugs would be abandoned after landing the men, each one of whom was to have his sack of provisions if they could land no more. The crews of the tugs as well as the small additional military force would join the garrison and share its fate.

In subsequent interviews with Generals Scott and Totten, Commander Ward became less confident and was finally convinced that relief was impracticable. He advised me that the scheme should be abandoned. Commodore Stringham came ultimately but reluctantly to the same conclusion, after the elaborate report of the two generals, who maintained that if supplies could be furnished the garrison, the fort itself could not hold out against the attack of the surrounding batteries which the Secessionists had been allowed to erect and fortify for the reduction of Sumter.

Mr. Seward, who from the first had viewed with no favor any attempt to relieve Sumter, soon became a very decisive and emphatic opponent of any proposition that was made; said he had entertained doubts, and the opinions and arguments of Major Anderson and his officers, confirmed by the distinguished military officers who were consulted, had fully convinced him that it would be abortive and useless. It was a duty to defer to these military gentlemen, whose profession and study made them experts, who had by long and faithful service justly acquired the positions they held, and who possessed the confidence of the country. It was, he was satisfied, impossible to relieve and reinforce the garrison; the attempt would provoke immediate hostilities, and if hostilities could not be avoided, he deemed it important that the Administration should not strike the first blow.

The President, though much distressed with the conclusions of the military officers, and the decisive concurrence of the Secretary of State in those conclusions, appeared to acquiesce in what seemed to be a military necessity, but was not disposed to yield until the last moment, and when there was no hope of accomplishing the work if attempted. In the mean time, he sent Mr. Lamon, his late law-partner, to Charleston and others also to make inquiries, among them Mr. Fox, who, like Commander Ward, had been a volunteer under the late administration to relieve Sumter and who never abandoned the idea of its practicability.

Commander Ward was so fully convinced by the arguments of General Scott and General Totten and the opinions of the officers of the garrison, so dissuaded by the opposition of Mr. Seward and the general current of views which prevailed, that he wholly abandoned the project, stating, however, that he held himself in readiness to obey orders and take charge of an expedition, if the Government should at any time deem it expedient that an effort should be made. On the 11th of March he left Washington, and returned to New York.

A strange state of things existed at that time in Washington. The atmosphere was thick with treason. Party spirit and old party differences prevailed, however, amidst these accumulating dangers. Secession was considered by most persons as a political party question, not as rebellion. Democrats to a large extent sympathized with the Rebels more than with the Administration, which they opposed, not that they wished secession to be successful and the Union divided, but they hoped that President Lincoln and the Republicans would, overwhelmed by obstacles and embarrassments, prove failures. The Republicans, on the other hand, were scarcely less partisan and unreasonable. Crowds of them at this period, when the storm of civil war was about bursting on the country, thronged the anterooms of the President and Secretaries, clamorous for the removal of all Democrats, indiscriminately, from office. Patriotism was with them no test, no shield from party malevolence. They demanded the proscription and exclusion of such Democrats as opposed the Rebel movements and clung to the Union, with the same vehemence that they demanded the removal of the worst Rebels who advocated a dissolution of the Union.

Neither party appeared to be apprehensive of or to realize the gathering storm. There was a general belief, indulged in by most persons, that an adjustment would in some way be brought about, without any extensive resort to extreme measures. It seemed probable there might be some outbreak in South Carolina, and perhaps in one or two other places, but such would, it was believed, be soon and easily suppressed. The threatened violence which the nullifiers had thundered for thirty years in the ears of the people had caused their threats to be considered as the harmless ebullitions of excited demagogues throughout the North, while at the South those utterances had so trained the Southern mind, and fired the Southern heart, as to cause them to be received as truthful. The South were, therefore, more united and earnest at this crisis, more determined on seceding, than either the Democrats or Republicans supposed. But, while the great body of the people and most of their leaders in the Northern States, listening to the ninety-day prophecies of Mr. Seward, were incredulous as to any extensive, serious disturbance, there were not a few whose forebodings were grave and sad. All the calamities which soon befell the country these men anticipated. Yet such as were in positions of responsibility would not permit themselves to despond, or despair of the Republic. Mr. Seward possessed a hopeful and buoyant spirit which did not fail him in that dark period, and at no time were his party feelings more decided than during the spring of 1861. Old Whig associates he clung to and strove to retain. All Democrats he distrusted, unless they became identified with the Republican Party. He had probably overestimated his own power and ability to allay the rising storm, and had not the personal influence he supposed. He had prophesied during the winter peace and harmony, within a very brief period after the change of administration was to be effected. These unfortunate prophecies, which became a matter of mirth with many of his friends and of ridicule among his opponents, were not entirely vain imaginings or without some foundation. In the confident belief that he could, if once in place and power, effect conciliation and peace, it had been an object with him to tide the difficulties past the 4th of March. He therefore had operated to that end, and so had Mr. Buchanan, though for different reasons.

Through Mr. Stanton, after that gentleman entered Mr. Buchanan's Cabinet, Mr. Seward and others were secretly advised in regard to the important measures of the Buchanan Administration, and in the course of the winter Mr. Seward came to an understanding, as was alleged and as events and circumstances indicated, with certain of the leading Secessionists. Among other things it was asserted that an agreement had been entered into that no assault should be made on Fort Sumter, provided the garrison should not be reinforced. Mr. Buchanan was to observe the status thus understood during the short remaining period of his administration, and Mr. Seward, as the coming premier, was, on the change of administration, to carry forward the policy of non-reinforcement of Sumter. If not supplied or reinforced, famine would certainly effect the downfall of the fortress without bloodshed on either side. Until blood was spilled, there was hope of conciliation. In fulfillment of this arrangement, Mr. Seward opposed any and every scheme to reinforce Sumter, and General Scott, who was old and much under his influence, if not a party to the understanding, seconded or took a leading part in that opposition.

On the 5th of March commissioners from the Rebel Government arrived in Washington and soon put themselves in communication with the Secretary of State, but the specific object which they had in view, and the negotiations or understanding between him and the parties were not immediately detailed to the Cabinet. They undoubtedly influenced the mind and course of Mr. Seward, who did not relinquish the hope of a peaceful adjustment of difficulties, and he in conversation continued to allure his friends with the belief that he should be able to effect reconciliation.

In the many, almost daily, discussions which for a time were held in regard to Sumter, the opposition to forwarding supplies gathered strength. Commodore Stringham, as well as Commander Ward, on a final application which I made to him, by request of the President, and finally by the President himself, said he was compelled to advise against it. The time had gone by. It was too late. The military gentlemen had satisfied him it was impossible, that nothing could be gained by it, were the attempt made, that it would be attended with a useless sacrifice of blood and treasure, and he felt constrained to state his belief of the inability of the Navy to give relief.

Postmaster-General Blair, who had been a close and near observer of what had taken place through the winter and spring, took an opposite view from Mr. Seward and General Scott. To some extent he was aware of the understanding which Mr. Seward had with the members of Buchanan's Administration, or was suspicious of it, and his indignation that any idea of abandoning Sumter should be entertained or thought of was unbounded. With the exception of Mr. Seward, all his colleagues concurred with Mr. Blair at the commencement, but as the subject was discussed, and the impossibility and inutility of the scheme was urged, with assurance from the first military men in the country, whose advice was sought and given, that it was a military necessity to leave Sumter to its fate, the opinions of men changed, or they began at least to waver. Mr. Blair saw these misgivings, in which he did not at all participate, and finally, observing that the President, with the acquiescence of the Cabinet, was about adopting the Seward and Scott policy, he wrote his resignation, determined not to continue in the Cabinet if no attempt were made to relieve Fort Sumter. Before handing in his resignation, a delay was made at the request of his father. The elder Blair sought an interview with the President, to whom he entered his protest against non-action, which he denounced as the offspring of intrigue. His earnestness and indignation aroused and electrified the President; and when, in his zeal, Blair warned the President that the abandonment of Sumter would be justly considered by the people, by the world, by history, as treason to the country, he touched a chord that responded to his invocation. The President decided from that moment that an attempt should be made to convey supplies to Major Anderson, and that he would reinforce Sumter. This determination he communicated to the members of the Cabinet as he saw them, without a general announcement in Cabinet-meeting. The resolve inspired all the members with hope and courage, except Mr. Seward, who was evidently disappointed. He said it was of vastly more importance to turn our attention to Fort Pickens. I told him this had been done and how; that we had a considerable naval force there, almost the whole of the Home Squadron, and we had sent, a fortnight before, orders to land the troops under Captain Vogdes from the Brooklyn. He said that still more should, in his opinion, be done; that it was practicable to save Fort Pickens, but it was confessedly impossible to retain Sumter. One would be a waste of effort and energy and life, would extinguish all hope of peace, and compel the Government to take the initiative in hostile demonstrations, while the other would be an effective and peaceable movement. Although, as already mentioned, stated Cabinet-meetings were not then established, the members were in those early days of the Administration frequently together, and the President had every day more or less interviews with them, individually or collectively. The Secretary of State spent much of each day at the Executive Mansion and was vigilant to possess himself of every act, move, and intention of the President and of each of his associates. Perhaps there was an equal desire on their part to be informed of the proceedings of the Administration in full, but less was known of the transactions of the State Department than of any other.

The President, after his interview with the elder Blair, asked me if a naval expedition could be promptly fitted out to relieve Sumter. Mr. Fox, who had in February proposed to the Buchanan Administration a plan for the relief of Sumter, again volunteered for the service, and was accepted by Mr. Lincoln.

The Firing on Fort Sumter from *A Diary from Dixie*

Mary Chesnut (1823–1886)

Mary Chesnut, one of the foremost diarists of the Civil War from a Southern perspective, was a "woman of society." From the planter class, she was in touch with many of the social, political, and military elite of the Civil War South. Her husband, James Chesnut, served as a U.S. Senator from South Carolina and as a Brigadier General in the Army of the Confederacy. Her diary, which she carefully edited in anticipation of its eventual publication, was first published in 1909 as *A Diary from Dixie*. A later version, edited and annotated by C. Vann Woodward, titled *Mary Chesnut's Civil War*, won a Pulitzer Prize in 1982.

April 8th.—Governor Manning walked in, bowed gravely, and seated himself by me. Again he bowed low in mock heroic style, and with a grand wave of his hand, said: "Madame, your country is invaded." When I had breath to speak, I asked, "What does he mean?" He meant this: there are six men-of-war outside the bar. Talbot and Chew have come to say that hostilities are to begin. Governor Pickens and Beauregard are holding a council of war. Mr. Chesnut then came in and confirmed the story. Wigfall next entered in boisterous spirits, and said: "There was a sound of revelry by night." In any stir or confusion my heart is apt to beat so painfully. Now the agony was so stifling I could hardly see or hear. The men went off almost immediately. And I crept silently to my room, where I sat down to a good cry.

Mrs. Wigfall came in and we had it out on the subject of civil war. We solaced ourselves with dwelling on all its known horrors, and then we added what we had a right to expect with Yankees in front and negroes in the rear. "The slave-owners must expect a servile insurrection, of course," said Mrs. Wigfall, to make sure that we were unhappy enough.

Suddenly loud shouting was heard. We ran out. Cannon after cannon roared. We met Mrs. Allen Green in the passageway with blanched cheeks and streaming eyes. Governor Means rushed out of his room in his dressing-gown and begged us to be calm. "Governor Pickens," said he, "has ordered in the plenitude of his wisdom, seven cannon to be fired as a signal to the Seventh Regiment. Anderson will hear as well as the Seventh Regiment. Now you go back and be quiet; fighting in the streets has not begun yet."

So we retired. Dr. Gibbes calls Mrs. Allen Green Dame Placid. There was no placidity to-day, with cannon bursting and Allen on the Island. No sleep for anybody last night. The streets were alive with soldiers, men shouting, marching, singing. Wigfall, the "stormy petrel," is in his glory, the only thoroughly happy person I see. To-day things seem to have settled down a little. One can but hope still. Lincoln, or Seward, has made such silly advances and then far sillier drawings back. There may be a chance for peace after all. Things are happening so fast. My husband has been made an aide-de-camp to General Beauregard.

Three hours ago we were quickly packing to go home. The Convention has adjourned. Now he tells me the attack on Fort Sumter may begin to-night; depends upon Anderson and the fleet outside. The Herald says that this show of war outside of the bar is intended for Texas. John Manning came in with his sword and red sash, pleased as a boy to be on Beauregard's staff, while the row goes on. He has gone with Wigfall to Captain Hartstein with instructions. Mr. Chesnut is finishing a report he had to make to the Convention.

Mrs. Hayne called. She had, she said, but one feeling; pity for those who are not here. Jack Preston, Willie Alston, "the take-life-easys," as they are called, with John Green, "the big brave," have gone down to the islands—volunteered as privates. Seven hundred men were sent over. Ammunition wagons were rambling along the streets all night. Anderson is burning blue lights, signs, and signals for the fleet outside, I suppose.

To-day at dinner there was no allusion to things as they stand in Charleston Harbor. There was an undercurrent of intense excitement. There could not have been a more brilliant circle. In addition to our usual quartette (Judge Withers, Langdon Cheves, and Trescott), our two ex-Governors dined with us, Means and

Manning. These men all talked so delightfully. For once in my life I listened. That over, business began in earnest. Governor Means had rummaged a sword and red sash from somewhere and brought it for Colonel Chesnut, who had gone to demand the surrender of Fort Sumter. And now patience—we must wait.

Why did that green goose Anderson go into Fort Sumter? Then everything began to go wrong. Now they have intercepted a letter from him urging them to let him surrender. He paints the horrors likely to ensue if they will not. He ought to have thought of all that before he put his head in the hole.

April 12th.—Anderson will not capitulate. Yesterday's was the merriest, maddest dinner we have had yet. Men were audaciously wise and witty. We had an unspoken foreboding that it was to be our last pleasant meeting. Mr. Miles dined with us to-day. Mrs. Henry King rushed in saying, "The news, I come for the latest news. All the men of the King family are on the Island," of which fact she seemed proud.

While she was here our peace negotiator, or envoy, came in—that is, Mr. Chesnut returned. His interview with Colonel Anderson had been deeply interesting, but Mr. Chesnut was not inclined to be communicative. He wanted his dinner. He felt for Anderson and had telegraphed to President Davis for instructions—what answer to give Anderson, etc. He has now gone back to Fort Sumter with additional instructions. When they were about to leave the wharf A. H. Boykin sprang into the boat in great excitement. He thought himself ill-used, with a likelihood of fighting and he to be left behind!

I do not pretend to go to sleep. How can I? If Anderson does not accept terms at four, the orders are, he shall be fired upon. I count four, St. Michael's bells chime out and I begin to hope. At half-past four the heavy booming of a cannon. I sprang out of bed, and on my knees prostrate I prayed as I never prayed before.

There was a sound of stir all over the house, pattering of feet in the corridors. All seemed hurrying one way. I put on my double-gown and a shawl and went, too. It was to the housetop. The shells were bursting. In the dark I heard a man say, "Waste of ammunition." I knew my husband was rowing about in a boat somewhere in that dark bay, and that the shells were roofing it over, bursting toward the fort. If Anderson was obstinate, Colonel Chesnut was to order the fort on one side to open fire. Certainly fire had begun. The regular roar of the cannon, there it was. And who could tell what each volley accomplished of death and destruction?

The women were wild there on the housetop. Prayers came from the women and imprecations from the men. And then a shell would light up the scene. To-night they say the forces are to attempt to land. We watched up there, and everybody wondered that Fort Sumter did not fire a shot.

To-day Miles and Manning, colonels now, aides to Beauregard, dined with us. The latter hoped I would keep the peace. I gave him only good words, for he was to be under fire all day and night, down in the bay carrying orders, etc.

Last night, or this morning truly, up on the housetop I was so weak and weary I sat down on something that looked like a black stool. "Get up, you foolish woman. Your dress is on fire," cried a man. And he put me out. I was on a chimney and the sparks had caught my clothes. Susan Preston and Mr. Venable then came up. But my fire had been extinguished before it burst out into a regular blaze.

Do you know, after all that noise and our tears and prayers, nobody has been hurt; sound and fury signifying nothing—a delusion and a snare.

Louisa Hamilton came here now. This is a sort of news center. Jack Hamilton, her handsome young husband, has all the credit of a famous battery, which is made of railroad iron. Mr. Petigru calls it the boomerang, because it throws the balls back the way they came; so Lou Hamilton tells us. During her first marriage, she had no children; hence the value of this lately achieved baby. To divert Louisa from the glories of "the Battery," of which she raves, we asked if the baby could talk yet. "No, not exactly, but he imitates the big gun when he hears that. He claps his hands and cries 'Boom, boom.'" Her mind is distinctly occupied by three things: Lieutenant Hamilton, whom she calls "Randolph," the baby, and the big gun, and it refuses to hold more.

Pryor, of Virginia, spoke from the piazza of the Charleston hotel. I asked what he said. An irreverent woman replied: "Oh, they all say the same thing, but he made great play with that long hair of his, which he is always tossing aside!"

Somebody came in just now and reported Colonel Chesnut asleep on the sofa in General Beauregard's room. After two such nights he must be so tired as to be able to sleep anywhere.

Just bade farewell to Langdon Cheves. He is forced to go home and leave this interesting place. Says he feels like the man that was not killed at Thermopylæ. I think he said that unfortunate had to hang himself when he got home for very shame. Maybe he fell on his sword, which was the strictly classic way of ending matters.

I do not wonder at Louisa Hamilton's baby; we hear nothing, can listen to nothing; boom, boom goes the cannon all the time. The nervous strain is awful, alone in this darkened room. "Richmond and Washington ablaze," say the papers—blazing with excitement. Why not? To us these last days' events seem frightfully great. We were all women on that iron balcony. Men are only seen at a distance now. Stark Means, marching under the piazza at the head of his regiment, held his cap in his hand all the time he was in sight. Mrs. Means was leaning over and looking with tearful eyes, when an unknown creature asked, "Why did he take his hat off?" Mrs. Means stood straight up and said: "He did that in honor of his mother; he saw me." She is a proud mother, and at the same time most unhappy. Her lovely daughter Emma is dying in there, before her eyes, of consumption. At that moment I am sure Mrs. Means had a spasm of the heart; at least, she looked as I feel sometimes. She took my arm and we came in.

April 13th.—Nobody has been hurt after all. How gay we were last night. Reaction after the dread of all the slaughter we thought those dreadful cannon were making. Not even a battery the worse for wear. Fort Sumter has been on fire. Anderson has not yet silenced any of our guns. So the aides, still with swords and red sashes by way of uniform, tell us. But the sound of those guns makes regular meals impossible. None of us go to table. Tea-trays pervade the corridors going everywhere. Some of the anxious hearts lie on their beds and moan in solitary misery. Mrs. Wigfall and I solace ourselves with tea in my room. These women have all a satisfying faith. "God is on our side," they say. When we are shut in Mrs. Wigfall and I ask "Why?" "Of course, He hates the Yankees, we are told. You'll think that well of Him."

Not by one word or look can we detect any change in the demeanor of these negro servants. Lawrence sits at our door, sleepy and respectful, and profoundly indifferent. So are they all, but they carry it too far. You could not tell that they even heard the awful roar going on in the bay, though it has been dinning in their ears night and day. People talk before them as if they were chairs and tables. They make no sign. Are they stolidly stupid? or wiser than we are; silent and strong, biding their time?

So tea and toast came; also came Colonel Manning, red sash and sword, to announce that he had been under fire, and didn't mind it. He said gaily: "It is one of those things a fellow never knows how he will come out until he has been tried. Now I know I am a worthy descendant of my old Irish hero of an ancestor, who held the British officer before him as a shield in the Revolution, and backed out of danger gracefully." We talked of St. Valentine's eve, or the maid of Perth, and the drop of the white doe's blood that sometimes spoiled all.

The war-steamers are still there, outside the bar. And there are people who thought the Charleston bar "no good" to Charleston. The bar is the silent partner, or sleeping partner, and in this fray it is doing us yeoman service.

April 15th.—I did not know that one could love such days of excitement. Some one called: "Come out! There is a crowd coming." A mob it was, indeed, but it was headed by Colonels Chesnut and Manning. The crowd was shouting and showing these two as messengers of good news. They were escorted to Beauregard's headquarters. Fort Sumter had surrendered! Those upon the housetops shouted to us "The fort is on fire." That had been the story once or twice before.

When we had calmed down, Colonel Chesnut, who had taken it all quietly enough, if anything more unruffled than usual in his serenity, told us how the surrender came about. Wigfall was with them on Morris Island when they saw the fire in the fort; he jumped in a little boat, and with his handkerchief as a white flag, rowed over. Wigfall went in through a porthole. When Colonel Chesnut arrived shortly after, and was received at the regular entrance, Colonel Anderson told him he had need to pick his way warily, for the place was all mined. As far as I can make out the fort surrendered to Wigfall. But it is all confusion. Our flag is flying there. Fire-engines have been sent for to put out the fire. Everybody tells you half of something and then rushes off to tell something else or to hear the last news.

In the afternoon, Mrs. Preston, Mrs. Joe Heyward, and I drove around the Battery. We were in an open carriage. What a changed scene—the very liveliest crowd I think I ever saw, everybody talking at once. All glasses were still turned on the grim old fort.

Russell, the correspondent of the London Times, was there. They took him everywhere. One man got out Thackeray to converse with him on equal terms. Poor Russell was awfully bored, they say. He only wanted to see the fort and to get news suitable to make up into an interesting article. Thackeray had become stale over the water.

Mrs. Frank Hampton and I went to see the camp of the Richland troops. South Carolina College had volunteered to a boy. Professor Venable (the mathematical) intends to raise a company from among them for the war, a permanent company. This is a grand frolic no more for the students, at least. Even the staid and severe of aspect, Clingman, is here. He says Virginia and North Carolina are arming to come to our rescue, for now the North will swoop down on us. Of that we may be sure. We have burned our ships. We are obliged to go on now. He calls us a poor, little, hot-blooded, headlong, rash, and troublesome sister State.

FROM *WITHIN FORT SUMTER*

Anonymous

On March 5, 1861, the day after his inauguration, Lincoln was informed that Major Robert Anderson's supplies at Fort Sumter in Charleston harbor were insufficient to last beyond mid-April. The fort was regarded by the South as part of the newly formed Confederacy, which was now being occupied by a foreign force, and the situation was rapidly unraveling.

The portion of *Within Fort Sumter* excerpted here gives a particularly intimate account of what went on inside the fort while both the president and his cabinet and the Confederate government, then located at Montgomery, Alabama, moved toward the confrontation of April 12–14. If, outside the fort, the situation was precarious and volatile, life at the fort was occupied with an expectation of desperately needed reinforcements and a certain amount of patriotic pugnacity among the interestingly diverse personnel.

The author of this account is not identified, though the document clearly represents the experience of someone who was present during the entire ordeal, well beyond the point at which women were evacuated from the fort. However, inscribed on the cover page of the original manuscript in a place usually reserved for the author's name is the name Mrs. Fletcher, so the reader is free to speculate on the gender of the writer.

All through the month of March the little garrison lived quietly and worked steadily. In spare hours they read the papers, and talked enthusiastically of what they, each, could achieve, in honor of their flag, when permitted to put forth their strength. They troubled their heads little about politics in general; it was enough for them to know that the UNION was assailed, and the Nation threatened with disruption. . . .

Toward the 1st of April the storage provisions had become so reduced in Fort Sumter that Major Anderson, in order to economize in that particular, arranged to send away the laborers employed in the fort; the State Authorities, however, refused to suffer them to depart. Of this interference with his movements and the circumstance preceding—namely, the reduction of his stock of provisions—the Major deemed it wise to apprise his Government; he, therefore, sent Lieutenants Talbott and Snyder with a flag of truce to Charleston, the former, by courtesy of the Governor, to proceed to Washington with dispatches. After the officers went ashore, and pending the return of Lieutenant Snyder to the boat, the men who rowed it took the opportunity of procuring tobacco and some other luxuries, but the police followed them and seized their purchases. This was on the 4th of April, and in two days after an order was issued by the State prohibiting the garrison of Fort Sumter any further supplies from Charleston Market.

Lieutenant Talbott made the journey to Washington and back in as short a time as possible; but on his return to Charleston he was refused permission to go to Fort Sumter. He, accordingly, returned immediately to Washington. The instructions to Major Anderson, of which he was the bearer, were, however, forwarded to the fort, and duly received there. They informed the Major that Government would immediately send him a supply of provisions, but as to the course he should pursue, they referred him entirely to his own judgment, expressing the utmost confidence in his bravery and military tact.

Upon this visit to Washington Mr. Talbott received promotion to a Captaincy, and, by the very next train for Charleston, returned thither as escort to Mr. Chew, a special messenger from the President to the Governor of South Carolina.

Mr. Chew's message was to inform Governor Pickens that it was the intention of the Government to send provisions to Fort Sumter, which would be landed there peaceably if permitted, but, if not, would be landed by force. This message was delivered on the 8th of April, and, after its delivery, Captain Talbott and Mr. Chew returned to Washington without delay.

Captain Talbott sincerely regretted his absence from Fort Sumter in this her hour of need. He knew the crisis had come, and that a sharp, severe struggle was before the gallant garrison, and, O! how he chafed under the necessity which compelled him away from the glory of sharing it with them.

The garrison was now on the look-out for the expected supplies, which must reach in a few days or not enter. The cause was this. Several weeks before the Carolinians had blocked the ship channel, by sinking the hulls of large vessels therein, leaving only a narrow passage, through which skillful piloting was necessary to lead large ships into harbor. The Charleston pilots had been forbidden by their State Government to steer into port any vessel bearing the United States Flag; it would, therefore, be impossible for the fleet to enter except during a very high tide, which would occur on the 10th and 11th of the month. Before that time, however, a storm arose which drove the vessels back; and when they at last arrived, it was too late—they could not enter.

Meanwhile they were expected; and the South Carolina authorities concluded to hurry up matters before their arrival. Accordingly, at two o'clock on Thursday, April 11th, a formal demand was sent by General Beauregard to Major Anderson for the evacuation of Fort Sumter. The Major's reply was as follows:

> *"Sir:—I have the honor to acknowledge the receipt of your communication, demanding the evacuation of this Fort, and to say in reply thereto that it is a demand with which I regret that my sense of honor and my obligations to my Government prevent my compliance.*
>
> *"Robert Anderson."*

The reception of this answer was immediately followed by a deputation from General Beauregard urging Major Anderson to evacuate, and proposing the most honorable terms, upon which he should be allowed to do so; but the Major, feeling his own strength, besides expecting the fleet from Washington, determined to hold out, and the deputation, after a long interview, in which they earnestly sought to persuade the Major to accept the offered terms, returned to Charleston to report their failure.

It was late on Thursday night when this interview closed; and at half past three o'clock, on Friday morning, the boat with its white flag, shrouded in darkness and mist, again drew up to the walls of Fort Sumter. It conveyed three of General Beauregard's Aide-de-camps, bearing the following notice:

> *"Major Anderson:*
>
> *"By virtue of Brigadier General Beauregard's command, we have the honor to notify you that he will open the line of his batteries on Fort Sumter in one hour from this time."*

Punctual to the minute, at half past four o'clock, the first gun was fired on Fort Sumtèr.

It was a dark, cloudy morning, not a star was visible, while a heavy mist covered earth and sea; but as through the sombre gloom came the brilliant flash of exploding shells from the batteries all around the bay, while the deep hoarse tones of talking cannon echoed over the waters, the scene was sublimely grand, and sensations wildly inspiriting swelled in every heart.

Major Anderson alone was calm, though the swollen veins of his temples, the dilating nostrils, the nervous lip, told that his great heart beat as ardently as any there.

He would allow of no hurry: he wished that his command should husband their strength as it would all be needed. With this view he desired that they should breakfast before proceeding to action.

Their simple meal was soon prepared. For a week they had been on short rations of salt pork, biscuit and coffee, with a little rice. This rice, the last they had received, had reached them through a rough sea, and, the boat being leaky, had become saturated with salt water. It had then been spread out in an empty room of the barracks to dry, with the expectation of its being very acceptable when the biscuit should give out. That extremity was reached now. The last few biscuits were divided, and the cook was ordered to boil some rice; but, lo! the very first fire had shattered the windows of the room where the precious article was spread, and particles of glass were thickly strewn amongst the grain—the food was useless.

But they still had a little pork and plenty of coffee; and, thankful for this same, the brave fellows eat and drank, then filed in order to their places in the casemates.

And all this time the enemy's shot rattled, thick and fast,

around our stronghold, which did but little execution beyond affording the Major an opportunity of observing the efficiency of each battery employed against him, and of tracing the plan which he had to oppose.

At five o'clock day began to break; but the heavy masses of clouds which obscured the sky, the sullen swell of the dark waters, the grey mist which hung, like a sombre veil, over nature's face, only became more apparent as the gathering light increased.

Shortly after the huge clouds burst, and a deluge of rain rushed down upon the scene, as if commissioned to quench the matricidal fire leveled against Columbia's breast. But all in vain. The moaning wind—the splashing shower were scarcely heeded, or made but feeble sounds, while the hoarse bellowing of deep-mouthed cannon still rolled fiercely on. An hour, and the elements ceased to strive, the wailing storm was hushed, and a still but troubled sky looked down upon the scene.

Meanwhile the Fort Sumter garrison coolly prepared for action. Major Anderson divided his command into three reliefs of four hours each, for service at the guns; the first under charge of Captain Doubleday, assisted by Dr. Crawford and Lieutenant Snyder; the second under charge of Captain Seymour, assisted by Lieutenant Hall; and the third under charge of Lieutenant Davis and Lieutenant Meade. The laborers, over forty of whom were in the fort, were appointed to carry ammunition, help make cartridges and assist the gunners where their aid could be available.

All was now ready, every man was in his place, and still, before giving the word to fire, our kind commander walked around to administer his last charge.

"Be careful," he said, "of your lives; make no imprudent exposure of your persons to the enemy's fire; do your duty coolly, determinedly and *cautiously.* Indiscretion is not valor; reckless disregard of life is not bravery. Manifest your loyalty and zeal by preserving yourselves from injury for the continued service of our cause; *and show your love to me by guarding all your powers to aid me through this important duty.*"

This admonition, delivered in sentences, with anxious brow and broken voice, will long be remembered by those who heard it:—no doubt it was the fulcrum sustaining and steadying the power which cast such deadly force from Sumter's walls.

It was just within ten minutes of seven o'clock when the order was given to fire. The first shot was from a forty-two pounder directed against the battery at Cumming's Point. Three of our guns bore upon this point and seven on Fort Moultrie. The famous floating battery—which, by the way, did not float at all, but stuck fast on a point of Sullivan's Island—also received some attention, besides a new battery in the same neighborhood, which had only been unmasked the day previous.

Before our firing commenced—when the storm had cleared off sufficiently to enable us to see around us—we discovered a fleet, which we supposed to be our long-expected succor, outside the bar. The Major signaled them, but the shoals being heavy and the tide low, they could not possibly cross. Shortly after this a fragment of a shell struck and cut through one of the flag halliards; but the flag, instead of falling, rose on the wind, and, with a whirl, flung the remaining halliard round the topmast, by which it was held securely all day:—Long live our gallant ensign!

To return. Major Anderson having opened fire continued to pour it forth with good effect. Almost every ball went home. One of the Fort Moultrie guns was soon disabled; the roofs and sides of the building were penetrated by shot; the flag-staff was struck seventeen times; its roof was penetrated, and several shots were sent square through it. The iron battery at Cumming's Point was struck several times, but not much impression was made. Two of its guns, however, were dismounted. The forty-two pound Paixhans of our lower tier worked well: not one of them opened her mouth without giving the enemy cause to shrink, while the ten-inch Columbiads of our second tier meant every word they said. The barbette guns were not manned. Early in the engagement three of them had been fired; but the number of shells descending upon the terre-plain of the parapet, and the flanks and faces of the work being taken in reverse by the enemy's batteries rendered the danger of serving in the ramparts so imminent that Major Anderson quickly withdrew his men from them, and kept them in the casemates.

When the cartridges became scarce, the men not engaged at the guns were employed to make them; the sheets and bedding from the hospital being brought out and used for that purpose.

Noon came, yet Fort Sumter was not hurt: the proud stronghold had resisted every effort to do it serious injury. A new species of attack, however, was now resorted to. The solid pile which was impervious to cold ball might feel the influence of *hot shot,* especially as the barracks were constructed mainly of timber; and so a red, hissing shower rushed from Fort Moultrie on this treacherous errand.

The officers' quarters soon caught fire;—the roof of this elegant building, being taller than those adjoining, received the assault first, but the bursting of the cistern, on top, which occurred about the same time, prevented the conflagration from spreading. Still down came the fierce hot shot upon the doomed dwellings, and were it not for the leaking cisterns, each of which had been perforated by ball, the whole would have been quickly consumed.

The ball from the enemy's batteries continued to rattle against the fort, and the latter paid back the compliment with interest. A strong, determined will actuated our men, astonishing to find in so small a number, surrounded and hemmed in by an armament of thousands.

"Aye! there's a great crowd o' them against us!" exclaimed one, as he leaned for a minute behind the column of an embrasure, "but it's the Republic they're fightin'—not us—and, in the name of the Republic, we're able for them."

"To be sure we are!" was the hearty response, "seventy true men to seventy thousand traitors, and the true side is the strongest!"

And at it they kept, loading and firing, firing and re-loading, without stopping for food or repose, except an occasional draught of coffee, to wash the powder from their throats, or a short rest for their weary shoulders against an arch or column.

Nor, all through the exciting day, did the officers ever flag in their duty. Cool, firm, and intrepid, with eyes like eagles, ears quick to hear, and limbs of agile motion, they saw every movement of the enemy, heard their leader's lightest command, and directed each action of their charge with a promptness and energy worthy of the important occasion.

The day seemed short, too, full as it was with labor and excitement; and the hearts which beat with hope and enthusiasm heeded not the flight of time. They would fain fight on after day had closed; but the sun went down in lowering gloom, night gathered over us murky and chill, and Major Anderson ordered the firing to cease, and the men to eat some supper and to go to bed.

The only supper they had was a little pork and coffee; but this, with a good sleep, would afford them some refreshment, preparatory to the next day's toil; so they took it cheerfully and laid down.

Still the enemy's fire continued. Even when, at seven o'clock, a mighty storm arose, and rain descended with the force of a cataract, an occasional bomb from one of the batteries mingled with the fury of the elements, as if bidding defiance to nature as well as law.

The condition of the fort was now examined, and the injuries sustained were found to be as follows: The crest of the parapet had been broken in many places; the gorge had been struck by shell and shot, and some of these had penetrated the wall to the depth of twelve inches. Several of the barbette guns had been injured; one had been struck by a ball and cracked; one was dismounted and two had been thrown over by a recoil. The lower casemates were uninjured, save one or two embrasures a little broken on the edges.

But the internal structure had received the most damage—the *wooden* building which had been treated to hot shot. Nothing saved it from being consumed but the riddling of the cisterns which sent the water flowing after the fire as fast as the red balls kindled it; and now the copious rain came down to quench every spark that might have remained in wall or roof.

Yet the pretty edifice was in a sad condition: between fire and water our pleasant quarters were spoiled.

And here we would say, in parenthesis, to military engineers: Never use timber to build the barracks of a fort, nor raise the roof of your officers' quarters higher than the outer wall, unless you calculate upon deserting your colors, turning traitor to your cause, and heading a host in attacking that very fort. In such case you will find that having used that material will serve your purpose—as did Beauregard.

That we should be again saluted with hot shot was pretty certain, and, the cisterns empty and the rain storm over, nothing could save the wood works from destruction. As much of the officers' effects as could be removed, were, therefore, carried to the casemates—the privates, many of whom were now sleeping soundly in their barracks, had not much to lose.

The next morning rose fair and mild. The rain clouds had discharged their burden, and now a clear, calm sky looked down upon the scene. As day broke the firing from the enemy's batteries was resumed, and our garrison arose and prepared to reply to them. The meagre breakfast of pork and coffee was again partaken, and at seven o'clock Fort Sumter opened fire, which was kept up vigorously during the remainder of the contest.

The first few shots directed at Fort Moultrie sent the chimneys off the officers' quarters, and considerably tore up the roof; nearly a dozen shots penetrated the floating battery below the water line, and several of the guns on Morris Island were disabled. The clear state of the atmosphere to-day enables us to see some of the effects of our fire upon the enemy—*all* the effects we do not expect ever to learn.

As anticipated, hot shot was fired again from Moultrie upon the doomed buildings inside Fort Sumter; and at a little after eight o'clock the officers' quarters were ablaze. All the men, not on duty at the guns, exerted themselves to extinguish the fire, but it spread rapidly, igniting here and there, as the red balls continued to drop, until every portion was in flames.

Attention was now directed to the magazines, which were situated at each of the southern corners of the fort, between the officers' quarters and the barracks. An intimacy with the internal arrangements of the fort had, doubtless, suggested to the gentleman in the opposite command the possibility of blowing up the garrison—hence the clever stratagem of firing the officers' quarters with hot shot; but against this danger Major Anderson provided by ordering all the powder to be taken from the upper magazines, and the lower magazines to be shut tight and thick mounds of earth to be heaped round the doors, through which no amount of heat could penetrate.

Afterwards, when the fire had spread through the barracks and reached the casemates, the Major ordered the powder, which had been removed thither from the magazines, to be thrown into the sea, and ninety barrels were thus disposed of.

As the fire increased the situation of the garrison was distressing beyond description. The water from the cisterns, followed by floods of rain, had saturated the riddled and broken buildings so that they burned with a hissing, smoldering flame, sending forth dense clouds of vapor and smoke, which soon filled the whole fort, rendering it difficult to breathe. The men were often obliged to lie down in the casemates, with wet cloths over their faces, to gain temporary relief.

Still the valiant fellows continued to serve their guns, and bomb after bomb, resounding from Sumter's walls, told that the spirit of American loyalty was not to be subdued, even by fire.

About half past twelve o'clock our flag-staff, which had been grazed several times, was shot through and the flag fell. Down, amid burning brands, surrounded by smoke and ruin, our war-worn ensign lay.

It was but a moment, and the next our young Lieutenant, Mr. Hall, rushed through the fire and, dashing all impediments out of his way, seized the prostrate colors. A buzz of admiration, mingled with words of fear for the officer's safety, and every man started forward, straining his eyes through the smoke until the object of quest emerged to view, begrimed with soot, choking and faint, his face and hair singed, his clothes scorched, and holding aloft, with almost spent strength, the rescued flag. A weak, but heartfelt cheer, from parched throats, greeted him as the precious burden was taken from his blistered hands, and he sunk down exhausted.

When the fire was all spent, the gay dwelling in ashes, and the noble fort was silent—standing, proud as ever, in stern, strong nakedness—Mr. Hall's epaulets were found on the spot from which he had raised the flag. In rushing through the fire they had become heated, and, oppressing his shoulders, he tore them off. They were now burnt—all but one little bunch of gold wire, which was embedded in ashes. That little relic is in the writer's possession; treasured as one of the precious trifles belonging to History's store-house.

In fifteen minutes from the fall of the flag it was up again; a jury-mast was hastily raised, to which it was nailed, and it floated out as before. The honor of nailing it up belongs to Mr. Peter Hart, a New York gentleman, who had come to Fort Sumter some time before, to visit Major Anderson, with whom he had served in the Mexican war, and had remained at the fort as his guest. Though he took no part in the actual battle, yet he made himself useful to the garrison in many ways, of which this, recorded, is not the least.

And still the fire raged within and the cannon roared without. The flames increased in strength and volume, the air became heated all through the fort; but the more the little garrison suffered the harder they fought, and each ball that flew from their embrasures performed its errand well.

At about half past one P. M. a boat was seen approaching from Cumming's Point. Arrived at Fort Sumter a gentleman sprang from it, and, with a white handkerchief tied to the point of his sword to represent a flag of truce, he ran up to a port-hole, which he entered, saying to a soldier, whom he met,

"I wish to see the commandant—my name is Wigfall, and I come from General Beauregard."

The soldier went to inform Major Anderson, and Mr. Wigfall passed into the casemate where he met Captain Foster and Lieutenant Davis. To them he also introduced himself, stating that he came from General Beauregard. Then he added excitedly:

"Let us stop this firing. You are on fire, and your flag is down—let us quit!"

Mr. Davis replied,

"No, Sir, our flag is not down. Step out here and you will see it waving over the ramparts."

He ran out and looked up, but the smoke filled his eyes and he exclaimed, impatiently extending his sword:

"Here's a white flag,—will any body wave it out of the embrasure?"

Captain Foster said one of the men might do so, and Corporal Bingham, who was present, took it in his hand and jumped into the embrasure. And so the first white flag that waved from Fort Sumter was Senator Wigfall's handkerchief, tied to the point of that gentleman's sword!

But the firing still continued, when Mr. Wigfall said:

"If you will show a white flag from your ramparts, they will cease firing."

Captain Foster replied:

"If you request that a white flag shall appear there while you hold a conference with Major Anderson, and for that purpose alone, Major Anderson may permit it."

Major Anderson, at that moment came up, and the white flag was ordered to be raised.

"Major Anderson," said Mr. Wigfall, "you have defended your flag nobly, Sir. You have done all that is possible for man to do, and General Beauregard wishes to stop the fight. On what terms, Major Anderson, will you evacuate this fort?"

"Terms?" said Major Anderson, raising himself to his full height, and speaking with emphasis, *"I shall evacuate on the most honorable terms, or—die here!"*

Mr. Wigfall inclined his head;—respect for the glorious soul in that slight, frail form could not be withheld by even an enemy.

"Will you, Major Anderson," he then asked, "evacuate this fort upon the terms proposed to you the other day?"

"On the terms *last proposed* I will," was the reply.

"Then, Sir, I understand that the fort is to be ours?"

"On those conditions *only*, I repeat."

"Well, Sir, I will return to General Beauregard," said Mr. Wigfall; and, bowing low, he retired.

The white flag was then hauled down, and the American flag run up.

The Major now ordered that the firing should not be renewed, but that the men should take such refreshment as they had and rest awhile. Poor fellows! they were nearly exhausted. Those who had not been engaged at the guns had been toiling to subdue the fire; and faint for lack of food, and suffocating with smoke, it was only their giant hearts sustained them through.

When the flames were at the highest the enemy blazed away the faster, in order to cut down the men who were working to extinguish the fire; but a Divine shield was over them, and *not one life of the gallant First was taken by traitor hands.*

Some "own correspondent" stated that the Major sent men outside the fort on a raft to procure water wherewith to quench the fire:—nonsense! there was plenty of water inside for the purpose, if there had only been hands enough to use it; but the guns must be kept manned, so only those who could be spared from that duty gave attention to the burning buildings.

Their exertions, however, were sufficient to prevent explosions and disaster to life. The fire was kept under, and prevented from communicating with the magazines, until every ounce of powder was removed out of our reach also, for, when hostilities ceased, we had but four barrels and three cartridges on hand.

But the fire had done its work, and was now gradually burning out. The barracks and officers' quarters were destroyed; and as the smoke thinned away, so that the eye could penetrate the scene, nothing but charred and smoldering ruins were visible.

About three o'clock P. M. a formal deputation came to Major Anderson from General Beauregard and Governor Pickens, proposing the same terms as had been previously offered, except that they were not willing the Major should salute his flag.

To this Major Anderson would not consent.

About six o'clock came another deputation, consisting of Colonel Prior, Colonel Miles, Major Jones, and Captain Hartstein, and presented to Major Anderson General Beauregard's final terms. They were as follows. The garrison to march out with their side and other arms, with all the honors, in their own way and at their own time; to salute their flag and take it with them, and to take all their individual and company property; the enemy also agreeing to furnish transports, as Major Anderson might select, to any part of the country, either by land or water.

With all this Major Anderson was satisfied except the last clause. He would not consent to accept traveling accommodations from the enemy beyond the use of a steam-tug to convey him to the Government vessels outside the bar. . . .

And now all was arranged according to the Major's dictation, nothing remained but for the garrison to pack their effects and prepare to depart. This occupied a great part of the night, and the next morning a Charleston steamer was in attendance to convey them to the fleet. The baggage was placed on board, then the men were drawn up under arms, on the parade, and a portion told off, as gunners, to salute their flag.

And now came the last solemn ceremony, to end even more solemnly than we expected. The guns began to fire. One after another their loud voices rolled out upon the Sabbath air until fifty were counted, and then—an explosion, a cry, a rush, and every gun was silent. A pile of cartridges, containing eighty pounds of powder, had been laid inside the bomb-proof, on the parapet, convenient to one of the guns. Among these cartridges a spark had fallen, and while the guns were firing, and the soldiers cheering, the powder exploded, tearing the strong sheets of iron, of which the bomb-proof was composed, into fragments, and scattering them abroad like feathers, at the same time sending a shock—a thrill of horror to every heart, for a group of men had been standing round, and Oh! where were they now?

A few moments and anxious faces were gathered to the scene of the disaster:—sad scene!—one of our brave fellows was dead—quite dead—rent almost in two; another was dying—fractured in every limb; another yet so mutilated that the Doctor only shook his head, and six others more or less injured.

The departure of the garrison was, of course, delayed by this accident—the dead and the wounded must be cared for; yet the process of evacuation must be concluded, and so, while with tender hands and moist eyes the soldiers removed their bleeding comrades, the flag, in vindicating whose honor this warm blood was spilt, drooped its proud pinions and slowly descended from the ramparts.

All that men in their circumstances could do was then done by the garrison for the dead and wounded: the former was prepared for decent burial, the latter tended with the kindest care.

The enemy, impatient to take possession of the fort, now arrived. Governor Pickens and General Beauregard with their aides landed and entered, but, seeing what had occurred, immediately tendered every assistance. A minister was accordingly sent for to Charleston, to perform the service for the dead, and physicians to take charge of those whom we should be obliged to leave behind living. Meanwhile a strong coffin was put together, a grave dug in the parade, and, shortly after the clergyman arrived, the funeral proceeded.

With military honors the scarcely cold remains were buried: the Major heading the procession with crape upon his sword. With the rites of the Church the coffin was lowered into the grave, and, awaiting the resurrection, when the justice of every cause shall be righteously proved, Daniel Howe was left sleeping in Fort Sumter.

The wounded men, all but two who were quite unfit to bear the voyage, were then removed to the steamer. These, under promise of the kindest treatment, were trusted to the hospitality of the South Carolinians; one of them, George Fielding, was, therefore, conveyed to the Charleston Hospital, the other, Edward Galway, whose hours were numbered, was made as comfortable as possible in the fort.

These sad details arranged, Major Anderson issued his final orders for embarkation; and, carrying their flag and even its shattered mast, with band playing *Yankee Doodle,* the garrison marched out of the fort and went on board the steamer. As the Major emerged from the gate the music changed into *Hail to the Chief*:—simple tribute but no less heart-felt!

It was now late in the afternoon, and the garrison had eaten nothing since their scanty breakfast of pork and coffee; it would, therefore, have been most desirable to have got out on board the transport without delay; but the state of the tide was such that the little steamer could not move, and all night she lay under the walls of Fort Sumter. Had they had only their own discomforts to think of, they would have felt more the inconveniences of that long delay without food or resting places; but thoughts of their dying comrade in the fort, whose groans almost reached their ears, filled their minds, even to the exclusion of self. Before they left, however, the sufferer was released. An officer came on board the steamer to inform Major Anderson of the death of Edward Galway, and to assure him that the deceased should be buried beside Howe, with the honors due to a brave soldier.

Those two men, Daniel Howe and Edward Galway, were natives of Ireland—the first from the County Tipperary, the last from the County Cork. They fought in the defence of our flag, they died in doing it honor:—their blood was the first that flowed—their lives were the first that were sacrificed in the cause of our glorious UNION.

Early on Monday morning, April 15th, with the rising of the tide, the Isabel, on board which our garrison lay, steamed out of the Charleston waters to where the United States vessels lay, waiting to receive the gallant freight. The little band were welcomed with cheers by the fleet, and the Baltic, on board which they were taken, felt honored by their presence. Every preparation had been made for their comfort, and nothing that could be done to atone for their past privation was neglected.

The Sumter flag, which had floated over the Isabel, was immediately hoisted on the Baltic, and a salute fired; and then Major Anderson was observed to bow his head and weep.

Lincoln's Call for Troops

(April 15, 1861)

Immediately following the attack on Fort Sumter, President Lincoln issued a call to state militias to provide seventy-five thousand men for three-month service in the Federal army. Though some in his cabinet urged him to call for as many as two hundred thousand, Lincoln, who was aware that arming and provisioning such a large force would take time, was satisfied initially to quadruple the size of the national army. The troops were due in Washington on May 2. He was, at that point, undoubtedly envisioning a short-term conflict. State quotas were established based on population, and the response from the states was immediate.

In issuing the call, Lincoln knew he was risking the fragile allegiance of the border states. Most significantly, the call effectively killed any hope that Virginia would remain in the Union. Fort Sumter was a blow to that hope, but raising troops to fight fellow slaveholding states was the final straw. On April 17, the Virginia Convention voted to secede.

O.R.—SERIES III—VOLUME I [S# 122]

CORRESPONDENCE, ORDERS, REPORTS, AND RETURNS OF THE UNION AUTHORITIES FROM NOVEMBER 1, 1860, TO MARCH 31, 1862.—#3

BY THE PRESIDENT OF THE UNITED STATES: A PROCLAMATION

Whereas the laws of the United States have been for some time past and now are opposed and the execution thereof obstructed in the States of South Carolina, Georgia, Alabama, Florida, Mississippi, Louisiana, and Texas by combinations too powerful to be suppressed by the ordinary course of judicial proceedings or by the powers vested in the marshals by law:

Now, therefore, I, Abraham Lincoln, President of the United States in virtue of the power in me vested by the Constitution and the laws, have thought fit to call forth, and hereby do call forth, the militia of the several States of the Union, to the aggregate number of 75,000, in order to suppress said combinations and to cause the laws to be duly executed.

The details of this object will be immediately communicated to the State authorities through the War Department.

I appeal to all loyal citizens to favor, facilitate, and aid this effort to maintain the honor, the integrity, and the existence of our National Union, and the perpetuity of popular government, and to redress wrongs already long enough endured.

I deem it proper to say that the first service assigned to the forces hereby called forth will probably be to repossess the forts, places, and property which have been seized from the Union, and in every event the utmost care will be observed, consistently with the objects aforesaid, to avoid any devastation, any destruction of or interference with property, or any disturbance of peaceful citizens in any part of the country.

And I hereby command the persons composing the combinations aforesaid to disperse and retire peaceably to their respective abodes within twenty days from date.

Deeming that the present condition of public affairs presents an extraordinary occasion, I do hereby, in virtue of the power in me vested by the Constitution, convene both houses of Congress.

Senators and Representatives are therefore summoned to assemble at their respective chambers at twelve o'clock noon on Thursday, the fourth day of July next, then and there to consider and determine such measures as in their wisdom the public safety and interest may seem to demand.

In witness whereof I have hereunto set my hand and caused the seal of the United States to be affixed.

Done at the city of Washington this fifteenth day of April, in the year of our Lord one thousand eight hundred and sixty-one, and of the Independence of the United States the eighty-fifth.

ABRAHAM LINCOLN.

By the President:
WILLIAM H. SEWARD,
Secretary of State.

TO ARMS!
TO ARMS!
YOUR COUNTRY CALLS.
THE UNION
IT MUST
AND SHALL BE PRESERVED!
VOLUNTEERS FOR THE WAR
ARE WANTED
IMMEDIATELY!
ENROLL IN THE INDEPENDENT COMPANY,
NOW RAISING FOR THE WAR!
A Meeting will be held at
The $100 Bounty Paid by the Government,
Capt. BILL YERKES.

The Anaconda Plan

The Anaconda Plan, sometimes referred to as Scott's Great Snake, was first developed by General Winfield Scott, a major hero of the Mexican-American War. In 1861, right before his resignation from the army, Scott proposed "strangulation" of the Confederacy by a blockade of the south Atlantic coast and the capture of Southern cities along

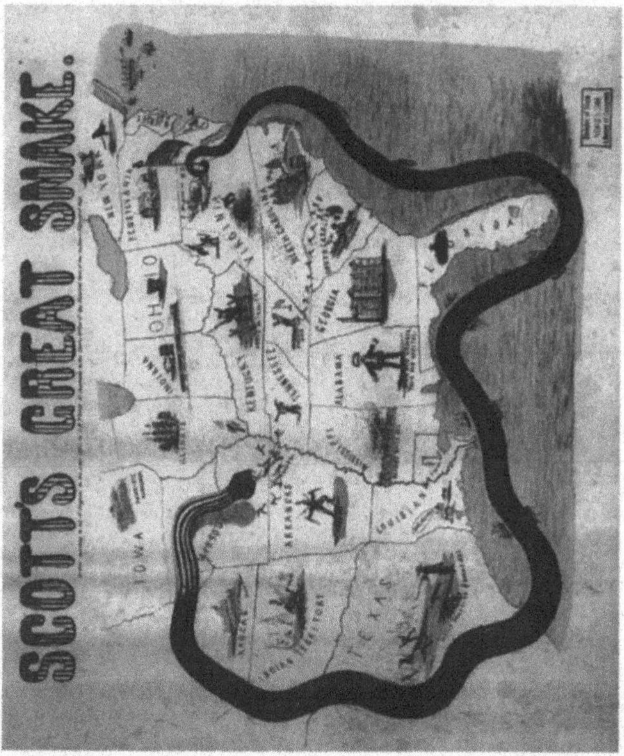

the Mississippi. At first the plan was derided as too simplistic, but, by the fall of Vicksburg on the Mississippi in 1863, it was clear that Scott's strategy was crucial to a Northern victory, and it was working.

"The Battle of Manassas"

Mary Bayard Clarke (1827–1886)

Mary Bayard Clarke was born in Raleigh, North Carolina, into a planter family. She traveled widely, living in Texas and Cuba, but returned to North Carolina, despite her husband's wishes, to be with him during the War. Mrs. Clarke wrote and sold poems and newspaper articles to augment the family income and after the War lived by her pen. "The Battle of Manassas" is one of a number of her poems published in William Shepperson's "War Songs of the South" (1862). As the poem evinces, she was a staunch supporter of the cause and would also be a sharp critic of Reconstruction.

Now glory to the "Lord of Hosts!" oh, bless and praise His
name,
For He hath battled in our cause, and brought our foes to
shame;
And honor to our BEAUREGARD, who conquered in His
might,
And for our children's children won Manassas' bloody fight.
Oh! let our thankful prayers ascend, our joyous praise re-
sound,
For God—the God of victory, our untried flag hath crowned!

They brought a mighty army, to crush us with a blow,
And in their pride they laughed to scorn the men they did not
know;
Fair women came to triumph, with the heroes of the day,
When the "boasting Southern rebels" should be scattered in
dismay,

And for their conquering Generals a lordly feast they spread;
But the wine in which we pledged them was all of ruby red!

The feast was like BELSHAZZAR'S—in terror and dismay,
Before *our* conquering heroes their Generals ran away.

God had weighed them in the balance; and His hand upon the wall,
At the taking of Fort Sumter, had fore-doomed them to their fall.
But they would not heed the warning, and scoffed in unbelief,
'Till their scorn was changed to wailing, and their laughter into grief!

All day the fight was raging, and amid the cannon's peal
Rang the cracking of our rifles, and the clashing of our steel;
But above the din of battle, our shout of triumph rose,
As we charged upon their batteries, and turned them on our foes.
We staid not for our fallen, and we thought not of our dead,
Until the day was ours, and the routed foe had fled.

But once our spirits faltered—BEE and BARTOW both were slain,
And our gallant Colonel HAMPTON lay wounded on the plain;
But BEAUREGARD, God bless him! led the legion in his stead,
And JOHNSTON seized the colors, and waved them o'er his head!
E'en coward must have followed, when such heroes led the way;
And no dastard blood was flowing in Southern veins that day!

But every arm was strengthened, and every heart wits stirred,
As shouts of "DAVIS! DAVIS!" along Our line were heard;
As he rode into the battle, the joyous news flew fast,
And the dying raised their voices, and cheered him as he passed.
Oh! with such glorious leaders, in Cabinet and field,
The gallant Southern chivalry will die, but never yield!

But from the wings of Victory the shifts of death were sped,
And our pride is dash'd with sorrow when we count our noble dead;
Though in our hearts they're living—and to our sons we'll tell
How gloriously our FISHER and our gallant JOHNSON fell;
And the name of each we'll cherish as an honor to his State,
And teach our boys to envy, and, need be, meet their fate.

Then "glory to the Lord of Hosts!" oh, bless and praise His name,
For He hath battled in our cause, and brought our foes to shame.
And honor to our BEAUREGARD, who conquered in His might.
And for our children's children, won Manassas' bloody fight.
Oh! let our grateful prayers ascend, our joyous praise resound,
For God, the God of victory, our untried flag hath crowned.

EYEWITNESS AT FIRST MANASSAS

William Howard Russell (1820–1896)

Russell was the first newspaper correspondent to actually report a war from the field. A veteran journalist of the Crimean War, he was sent by the *London Times* to Washington to cover the American Civil War and was regarded as influential in forming British public opinion. In 1861, he joined General McDowell's troops at Manassas and described the high expectations of the civilians and politicians who had come out from the capital, with opera glasses, parasols, and picnic baskets, to enjoy the spectacle of what they believed would be the single battle of the War. His highly critical coverage of the panic and disarray that followed the Confederate rout of the Union Army earned him the deep resentment of the Lincoln administration, and he was denied access to further Union battlefields. Completely isolated, he returned to London, but not before commenting in his diary about the first lady: "Poor Mrs. Lincoln. A more preposterous-looking female I never saw." In England he continued to be a supporter of the Union cause. He was knighted in 1895.

It was a strange scene before us. From the hill a densely wooded country, dotted at intervals with green fields and cleared lands, spread five or six miles in front, bounded by a line of blue and purple ridges, terminating abruptly in escarpments towards the left front, and swelling gradually towards the right into the lower spines of an offshoot from the Blue Ridge Mountains. On our left the view was circumscribed by a forest which clothed the side of the ridge on which we stood, and covered its shoulder far down into the plain. A gap in the nearest chain of the hills in our front was pointed out by the by-standers as the

Pass of Manassas, by which the railway from the West is carried into the plain, and still nearer at hand, before us, is the junction of that rail with the line from Alexandria, and with the railway leading southwards to Richmond. The intervening space was not a deal level; undulating lines of forest marked the course of the streams which intersected it, and gave, by their variety of color and shading an additional charm to the landscape which, enclosed in a framework of blue and purple hills, softened into violet in the extreme distance, presented one of the most agreeable displays of simple pastoral woodland scenery that could be conceived.

But the sounds which came upon the breeze, and the sights which met our eyes, were in terrible variance with the tranquil character of the landscape. The woods far and near echoed to the roar of cannon, and thin frayed lines of blue smoke marked the spots whence came the muttering sound of rolling musketry; the white puffs of smoke burst high above the tree-tops, and the gunners' rings from shell and howitzer marked the fire of the artillery.

Clouds of dust shifted and moved through the forest; and through the wavering mists of light-blue smoke, and the thicker masses which rose commingling from the feet of men and the mouths of cannon, I could see the gleam of arms and the twinkling of bayonets.

On the hill beside me there was a crowd of civilians on horseback, and in all sorts of vehicles, with a few of the fairer, if not gentler sex. A few officers and some soldiers, who had straggled from the regiments in reserve, moved about among the spectators, and pretended to explain the movements of the troops below, of which they were profoundly ignorant.

The cannonade and musketry had been exaggerated by the distance and by the rolling echoes of the hills; and sweeping the position narrowly with my glass from point to point, I failed to discover any traces of close encounter or very severe fighting. The spectators were all excited, and a lady with an opera-glass who was near me, was quite beside herself when an unusually heavy discharge roused the current of her blood—"That is splendid. Oh, my! Is not that first-rate? I guess we will be in Richmond this time to-morrow." These, mingled with coarser exclamations, burst from the politicians who had come out to see the triumph of the Union arms. I was particularly irritated by constant applications for the loan of my glass. One broken-down looking soldier observing my flask, asked me for a drink, and took a startling pull, which left but little between the bottom and utter vacuity.

"Stranger, that's good stuff and no mistake. I have not had such a drink since I come South. I feel now as if I'd like to whip ten Seceshers."

From the line of the smoke it appeared to me that the action was in an oblique line from our left, extending farther outwards towards the right, bisected by a road from Centreville, which descended the hill close at hand and ran right across the undulating plain, its course being marked by the white covers of the baggage and commissariat wagons as far as a turn of the road, where the trees closed in upon them. Beyond the right of the curling smoke clouds of dust appeared from time to time in the distance, as if bodies of cavalry where moving over a sandy plain.

Notwithstanding all the exultation and boastings of the people at Centreville, I was well convinced no advance of any importance or any great success had been achieved, because the ammunition and baggage wagons had never moved, nor had the reserves received any orders to follow in the line of the army.

The clouds of dust on the right were quite inexplicable. As we were looking, my philosophic companion asked me in perfect seriousness, "Are we really seeing a battle now? Are they supposed to be fighting where all that smoke is going on? This is rather interesting, you know."

Up came our black boy. "Not find a bit to eat, sir, in all the place." We had, however, my little paper of sandwiches, and descended the hill to a by-lane off the village, where, seated in the shade of the gig, Mr. Warre and myself, dividing our provision with the driver, wound up a very scanty, but much relished, repast with a bottle of tea and half the bottle of Bordeaux and water, the remainder being prudently reserved at my request for contingent remainders. Leaving orders for the saddle-horse, which was eating his first meal, to be brought up the moment he was ready—I went with Mr. Warre to the hill once more and observed that the line had not sensibly altered whilst we were away.

An English gentleman, who came up flushed and heated from the plain, told us that the Federals had been advancing steadily, in spite of a stubborn resistance, and had behaved most gallantly.

Loud cheers suddenly burst from the spectators, as a man dressed in the uniform of an officer, whom I had seen riding violently across the plain in an open space below, galloped along the front, waving his cap and shouting at the top of his voice. He was brought up by the press of people round his horse close to where I stood. "We've whipped them on all points," he cried. "We have taken all their batteries. They are retreating as fast as they can, and we are after them." Such cheers as rent the welkin! The congressmen shook hands with each other, and cried out, "Bully for us. Bravo! Didn't I tell you so." The Germans uttered their martial cheers and the Irish hurrahed wildly. At this moment my horse was brought up the hill, and I mounted and turned towards the road to the front, whilst Mr. Warre and his companion proceeded straight down the hill.

By the time I reached the lane, already mentioned, which was in a few minutes, the string of commissariat wagons was moving onwards pretty briskly, and I was detained until my friends appeared at the roadside. I told Mr. Warre I was going forward to the front as fast as I could, but that I would come back, under any circumstances, about an hour before dusk, and would go straight to the spot where we had put up the gig by the road-side, in order to return to Washington. Then getting into the fields, I pressed my horse, which was quite recovered from his twenty-seven miles' ride and full of spirit and mettle, as fast as I could, making detours here and there to get through the ox fences, and by the small streams which cut up the country. The firing did not increase but rather diminished in volume, though it now sounded close at hand.

I had ridden between three and a half and four miles, as well as I could judge, when I was obliged to turn for the third and fourth time into the road by a considerable stream, which was spanned by a bridge, towards which I was threading my way, when my attention was attracted by loud shouts in advance, and I perceived several wagons coming from the direction of the battle-field, the drivers of which were endeavoring to force their horses past the ammunition carts going in the contrary direction near the bridge; a thick cloud of dust rose behind them, and running by the side of the wagons, were a number of men in uniform whom I supposed to be the guard. My first impression was that the wagons were returning for fresh supplies of ammunition. But every moment the crowd increased, drivers and men cried out with the most vehement gestures, "Turn back! Turn back! We are whipped." They seized the heads of the horses and swore at the opposing drivers. Emerging from the crowd a breathless man in the uniform of an officer with an empty scabbard dangling by his side, was cut off by getting between my horse and a cart for a moment. "What is the matter, sir? What is all this about?" "Why, it means we are pretty badly whipped, that's the truth," and continued.

By this time the confusion had been communicating itself through the line of wagons towards the rear, and the drivers endeavored to turn round their vehicles in the narrow road, which caused the usual amount of imprecations from the men and plunging and kicking from the horses.

The crowd from the front continually increased, the heat, the uproar, and the dust were beyond description, and these were augmented when some cavalry soldiers, flourishing their sabres and preceded by an officer who cried out, "Make way there—make way there for the General," attempted to force a covered wagon in which was seated a man with a bloody handkerchief round his head through the press.

I had succeeded in getting across the bridge with great difficulty before the wagon came up, and I saw the crowd on the road was still gathering thicker and thicker. Again I asked an officer, who was on foot, with his sword under his arm, "What is all this for?" "We are whipped, sir. We are all in retreat. You are all to go back." "Can you tell me where I can find General McDowell?" "No! nor can any one else."

A few shells could be heard bursting not very far off, but there was nothing to account for such an extraordinary scene. A third officer, however, confirmed the report that the whole army was in retreat, and that the Federals were beaten on all points, but there was nothing in this disorder to indicate a general rout. All these things took place in a few seconds. I got up out of the road into a corn-field, through which men were hastily walking or running, their faces streaming with perspiration, and generally without arms, and worked my way for about half a mile or so, as well as I could judge, against an increasing stream of fugitives, the ground being strewed with coats, blankets, firelocks, cooking tins, caps, belts, bayonets—asking in vain where General McDowell was.

Again I was compelled by the condition of the fields to come into the road; and having passed a piece of wood and a regiment which seemed to be moving back in column of march in tolerably good order, I turned once more into an opening close to a white house, not far from the lane, beyond which there was a belt of forest. Two field-pieces unlimbered near the house, with panting horses in the rear, were pointed towards the front, and along the road beside them there swept a tolerably steady column of men mingled with field ambulances and light baggage carts, back to Centreville. I had just stretched out my hand to get a cigar-light from a German gunner, when the dropping shots which had been sounding through the woods in front of us, suddenly swelled into an animated fire. In a few seconds a crowd of men rushed out of the wood down toward the guns, and the artillerymen near me seized the trail of a piece, and were wheeling it round to fire, when an officer or sergeant called out, "Stop! stop! They are our own men"; and in two or three minutes the whole battalion came sweeping past the guns at the double, and in the utmost disorder. Some of the artillerymen dragged the horses out of the tumbrils; and for a moment the confusion was so great I could not understand what had taken place; but a soldier whom I stopped, said, "We are pursued by their cavalry; they have cut us all to pieces."

Murat himself would not have dared to move a squadron on such ground. However, it could not be doubted that something serious was taking place; and at that moment a shell burst in front of the house, scattering the soldiers near it, which was followed by another that bounded along the road; and in a few minutes more out came another regiment from the wood, almost as broken as the first. The scene on the road had now assumed an aspect which has not a parallel in any description I have ever read. Infantry soldiers on mules and draught horses, with the harness clinging to their heels, as much frightened as their riders; negro servants on their masters' chargers; ambulances crowded with unwounded soldiers; wagons swarming with men who threw out the contents in the road to make room, grinding through a shouting, screaming mass of men on foot, who were literally yelling with rage at every halt, and shrieking out, "Here are the cavalry! Will you get on?" This portion of the force was evidently in discord.

There was nothing left for it but to go with the current one could not stem. I turned round my horse from the deserted guns, and endeavored to find out what had occurred as I rode quietly back on the skirts of the crowd. I talked with those on all sides of me. Some uttered prodigious nonsense, describing batteries tier over tier, and ambuscades, and blood running knee-deep. Others described how their boys had carried whole lines of intrenchments, but were beaten back for want of reinforcements. The names of many regiments were mentioned as being utterly destroyed. Cavalry and bayonet charges and masked batteries played prominent parts in all the narrations. Some of the officers seemed to feel the disgrace of defeat; but the strangest thing was the general indifference with which the event seemed to be regarded by those who collected their senses as soon as they got out of fire, and who said they were just going as far as Centreville, and would have a big fight to-morrow.

By this time I was unwillingly approaching Centreville in the midst of heat, dust, confusions, imprecations inconceivable. On arriving at the place where a small rivulet crossed the road, the throng increased still more. The ground over which I had passed going out was now covered with arms, clothing of all kinds, accoutrements thrown off and left to be trampled in the dust under the hoofs of men and horses. The runaways ran along-side the wagons, striving to force themselves in among the occupants, who resisted tooth and nail. The drivers spurred and whipped and urged the horses to the utmost of their bent. I felt an inclination to laugh, which was overcome by disgust, and by that vague sense of something extraordinary taking place which is experienced when a man sees a number of people acting as if driven by some unknown terror. As I rode in the crowd with men clinging to the stirrup-leathers, or holding on by anything they could lay hands on, so that I had some apprehension of being pulled off, I spoke to the men, and asked them over and over again not to be in such a hurry. "There's no enemy to pursue you. All the cavalry in the world could not get at you." But I might as well have talked to the stones.

For my own part, I wanted to get out of the ruck as fast as I could, for the heat and dust were very distressing, particularly to a half-starved man. Many of the fugitives were in the last stages of exhaustion, and some actually sank down by the fences, at the risk of being trampled to death. Above the roar of the flight, which was like the rush of a great river, the guns burst forth from time to time.

The road at last became somewhat clearer; for I had got ahead of some of the ammunition train and wagons, and the others were dashing up the hill towards Centreville. The men's great-coats and blankets had been stowed in the trains; but the fugitives had apparently thrown them out on the road, to make room for themselves. Just beyond the stream I saw a heap of clothing tumble out of a large covered cart, and cried out after the driver, "Stop! stop! All the things are tumbling out of the cart." But my zeal was checked by a scoundrel putting his head out, and shouting with a curse, "If you try to stop the team, I'll blow your —— brains out." My brains advised me to adopt the principle of non-intervention.

A Final Letter

Major Sullivan Ballou (1829–1861)

Major Sullivan Ballou withdrew from a promising political career to become an officer in the 2nd Rhode Island Volunteers. On July 14, 1861, seven days before the battle of Manassas, he wrote a letter to his wife, a simple classic testimony to his love for her and their sons and his devotion to the Union. He died on July 29 from wounds received during the battle and the subsequent amputation of his leg, and was hastily buried at Sudley Church near the battlefield as the Union Army retreated to Washington. When Union soldiers returned to the site to recover his body, it was found to have been dug up and desecrated by Confederate soldiers.

The letter was never sent but was retrieved from his trunk after his death and delivered to his wife. Several versions of the letter exist, but none in Ballou's hand; the original appears not to have survived.

July the 14th, 1861
Washington DC

My very dear Sarah:

The indications are very strong that we shall move in a few days—perhaps tomorrow. Lest I should not be able to write you again, I feel impelled to write lines that may fall under your eye when I shall be no more.

Our movement may be one of a few days' duration and full of pleasure—and it may be one of severe conflict and death to me. Not my will, but thine O God, be done. If it is necessary that I should fall on the battlefield for my country, I am ready. I have no misgivings about, or lack of confidence in, the cause in which I am engaged, and my courage does not halt or falter. I know how strongly American Civilization now leans upon the triumph of the Government, and how great a debt we owe to those who went before us through the blood and suffering of the Revolution. And I am willing—perfectly willing—to lay down all my joys in this life, to help maintain this Government, and to pay that debt.

But, my dear wife, when I know that with my own joys I lay down nearly all of yours, and replace them in this life with cares and sorrows—when, after having eaten for long years the bitter fruit of orphanage myself, I must offer it as their only sustenance to my dear little children—is it weak or dishonorable, while the banner of my purpose floats calmly and proudly in the breeze, that my unbounded love for you, my darling wife and children, should struggle in fierce, though useless, contest with my love of country?

I cannot describe to you my feelings on this calm summer night, when two thousand men are sleeping around me, many of them enjoying the last, perhaps, before that of death—and I, suspicious that Death is creeping behind me with his fatal dart, am communing with God, my country, and thee.

I have sought most closely and diligently, and often in my breast, for a wrong motive in thus hazarding the happiness of those I loved and I could not find one. A pure love of my country and of the principles I have often advocated before the people and "the name of honor that I love more than I fear death" have called upon me, and I have obeyed.

Sarah, my love for you is deathless, it seems to bind me to you with mighty cables that nothing but Omnipotence could break; and yet my love of Country comes over me like a strong wind and bears me irresistibly on with all these chains to the battlefield.

The memories of the blissful moments I have spent with you come creeping over me, and I feel most gratified to God and to you that I have enjoyed them so long. And hard it is for me to give them up and burn to ashes the hopes of future years, when God willing, we might still have lived and loved together and seen our sons grow up to honorable manhood around us. I have, I know, but few and small claims upon Divine Providence, but something whispers to me—perhaps it is the wafted prayer of my little Edgar—that I shall return to my loved ones unharmed. If I do not, my dear Sarah, never forget how much I love you, and when my last breath escapes me on the battlefield, it will whisper your name.

Forgive my many faults, and the many pains I have caused you. How thoughtless and foolish I have oftentimes been! How gladly would I wash out with my tears every little spot upon your happiness, and struggle with all the misfortune of this world, to shield you and my children from harm. But I cannot. I must watch you from the spirit land and hover near you, while you buffet the storms with your precious little freight, and wait with sad patience till we meet to part no more.

But, O Sarah! If the dead can come back to this earth and flit unseen around those they loved, I shall always be near you; in the garish day and in the darkest night—amidst your happiest scenes and gloomiest hours—always, always; and if there be a soft breeze upon your cheek, it shall be my breath; or the cool air fans your throbbing temple, it shall be my spirit passing by.

Sarah, do not mourn me dead; think I am gone and wait for thee, for we shall meet again.

As for my little boys, they will grow as I have done, and never know a father's love and care. Little Willie is too young to remember me long, and my blue eyed Edgar will keep my frolics with him among the dimmest memories of his childhood. Sarah, I have unlimited confidence in your maternal care and your development of their characters. Tell my two mothers his and hers I call God's blessing upon them. O Sarah, I wait for you there! Come to me, and lead thither my children.

Sullivan

The United States Sanitary Commission (USSC)

Mary Livermore (1820–1905)

The War claimed an appalling number of lives. It is estimated that for every man killed in battle, two died from diseases such as dysentery, diarrhea, typhoid, and malaria fostered by overcrowded and unsanitary conditions on the field. In June 1861, President Lincoln authorized the United States Sanitary Commission, modeled after the British Sanitary Commission established during the Crimean War. It was a civilian agency organized to give oversight to the welfare of Union soldiers in army camps, field and military hospitals, and so-called soldiers homes, which supported discharged veterans in need. It is estimated that these services cut the disease rate, a major cause of mortality during the War, in half. Women numbering in the thousands served as volunteers, as nurses and organizers. Operating from headquarters in Gettysburg and numerous local outposts, the commission raised and distributed an estimated twenty-five million dollars in money and donated supplies. It also provided women with managerial experience that, in some cases, outlasted the War and influenced the Women's Rights Movement. The USSC also assisted veterans in gaining benefits until it was disbanded in 1866 and replaced by other postwar relief organizations; it was a forerunner of the American Red Cross.

Mary Livermore, who became a teacher and abolitionist after tutoring at a Virginia plantation before the War, joined the U.S. Sanitary Commission and organized a Sanitary Fair in Chicago, which raised more than $70,000. Lincoln donated his personal copy of the Emancipation Proclamation to the fair to be auctioned for $10,000. Here

Livermore describes the work of her colleague Mary Ann Bickerdyke, Grant's chief of nursing.

After the battle of Donelson, Mother Bickerdyke went from Cairo in the first hospital boat, and assisted in the removal of the wounded to Cairo, St. Louis, and Louisville, and in nursing those too badly wounded to be moved. The Sanitary Commission had established a depot of stores at Cairo, and on these she was allowed to make drafts *ad libitum:* for she was as famous for her economical use of sanitary stores as she had been before the war for her notable housewifery. The hospital boats at that time were poorly equipped for the sad work of transporting the wounded. But this thoughtful woman, who made five of the terrible trips from the battle-field of Donelson to the hospital, put on board the boat with which she was connected, before it started from Cairo, an abundance of necessaries. There was hardly a want expressed for which she could not furnish some sort of relief.

On the way to the battle-field, she systematized matters perfectly. The beds were ready for the occupants, tea, coffee, soup and gruel, milk punch and ice water were prepared in large quantities, under her supervision, and sometimes by her own hand. When the wounded were brought on board,—mangled almost out of human shape; the frozen ground from which they had been cut adhering to them; chilled with the intense cold in which some had lain for twenty-four hours; faint with loss of blood, physical agony, and lack of nourishment; racked with a terrible five-mile ride over frozen roads, in ambulances, or common Tennessee farm wagons, without springs; burning with fever; raving in delirium, or in the faintness of death,—Mother Bickerdyke's boat was in readiness for them.

"I never saw anybody like her," said a volunteer surgeon who came on the boat with her. "There was really nothing for us surgeons to do but dress wounds and administer medicines. She drew out clean shirts or drawers from some corner, whenever they were needed. Nourishment was ready for every man as soon as he was brought on board. Every one was sponged from blood and the frozen mire of the battle-field, as far as his condition allowed. His blood-stiffened, and sometimes horribly filthy uniform, was exchanged for soft and clean hospital garments. Incessant cries of 'Mother! Mother! Mother!' rang through the boat, in every note of beseeching and anguish. And to every man she turned with a heavenly tenderness, as if he were indeed her son. She moved about with a decisive air, and gave directions in such decided, clarion tones as to ensure prompt obedience. We all had an impression that she held a commission from the Secretary of War, or at least from the Governor of Illinois. To every surgeon who was superior, she held herself subordinate, and was as good at obeying as at commanding." And yet, at that time, she held no position whatever, and was receiving no compensation for her services; not even the beggarly pittance of thirteen dollars per month allowed by government to army nurses.

At last it was believed that all the wounded had been removed from the field, and the relief parties discontinued their work. Looking from his tent at midnight, an officer observed a faint light flitting hither and thither on the abandoned battlefield, and, after puzzling over it for some time, sent his servant to ascertain the cause. It was Mother Bickerdyke, with a lantern, still groping among the dead. Stooping down, and turning their cold faces towards her, she scrutinized them searchingly, uneasy lest some might be left to die uncared for. She could not rest while she thought any were overlooked who were yet living.

Up to this time, no attempt had been made to save the clothing and bedding used by the wounded men on the transports and in the temporary hospitals. Saturated with blood, and the discharges of healing wounds, and sometimes swarming with vermin, it had been collected, and burned or buried. But this involved much waste; and as these articles were in constant need, Mother Bickerdyke conceived the idea of saving them. She sent to the Commission at Chicago for washing-machines, portable kettles, and mangles, and caused all this offensive clothing to be collected. She then obtained from the authorities a full detail of contrabands, and superintended the laundering of all these hideously foul garments. Packed in boxes, it all came again into use at the next battle.

This work once begun, Mother Bickerdyke never intermitted. Her washing-machines, her portable kettles, her posse of contrabands, an ambulance or two, and one or two handy detailed soldiers, were in her retinue after this, wherever she went. How much she saved to the government, and to the Sanitary Commission, may be inferred from the fact that it was no unusual thing for three or four thousand pieces to pass through her extemporized laundry in a day. Each piece was returned to the hospital from which it was taken, or, if it belonged to no place in particular, was used *in transitu*. She saw it boxed, and the boxes deposited in some safe place, where she could easily reach them in time of need.

During a large part of her army life, Mrs. Bickerdyke was associated with, and most efficiently supplemented by, Mrs. Eliza Porter, wife of a Congregationalist clergyman of Chicago. She entered the service in the beginning, as did her associate, and turned not from the work until the war ended. Together they worked in the hospitals, enduring cold and hunger, dwelling amid constant alarms, breathing the tainted air of wounds and sickness, and foregoing every species of enjoyment save that which comes from the consciousness of duties well done. Unlike in all respects, they harmonized admirably; and each helped the other. Mrs. Bickerdyke came less frequently into collision with officials when in company with Mrs. Porter; and the obstacles in the way of the latter were more readily overcome when the energy of Mrs. Bickerdyke opposed them. Mrs. Porter patiently won her way, and urged her claims mildly but persistently. Mrs. Bickerdyke was heedless of opposition, which only nerved her to a more invincible energy; and she took what she claimed, no matter who opposed. Both were very dear to the soldiers, from each of whom they expected sympathy and pity, as well as courage and help.

After the wounded of Donelson were cared for, Mrs. Bickerdyke left the hospitals, and went back into the army. There was great sickness among our troops at Savannah, Tenn. She had already achieved such a reputation for devotion to the men, for executive ability, and versatility of talent, that the spirits of the sick and wounded revived at the very sound of her voice, and at the sight of her motherly face. While busy here, the battle of Shiloh occurred, nine miles distant by the river, but only six in a direct line. There had been little provision made for the terrible needs of the battle-field in advance of the conflict. The battle occurred unexpectedly, and was a surprise to our men,—who nearly suffered defeat,—and again there was utter destitution and incredible suffering. Three days after the battle, the boats of the Sanitary Commission arrived at the Landing, laden with every species of relief,—condensed food, stimulants, clothing, bedding, medicines, chloroform, surgical instruments, and carefully selected volunteer nurses and surgeons. They were on the ground some days in advance of the government boats.

Here Mother Bickerdyke was found, carrying system, order, and relief wherever she went. One of the surgeons went to the rear with a wounded man, and found her wrapped in the gray overcoat of a rebel officer, for she had disposed of her blanket shawl to some poor fellow who needed it. She was wearing a soft slouch hat, having lost her inevitable Shaker bonnet. Her kettles had been set up, the fire kindled underneath, and she was dispensing hot soup, tea, crackers, panado, whiskey and water, and other refreshments, to the shivering, fainting, wounded men.

"Where did you get these articles?" he inquired; "and under whose authority are you at work?"

She paid no heed to his interrogatories, and, indeed, did not hear them, so completely absorbed was she in her work of compassion. Watching her with admiration for her skill, administrative ability, and intelligence,—for she not only fed the wounded men, but temporarily dressed their wounds in some cases,—he approached her again:—

"Madam, you seem to combine in yourself a sick-diet kitchen and a medical staff. May I inquire under whose authority you are working?"

Without pausing in her work, she answered him, "I have received my authority from the Lord God Almighty; have you anything that ranks higher than that?" The truth was, she held no position whatever at that time. She was only a "volunteer nurse," having received no appointment, and being attached to no corps of relief.

The Chicago boat took down over one hundred boxes of sanitary stores, on which she was allowed to draw. But they were only as a drop in the bucket among the twelve thousand wounded, lying in extemporized hospitals in and around Savannah. Other consignments of sanitary goods were made to her from Chicago and Springfield, Ill. The agents of the St. Louis and Cincinnati Commissions gave to her freely, when she made requisition on them. When every other resource failed, Mother Bickerdyke would take an ambulance, and one of her detailed soldiers as driver, and go out foraging. Never returned she empty-handed. The contrabands were her friends and allies; and she always came back with eggs, milk, butter, and fowls, which were the main objects of her quest. These foraging expeditions sometimes placed her in great peril; but she scorned any thought of danger where the welfare of the boys was concerned.

After she became an agent of the Sanitary Commission, we endeavored to keep her supplied with what she needed. But emergencies were constantly arising which she could not foresee, and for which the Commission could not provide, which would throw her on her own resources; and these never failed her. Sometimes, when opportunities for purchasing hospital supplies came in her way, she would buy largely, and send the bills to the Commission with her endorsement. Again, at other times of great need, she would borrow money, expend it for the boys in her charge, and, sending to Mrs. Hoge and myself vouchers and notes, would leave the affair with us to settle.

The gentlemen of the Commission, while they had no doubt that the good woman made a legitimate use of the money and of the articles purchased, objected to these irregular and unbusiness-like transactions; and they were in the right. Again and again have we taken these bills, notes, and vouchers into our hands, and raised money to pay them outside the Commission, among personal friends who knew Mrs. Bickerdyke through sons, husbands, and brothers. They believed she should be sustained in her wonderful work, even though she were a little irregular in her proceedings.

The ladies of the city and country were continually sending Mrs. Bickerdyke boxes of clothing for her own use. In her life of hard work, her clothes were soon worn out; and as she never had time to bestow on herself, she was greatly in need of such kindnesses. Reserving for herself a few articles of which she had imperative need, she would take the remainder of the garments in her ambulance to the Southern women in the neighboring country, and peddle them for honey, fruit, milk, eggs, and butter, of which she never could have too much.

Among the articles sent her at one time were two very elegant long night-dresses, embroidered, and trimmed with ruffles and lace. They were the gift of very dear friends; and she had some scruples about bartering them away as she did other garments. Returning with the "plunder" she had received in exchange for her superfluous clothing, she crossed a railroad track, on which stood a train of box cars. Stopping the ambulance, she began to explore them, according to her usual custom. Inside of one were two wounded soldiers going home on furlough. Their unhealed wounds were undressed, and full of vermin; they were weak for lack of food, were depressed and discouraged, and in all respects were in a very sorry plight.

"Humph!" said Mother Bickerdyke; "now I see what them furbelowed night-gowns were sent down here for. The Lord meant I should put 'em to a good use, after all."

The wounds of the poor fellows were washed and cleansed. Tearing off bandages from the bottom of the night-dresses, she properly dressed and bandaged them. Socks, and drawers, and handkerchiefs were found in the ambulance; but she was entirely destitute of shirts. A happy thought came to her.

"Here, boys," she said; "put on the upper half of these night-gowns; they're just the thing. My sakes! but this *is* lucky!"

But to this the men decidedly objected. "They would wear the dirty, tattered shirts, that had not been changed in two months, rather than go home in a woman's night-gown!"

"Oh, pshaw, boys! don't be fools!" persisted practical Mother Bickerdyke. "Night *gowns,* or night *shirts*; what's the odds? These will be softer to your wounds; and Heaven knows they're enough sight cleaner. Put 'em on, and wear 'em home. If anybody says anything, tell them you've jerked 'em from the secesh, and the folks will think a heap sight more of you for it."

1862

Holding on desperately to the hope for a short war and a critical decisive victory, President Lincoln issued War Order # 1 calling for action and movement by the Union armies. This order directed at his generals was an expression of his anxiety about political dangers of a lengthy war undoing the delicate balance of limited aims. Time favored the South, the Northern Democrats opposed to the War, and even his political opponents in the cabinet and the Republican Party.

There was good news from Tennessee in February with victories at Fort Henry and Fort Donelson, opening the Cumberland and Tennessee rivers to Union forces and precipitating the evacuation of Nashville in February. These battles underscored the importance of rivers as theaters of battle and centers of commerce and troop movement.

Not only were these victories celebrated in the North, but General Ulysses S. Grant's refusal to negotiate surrender terms at Donelson earned him the nom de guerre "Unconditional Surrender Grant" in recognition of the very tough approach Lincoln so desperately wanted. Here was a warrior ready and eager to fight. Grant would in time eclipse McClellan, who lost his supreme command and, as General of the Army of the Potomac, was ordered by Lincoln to attack Richmond. The beginning of the Peninsula Campaign in March was a logistical challenge for McClellan involving the training, equipping, and transporting of more than one hundred thousand men, drawing on all his organizational skills.

If the South was to offset the North's superiority in men, money, and manufacturing, they needed innovation and guile. The Confederate ironclad the *Virginia,* which was a new kind of threat to the wooden-hulled Union navy, was neutralized by the *Monitor* designed by John Ericsson in the Brooklyn Navy Yard. The industrial age had gone to war and would change the character of the battlefield and introduce more deadly and powerful weaponry.

While the ironclads engaged in direct frontal assaults until they were both exhausted and spent, Little Mac's Army of the Potomac moved cautiously up the Peninsula toward Richmond—only to pause at Williamsburg waiting for reinforcements. McClellan had a penchant for overestimating the size of the opposing forces and the potential danger to his army. This was a prescription for hesitation and indecision. After the Seven Days Battle, Union forces pulled back and did not pursue their advantage, allowing the Confederates to withdraw to Richmond. President Lincoln concluded that McClellan had a serious case of the "slows."

In the west, more than forty thousand Confederate soldiers attacked Grant's army of sixty thousand at Shiloh on the Tennessee River in a fierce two-day battle with twenty-five thousand casualties. In the face of this kind of bloodletting, it was not surprising that both sides were numb. The term "victory" was taking on a new definition in which strategic advantage seemed to matter less when measured against the unprecedented number of casualties. Grant wrote of Shiloh that "it would have been possible to walk across the clearing in any direction stepping on dead bodies without a foot touching the ground." All Americans—North and South—wondered if this was the war of "remorseless revenge" all had feared. Romantic notions of a short war with chivalrous heroes and noble battles were one of the major casualties of Shiloh. Inexorably the divided country was about to be introduced to modern warfare, which featured more deadly weapons and obliterated the boundaries between civilian life and the battlefield. All was now fair game. Shiloh was described as Hell, and the term soon became a descriptor for the War itself.

The shattered ground now seemed increasingly to be drenched in blood. The death that year of the president's eleven-year-old son, Willie, linked personal tragedy with the national loss. The development of photography compelled many Americans to face the awfulness of the War. Many pondered how they would go forward, even what they were fighting for. The limited objectives of the early War years—to preserve the Union or maintain slavery—served to contain secession and ensure the neutrality of the border states. The blood of Shiloh, and later that year Antietam, obliterated all these self-imposed boundaries. If the nightmare of "remorseless revenge" was upon the nation, then slavery must end and the South be remade.

The issue of slavery was tugging at the fringes of the War, with a growing number of slaves escaping to the safety of the Union Army, in some cases with the support of field commanders, the increasing pressure of abolitionists, colonizers, radical republicans, and the powerful voice of Frederick Douglass, who was pressuring the president to strike a blow for freedom. In March, Lincoln invited slave states in the Union to perform acts of voluntary emancipation. Slavery was abolished in the capital and a national blot at the center of government was removed. Throughout the year, within the confines of cabinet deliberations, Lincoln concluded he must act. But always for Lincoln morality was married to politics, and his preliminary (this was the term that was used) proclamation freed slaves only in the rebellious states. While the measure had only limited goals, it fundamentally changed the character of the Civil War. The president now waited for a battlefield success to make the proclamation the law of the land.

On the Southern front, Lee followed up on the success of the Second Battle of Manassas in August and pressed his advantage by invading Maryland and sending shock waves into Washington, where many feared the capital would fall. Lee began to personify the guile that the South needed in order to overcome innate Northern economic and demographic advantages. His reputation assumed mythical proportions as more and more Northern soldiers expressed the fear that he was invincible and had taken the measure of his Union counterparts. However, at Antietam after a day of fierce fighting and more than five thousand dead, Lee withdrew. McClellan claimed victory, and the French and British waffled in their support for the Confederate cause.

The bloodiest day in the War paved the way for Lincoln's announcement of the preliminary Emancipation Proclamation on September 22.

Nevertheless, a frustrated Lincoln removed McClellan in November for his failure to press his advantage and ordered Ambrose Burnside to pursue Lee. In December, Burnside moved against Lee's heavily entrenched forces at Fredericksburg, lost the battle, and suffered twelve thousand casualties. Burnside was quickly replaced by General Joseph Hooker and the revolving door of Union generals was under way.

"The Death of Willie Lincoln"

Elizabeth Keckley (1818–1907)

The death from typhoid fever of her third and favorite son, Willie, at the age of eleven, on February 20, 1862, undoubtedly contributed to the emotional fragility that Mary Todd Lincoln fully succumbed to after her husband's death. So distraught that she was unable to attend either Willie's funeral or burial, she would not be comforted. Lincoln's ominously pointing out the asylum in view outside a White House window may have held her back from the edge. After the president's assassination, Willie's coffin was disinterred and placed beside his father's for the journey to the family burial plot in Springfield, Illinois. (Ironically and poignantly, Jefferson Davis's five-year-old son, Joe, also died during the War, falling from a banister outside the Confederate White House.) Elizabeth Keckley was Mrs. Lincoln's dressmaker and personal friend. Born into slavery, she became a talented seamstress and eventually purchased her freedom with $1,200 borrowed from a customer. With other black women, Keckley established the Contraband Relief Organization to assist slaves seeking refuge in Washington. In 1868, in an effort to assist Mary Lincoln financially, she published her diaries, *Behind the Scenes; or, Thirty Years a Slave and Four Years in the White House.*

Mrs. Lincoln returned to Washington in November, and again duty called me to the White House. The war was now in progress, and every day brought stirring news from the front—the front, where the Gray opposed the Blue, where flashed the bright sabre in the sunshine, where were heard the angry notes of battle, the deep roar of cannon, and the fearful rattle of musketry; where new graves were being made every day, where brother forgot a mother's early blessing and sought the life-blood of brother, and friend raised the deadly knife against friend. Oh, the front, with its stirring battle-scenes! Oh, the front, with its ghastly heaps of dead! The life of the nation was at stake; and when the land was full of sorrow, there could not be much gayety at the capital. The days passed quietly with me. I soon learned that some people had an intense desire to penetrate the inner circle of the White House. No President and his family, heretofore occupying this mansion, ever excited so much curiosity as the present incumbents. Mr. Lincoln had grown up in the wilds of the West, and evil report had said much of him and his wife. The polite world was shocked, and the tendency to exaggerate intensified curiosity. As soon as it was known that I was the modiste of Mrs. Lincoln, parties crowded around and affected friendship for me, hoping to induce me to betray the secrets of the domestic circle. One day a woman, I will not call her a lady, drove up to my rooms, gave me an order to make a dress, and insisted on partly paying me in advance. She called on me every day, and was exceedingly kind. When she came to take her dress away, she cautiously remarked:

"Mrs. Keckley, you know Mrs. Lincoln?"

"Yes."

"You are her modiste; are you not?"

"Yes."

"You know her very well; do you not?"

"I am with her every day or two."

"Don't you think you would have some influence with her?"

"I cannot say. Mrs. Lincoln, I presume, would listen to anything I should suggest, but whether she would be influenced by a suggestion of mine is another question."

"I am sure that you could influence her, Mrs. Keckley. Now listen; I have a proposition to make. I have a great desire to become an inmate of the White House. I have heard so much of Mr. Lincoln's goodness that I should like to be near him; and if I can enter the White House no other way, I am willing to go as a menial. My dear Mrs. Keckley, will you not recommend me to Mrs. Lincoln as a friend of yours out of employment, and ask her to take me as a chambermaid? If you will do this you shall be well rewarded. It may be worth several thousand dollars to you in time."

I looked at the woman in amazement. A bribe, and to betray the confidence of my employer! Turning to her with a glance of scorn, I said:

"Madam, you are mistaken in regard to my character. Sooner than betray the trust of a friend, I would throw myself into the Potomac river. I am not so base as that. Pardon me, but there is the door, and I trust that you will never enter my room again."

She sprang to her feet in deep confusion, and passed through the door, murmuring: "Very well; you will live to regret your action today."

"Never, never!" I exclaimed, and closed the door after her with a bang. I afterwards learned that this woman was an actress, and that her object was to enter the White House as a servant, learn its secrets, and then publish a scandal to the world. I do not give her name, for such publicity would wound the sensitive feelings of friends, who would have to share her disgrace, without being responsible for her faults. I simply record the incident to show how I often was approached by unprincipled parties. It is unnecessary to say that I indignantly refused every bribe offered.

The first public appearance of Mrs. Lincoln that winter was at the reception on New Year's Day. This reception was shortly followed by a brilliant levee. The day after the levee I went to the White House, and while fitting a dress to Mrs. Lincoln, she said:

"Lizabeth"—she had learned to drop the E—"Lizabeth, I have an idea. These are war times, and we must be as economical as possible. You know the President is expected to give a series of state dinners every winter, and these dinners are very costly; now I want to avoid this expense; and my idea is, that if I give three large receptions, the state dinners can be scratched from the programme. What do you think, Lizabeth?"

"I think that you are right, Mrs. Lincoln."

"I am glad to hear you say so. If I can make Mr. Lincoln take the same view of the case, I shall not fail to put the idea into practice."

Before I left her room that day, Mr. Lincoln came in. She at once stated the case to him. He pondered the question a few moments before answering.

"Mother, I am afraid your plan will not work."

"But it *will* work, if you will only determine that it *shall* work."

"It is breaking in on the regular custom," he mildly replied.

"But you forget, father, these are war times, and old customs can be done away with for the once. The idea is economical, you must admit."

"Yes, mother, but we must think of something besides economy."

"I do think of something else. Public receptions are more democratic than stupid state dinners—are more in keeping with the spirit of the institutions of our country, as you would say if called upon to make a stump speech. There are a great many strangers in the city, foreigners and others, whom we can entertain at our receptions, but whom we cannot invite to our dinners."

"I believe you are right, mother. You argue the point well. I think that we shall have to decide on the receptions."

So the day was carried. The question was decided, and arrangements were made for the first reception. It now was January, and cards were issued for February.

The children, Tad and Willie, were constantly receiving presents. Willie was so delighted with a little pony, that he insisted on riding it every day. The weather was changeable, and exposure resulted in a severe cold, which deepened into fever. He was very sick, and I was summoned to his bedside. It was sad to see the poor boy suffer. Always of a delicate constitution, he could not resist the strong inroads of disease. The days dragged wearily by, and he grew weaker and more shadow-like. He was his mother's favorite child, and she doted on him. It grieved her heart sorely to see him suffer. When able to be about, he was almost constantly by her side. When I would go in her room, almost always I found blue-eyed Willie there, reading from an open book, or curled up in a chair with pencil and paper in hand. He had decidedly a literary taste, and was a studious boy. A short time before his death he wrote this simple little poem:

"WASHINGTON, D. C., October 30, 1861.

"DEAR SIR:—I enclose you my first attempt at poetry.

"Yours truly,

"WM. W. LINCOLN.

"To the Editor of the National Republican."

LINES
ON THE DEATH OF COLONEL EDWARD BAKER.

THERE was no patriot like Baker,
So noble and so true;
He fell as a soldier on the field,
His face to the sky of blue.

His voice is silent in the hall
Which oft his presence graced;
No more he'll hear the loud acclaim
Which rang from place to place.

No squeamish notions filled his breast,
The Union was his theme;
No surrender and no compromise,
His day-thought and night's dream.

His Country has *her* part to play
To'rds those he has left behind;
His widow and his children all,
She must always keep in mind.

Finding that Willie continued to grow worse, Mrs. Lincoln determined to withdraw her cards of invitation and postpone the reception. Mr. Lincoln thought that the cards had better not be withdrawn. At least he advised that the doctor be consulted before any steps were taken. Accordingly Dr. Stone was called in. He pronounced Willie better, and said that there was every reason for an early recovery. He thought, since the invitations had been issued, it would be best to go on with the reception. Willie, he insisted, was in no immediate danger. Mrs. Lincoln was guided by these counsels, and no postponement was announced. On the evening of the reception Willie was suddenly taken worse. His mother sat by his bedside a long while, holding his feverish hand in her own, and watching his labored breathing. The doctor claimed there was no cause for alarm. I arranged Mrs. Lincoln's hair, then assisted her to dress. Her dress was white satin, trimmed with black lace. The trail was very long, and as she swept through the room, Mr. Lincoln was standing with his back to the fire, his hands behind him, and his eyes on the carpet. His face wore a thoughtful, solemn look. The rustling of the satin dress attracted his attention. He looked at it a few moments; then, in his quaint, quiet way remarked—

"Whew! our cat has a long tail to-night."

Mrs. Lincoln did not reply. The President added:

"Mother, it is my opinion, if some of that tail was nearer the head, it would be in better style;" and he glanced at her bare arms and neck. She had a beautiful neck and arm, and low dresses were becoming to her. She turned away with a look of offended dignity, and presently took the President's arm, and both went down-stairs to their guests, leaving me alone with the sick boy.

The reception was a large and brilliant one, and the rich notes of the Marine Band in the apartments below came to the sick-room in soft, subdued murmurs, like the wild, faint sobbing of far-off spirits. Some of the young people had suggested dancing, but Mr. Lincoln met the suggestion with an emphatic veto. The brilliance of the scene could not dispel the sadness that rested upon the face of Mrs. Lincoln. During the evening she came up-stairs several times, and stood by the bedside of the suffering boy. She loved him with a mother's heart, and her anxiety was great. The night passed slowly; morning came, and Willie was worse. He lingered a few days, and died. God called the beautiful spirit home, and the house of joy was turned into the house of mourning. I was worn out with watching, and was not in the room when Willie died, but was immediately sent for. I assisted in washing him and dressing him, and then laid him on the bed, when Mr. Lincoln came in. I never saw a man so bowed down with grief. He came to the bed, lifted the cover from the face of his child, gazed at it long and earnestly, murmuring, "My poor boy, he was too good for this earth. God has called him home. I know that he is much better off in heaven, but then we loved him so. It is hard, hard to have him die!"

Great sobs choked his utterance. He buried his head in his hands, and his tall frame was convulsed with emotion. I stood at the foot of the bed, my eyes full of tears, looking at the man in silent, awe-stricken wonder. His grief unnerved him, and made him a weak, passive child. I did not dream that his rugged nature could be so moved. I shall never forget those solemn moments—genius and greatness weeping over love's idol lost. There is a grandeur as well as a simplicity about the picture that will never fade. With me it is immortal—I really believe that I shall carry it with me across the dark, mysterious river of death.

Mrs. Lincoln's grief was inconsolable. The pale face of her dead boy threw her into convulsions. Around him love's tendrils had been twined, and now that he was dressed for the tomb, it was like tearing the tendrils out of the heart by their roots. Willie, she often said, if spared by Providence, would be the hope and stay of her old age. But Providence had not spared him. The light faded from his eyes, and the death-dew had gathered on his brow.

In one of her paroxysms of grief the President kindly bent over his wife, took her by the arm, and gently led her to the window. With a stately, solemn gesture, he pointed to the lunatic asylum.

"Mother, do you see that large white building on the hill yonder? Try and control your grief, or it will drive you mad, and we may have to send you there."

Mrs. Lincoln was so completely overwhelmed with sorrow that she did not attend the funeral. Willie was laid to rest in the cemetery, and the White House was draped in mourning. Black crape everywhere met the eye, contrasting strangely with the gay and brilliant colors of a few days before. Party dresses were laid aside, and every one who crossed the threshold of the Presidential mansion spoke in subdued tones when they thought of the sweet boy at rest—

"Under the sod and the dew."

Previous to this I had lost my son. Leaving Wilberforce, he went to the battle-field with the three months troops, and was killed in Missouri—found his grave on the battle-field where the gallant General Lyon fell. It was a sad blow to me, and the kind womanly letter that Mrs. Lincoln wrote to me when she heard of my bereavement was full of golden words of comfort.

Nathaniel Parker Willis, the genial poet, now sleeping in his grave, wrote this beautiful sketch of Willie Lincoln, after the sad death of the bright-eyed boy:

"This little fellow had his acquaintances among his father's friends, and I chanced to be one of them. He never failed to seek me out in the crowd, shake hands, and make some pleasant remark; and this, in a boy of ten years of age, was, to say the least, endearing to a stranger. But he had more than mere affectionateness. His self-possession—*aplomb,* as the French call it—was extraordinary. I was one day passing the White House, when he was outside with a play-fellow on the sidewalk. Mr. Seward drove in, with Prince Napoleon and two of his *suite* in the carriage; and, in a mock-heroic way—terms of intimacy evidently existing between the boy and the Secretary—the official gentleman took off his hat, and the Napoleon did the same, all making the young Prince President a ceremonious salute. Not a bit staggered with the homage, Willie drew himself up to his full height, took off his little cap with graceful self-possession, and bowed down formally to the ground, like a little ambassador. They drove past, and he went on unconcernedly with his play: the impromptu readiness and good judgment being clearly a part of his nature. His genial and open expression of countenance was none the less ingenuous and fearless for a certain tincture of fun; and it was in this mingling of qualities that he so faithfully resembled his father.

"With all the splendor that was around this little fellow in his new home, he was so bravely and beautifully *himself*—and that only. A wild flower transplanted from the prairie to the hothouse, he retained his prairie habits, unalterably pure and simple, till he died. His leading trait seemed to be a fearless and kindly frankness, willing that everything should be as different as it pleased, but resting unmoved in his own conscious single-heartedness. I found I was studying him irresistibly, as one of the sweet problems of childhood that the world is blessed with in rare places; and the news of his death (I was absent from Washington, on a visit to my own children, at the time) came to me like a knell heard unexpectedly at a merry-making.

"On the day of the funeral I went before the hour, to take a near farewell look at the dear boy; for they had embalmed him to send home to the West—to sleep under the sod of his own valley—and the coffin-lid was to be closed before the service. The family had just taken their leave of him, and the servants and nurses were seeing him for the last time—and with tears and sobs wholly unrestrained, for he was loved like an idol by every one of them. He lay with eyes closed—his brown hair parted as we had known it—pale in the slumber of death; but otherwise unchanged, for he was dressed as if for the evening, and held in one of his hands, crossed upon his breast, a bunch of exquisite flowers—a message coming from his mother, while we were looking upon him, that those flowers might be preserved for her. She was lying sick in her bed, worn out with grief and overwatching.

"The funeral was very touching. Of the entertainments in the East Room the boy had been—for those who now assembled more especially—a most life-giving variation. With his bright face, and his apt greetings and replies, he was remembered in every part of that crimson-curtained hall, built only for pleasure—of all the crowds, each night, certainly the one least likely to be death's first mark. He was his father's favorite. They were intimates—often seen hand in hand. And there sat the man, with a burden on his brain at which the world marvels—bent now with the load at both heart and brain—staggering under a blow like the taking from him of his child! His men of power sat around him—McClellan, with a moist eye when he bowed to the prayer, as I could see from where I stood; and Chase and Seward, with their austere features at work; and senators, and ambassadors, and soldiers, all struggling with their tears—great hearts sorrowing with the President as a stricken man and a brother. That God may give him strength for all his burdens is, I am sure, at present the prayer of a nation."

This sketch was very much admired by Mrs. Lincoln. I copy it from the scrap-book in which she pasted it, with many tears, with her own hands.

THE *MONITOR* AND THE *MERRIMAC*
(March 6–8, 1862)
Israel N. Stiles (1823–1895)

Immediately after the surrender of Fort Sumter, Lincoln called for a naval blockade of Confederate ports along the Atlantic coast. The Confederate Navy, in an effort to accelerate the production of an ironclad ship, raised the USS *Merrimac*, which had been sunk by the Union when it abandoned Norfolk Navy Yard, and refitted it as an ironclad. Renamed the *Virginia*, it subsequently did considerable damage to wooden blockading ships at Hampton Roads.

Meanwhile the Union hastily prepared its mythic adversary, the *Monitor*, built at the Brooklyn Navy Yard, which entered the harbor at Hampton Roads to engage the *Merrimac*—the name that has continued, perhaps merely for alliterative purposes, to designate the *Virginia*.

Though history has deemed the battle a draw, each side drew moral encouragement from its presumptive victory. Neither ship ever fought again. Rather than allowing the unwieldy *Merrimac* to fall into Union hands, the Confederate Navy destroyed her by explosion in May 1862, and the blockade of the Confederate ports continued. In December, the *Monitor* sank, with sixteen lives lost, in rough seas off Cape Hatteras, North Carolina. Despite the somewhat ignominious ending of both ships, the undisputed winner was innovation in maritime technology.

The great battle between the two iron-clads— the "Monitor" and the "Merrimac"—was fought in Hampton Roads Sunday, March 9, 1862. It was witnessed by the Union troops at Newport News, and by the Confederates across the bay at Ragged Island. Several accounts of this great contest have been lately printed, written by actual participants in the fight. My own narrative will be confined to such incidents as came under my own observation from on shore at Newport News.

I was at that time an officer of the Twentieth Indiana Volunteer Infantry. On the 8th of March, at about one o'clock P. M., the long-roll sounded, and the cry ran through the camp, "The 'Merrimac' is coming." She was now about five or six miles away, and looked very like a house submerged to the eaves, borne onward by a flood. We had been expecting her for some weeks. Our position was strongly fortified; we had heavy guns commanding our front; and we thought we were ready to receive her becomingly should she come within our range. Near by and at anchor were two of our largest sailing frigates, the "Congress" and "Cumberland," carrying fifty and thirty guns respectively. They also were ready, prepared as well as wooden ships could be to contend with an iron-clad. A few miles away were also the Union frigates "Minnesota," "Roanoke," and "St. Lawrence," and several gun-boats.

The "Merrimac" moved very slowly, accompanied by the "Beaufort" and "Raleigh," two small boats carrying one gun each. Not until she fired her first gun was there any outward sign of life on board, or of any armament, although she bore a crew of three hundred, and carried ten heavy guns. She had practically no visible deck; her crew were somewhere under her roof, but out of sight; her gun-ports were covered by hinged lids, which were raised only when her guns were brought forward for firing, and closed when they were withdrawn. She moved directly for the "Cumberland," which had cleared for action when the enemy was first sighted, and for the last half-hour had been ready with every man at his post. On her way she passed the "Congress" on her starboard side, and within easy range. The latter greeted her with a terrific broadside, to which the "Merrimac" responded, but kept on her course. Soon she came within range of the shore batteries, which opened upon her, and a minute or two later the thirty guns of the "Cumberland" were doing their duty. Many of the shots struck her, but they rebounded from her sides like marbles thrown by boys against a brick wall. Approaching the "Cumberland," she fired her bow gun, and struck her at full speed on her port bow, delivering another shot at the same time. The blow opened an immense hole in the frigate, and the force of it was so great that the "Merrimac's" iron prow, or beak, was wrenched off as she withdrew, and was left sticking in the side of the ship. The two shots which had been delivered from her bow gun had been terribly destructive. One entered the "Cumberland's" port, killing or wounding every man at one of her guns; the other raked her gun-deck from one end to the other. Withdrawing from the frigate, the "Merrimac" steamed slowly up the river, and turning, chose her own position, from which she delivered broadside after broadside into the now sinking ship, and then, changing her position, raked her fore and aft with shell and grape.

Meantime the shore batteries had kept up their fire, while the "Congress" had been towed up into position, and with her thirty guns pounded away at the iron monster. It was plain to us on shore that all combined were not a match for her. This must have been plain to the officers and men of the "Cumberland" as well; yet with their ship sinking under them, they continued the fight with a courage and desperation which is recorded of no other naval battle. It was stated at the time that while her bow guns were under water, those in the after part of the ship were made to do double duty. Her commander was called upon to surrender; he refused, and his men cheered him. Still she sank, and the men were ordered to save themselves by swimming ashore. The water closed over her with her flag still flying. In the month of August following, as I came down the James River on my return from Libby Prison, we passed near the place where she sank. Her topmast was still visible, and at its head still waved the old flag.

While the "Merrimac" was occupied with the "Cumberland," three Confederate steamers—the "Patrick Henry," "Jamestown," and "Teaser"—had come down the James River, and with the two gun-boats "Beaufort" and "Raleigh" had already engaged the "Congress." On our side, the screw frigate "Minnesota" had worked her way from the fort, but had grounded a mile and a half away. The "Roanoke," which was disabled by a broken shaft, was towed up by a couple of tugs, but from her great draught failed to get into position ; and the "St. Lawrence" was unable to use her fifty guns, for like reasons. For half an hour or more the "Merrimac" alternated her attentions between the

"Congress" and the "Minnesota." Owing to her great draught of water, she could not get near enough to the latter to do much damage, although the other gun-boats worried her exceedingly. She chose her own position with regard to the "Congress," and the utter destruction of the frigate became only a question of time. She had repeatedly been set on fire; her decks were covered with the dead and wounded; and the loss of life (including that of her commander) had been very great. She was run ashore, head on, and not long after hoisted the white flag. Two tugs were sent by the enemy alongside the "Congress" to take possession and to remove the prisoners, but a sharp fire of artillery and small arms from the shore drove them off. General Mansfield had directed the Twentieth Indiana to deploy along the beach and behind a sand ridge; and a couple of field-guns under command of Lieutenant Sanger were also wheeled into position to prevent the enemy from hauling away their prize. Captain Reed, of the Twentieth,—who had been as good a lawyer as he was now a good soldier,—raised a question of military law: "Since the ship has surrendered, has not the enemy the right to take possession of her?" The question was answered by General Mansfield (Judge Mansfield in this instance), in one of the shortest and most conclusive opinions on record. "I know the d—d ship has surrendered," said he, "but *we* have n't." That settled it. During the firing which was kept up by the infantry, Commander Buchanan, of the "Merrimac," received a wound which disabled him from further participation in the fight. Being unable to take possession of the frigate, the iron-clad again opened fire upon her, —this time with incendiary shot,—and the ship was soon on fire in several places.

It was now nearly dark, and the "Merrimac" hauled off, and anchored under the guns at Sewell's Point. She had received no substantial injury, and had demonstrated her ability to sink any wooden ship which might dare cope with her. Indeed, it looked that night as if the entire fleet would be wholly at her mercy on the morrow. The crew of the "Congress," such as were able, had escaped, and during the early hours of the evening the wounded had been brought ashore. They and those of the "Cumberland" filled the little hospital. Officers and men gathered around those brave fellows and listened with moistened eyes to their accounts of the fight. Some of them were very touching. One gunner, who had had both legs shot away just before the "Cumberland" sunk, hobbled several steps on his bloody stumps and seized the lanyard, that he might fire one more shot. An officer of the "Congress," who had both arms shot away, on being offered assistance, cried out: "Back to your guns, boys! give 'em hell! hurrah for the old flag!" The surgeons were kept busy. "Are you going to cut my leg off?" said a wounded man from the "Congress." "It's not much use," said the surgeon; "it would have to be taken off at the hip-joint, and not one in seventy of such cases ever recover; however, if you say so, we will take it off." "Go ahead, sir," said the sailor. He refused stubbornly to be placed under the influence of an anæsthetic, seemingly because to do so would be to admit that he lacked courage. He insisted upon having his head propped up, that he might observe the surgeon's work, which he did. Old Nature stood by him, and during the whole operation he did not apparently move a muscle. But she deserted him soon afterward, for he fainted dead away, and died two days later.

I found one poor fellow who bore the same name as my own, the surface of whose body was burned from head to heel. "I am all right," said he, "I have no pain. I shall get along." "His sensory nerves are destroyed," said the surgeon to me; "he will not live five hours." And so it proved.

The "Congress" continued to burn, her loaded guns discharging as the fire reached them, until about one o'clock A. M., when the fire reached her magazine, and she blew up with a tremendous noise, and with a shock so great that many of us on shore were prostrated, although we had retired to what we considered a perfectly safe distance. We were not sleepy that night, and before morning we heard of the arrival at the fort of "Ericsson's Battery." The surgeon of our regiment gave us a pretty good idea of what it was. "It is a floating battery," said he, "lying very low in the water, with its guns enclosed in a revolving turret which will, by its motion, cause shots striking it to glance off, and there's very little else of the thing above water to be struck." He was well up in the details of the construction, and had great confidence in the thing. "I believe the Doctor knows what he is talking about," said our colonel.

Morning came, and with it a hazy condition of the atmosphere, which for some time after daylight obscured everything from view in front but the charred wreck of the "Congress." After a while there came into view the great hull of the "Minnesota," and looking beyond and toward Sewell's Point, there appeared also the "Merrimac" and her attendants, the "Yorktown" and the "Patrick Henry." Alongside the "Minnesota" lay "Ericsson's Battery,"—a most insignificant-looking thing, a "cheese-box on a raft." The "Merrimac" and her companions were stationary, and seemed to be in consultation. At seven o'clock a plan seemed to have been adopted, and the "Merrimac" steamed in the direction of the "Minnesota." She was followed in the distance by the "Yorktown" and the "Patrick Henry," which were crowded with troops. The "Minnesota" was still hard aground, and the "Merrimac" evidently counted upon choosing her own position and disposing of her as she had done with the "Cumberland" and "Congress" the day before; but now a lion was in her path. The "Monitor" had steamed around the bow of the "Minnesota," and like another David, marched out to meet this Goliath. At 8.10 o'clock the fire opened, and the first shot was fired by the "Merrimac" at the "Minnesota." The next shot was from the "Monitor," which struck the "Merrimac" near her water-line, but with little effect. The iron-clads now came very near together—as it seemed to us on shore, less than one hundred feet apart,—and the firing was very rapid. Occasionally the "Merrimac" varied the entertainment by a few shots at the "Minnesota," and as often as the position would enable her to do so, the frigate would give her a broadside. Frequently the "Merrimac" would try to ram her little antagonist; but the ease with which the latter was handled enabled her to avoid a direct shock. In turn, the "Monitor" attempted to disable her enemy's screw, but without success. In vain the "Merrimac" tried to work her way up to close quarters with the "Minnesota;" the "Monitor" would not consent. Occasionally we could see the shots rebound from the sides of the "Merrimac," and every now and then one of the shells aimed at the "Minnesota" would pass over her and greet the quartermasters in the rear of our camp. One of them passed through the headquarters of General Mansfield. The shores, which were but a few miles apart, were lined with Union and Confederate soldiers, and the ramparts of the fort and the rigging of the ships at anchor were also crowded with witnesses of the fight.

At ten o'clock no perceptible damage had been sustained by either of the contestants. At about this time a dense smoke concealed both from view for several minutes, and when it lifted, the "Monitor" was observed moving off, whereat some of us concluded that she was disabled. "She's gone off to get her wind," said a soldier, who all along had been comparing the contest to a cock-fight. "She has but two guns," said our surgeon, "and has probably gone out of range to cool them." One of her officers told us later that she steamed off while she was hoisting shot into her turret. She returned within half an hour, and the fight was renewed, and at very close quarters. With her ten guns the "Merrimac" was able to return two or three shots for every one she received. She had no solid shot, as she expected to meet only wooden ships. Twenty-one in all of her shells struck the "Monitor," but without doing any injury that needed repairing. The "Merrimac" presented a large mark, and during the last two hours of the fight nearly every shot from the "Monitor" struck her. Her armor was broken in several places, and in three instances, when two or more shots had struck the same place, the wood backing was badly shattered. As the fight continued, nearly all of the smaller craft ventured near enough to fire a few shots, and when at one time the batteries at Sewell's Point joined in, the soldiers declared that there was "music by the entire band." The fight continued till 12.15, when the "Merrimac" quit, and steamed toward Norfolk. The commander of the "Monitor" wanted to follow her, but was prevented by orders from the flag officer, who thought the risk too great. The official report of the "Merrimac" says: "Our loss is two killed and nineteen wounded. The stern is twisted, and the ship leaks. We have lost the prow, starboard anchor, all the boats; the armor is somewhat damaged, the steam-pipe and smoke-stack both riddled, and the muzzles of two guns shot away. It was not easy to keep a flag flying; the flagstaffs were repeatedly shot away, the colors were hoisted to the smoke-stack, and several times cut down from it." She was placed in the dry dock at Norfolk, and every effort was made to put her in complete repair. Jones, who took command of her after Buchanan was wounded, says of the forty-five days during which Commodore Tatnell was in command of her: "There were only thirteen days that she was not in dock or in the hands of the navy-yard. Yet we succeeded in impressing the enemy that we were ready for active service. It was evident that the enemy very much overrated our power and efficiency."

So it seemed to us on shore. The "Merrimac" came down to the old fighting-ground on two or three occasions afterward, and dared the "Monitor" to fight her single-handed. The "Monitor" refused to meet her except in waters where the whole Union fleet could have pounced upon her. "We on our side," said Commodore Greene, "had received particular orders not to attack in the comparatively shoal waters above Hampton Roads, where the Union fleet could not manœuvre." These orders were obeyed; and although the "Merrimac" sent her consorts "Jamestown" and "Raleigh," and hauled off two brigs and a schooner from right under the very noses of our fleet, the "Monitor" refused to budge. Our surgeon guessed rightly the reason that the "Merrimac's" challenge was refused. The "Monitor" was the only vessel that could possibly cope with her, and should some mishap befall her, the rest of the fleet would be wholly at the "Merrimac's" mercy. So the position taken by the flag officer must have been a wise one; but that did not prevent us land-lubbers from thinking that we saw a big white feather.

On the 10th of May the enemy abandoned Norfolk, on the 11th blew up the "Merrimac," and on the 12th we marched in. On visiting the navy-yard we saw the two guns of the "Merrimac," the muzzles of which had been knocked off in the fight. We talked with one of the engineers who had charge of the repairs made upon the "Merrimac." He stated to us that a shot from the "Monitor" entered one of her ports, lodged in the backing of the opposite side, and so "shivered her timbers that she never afterward could be made seaworthy. . . . She could not have been kept afloat for twelve hours, and her officers knew it when they went out and dared the 'Monitor' to fight her. It was a case of pure bluff; we didn't hold a single pair." Let me quote again the remark of her commander, Jones: "It was evident that the enemy very much overrated our power and efficiency."

"TARDY GEORGE"

George Henry Boker (1826–1885)

George Brinton McClellan, a precocious graduate of West Point (he was admitted at fifteen and graduated second in his class), was appointed by Lincoln as Commander of the Army of the Potomac, which he turned into a highly disciplined fighting force. Known as "Little Mac" for his small stature, he was greatly respected by his troops, but irritated Washington for his seeming indecision. The 1862 poem "Tardy George" satirizes McClellan's apparent unwillingness to move beyond readying his troops for battles that went unfought. Lincoln described McClellan as having a case of the "slows," and, after McClellan failed to press his advantage against Lee's Army of Northern Virginia following the battle of Antietam, Lincoln removed him from command, ending his military career. In the 1864 election, McClellan ran against Lincoln as a "Copperhead" Democrat and peace candidate.

"Tardy George" is one of a number of Civil War poems written by Philadelphian George Henry Boker, generally regarded as a minor poet and playwright.

What are you waiting for, George, I pray?—
To scour your cross-belts with fresh pipe-clay?
To burnish your buttons, to brighten your guns;
Or wait you for May-day and warm Spring suns?
Are you blowing your fingers because they are cold,
Or catching your breath ere you take a hold?
Is the mud knee-deep in valley and gorge?
What are you waiting for, tardy George?

Want you a thousand more cannon made,
To add to the thousand now arrayed?

Want you more men, more money to pay?
Are not two millions enough per day?
Wait you for gold and credit to go,
Before we shall see your martial show;
Till Treasury Notes will not pay to forge?
What are you waiting for, tardy George?

Are you waiting for your hair to turn,
Your heart to soften, your bowels to yearn
A little more towards 'our Southern friends,'
As at home and abroad they word their ends?
'Our Southern friends!' whom you hold so dear
That you do no harm and give no fear,
As you tenderly take them by the gorge?
What are you waiting for, tardy George?

Now that you've marshaled your whole command,
Planned what you would, and changed what you planned;
Practiced with shot and practiced with shell,
Know to a hair where every one fell,
Made signs by day and signals by night;
Was it all done to keep out of a fight?
Is the whole matter too heavy a charge?
What are you waiting for, tardy George?

Shall we have more speeches, more reviews?
Or are you waiting to hear the news;
To hold up your hands in mute surprise
When France and England shall 'recognize'?
Are you too grand to fight traitors small?
Must you have a Nation to cope withal?
Well, hammer the anvil and blow the forge;
You'll soon have a dozen, tardy George!

Suppose for a moment, George, my friend—
Just for a moment—you condescend
To use the means that are in your hands,
The eager muskets, and guns, and brands;
Take one bold step on the Southern sod,
And leave the issue to watchful God!
For now the Nation raises its gorge,
Waiting and watching you, tardy George!

I should not much wonder, George, my boy,
If Stanton get in his head a toy,
And some fine morning, ere you are out,
He send you all 'to the right about'—
You and Jomini, and all the crew
Who think that war is nothing to do
But drill, and cipher, and hammer, and forge—
What are you waiting for, tardy George?

The Battle of Shiloh
(April 6–7, 1862)
Ulysses S. Grant (1822–1885)

Fought just one year into the War, Shiloh was the bloodiest battle so far in American history. The extent of the casualties shocked both sides, effectively ending any lingering hopes that the War would be short. Ironically the battle, referred to in the North as the battle of Pittsburg Landing, gets its name from a small log chapel at the site, whose name means "peace."

Grant was in command of the Army of the Tennessee, a force of just under fifty thousand men. On the morning of April 6, the Confederates attacked by surprise, inflicting very heavy losses. During an agonizing night, Grant pondered the casualties and suffering of his wounded men being triaged nearby, but rallied the next day and forced the Confederates to abandon their objective.

Some journalists criticized Grant's leadership on the first day of battle, particularly his being taken by surprise; they suggested erroneously that he was drunk and called for his removal. Lincoln, no doubt remembering his struggles with McClellan's indecisiveness, reportedly responded, "I can't spare this man; he fights."

During the night rain fell in torrents, and our troops were exposed to the storm without shelter. I made my headquarters under a tree a few hundred yards back from the river bank. My ankle was so much swollen from the fall of my horse the Friday night preceding, and the bruise was so painful, that I could get no rest. The drenching rain would have precluded the possibility of sleep, without this additional cause. Some time after midnight, growing restive under the storm and the continuous pain, I moved back to the log house on the bank. This had been taken as a hospital, and all night wounded men were being brought in, their wounds dressed, a leg or an arm amputated, as the case might require, and everything being done to save life or alleviate suffering. The sight was more unendurable than encountering the rebel fire, and I returned to my tree in the rain . . .

In a very short time the battle became general all along the line. This day everything was favorable to the Federal side. We now had become the attacking party. The enemy was driven back all day, as we had been the day before, until finally he beat a precipitate retreat. The last point held by him was near the road from the landing to Corinth, on the left of Sherman and right of McClernand. About three o'clock, being near that point, and seeing that the enemy was giving way everywhere else, I gathered up a couple of regiments, or parts of regiments, from troops near by, formed them in line of battle and marched them forward, going in front myself to prevent premature or long-range firing. At this point there was a clearing between us and the enemy favorable for charging, although exposed. I knew the enemy were ready to break, and only wanted a little encouragement from us to go quickly and join their friends who had started earlier. After marching to within musket-range, I stopped and let the troops pass. The command, *Charge,* was given, and was executed with loud cheers, and with a run, when the last of the enemy broke.

During this second day I had been moving from right to left and back, to see for myself the progress made. In the early part of the afternoon, while riding with Colonel McPherson and Major Hawkins, then my chief commissary, we got beyond the left of our troops. We were moving along the northern edge of a clearing, very leisurely, toward the river above the landing. There did not appear to be an enemy to our right, until suddenly a battery with musketry opened upon us from the edge of the woods on the other side of the clearing. The shells and balls whistled about our ears very fast for about a minute. I do not think it took us longer than that to get out of range and out of sight. In the sudden start we made, Major Hawkins lost his hat. He did not stop to pick it up. When we arrived at a perfectly safe position we halted to take an account of damages. McPherson's horse was panting as if ready to drop. On examination it was found that a ball had struck him forward of the flank just back of the saddle, and had gone entirely through. In a few minutes the poor beast dropped dead; he had given no sign of injury until we came to a stop. A ball had struck the metal scabbard of my sword, just below the hilt, and broken it nearly off; before the battle was over, it had broken off entirely. There were three of us: We had lost a horse, killed, one a hat, and one a sword-scabbard. All were thankful that it was no worse. After the rain of the night before and the frequent and heavy rains for some days previous, the roads were almost impassable. The enemy, carrying his artillery and supply trains over them in his retreat, made them still worse for troops following. I wanted to pursue, but had not the heart to order the men who had fought desperately for two days, lying in the mud and rain whenever not fighting, and I did not feel disposed to positively order Buell, or any part of his command, to pursue. Although the senior in rank at the time, I had been so only a few weeks. Buell was, and had been for some time past, a department commander, while I only commanded a district. I did not meet Buell in person until too late to get troops ready and pursue with effect; but had I seen him at the moment of the last charge, I should have at least requested him to follow. The enemy had hardly started in retreat from his last position, when, looking back toward the river, I saw a division of troops coming up in beautiful order, as if going on parade or review. The commander was at the head of the column, and the staff seemed to be disposed about as they would have been had they been going on parade. When the head of the column came near where I was standing, it was halted, and the commanding officer, General A. McD. McCook, rode up to where I was and appealed to me not to send his division any farther, saying that they were worn out with marching and fighting. This division had marched on the 6th from a point ten or twelve miles east of Savanna, over bad roads; the men had also lost rest during the night while crossing the Tennessee, and had been engaged in the battle of the 7th. It was not, however, the rank and file or the junior officers who asked to be excused, but the division commander. I rode forward several miles the day after the battle, and found that the enemy had dropped much, if not all, of their provisions, some ammunition, and the extra wheels of their caissons, lightening their loads to enable them to get off their guns. About five miles out we found their field hospital abandoned. An immediate pursuit must have resulted in the capture of a considerable number of prisoners and probably some guns.

Shiloh was the most severe battle fought at the West during the war, and but few in the East equaled it for hard, determined fighting. I saw an open field, in our possession on the second day, over which the Confederates had made repeated charges the day before, so covered with dead that it would have been possible to walk across the clearing, in any direction, stepping on dead bodies, without a foot touching the ground. On our side Federal and Confederate were mingled together in about equal proportions; but on the remainder of the field nearly all were Confederates. On one part, which had evidently not been plowed for several years, probably because the land was poor, bushes had grown up, some to the height of eight or ten feet. There was not one of these left standing unpierced by bullets. The smaller ones were all cut down.

Contrary to all my experience up to that time, and to the experience of the army I was then commanding, we were on the defensive. We were without intrenchments or defensive advantages of any sort, and more than half the army engaged the first day was without experience or even drill as soldiers. The officers with them, except the division commanders, and possibly two or three of the brigade commanders, were equally inexperienced in war. The result was a Union victory that gave the men who achieved it great confidence in themselves ever after.

The enemy fought bravely, but they had started out to defeat and destroy an army and capture a position. They failed in both, with very heavy loss in killed and wounded, and must have gone back discouraged and convinced that the "Yankee" was not an enemy to be despised.

After the battle I gave verbal instructions to division commanders to let the regiments send out parties to bury their own dead, and to detail parties, under commissioned officers from each division, to bury the Confederate dead in their respective fronts, and to report the numbers so buried. The latter part of these instructions was not carried out by all, but they were by those sent from Sherman's division, and by some of the parties sent out by McClernand. The heaviest loss sustained by the enemy was in front of these two divisions.

The criticism has often been made that the Union troops should have been intrenched at Shiloh. But up to that time the pick and spade had been but little resorted to at the West. I had, however, taken this subject under consideration soon after reassuming command in the field. McPherson, my only military engineer, had been directed to layout a line to intrench. He did so, but reported that it would have to be made in rear of the line of encampment as it then ran. The new line, while it would be nearer the river, was yet too far away from the Tennessee, or even from the creeks, to be easily supplied with water from them; and in case of attack, these creeks would be in the hands of the enemy. But, besides this, the troops with me, officers and men, needed discipline and drill more than they did experience with the pick, shovel, and axe. Reenforcements were arriving almost daily, composed of troops that had been hastily thrown together into companies and regiments—fragments of incomplete organizations, the men and officers strangers to each other. Under all these circumstances I concluded that drill and discipline were worth more to our men than fortifications.

General Buell was a brave, intelligent officer, with as much professional pride and ambition of a commendable sort as I ever knew. I had been two years at West Point with him, and had served with him afterward, in garrison and in the Mexican war, several years more. He was not given in early life or in mature years to forming intimate acquaintances. He was studious by habit, and commanded the confidence and respect of all who knew him. He was a strict disciplinarian, and perhaps did not distinguish sufficiently the difference between the volunteer who "enlisted for the war" and the soldier who serves in time of peace. One system embraced men who risked life for a principle, and often men of social standing, competence, or wealth, and independence of character. The other includes, as a rule, only men who could not do as well in any other occupation. General Buell became an object of harsh criticism later, some going so far as to challenge his loyalty. No one who knew him ever believed him capable of a dishonorable act, and nothing could be more dishonorable than to accept high rank and command in war and then betray his trust. When I came into command of the army, in 1864, I requested the Secretary of War to restore General Buell to duty.

After the war, during the summer of 1865, I traveled considerably through the North and was everywhere met by large numbers of people. Every one had his opinion about the manner in which the war had been conducted; who among the generals had failed, how, and why. Correspondents of the press were ever on hand to hear every word dropped, and were not always disposed to report correctly what did not confirm their preconceived notions, either about the conduct of the war or the individuals concerned in it. The opportunity frequently occurred for me to defend General Buell against what I believed to be most unjust charges. On one occasion a correspondent put in my mouth the very charge I had so often refuted—of disloyalty. This brought from General Buell a very severe retort, which I saw in the New York "World" some time before I received the letter itself. I could very well understand his grievance at seeing untrue and disgraceful charges apparently sustained by an officer who, at the time, was at the head of the army. I replied to him, but not through the press. I kept no copy of my letter, nor did I ever see it in print, neither did I receive an answer. . . .

After nightfall, when firing had entirely ceased on land, the commander of the fleet informed himself, proximately, of the position of our troops, and suggested the idea of dropping a shell within the lines of the enemy every fifteen minutes during the night. This was done with effect as is proved by the Confederate reports. Up to the battle of Shiloh, I, as well as thousands of other citizens, believed that the rebellion against the Government would collapse suddenly and soon if a decisive victory could be gained over any of its armies. Donelson and Henry were such victories. An army of more than 25,000 men was captured or destroyed. Bowling Green, Columbus, and Hickman, Kentucky, fell in consequence; Clarkesville and Nashville, Tennessee, with an immense amount of stores, also fell into our hands. The Tennessee and Cumberland rivers, from their mouths to the head of navigation, were secured. But when Confederate armies were collected which not only attempted to hold a line farther south, from Memphis to Chattanooga, and Knoxville, and on to the Atlantic, but assumed the offensive, and made such a gallant effort to regain what had been lost, then, indeed, I gave up all idea of saving the Union except by complete conquest. Up to that time it had been the policy of our army, certainly of that portion commanded by me, to protect the property of the citizens whose territory was invaded, without regard to their sentiments, whether Union or Secession. After this, however, I regarded it as humane to both sides to protect the persons of those found at their homes, but to consume everything that could be used to support or supply armies. Protection was still continued over such supplies as were within lines held by us, and which we expected to continue to hold. But such supplies within the reach of Confederate armies I regarded as much contraband as arms or ordnance stores. Their destruction was accomplished without bloodshed, and tended to the same result as the destruction of armies. I continued this policy to the close of the war. Promiscuous pillaging, however, was discouraged and punished. Instructions were always given to take provisions and forage under the direction of commissioned officers, who should give receipts to owners, if at home, and turn the property over to officers of the quartermaster or commissary departments; to be issued as if furnished from our Northern depots. But much was destroyed without receipts to owners, which could not be brought within our lines, and would otherwise have gone to the support of secession and rebellion.

This policy, I believe, exercised a material influence in hastening the end.

U. S. Grant.

"What I Saw of Shiloh"

Ambrose Bierce (1842–1914)

Early in the conflict, in response to Lincoln's call for troops, Ambrose Bierce joined an Ohio company formed by his uncle and became part of an invasion force led by George McClellan in West Virginia. On April 6, 1862, some fifty-five thousand Confederate troops attacked the army of General Grant near Shiloh Church in Hardin, Tennessee, and the Union forces suffered heavy losses. Bierce was deeply shocked by what he experienced at Shiloh and used it as the basis of several short stories and this narrative account. The cynicism that came to characterize his writing may well stem from military behaviors he observed during this period.

This is a simple story of a battle; such a tale as may be told by a soldier who is no writer to a reader who is no soldier.

The morning of Sunday, the sixth day of April, 1862, was bright and warm. Reveille had been sounded rather late, for the troops, wearied with long marching, were to have a day of rest. The men were idling about the embers of their bivouac fires; some preparing breakfast, others looking carelessly to the condition of their arms and accoutrements, against the inevitable inspection; still others were chatting with indolent dogmatism on that never-failing theme, the end and object of the campaign. Sentinels paced up and down the confused front with a lounging freedom of mien and stride that would not have been tolerated at another time. A few of them limped unsoldierly in deference to blistered feet. At a little distance in rear of the stacked arms were a few tents out of which frowsy-headed officers occasionally peered, languidly calling to their servants to fetch a basin of water, dust a coat or polish a scabbard. Trim young mounted orderlies, bearing dispatches obviously unimportant, urged their lazy nags by devious ways amongst the men, enduring with unconcern their good-humored raillery, the penalty of superior station. Little negroes of not very clearly defined status and function lolled on their stomachs, kicking their long, bare heels in the sunshine, or slumbered peacefully, unaware of the practical waggery prepared by white hands for their undoing.

Presently the flag hanging limp and lifeless at headquarters was seen to lift itself spiritedly from the staff. At the same instant was heard a dull, distant sound like the heavy breathing of some great animal below the horizon. The flag had lifted its head to listen. There was a momentary lull in the hum of the human swarm; then, as the flag drooped the hush passed away. But there were some hundreds more men on their feet than before; some thousands of hearts beating with a quicker pulse.

Again the flag made a warning sign, and again the breeze bore to our ears the long, deep sighing of iron lungs. The division, as if it had received the sharp word of command, sprang to its feet, and stood in groups at "attention." Even the little blacks got up. I have since seen similar effects produced by earthquakes; I am not sure but the ground was trembling then. The mess-cooks, wise in their generation, lifted the steaming camp-kettles off the fire and stood by to cast out. The mounted orderlies had somehow disappeared. Officers came ducking from beneath their tents and gathered in groups. Headquarters had become a swarming hive.

The sound of the great guns now came in regular throbbings—the strong, full pulse of the fever of battle. The flag flapped excitedly, shaking out its blazonry of stars and stripes with a sort of fierce delight. Toward the knot of officers in its shadow dashed from somewhere—he seemed to have burst out of the ground in a cloud of dust—a mounted aide-de-camp, and on the instant rose the sharp, clear notes of a bugle, caught up and repeated, and passed on by other bugles, until the level reaches of brown fields, the line of woods trending away to far hills, and the unseen valleys beyond were "telling of the sound," the farther, fainter strains half drowned in ringing cheers as the men ran to range themselves behind the stacks of arms. For this call was not the wearisome "general" before which the tents go down; it was the exhilarating "assembly," which goes to the heart as wine and stirs the blood like the kisses of a beautiful woman. Who that has heard it calling to him above the grumble of great guns can forget the wild intoxication of its music?

II

The Confederate forces in Kentucky and Tennessee had suffered a series of reverses, culminating in the loss of Nashville. The blow was severe: immense quantities of war material had fallen to the victor, together with all the important strategic points. General Johnston withdrew Beauregard's army to Corinth, in northern Mississippi, where he hoped so to recruit and equip it as to enable it to assume the offensive and retake the lost territory.

The town of Corinth was a wretched place—the capital of a swamp. It is two days' march west of the Tennessee River, which here and for a hundred and fifty miles farther, to where it falls into the Ohio at Paducah, runs nearly north. It is navigable to this point—that is to say, to Pittsburg Landing, where Corinth got to it by a road worn through a thickly wooded country seamed with ravines and bayous, rising nobody knows where and running into the river under sylvan arches heavily draped with Spanish moss. In some places they were obstructed by fallen trees. The Corinth road was at certain seasons a branch of the Tennessee River. Its mouth was Pittsburg Landing. Here in 1862 were some fields and a house or two; now there are a national cemetery and other improvements.

It was at Pittsburg Landing that Grant established his army, with a river in his rear and two toy steamboats as a means of communication with the east side, whither General Buell with thirty thousand men was moving from Nashville to join him. The question has been asked, Why did General Grant occupy the enemy's side of the river in the face of a superior force before the arrival of Buell? Buell had a long way to come; perhaps Grant was weary of waiting. Certainly Johnston was, for in the gray of the morning of April 6th, when Buell's leading division was en bivouac near the little town of Savannah, eight or ten miles below, the Confederate forces, having moved out of Corinth two days before, fell upon Grant's advance brigades and destroyed them. Grant was at Savannah, but hastened to the Landing in time to find his camps in the hands of the enemy and the remnants of his beaten army cooped up with an impassable river at their backs for moral support. I have related how the news of this affair came to us at Savannah. It came on the wind—a messenger that does not bear copious details.

III

On the side of the Tennessee River, over against Pittsburg Landing, are some low bare hills, partly inclosed by a forest. In the dusk of the evening of April 6 this open space, as seen from the other side of the stream—whence, indeed, it was anxiously watched by thousands of eyes, to many of which it grew dark long before the sun went down—would have appeared to have been ruled in long, dark lines, with new lines being constantly drawn across. These lines were the regiments of Buell's leading division, which having moved from Savannah through a country presenting nothing but interminable swamps and pathless "bottom lands," with rank overgrowths of jungle, was arriving at the scene of action breathless, footsore and faint with hunger. It had been a terrible race; some regiments had lost a third of their number from fatigue, the men dropping from the ranks as if shot, and left to recover or die at their leisure. Nor was the scene to which they had been invited likely to inspire the moral confidence that medicines physical fatigue. True, the air was full of thunder and the earth was trembling beneath their feet; and if there is truth in the theory of the conversion of force, these men were storing up energy from every shock that burst its waves upon their bodies. Perhaps this theory may better than another explain the tremendous endurance of men in battle. But the eyes reported only matter for despair.

Before us ran the turbulent river, vexed with plunging shells and obscured in spots by blue sheets of low-lying smoke. The two little steamers were doing their duty well. They came over to us empty and went back crowded, sitting very low in the water, apparently on the point of capsizing. The farther edge of the water could not be seen; the boats came out of the obscurity, took on their passengers and vanished in the darkness. But on the heights above, the battle was burning brightly enough; a thousand lights kindled and expired in every second of time. There were broad flashings in the sky, against which the branches of the trees showed black. Sudden flames burst out here and there, singly and in dozens. Fleeting streaks of fire crossed over to us by way of welcome. These expired in blinding flashes and fierce little rolls of smoke, attended with the peculiar metallic ring of bursting shells, and followed by the musical humming of the fragments as they struck into the ground on every side, making us wince, but doing little harm. The air was full of noises. To the right and the left the musketry rattled smartly and petulantly; directly in front it sighed and growled. To the experienced ear this meant that the death-line was an arc of which the river was the chord. There were deep, shaking explosions and smart shocks; the whisper of stray bullets and the hurtle of conical shells; the rush of round shot. There were faint, desultory cheers, such as announce a momentary or partial triumph. Occasionally, against the glare behind the trees, could be seen moving black figures, singularly distinct but apparently no longer than a thumb. They seemed to me ludicrously like the figures of demons in old allegorical prints of hell. To destroy these and all their belongings the enemy needed but another hour of daylight; the steamers in that case would have been doing him fine service by bringing more fish to his net. Those of us who had the good fortune to arrive late could then have eaten our teeth in impotent rage. Nay, to make his victory sure it did not need that the sun should pause in the heavens; one of many random shots falling into the river would have done the business had chance directed it into the engine-room of a steamer. You can perhaps fancy the anxiety with which we watched them leaping down.

But we had two other allies besides the night. Just where the enemy had pushed his right flank to the river was the mouth of a wide bayou, and here two gunboats had taken station. They too were of the toy sort, plated perhaps with railway metals, perhaps with boiler-iron. They staggered under a heavy gun or two each. The bayou made an opening in the high bank of the river. The bank was a parapet, behind which the gunboats crouched, firing up the bayou as through an embrasure. The enemy was at this disadvantage: he could not get at the gunboats, and he could advance only by exposing his flank to their ponderous missiles, one of which would have broken a half-mile of his bones and made nothing of it. Very annoying this must have been—these twenty gunners beating back an army because a sluggish creek had been pleased to fall into a river at one point rather than another. Such is the part that accident may play in the game of war.

As a spectacle this was rather fine. We could just discern the black bodies of these boats, looking very much like turtles. But when they let off their big guns there was a conflagration. The river shuddered in its banks, and hurried on, bloody, wounded, terrified! Objects a mile away sprang toward our eyes as a snake strikes at the face of its victim. The report stung us to the brain, but we blessed it audibly. Then we could hear the great shell tearing away through the air until the sound died out in the distance; then, a surprisingly long time afterward, a dull, distant explosion and a sudden silence of small-arms told their own tale.

IV

There was, I remember, no elephant on the boat that passed us across that evening, nor, I think, any hippopotamus. These would have been out of place. We had, however, a woman. Whether the baby was somewhere on board I did not learn. She was a fine creature, this woman; somebody's wife. Her mission, as she understood it, was to inspire the failing heart with courage; and when she selected mine I felt less flattered by her preference than astonished by her penetration. How did she learn? She stood on the upper deck with the red blaze of battle bathing her beautiful face, the twinkle of a thousand rifles mirrored in her eyes; and displaying a small ivory-handled pistol, she told me in a sentence punctuated by the thunder of great guns that if it came to the worst she would do her duty like a man! I am proud to remember that I took off my hat to this little fool.

V

Along the sheltered strip of beach between the river bank and the water was a confused mass of humanity—several thousands of men. They were mostly unarmed; many were wounded; some dead. All the camp-following tribes were there; all the cowards; a few officers. Not one of them knew where his regiment was, nor if he had a regiment. Many had not. These men were defeated, beaten, cowed. They were deaf to duty and dead to shame. A more demented crew never drifted to the rear of broken battalions. They would have stood in their tracks and been shot down to a man by a provost-marshal's guard, but they could not have been urged up that bank. An army's bravest men are its cowards. The death which they would not meet at the hands of the enemy they will meet at the hands of their officers, with never a flinching.

Whenever a steamboat would land, this abominable mob had to be kept off her with bayonets; when she pulled away, they sprang on her and were pushed by scores into the water, where they were suffered to drown one another in their own way. The men disembarking insulted them, shoved them, struck them. In return they expressed their unholy delight in the certainty of our destruction by the enemy.

By the time my regiment had reached the plateau night had put an end to the struggle. A sputter of rifles would break out now and then, followed perhaps by a spiritless hurrah. Occasionally a shell from a faraway battery would come pitching down somewhere near, with a whir crescendo, or flit above our heads with a whisper like that made by the wings of a night bird, to smother itself in the river. But there was no more fighting. The gunboats, however, blazed away at set intervals all night long, just to make the enemy uncomfortable and break him of his rest.

For us there was no rest. Foot by foot we moved through the dusky fields, we knew not whither. There were men all about us, but no camp-fires; to have made a blaze would have been madness. The men were of strange regiments; they mentioned the names of unknown generals. They gathered in groups by the wayside, asking eagerly our numbers. They recounted the depressing incidents of the day. A thoughtful officer shut their mouths with a sharp word as he passed; a wise one coming after encouraged them to repeat their doleful tale all along the line.

Hidden in hollows and behind clumps of rank brambles were large tents, dimly lighted with candles, but looking comfortable. The kind of comfort they supplied was indicated by pairs of men entering and reappearing, bearing litters; by low moans from within and by long rows of dead with covered faces outside. These tents were constantly receiving the wounded, yet were never full; they were continually ejecting the dead, yet were never empty. It was as if the helpless had been carried in and murdered, that they might not hamper those whose business it was to fall to-morrow.

The night was now black-dark; as is usual after a battle, it had begun to rain. Still we moved; we were being put into position by somebody. Inch by inch we crept along, treading on one another's heels by way of keeping together. Commands were passed along the line in whispers; more commonly none were given. When the men had pressed so closely together that they could advance no farther they stood stock-still, sheltering the locks of their rifles with their ponchos. In this position many fell asleep. When those in front suddenly stepped away those in the rear, roused by the tramping, hastened after with such zeal that the line was soon choked again. Evidently the head of the division was being piloted at a snail's pace by some one who did not feel sure of his ground. Very often we struck our feet against the dead; more frequently against those who still had spirit enough to resent it with a moan. These were lifted carefully to one side and abandoned. Some had sense enough to ask in their weak way for water. Absurd! Their clothes were soaked, their hair dank; their white faces, dimly discernible, were clammy and cold. Besides, none of us had any water. There was plenty coming, though, for before midnight a thunderstorm broke upon us with great violence. The rain, which had for hours been a dull drizzle, fell with a copiousness that stifled us; we moved in running water up to our ankles. Happily, we were in a forest of great trees heavily "decorated" with Spanish moss, or with an enemy standing to his guns the disclosures of the lightning might have been inconvenient. As it was, the incessant blaze enabled us to consult our watches and encouraged us by displaying our numbers; our black, sinuous line, creeping like a giant serpent beneath the trees, was apparently interminable. I am almost ashamed to say how sweet I found the companionship of those coarse men.

So the long night wore away, and as the glimmer of morning crept in through the forest we found ourselves in a more open country. But where? Not a sign of battle was here. The trees were neither splintered nor scarred, the underbrush was unmown, the ground had no footprints but our own. It was as if we had broken into glades sacred to eternal silence. I should not have been surprised to see sleek leopards come fawning about our feet, and milkwhite deer confront us with human eyes.

A few inaudible commands from an invisible leader had placed us in order of battle. But where was the enemy? Where, too, were the riddled regiments that we had come to save? Had our other divisions arrived during the night and passed the river to assist us? or were we to oppose our paltry five thousand breasts to an army flushed with victory? What protected our right? Who lay upon our left? Was there really anything in our front?

There came, borne to us on the raw morning air, the long weird note of a bugle. It was directly before us. It rose with a low clear, deliberate warble, and seemed to float in the gray sky like the note of a lark. The bugle calls of the Federal and the Confederate armies were the same: it was the "assembly"! As it died away I observed that the atmosphere had suffered a change; despite the equilibrium established by the storm, it was electric. Wings were growing on blistered feet. Bruised muscles and jolted bones, shoulders pounded by the cruel knapsack, eyelids leaden from lack of sleep—all were pervaded by the subtle fluid, all were unconscious of their clay. The men thrust forward their heads, expanded their eyes and clenched their teeth. They breathed hard, as if throttled by tugging at the leash. If you had laid your hand in the beard or hair of one of these men it would have crackled and shot sparks.

VI

I suppose the country lying between Corinth and Pittsburg Landing could boast a few inhabitants other than alligators. What manner of people they were it is impossible to say, inasmuch as the fighting dispersed, or possibly exterminated them; perhaps in merely classing them as non-saurian I shall describe them with sufficient particularity and at the same time avert from myself the natural suspicion attaching to a writer who points out to persons who do not know him the peculiarities of persons whom he does not know. One thing, however, I hope I may without offense affirm of these swamp-dwellers—they were pious. To what deity their veneration was given—whether, like the Egyptians, they worshiped the crocodile, or, like other Americans, adored themselves, I do not presume to guess. But whoever, or whatever, may have been the divinity whose ends they shaped, unto Him, or It, they had builded a temple. This humble edifice, centrally situated in the heart of a solitude, and conveniently accessible to the supersylvan crow, had been christened Shiloh Chapel, whence the name of the battle. The fact of a Christian church—assuming it to have been a Christian church—giving name to a wholesale cutting of Christian throats by Christian hands need not be dwelt on here; the frequency of its recurrence in the history of our species has somewhat abated the moral interest that would otherwise attach to it.

VII

Owing to the darkness, the storm and the absence of a road, it had been impossible to move the artillery from the open ground about the Landing. The privation was much greater in a moral than in a material sense. The infantry soldier feels a confidence in his cumbrous arm quite unwarranted by its actual achievements in thinning out the opposition. There is something that inspires confidence in the way a gun dashes up to the front, shoving fifty or a hundred men to one side as if it said, "Permit me!" Then it squares its shoulders, calmly dislocates a joint in its back, sends away its twenty-four legs and settles down with a quiet rattle which says as plainly as possible, "I've come to stay." There is a superb scorn in its grimly defiant attitude, with its nose in the air; it appears not so much to threaten the enemy as deride him.

Our batteries were probably toiling after us somewhere; we could only hope the enemy might delay his attack until they should arrive. "He may delay his defense if he likes," said a sententious young officer to whom I had imparted this natural wish. He had read the signs aright; the words were hardly spoken when a group of staff officers about the brigade commander shot away in divergent lines as if scattered by a whirlwind, and galloping each to the commander of a regiment gave the word. There was a momentary confusion of tongues, a thin line of skirmishers detached itself from the compact front and pushed forward, followed by its diminutive reserves of half a company each—one of which platoons it was my fortune to command. When the straggling line of skirmishers had swept four or five hundred yards ahead, "See," said one of my comrades, "she moves!" She did indeed, and in fine style, her front as straight as a string, her reserve regiments in columns doubled on the center, following in true subordination; no braying of brass to apprise the enemy, no fifing and drumming to amuse him; no ostentation of gaudy flags; no nonsense. This was a matter of business.

In a few moments we had passed out of the singular oasis that had so marvelously escaped the desolation of battle, and now the evidences of the previous day's struggle were present in profusion. The ground was tolerably level here, the forest less dense, mostly clear of undergrowth, and occasionally opening out into small natural meadows. Here and there were small pools—mere discs of rainwater with a tinge of blood. Riven and torn with cannon-shot, the trunks of the trees protruded bunches of splinters like hands, the fingers above the wound interlacing with those below. Large branches had been lopped, and hung their green heads to the ground, or swung critically in their netting of vines, as in a hammock. Many had been cut clean off and their masses of foliage seriously impeded the progress of the troops. The bark of these trees, from the root upward to a height of ten or twenty feet, was so thickly pierced with bullets and grape that one could not have laid a hand on it without covering several punctures. None had escaped. How the human body survives a storm like this must be explained by the fact that it is exposed to it but a few moments at a time, whereas these grand old trees had had no one to take their places, from the rising to the going down of the sun. Angular bits of iron, concavo-convex, sticking in the sides of muddy depressions, showed where shells had exploded in their furrows. Knapsacks, canteens, haversacks distended with soaken and swollen biscuits, gaping to disgorge, blankets beaten into the soil by the rain, rifles with bent barrels or splintered stocks, waist-belts, hats and the omnipresent sardine-box—all the wretched debris of the battle still littered the spongy earth as far as one could see, in every direction. Dead horses were everywhere; a few disabled caissons, or limbers, reclining on one elbow, as it were; ammunition wagons standing disconsolate behind four or six sprawling mules. Men? There were men enough; all dead apparently, except one, who lay near where I had halted my platoon to await the slower movement of the line—a Federal sergeant, variously hurt, who had been a fine giant in his time. He lay face upward, taking in his breath in convulsive, rattling snorts, and blowing it out in sputters of froth which crawled creamily down his cheeks, piling itself alongside his neck and ears. A bullet had clipped a groove in his skull, above the temple; from this the brain protruded in bosses, dropping off in flakes and strings. I had not previously known one could get on, even in this unsatisfactory fashion, with so little brain. One of my men whom I knew for a womanish fellow, asked if he should put his bayonet through him. Inexpressibly shocked by the cold-blooded proposal, I told him I thought not; it was unusual, and too many were looking.

VIII

It was plain that the enemy had retreated to Corinth. The arrival of our fresh troops and their successful passage of the river had disheartened him. Three or four of his gray cavalry videttes moving amongst the trees on the crest of a hill in our front, and galloping out of sight at the crack of our skirmishers' rifles, confirmed us in the belief; an army face to face with its enemy does not employ cavalry to watch its front. True, they might be a general and his staff. Crowning this rise we found a level field, a quarter of a mile in width; beyond it a gentle acclivity, covered with an undergrowth of young oaks, impervious to sight. We pushed on into the open, but the division halted at the edge. Having orders to conform to its movements, we halted too; but that did not suit; we received an intimation to proceed. I had performed this sort of service before, and in the exercise of my discretion deployed my platoon, pushing it forward at a run, with trailed arms, to strengthen the skirmish line, which I overtook some thirty or forty yards from the wood. Then—I can't describe it—the forest seemed all at once to flame up and disappear with a crash like that of a great wave upon the beach—a crash that expired in hot hissings, and the sickening "spat" of lead against flesh. A dozen of my brave fellows tumbled over like ten-pins. Some struggled to their feet only to go down again, and yet again. Those who stood fired into the smoking brush and doggedly retired. We had expected to find, at most, a line of skirmishers similar to our own; it was with a view to overcoming them by a sudden coup at the moment of collision that I had thrown forward my little reserve. What we had found was a line of battle, coolly holding its fire till it could count our teeth. There was no more to be done but get back across the open ground, every superficial yard of which was throwing up its little jet of mud provoked by an impinging bullet. We got back, most of us, and I shall never forget the ludicrous incident of a young officer who had taken part in the affair walking up to his colonel, who had been a calm and apparently impartial spectator, and gravely reporting: "The enemy is in force just beyond this field, sir."

IX

In subordination to the design of this narrative, as defined by its title, the incidents related necessarily group themselves about my own personality as a center; and, as this center, during the few terrible hours of the engagement, maintained a variably constant relation to the open field already mentioned, it is important that the reader should bear in mind the topographical and tactical features of the local situation. The hither side of the field was occupied by the front of my brigade—a length of two regiments in line, with proper intervals for field batteries. During the entire fight the enemy held the slight wooded acclivity beyond. The debatable ground to the right and left of the open was broken and thickly wooded for miles, in some places quite inaccessible to artillery and at very few points offering opportunities for its successful employment. As a consequence of this the two sides of the field were soon studded thickly with confronting guns, which flamed away at one another with amazing zeal and rather startling effect. Of course, an infantry attack delivered from either side was not to be thought of when the covered flanks offered inducements so unquestionably superior; and I believe the riddled bodies of my poor skirmishers were the only ones left on this "neutral ground" that day. But there was a very pretty line of dead continually growing in our rear, and doubtless the enemy had at his back a similar encouragement.

The configuration of the ground offered us no protection. By lying flat our faces between the guns we were screened from view by a straggling row of brambles, which marked the course of an obsolete fence; but the enemy's grape was sharper than his eyes, and it was poor consolation to know that his gunners could not see what they were doing, so long as they did it. The shock of our own pieces nearly deafened us, but in the brief intervals we could hear the battle roaring and stammering in the dark reaches of the forest to the right and left, where our other divisions were dashing themselves again and again into the smoking jungle. What would we not have given to join them in their brave, hopeless task! But to lie inglorious beneath showers of shrapnel darting divergent from the unassailable sky—meekly to be blown out of life by level gusts of grape—to clench our teeth and shrink helpless before big shot pushing noisily through the consenting air—this was horrible! "Lie down, there!" a captain would shout, and then get up himself to see that his order was obeyed. "Captain, take cover, sir!" the lieutenant-colonel would shriek, pacing up and down in the most exposed position that he could find.

O those cursed guns!—not the enemy's, but our own. Had it not been for them, we might have died like men. They must be supported, forsooth, the feeble, boasting bullies! It was impossible to conceive that these pieces were doing the enemy as excellent a mischief as his were doing us; they seemed to raise their "cloud by day" solely to direct aright the streaming procession of Confederate missiles. They no longer inspired confidence, but begot apprehension; and it was with grim satisfaction that I saw the carriage of one and another smashed into matchwood by a whooping shot and bundled out of the line.

X

The dense forests wholly or partly in which were fought so many battles of the Civil War, lay upon the earth in each autumn a thick deposit of dead leaves and stems, the decay of which forms a soil of surprising depth and richness. In dry weather the upper stratum is as inflammable as tinder. A fire once kindled in it will spread with a slow, persistent advance as far as local conditions permit, leaving a bed of light ashes beneath which the less combustible accretions of previous years will smolder until extinguished by rains. In many of the engagements of the war the fallen leaves took fire and roasted the fallen men. At Shiloh, during the first day's fighting, wide tracts of woodland were burned over in this way and scores of wounded who might have recovered perished in slow torture. I remember a deep ravine a little to the left and rear of the field I have described, in which, by some mad freak of heroic incompetence, a part of an Illinois regiment had been surrounded, and refusing to surrender was destroyed, as it very well deserved. My regiment having at last been relieved at the guns and moved over to the heights above this ravine for no obvious purpose, I obtained leave to go down into the valley of death and gratify a reprehensible curiosity.

Forbidding enough it was in every way. The fire had swept every superficial foot of it, and at every step I sank into ashes to the ankle. It had contained a thick undergrowth of young saplings, every one of which had been severed by a bullet, the foliage of the prostrate tops being afterward burnt and the stumps charred. Death had put his sickle into this thicket and fire had gleaned the field. Along a line which was not that of extreme depression, but was at every point significantly equidistant from the heights on either hand, lay the bodies half buried in ashes; some in the unlovely looseness of attitude denoting sudden death by the bullet, but by far the greater number in postures of agony that told of the tormenting flame. Their clothing was half burnt away—their hair and beard entirely; the rain had come too late to save their nails. Some were swollen to double girth; others shriveled to manikins. According to degree of exposure, their faces were bloated and black or yellow and shrunken. The contraction of muscles which had given them claws for hands had cursed each countenance with a hideous grin. Faugh! I cannot catalogue the charms of these gallant gentlemen who had got what they enlisted for.

XI

It was now three o'clock in the afternoon and raining. For fifteen hours we had been wet to the skin. Chilled, sleepy, hungry and disappointed—profoundly disgusted with the inglorious part to which they had been condemned—the men of my regiment did everything doggedly. The spirit had gone quite out of them. Blue sheets of powder smoke, drifting amongst the trees, settling against the hillsides and beaten into nothingness by the falling rain, filled the air with their peculiar pungent odor, but it no longer stimulated. For miles on either hand could be heard the hoarse murmur of the battle, breaking out nearby with frightful distinctness, or sinking to a murmur in the distance; and the one sound aroused no more attention than the other.

We had been placed again in rear of those guns, but even they and their iron antagonists seemed to have tired of their feud, pounding away at one another with amiable infrequency. The right of the regiment extended a little beyond the field. On the prolongation of the line in that direction were some regiments of another division, with one in reserve. A third of a mile back lay the remnant of somebody's brigade looking to its wounds. The line of forest bounding this end of the field stretched as straight as a wall from the right of my regiment to Heaven knows what regiment of the enemy. There suddenly appeared, marching down along this wall, not more than two hundred yards in our front, a dozen files of gray-clad men with rifles on the right shoulder. At an interval of fifty yards they were followed by perhaps half as many more; and in fair supporting distance of these stalked with confident mien a single man! There seemed to me something indescribably ludicrous in the advance of this handful of men upon an army, albeit with their left flank protected by a forest. It does not so impress me now. They were the exposed flanks of three lines of infantry, each half a mile in length. In a moment our gunners had grappled with the nearest pieces, swung them half round, and were pouring streams of canister into the invaded wood. The infantry rose in masses, springing into line. Our threatened regiments stood like a wall, their loaded rifles at "ready," their bayonets hanging quietly in the scabbards. The right wing of my own regiment was thrown slightly backward to threaten the flank of the assault. The battered brigade away to the rear pulled itself together.

Then the storm burst. A great gray cloud seemed to spring out of the forest into the faces of the wailing battalions. It was received with a crash that made the very trees turn up their leaves. For one instant the assailants paused above their dead, then struggled forward, their bayonets glittering in the eyes that shone behind the smoke. One moment, and those unmoved men in blue would be impaled. What were they about? Why did they not fix bayonets? Were they stunned by their own volley? Their inaction was maddening! Another tremendous crash!—the rear rank had fired! Humanity, thank Heaven! is not made for this, and the shattered gray mass drew back a score of paces, opening a feeble fire. Lead had scored its old-time victory over steel; the heroic had broken its great heart against the commonplace. There are those who say that it is sometimes otherwise.

All this had taken but a minute of time, and now the second Confederate line swept down and poured in its fire. The line of blue staggered and gave way; in those two terrific volleys it seemed to have quite poured out its spirit. To this deadly work our reserve regiment now came up with a run. It was surprising to see it spitting fire with never a sound, for such was the infernal din that the ear could take in no more. This fearful scene was enacted within fifty paces of our toes, but we were rooted to the ground as if we had grown there. But now our commanding officer rode from behind us to the front, waved his hand with the courteous gesture that says apres vous, and with a barely audible cheer we sprang into the fight. Again the smoking front of gray receded, and again, as the enemy's third line emerged from its leafy covert, it pushed forward across the piles of dead and wounded to threaten with protruded steel. Never was seen so striking a proof of the paramount importance of numbers. Within an area of three hundred yards by fifty there struggled for front places no fewer than six regiments; and the accession of each, after the first collision, had it not been immediately counterpoised, would have turned the scale.

As matters stood, we were now very evenly matched, and how long we might have held out God only knows. But all at once something appeared to have gone wrong with the enemy's left; our men had somewhere pierced his line. A moment later his whole front gave way, and springing forward with fixed bayonets we pushed him in utter confusion back to his original line. Here, among the tents from which Grant's people had been expelled the day before, our broken and disordered regiments inextricably intermingled, and drunken with the wine of triumph, dashed confidently against a pair of trim battalions, provoking a tempest of hissing lead that made us stagger under its very weight. The sharp onset of another against our flank sent us whirling back with fire at our heels and fresh foes in merciless pursuit—who in their turn were broken upon the front of the invalided brigade previously mentioned, which had moved up from the rear to assist in this lively work.

As we rallied to reform behind our beloved guns and noted the ridiculous brevity of our line—as we sank from sheer fatigue, and tried to moderate the terrific thumping of our hearts—as we caught our breath to ask who had seen such-and-such a comrade, and laughed hysterically at the reply—there swept past us and over us into the open field a long regiment with fixed bayonets and rifles on the right shoulder. Another followed, and another; two—three—four! Heavens! where do all these men come from, and why did they not come before? How grandly and confidently they go sweeping on like long blue waves of ocean chasing one another to the cruel rocks! Involuntarily we draw in our weary feet beneath us as we sit, ready to spring up and interpose our breasts when these gallant lines shall come back to us across the terrible field, and sift brokenly through among the trees with spouting fires at their backs. We still our breathing to catch the full grandeur of the volleys that are to tear them to shreds. Minute after minute passes and the sound does not come. Then for the first time we note that the silence of the whole region is not comparative, but absolute. Have we become stone deaf? See; here comes a stretcher-bearer, and there a surgeon! Good heavens! a chaplain!

The battle was indeed at an end.

XII

And this was, O so long ago! How they come back to me—dimly and brokenly, but with what a magic spell—those years of youth when I was soldiering! Again I hear the far warble of blown bugles. Again I see the tall, blue smoke of camp-fires ascending from the dim valleys of Wonderland. There steals upon my sense the ghost of an odor from pines that canopy the ambuscade. I feel upon my cheek the morning mist that shrouds the hostile camp unaware of its doom, and my blood stirs at the ringing rifle-shot of the solitary sentinel. Unfamiliar landscapes, glittering with sunshine or sullen with rain, come to me demanding recognition, pass, vanish and give place to others. Here in the night stretches a wide and blasted field studded with half-extinct fires burning redly with I know not what presage of evil. Again I shudder as I note its desolation and its awful silence. Where was it? To what monstrous inharmony of death was it the visible prelude?

O days when all the world was beautiful and strange; when unfamiliar constellations burned in the Southern midnights, and the mocking-bird poured out his heart in the moon-gilded magnolia; when there was something new under a new sun; will your fine, far memories ever cease to lay contrasting pictures athwart the harsher features of this later world, accentuating the ugliness of the longer and tamer life? Is it not strange that the phantoms of a blood-stained period have so airy a grace and look with so tender eyes?—that I recall with difficulty the danger and death and horrors of the time, and without effort all that was gracious and picturesque? Ah, Youth, there is no such wizard as thou! Give me but one touch of thine artist hand upon the dull canvas of the Present; gild for but one moment the drear and somber scenes of to-day, and I will willingly surrender another life than the one that I should have thrown away at Shiloh.

Shiloh Songs

Different types of music played a vital role in the Civil War. Bugles, fifes, and drums were used on the battlefield to rally troops and to communicate with soldiers in combat because the sounds of these instruments could be heard above the din of battle.

The songs of the War must be understood as vehicles and outlets for the emotional distress of the period, both on the home front and in the military camps. What may appear on the page as clichés of Victorian sentimentality—the trope of the child soldier and the pointed calls for divine guidance and protection—communicate not so much the realities of the field as the need for a soothing balm for the emotional wounds, homesickness, and terrors of the War. The battle of Shiloh, resulting in 25 percent casualties on both sides, ended in what was probably a statistical draw and killed all hope of a quick end to the War.

Shiloh's Hill

(M. G. Smith)

Come all ye valiant soldiers—a story I will tell
About the bloody battle that was fought on Shiloh Hill.
It was an awful struggle and will cause your blood to chill;
It was the famous battle, that was fought on Shiloh Hill.

'Twas on the sixth of April, just at the break of day;
The drums and fifes were playing for us to march away.
The feeling of that hour I do remember still,
When first my feet were tromping on the top of Shiloh Hill.

About the hour of sunrise the battle it began;
Before the day was ended, we fought 'em hand to hand.

The horrors of that field did my heart with anguish fill
For the wounded and the dying that lay on Shiloh Hill.

There were men from every nation laid on those bloody plains,
Fathers, sons, and brothers were numbered with the slain,
That has caused so many homes with deep mourning to be
filled,
All from the bloody battle that was fought on Shiloh Hill.

The wounded men were crying for help from everywhere,
While others who were dying were offering God their prayer,
"Protect my wife and children if it is Thy holy will!"
Such were the prayers I heard that night on Shiloh Hill.

And early the next morning we were called to arms again,
Unmindful of the wounded and unuseful to the slain;
The struggle was renewed again, and ten thousand men were
killed;
This was the second conflict of the famous Shiloh Hill.

The battle it raged on, though dead and dying men
Lay thick all o'er the ground, on the hill and on the glen;
And from their deadly wounds, the blood ran like a rill;
Such were the mournful sights that I saw on Shiloh Hill.

Before the day was ended, the battle ceased to roar,
And thousands of brave soldiers had fell to rise no more;
They left their vacant ranks for some other ones to fill,
And now their mouldering bodies all lie on Shiloh Hill.

And now my song is ended about those bloody plains;
I hope the sight by mortal man may ne'er be seen again!
But I pray to God, the Saviour, "If consistent with Thy will,
To save the souls of all who fell on bloody Shiloh Hill."

The Drummer Boy of Shiloh

(Will S. Hays)

On Shiloh's dark and bloody ground
The dead and wounded lay,
Amongst them was a drummer boy
Who beat the drums that day.

A wounded soldier held him up
His drum was by his side;
He clasped his hands, then raised his eyes
And prayed before he died.
He clasped his hands, then raised his eyes
And prayed before he died.

Look down upon the battle field,
Oh, Thou our Heavenly Friend!
Have mercy on our sinful souls!
The soldiers cried, "Amen!"
For gathered 'round a little group,
Each brave man knelt and cried.
They listened to the drummer boy
Who prayed before he died.
They listened to the drummer boy
Who prayed before he died.

"Oh, mother," said the dying boy,
"Look down from Heaven on me,
Receive me to thy fond embrace—
Oh, take me home to thee.
I've loved my country as my God;
To serve them both I've tried."
He smiled, shook hands—death seized the boy
Who prayed before he died;
He smiled, shook hands—death seized the boy
Who prayed before he died;

Each soldier wept, then, like a child,
Stout hearts were they, and brave;
The flag his winding sheet, God's Book
The key unto his grave.
They wrote upon a simple board
These words: "This is a guide
To those who'd mourn the drummer boy
Who prayed before he died;
To those who'd mourn the drummer boy
Who prayed before he died."

Ye angels round the Throne of Grace,
Look down upon the braves
Who fought and died on Shiloh's plain,

Now slumb'ring in their graves!
How many homes made desolate?
How many hearts have sighed?
How many, like that drummer boy,
Who prayed before they died;
How many, like that drummer boy,
Who prayed before they died!

"Shiloh: A Requiem"

Herman Melville (1819–1891)

By 1857, his novels largely unnoticed by the literary public, Melville had stopped writing fiction and begun to concentrate on writing poetry. The Civil War made a profound impression on him and became the focus of his verse. Melville's first published book of poems was *Battle-Pieces and Aspects of the War* (1866). Many readers find Melville's poetry as rich and engaging as any of his novels, though he remains relatively unrecognized as a poet. The fusion of irony and serenity in this poem is in disturbing contrast to the gruesome accounts of the battle, a slaughterfest on both sides.

Skimming lightly, wheeling still,
The swallows fly low
Over the field in clouded days,
The forest-field of Shiloh—
Over the field where April rain
Solaced the parched one stretched in pain
Through the pause of night
That followed the Sunday fight
Around the church of Shiloh—
The church so lone, the log-built one,
That echoed to many a parting groan
And natural prayer
Of dying foemen mingled there—
Foemen at morn, but friends at eve—
Fame or country least their care:
(What like a bullet can undeceive!)
But now they lie low,
While over them the swallows skim
And all is hushed at Shiloh.

"The Private History of a Campaign That Failed"

Mark Twain (1835–1910)

"The Private History of a Campaign that Failed," published in *Century Magazine* in 1885, is a fictionalized version of two weeks Mark Twain spent as part of a pro-Confederate Missouri State Guard, called the Marion Rangers, whose "campaign" consisted of constant retreat from the enemy and killing an innocent passerby mistaken for a Yankee. At the end of the sketch, Twain rescues his piece from the charge of mere slapstick by reminding his reader exactly what it meant to cease to be a *raw* recruit: ". . . it is not an unfair picture of what went on in many a militia camp in the first months of the rebellion, when the green recruits were without discipline, without the steadying and heartening influence of trained leaders, when all their circumstances were new and strange and charged with exaggerated terrors, and before the invaluable experience of actual collision in the field had turned them from rabbits into soldiers." Twain's ever-present satire takes the reader just a bit further than expected.

You have heard from a great many people who did something in the war; is it not fair and right that you listen a little moment to one who started out to do something in it, but didn't? Thousands entered the war, got just a taste of it, and then stepped out again permanently. These, by their very numbers, are respectable, and are therefore entitled to a sort of voice—not a loud one, but a modest one; not a boastful one, but an apologetic one. They ought not to be allowed much space among better people—people who did something. I grant that; but they ought at least to be allowed to state why they didn't do anything, and also to explain the process by which they didn't do anything. Surely this kind of light must have a sort of value.

Out West there was a good deal of confusion in men's minds during the first months of the great trouble—a good deal of unsettledness, of leaning first this way, then that, then the other way. It was hard for us to get our bearings. I call to mind an instance of this. I was piloting on the Mississippi when the news came that South Carolina had gone out of the Union on the 20th of December, 1860. My pilot mate was a New-Yorker. He was strong for the Union; so was I. But he would not listen to me with any patience; my loyalty was smirched, to his eye, because my father had owned slaves. I said, in palliation of this dark fact, that I had heard my father say, some years before he died, that slavery was a great wrong, and that he would free the solitary negro he then owned if he could think it right to give away the property of the family when he was so straitened in means. My mate retorted that a mere impulse was nothing—anybody could pretend to a good impulse; and went on decrying my Unionism and libeling my ancestry. A month later the secession atmosphere had considerably thickened on the Lower Mississippi, and I became a rebel; so did he. We were together in New Orleans the 26th of January, when Louisiana went out of the Union. He did his full share of the rebel shouting, but was bitterly opposed to letting me do mine. He said that I came of bad stock—of a father who had been willing to set slaves free. In the following summer he was piloting a Federal gunboat and shouting for the Union again, and I was in the Confederate army. I held his note for some borrowed money. He was one of the most upright men I ever knew, but he repudiated that note without hesitation because I was a rebel and the son of a man who owned slaves.

In that summer—of 1861—the first wash of the wave of war broke upon the shores of Missouri. Our state was invaded by the Union forces. They took possession of St. Louis, Jefferson Barracks, and some other points. The Governor, Claib Jackson, issued his proclamation calling out fifty thousand militia to repel the invader.

I was visiting in the small town where my boyhood had been spent—Hannibal, Marion County. Several of us got together in a secret place by night and formed ourselves into a military company. One Tom Lyman, a young fellow of a good deal of spirit but of no military experience, was made captain; I was made second lieutenant. We had no first lieutenant; I do not know why; it was long ago. There were fifteen of us. By the advice of an innocent connected with the organization we called ourselves the Marion Rangers. I do not remember that any one found fault with the name. I did not; I thought it sounded quite well. The young fellow who proposed this title was perhaps a fair sample of the kind of stuff we were made of. He was young, ignorant, good-natured, well-meaning, trivial, full of romance, and given to reading chivalric novels and singing forlorn love-ditties. He had some pathetic little nickel-plated aristocratic instincts, and detested his name, which was Dunlap; detested it, partly because it was nearly as common in that region as Smith, but mainly because it had a plebeian sound to his ear. So he tried to ennoble it by writing it in this way: *d'Unlap.* That contented his eye, but left his ear unsatisfied, for people gave the new name the same old pronunciation—emphasis on the front end of it. He then did the bravest thing that can be imagined—a thing to make one shiver when one remembers how the world is given to resenting shams and affectations; he began to write his name so: *d'Un Lap.* And he waited patiently through the long storm of mud that was flung at this work of art, and he had his reward at last; for he lived to see that name accepted, and the emphasis put where he wanted it by people who had known him all his life, and to whom the tribe of Dunlaps had been as familiar as the rain and the sunshine for forty years. So sure of victory at last is the courage that can wait. He said he had found, by consulting some ancient French chronicles, that the name was rightly and originally written d'Un Lap; and said that if it were translated into English it would mean Peterson: *Lap,* Latin or Greek, he said, for stone or rock, same as the French *pierre,* that is to say, Peter: *d',* of or from; *un,* a or one; hence, d'Un Lap, of or from a stone or a Peter; that is to say, one who is the son of a stone, the son of a Peter—Peterson. Our militia company were not learned, and the explanation confused them; so they called him Peterson Dunlap. He proved useful to us in his way; he named our camps for us, and he generally struck a name that was "no slouch," as the boys said.

That is one sample of us. Another was Ed Stevens, son of the town jeweler—trim-built, handsome, graceful, neat as a cat; bright, educated, but given over entirely to fun. There was nothing serious in life to him. As far as he was concerned, this military expedition of ours was simply a holiday. I should say that about half of us looked upon it in the same way; not consciously, perhaps, but unconsciously. We did not think; we were not capable of it. As for myself, I was full of unreasoning joy to be done with turning out of bed at midnight and four in the morning for a while; grateful to have a change, new scenes, new occupations, a new interest. In my thoughts that was as far as I went; I did not go into the details; as a rule, one doesn't at twenty-four.

Another sample was Smith, the blacksmith's apprentice. This vast donkey had some pluck, of a slow and sluggish nature, but a soft heart; at one time he would knock a horse down for some impropriety, and at another he would get homesick and cry. However, he had one ultimate credit to his account which some of us hadn't; he stuck to the war, and was killed in battle at last.

Jo Bowers, another sample, was a huge, good-natured, flax-headed lubber; lazy, sentimental, full of harmless brag, a grumbler by nature; an experienced, industrious, ambitious, and often quite picturesque liar, and yet not a successful one, for he had had no intelligent training, but was allowed to come up just any way. This life was serious enough to him, and seldom satisfactory. But he was a good fellow, anyway, and the boys all liked him. He was made orderly sergeant; Stevens was made corporal.

These samples will answer—and they are quite fair ones. Well, this herd of cattle started for the war. What could you expect of them? They did as well as they knew how; but, really, what was justly to be expected of them? Nothing, I should say. That is what they did.

We waited for a dark night, for caution and secrecy were necessary; then, toward midnight, we stole in couples and from various directions to the Griffith place, beyond the town; from that point we set out together on foot. Hannibal lies at the extreme southeastern corner of Marion County, on the Mississippi River; our objective point was the hamlet of New London, ten miles away, in Ralls County.

The first hour was all fun, all idle nonsense and laughter. But that could not be kept up. The steady trudging came to be like work; the play had somehow oozed out of it; the stillness of the woods and the somberness of the night began to throw a depressing influence over the spirits of the boys, and presently the talking died out and each person shut himself up in his own thoughts. During the last half of the second hour nobody said a word.

Now we approached a log farm-house where, according to report, there was a guard of five Union soldiers. Lyman called a halt; and there, in the deep gloom of the overhanging branches, he began to whisper a plan of assault upon that house, which made the gloom more depressing than it was before. It was a crucial moment; we realized, with a cold suddenness, that here was no jest—we were standing face to face with actual war. We were equal to the occasion. In our response there was no hesitation, no indecision: we said that if Lyman wanted to meddle with those soldiers, he could go ahead and do it; but if he waited for us to follow him, he would wait a long time.

Lyman urged, pleaded, tried to shame us, but it had no effect. Our course was plain, our minds were made up: we would flank the farm-house—go out around. And that was what we did.

We struck into the woods and entered upon a rough time, stumbling over roots, getting tangled in vines, and torn by briers. At last we reached an open place in a safe region, and sat down, blown and hot, to cool off and nurse our scratches and bruises. Lyman was annoyed, but the rest of us were cheerful; we had flanked the farm-house, we had made our first military movement, and it was a success; we had nothing to fret about, we were feeling just the other way. Horse-play and laughing began again; the expedition was become a holiday frolic once more.

Then we had two more hours of dull trudging and ultimate silence and depression; then, about dawn, we straggled into New London, soiled, heel-blistered, fagged with our little march, and all of us except Stevens in a sour and raspy humor and privately down on the war. We stacked our shabby old shotguns in Colonel Ralls's barn, and then went in a body and breakfasted with that veteran of the Mexican War. Afterward he took us to a distant meadow, and there in the shade of a tree we listened to an old-fashioned speech from him, full of gunpowder and glory, full of that adjective-piling, mixed metaphor and windy declamation which were regarded as eloquence in that ancient time and that remote region; and then he swore us on the Bible to be faithful to the State of Missouri and drive all invaders from her soil, no matter whence they might come or under what flag they might march. This mixed us considerably, and we could not make out just what service we were embarked in; but Colonel

Ralls, the practised politician and phrase-juggler, was not similarly in doubt; he knew quite clearly that he had invested us in the cause of the Southern Confederacy. He closed the solemnities by belting around me the sword which his neighbor, Colonel Brown, had worn at Buena Vista and Molino del Rey; and he accompanied this act with another impressive blast.

Then we formed in line of battle and marched four miles to a shady and pleasant piece of woods on the border of the far-reaching expanses of a flowery prairie. It was an enchanting region for war—our kind of war.

We pierced the forest about half a mile, and took up a strong position, with some low, rocky, and wooded hills behind us, and a purling, limpid creek in front. Straightway half the command were in swimming and the other half fishing. The ass with the French name gave this position a romantic title, but it was too long, so the boys shortened and simplified it to Camp Ralls.

We occupied an old maple-sugar camp, whose half-rotted troughs were still propped against the trees. A long corn-crib served for sleeping-quarters for the battalion. On our left, half a mile away, were Mason's farm and house; and he was a friend to the cause. Shortly after noon the farmers began to arrive from several directions, with mules and horses for our use, and these they lent us for as long as the war might last, which they judged would be about three months. The animals were of all sizes, all colors, and all breeds. They were mainly young and frisky, and nobody in the command could stay on them long at a time; for we were town boys, and ignorant of horsemanship. The creature that fell to my share was a very small mule, and yet so quick and active that it could throw me without difficulty; and it did this whenever I got on it. Then it would bray—stretching its neck out, laying its ears back, and spreading its jaws till you could see down to its works. It was a disagreeable animal in every way. If I took it by the bridle and tried to lead it off the grounds, it would sit down and brace back, and no one could budge it. However, I was not entirely destitute of military resources, and I did presently manage to spoil this game; for I had seen many a steamboat aground in my time, and knew a trick or two which even a grounded mule would be obliged to respect. There was a well by the corn-crib; so I substituted thirty fathom of rope for the bridle, and fetched him home with the windlass.

I will anticipate here sufficiently to say that we did learn to ride, after some days' practice, but never well. We could not learn to like our animals; they were not choice ones, and most of them had annoying peculiarities of one kind or another. Stevens's horse would carry him, when he was not noticing, under the huge excrescences which form on the trunks of oak-trees, and wipe him out of the saddle; in this way Stevens got several bad hurts. Sergeant Bowers's horse was very large and tall, with slim, long legs, and looked like a railroad bridge. His size enabled him to reach all about, and as far as he wanted to, with his head; so he was always biting Bowers's legs. On the march, in the sun, Bowers slept a good deal; and as soon as the horse recognized that he was asleep he would reach around and bite him on the leg. His legs were black and blue with bites. This was the only thing that could ever make him swear, but this always did; whenever his horse bit him he always swore, and of course Stevens, who laughed at everything, laughed at this, and would even get into such convulsions over it as to lose his balance and fall off his horse; and then Bowers, already irritated by the pain of the horse-bite, would resent the laughter with hard language, and there would be a quarrel; so that horse made no end of trouble and bad blood in the command.

However, I will get back to where I was—our first afternoon in the sugar-camp. The sugar-troughs came very handy as horse-troughs, and we had plenty of corn to fill them with. I ordered Sergeant Bowers to feed my mule; but he said that if I reckoned he went to war to be a dry-nurse to a mule it wouldn't take me very long to find out my mistake. I believed that this was insubordination, but I was full of uncertainties about everything military, and so I let the thing pass, and went and ordered Smith, the blacksmith's apprentice, to feed the mule; but he merely gave me a large, cold, sarcastic grin, such as an ostensibly seven-year-old horse gives you when you lift his lip and find he is fourteen, and turned his back on me. I then went to the captain, and asked if it were not right and proper and military for me to have an orderly. He said it was, but as there was only one orderly in the corps, it was but right that he himself should have Bowers on his staff. Bowers said he wouldn't serve on anybody's staff; and if anybody thought he could make him, let him try it. So, of course, the thing had to be dropped; there was no other way.

Next, nobody would cook; it was considered a degradation; so we had no dinner. We lazied the rest of the pleasant afternoon away, some dozing under the trees, some smoking cob-pipes and talking sweethearts and war, some playing games. By late supper-time all hands were famished; and to meet the difficulty all hands turned to, on an equal footing, and gathered wood, built fires, and cooked the meal. Afterward everything was smooth for a while; then trouble broke out between the corporal and the sergeant, each claiming to rank the other. Nobody knew which was the higher office; so Lyman had to settle the matter by making the rank of both officers equal. The commander of an ignorant crew like that has many troubles and vexations which probably do not occur in the regular army at all. However, with the song-singing and yarn-spinning around the camp-fire, everything presently became serene again; and by and by we raked the corn down level in one end of the crib, and all went to bed on it, tying a horse to the door, so that he would neigh if any one tried to get in.*

We had some horsemanship drill every forenoon; then, afternoons, we rode off here and there in squads a few miles, and visited the farmers' girls, and had a youthful good time, and got an honest good dinner or supper, and then home again to camp, happy and content.

For a time life was idly delicious, it was perfect; there was nothing to mar it. Then came some farmers with an alarm one day. They said it was rumored that the enemy were advancing in our direction from over Hyde's prairie. The result was a sharp stir among us, and general consternation. It was a rude awakening from our pleasant trance. The rumor was but a rumor—nothing definite about it; so, in the confusion, we did not know which way to retreat. Lyman was for not retreating at all in these uncertain circumstances; but he found that if he tried to maintain that attitude he would fare badly, for the command were in no

*It was always my impression that that was what the horse was there for, and I know that it was also the impression of at least one other of the command, for we talked about it at the time, and admired the military ingenuity of the device; but when I was out West, three years ago, I was told by Mr. A. G. Fuqua, a member of our company, that the horse was his; that the leaving him tied at the door was a matter of mere forgetfulness, and that to attribute it to intelligent invention was to give him quite too much credit. In support of his position he called my attention to the suggestive fact that the artifice was not employed again. I had not thought of that before.

humor to put up with insubordination. So he yielded the point and called a council of war—to consist of himself and the three other officers; but the privates made such a fuss about being left out that we had to allow them to remain, for they were already present, and doing the most of the talking too. The question was, which way to retreat; but all were so flurried that nobody seemed to have even a guess to offer. Except Lyman. He explained in a few calm words that, inasmuch as the enemy were approaching from over Hyde's prairie, our course was simple: all we had to do was not to retreat *toward* him; any other direction would answer our needs perfectly. Everybody saw in a moment how true this was, and how wise; so Lyman got a great many compliments. It was now decided that we should fall back on Mason's farm.

It was after dark by this time, and as we could not know how soon the enemy might arrive, it did not seem best to try to take the horses and things with us; so we only took the guns and ammunition, and started at once. The route was very rough and hilly and rocky, and presently the night grew very black and rain began to fall; so we had a troublesome time of it, struggling and stumbling along in the dark; and soon some person slipped and fell, and then the next person behind stumbled over him and fell, and so did the rest, one after the other; and then Bowers came, with the keg of powder in his arms, while the command were all mixed together, arms and legs, on the muddy slope; and so he fell, of course, with the keg, and this started the whole detachment down the hill in a body, and they landed in the brook at the bottom in a pile, and each that was undermost pulling the hair and scratching and biting those that were on top of him; and those that were being scratched and bitten scratching and biting the rest in their turn, and all saying they would die before they would ever go to war again if they ever got out of this brook this time, and the invader might rot for all they cared, and the country along with him—and all such talk as that, which was dismal to hear and take part in, in such smothered, low voices, and such a grisly dark place and so wet, and the enemy, maybe, coming any moment.

The keg of powder was lost, and the guns, too; so the growling and complaining continued straight along while the brigade pawed around the pasty hillside and slopped around in the brook hunting for these things; consequently we lost considerable time at this; and then we heard a sound, and held our breath and listened, and it seemed to be the enemy coming, though it could have been a cow, for it had a cough like a cow; but we did not wait, but left a couple of guns behind and struck out for Mason's again as briskly as we could scramble along in the dark. But we got lost presently among the rugged little ravines, and wasted a deal of time finding the way again, so it was after nine when we reached Mason's stile at last; and then before we could open our mouths to give the countersign several dogs came bounding over the fence, with great riot and noise, and each of them took a soldier by the slack of his trousers and began to back away with him. We could not shoot the dogs without endangering the persons they were attached to; so we had to look on helpless at what was perhaps the most mortifying spectacle of the Civil War. There was light enough, and to spare, for the Masons had now run out on the porch with candles in their hands. The old man and his son came and undid the dogs without difficulty, all but Bowers's; but they couldn't undo his dog, they didn't know his combination; he was of the bull kind, and seemed to be set with a Yale time-lock; but they got him loose at last with some scalding water, of which Bowers got his share and returned thanks. Peterson Dunlap afterward made up a fine name for this engagement, and also for the night march which preceded it, but both have long ago faded out of my memory.

We now went into the house, and they began to ask us a world of questions, whereby it presently came out that we did not know anything concerning who or what we were running from; so the old gentleman made himself very frank, and said we were a curious breed of soldiers, and guessed we could be depended on to end up the war in time, because no government could stand the expense of the shoe-leather we should cost it trying to follow us around. "Marion *Rangers*! good name, b'gosh!" said he. And wanted to know why we hadn't had a picket-guard at the place where the road entered the prairie, and why we hadn't sent out a scouting party to spy out the enemy and bring us an account of his strength, and so on, before jumping up and stampeding out of a strong position upon a mere vague rumor—and so on, and so forth, till he made us all feel shabbier than the dogs had done, not half so enthusiastically welcome. So we went to bed shamed and low-spirited; except Stevens. Soon Stevens began to devise a garment for Bowers which could be made to automatically display his battle-scars to the grateful, or conceal them from the envious, according to his occasions; but Bowers was in no humor for this, so there was a fight, and when it was over Stevens had some battle-scars of his own to think about.

Then we got a little sleep. But after all we had gone through, our activities were not over for the night; for about two o'clock in the morning we heard a shout of warning from down the lane, accompanied by a chorus from all the dogs, and in a moment everybody was up and flying around to find out what the alarm was about. The alarmist was a horseman who gave notice that a detachment of Union soldiers was on its way from Hannibal with orders to capture and hang any bands like ours which it could find, and said we had no time to lose. Farmer Mason was in a flurry this time himself. He hurried us out of the house with all haste, and sent one of his negroes with us to show us where to hide ourselves and our telltale guns among the ravines half a mile away. It was raining heavily.

We struck down the lane, then across some rocky pasture-land which offered good advantages for stumbling; consequently we were down in the mud most of the time, and every time a man went down he blackguarded the war, and the people that started it, and everybody connected with it, and gave himself the master dose of all for being so foolish as to go into it. At last we reached the wooded mouth of a ravine, and there we huddled ourselves under the streaming trees, and sent the negro back home. It was a dismal and heart-breaking time. We were like to be drowned with the rain, deafened with the howling wind and the booming thunder, and blinded by the lightning. It was, indeed, a wild night. The drenching we were getting was misery enough, but a deeper misery still was the reflection that the halter might end us before we were a day older. A death of this shameful sort had not occurred to us as being among the possibilities of war. It took the romance all out of the campaign, and turned our dreams of glory into a repulsive nightmare. As for doubting that so barbarous an order had been given, not one of us did that.

The long night wore itself out at last, and then the negro came to us with the news that the alarm had manifestly been a false one, and that breakfast would soon be ready. Straightway we were light-hearted again, and the world was bright, and life as full of hope and promise as ever—for we were young then. How long ago that was! Twenty-four years.

The mongrel child of philology named the night's refuge Camp Devastation, and no soul objected. The Masons gave us a Missouri country breakfast, in Missourian abundance, and we needed it: hot biscuits; hot "wheat bread," prettily criss-crossed in a lattice pattern on top; hot corn-pone; fried chicken; bacon, coffee, eggs, milk, buttermiik, etc.; and the world may be confidently challenged to furnish the equal of such a breakfast, as it is cooked in the South.

We stayed several days at Mason's; and after all these years the memory of the dullness, and stillness, and lifelessness of that slumberous farm-house still oppresses my spirit as with a sense of the presence of death and mourning. There was nothing to do, nothing to think about; there was no interest in life. The male part of the household were away in the fields all day, the women were busy and out of our sight; there was no sound but the plaintive wailing of a spinning-wheel, forever moaning out from some distant room—the most lonesome sound in nature, a sound steeped and sodden with homesickness and the emptiness of life. The family went to bed about dark every night, and as we were not invited to intrude any new customs we naturally followed theirs. Those nights were a hundred years long to youths accustomed to being up till twelve. We lay awake and miserable till that hour every time, and grew old and decrepit waiting through the still eternities for the clock-strikes. This was no place for town boys. So at last it was with something very like joy that we received news that the enemy were on our track again. With a new birth of the old warrior spirit we sprang to our places in line of battle and fell back on Camp Ralls.

Captain Lyman had taken a hint from Mason's talk, and he now gave orders that our camp should be guarded against surprise by the posting of pickets. I was ordered to place a picket at the forks of the road in Hyde's prairie. Night shut down black and threatening. I told Sergeant Bowers to go out to that place and stay till midnight, and, just as I was expecting, he said he wouldn't do it. I tried to get others to go, but all refused. Some excused themselves on account of the weather; but the rest were frank enough to say they wouldn't go in any kind of weather. This kind of thing sounds odd now, and impossible, but there was no surprise in it at the time. On the contrary, it seemed a perfectly natural thing to do. There were scores of little camps scattered over Missouri where the same thing was happening. These camps were composed of young men who had been born and reared to a sturdy independence, and who did not know what it meant to be ordered around by Tom, Dick, and Harry, whom they had known familiarly all their lives, in the village or on the farm. It is quite within the probabilities that this same thing was happening all over the South. James Redpath recognized the justice of this assumption, and furnished the following instance in support of it. During a short stay in East Tennessee he was in a citizen colonel's tent one day talking, when a big private appeared at the door, and, without salute or other circumlocution, said to the colonel:

"Say, Jim, I'm a-goin' home for a few days."

"What for?"

"Well, I hain't b'en there for a right smart while, and I'd like to see how things is comin' on."

"How long are you going to be gone?"

" 'Bout two weeks."

"Well, don't be gone longer than that; and get back sooner if you can."

That was all, and the citizen officer resumed his conversation where the private had broken it off. This was in the first months of the war, of course. The camps in our part of Missouri were under Brigadier-General Thomas H. Harris. He was a townsman of ours, a first-rate fellow, and well liked; but we had all familiarly known him as the sole and modest-salaried operator in our telegraph-office, where he had to send about one despatch a week in ordinary times, and two when there was a rush of business; consequently, when he appeared in our midst one day, on the wing, and delivered a military command of some sort, in a large military fashion, nobody was surprised at the response which he got from the assembled soldiery:

"Oh, now, what'll you take to *don't,* Tom Harris?"

It was quite the natural thing. One might justly imagine that we were hopeless material for war. And so we seemed, in our ignorant state; but there were those among us who afterward learned the grim trade; learned to obey like machines; became valuable soldiers; fought all through the war, and came out at the end with excellent records. One of the very boys who refused to go out on picket duty that night, and called me an ass for thinking he would expose himself to danger in such a foolhardy way, had become distinguished for intrepidity before he was a year older.

I did secure my picket that night—not by authority, but by diplomacy. I got Bowers to go by agreeing to exchange ranks with him for the time being, and go along and stand the watch with him as his subordinate. We stayed out there a couple of dreary hours in the pitchy darkness and the rain, with nothing to modify the dreariness but Bowers's monotonous growlings at the war and the weather; then we began to nod, and presently found it next to impossible to stay in the saddle; so we gave up the tedious job, and went back to the camp without waiting for the relief guard. We rode into camp without interruption or objection from anybody, and the enemy could have done the same, for there were no sentries. Everybody was asleep; at midnight there was nobody to send out another picket, so none was sent. We never tried to establish a watch at night again, as far as I remember, but we generally kept a picket out in the daytime.

In that camp the whole command slept on the corn in the big corn-crib; and there was usually a general row before morning, for the place was full of rats, and they would scramble over the boys' bodies and faces, annoying and irritating everybody; and now and then they would bite some one's toe, and the person who owned the toe would start up and magnify his English and begin to throw corn in the dark. The ears were half as heavy as bricks, and when they struck they hurt. The persons struck would respond, and inside of five minutes every man would be locked in a death-grip with his neighbor. There was a grievous deal of blood shed in the corn-crib, but this was all that was spilt while I was in the war. No, that is not quite true. But for one circumstance it would have been all. I will come to that now.

Our scares were frequent. Every few days rumors would come that the enemy were approaching. In these cases we always fell back on some other camp of ours; we never stayed where we were. But the rumors always turned out to be false; so at last even we began to grow indifferent to them. One night a negro was sent to our corn-crib with the same old warning: the enemy was hovering in our neighborhood. We all said let him hover. We resolved to stay still and be comfortable. It was a fine warlike resolution, and no doubt we all felt the stir of it in our veins—for a moment. We had been having a very jolly time, that was full of horse-play and school-boy hilarity; but that cooled down now, and presently the fast-waning fire of forced jokes and forced laughs died out altogether, and the company became silent. Silent and nervous. And soon uneasy—worried—apprehensive. We had said we would stay, and we were committed. We could have been persuaded to go, but there was nobody brave enough to suggest it. An almost noiseless movement presently began in the dark by a general but unvoiced impulse. When the movement was completed each man knew that he was not the only person who had crept to the front wall and had his eye at a crack between the logs. No, we were all there; all there with our hearts in our throats, and staring out toward the sugar-troughs where the forest footpath came through. It was late, and there was a deep woodsy stillness everywhere. There was a veiled moonlight, which was only just strong enough to enable us to mark the general shape of objects. Presently a muffled sound caught our ears, and we recognized it as the hoof-beats of a horse or horses. And right away a figure appeared in the forest path; it could have been made of smoke, its mass had so little sharpness of outline. It was a man on horseback, and it seemed to me that there were others behind him. I got hold of a gun in the dark, and pushed it through a crack between the logs, hardly knowing what I was doing, I was so dazed with fright. Somebody said "Fire!" I pulled the trigger. I seemed to see a hundred flashes and hear a hundred reports; then I saw the man fall down out of the saddle. My first feeling was of surprised gratification; my first impulse was an apprentice-sportsman's impulse to run and pick up his game. Somebody said, hardly audibly, "Good—we've got him!—wait for the rest." But the rest did not come. We waited—listened—still no more came. There was not a sound, not the whisper of a leaf; just perfect stillness; an uncanny kind of stillness, which was all the more uncanny on account of the damp, earthy, late-night smells now rising and pervading it. Then, wondering, we crept stealthily out, and approached the man. When we got to him the moon revealed him distinctly. He was lying on his back, with his arms abroad; his mouth was open and his chest heaving with long gasps, and his white shirt-front was all splashed with blood. The thought shot through me that I was a murderer; that I had killed a man—a man who had never done me any harm. That was the coldest sensation that ever went through my marrow. I was down by him in a moment, helplessly stroking his forehead; and I would have given anything then—my own life freely—to make him again what he had been five minutes before. And all the boys seemed to be feeling in the same way; they hung over him, full of pitying interest, and tried all they could to help him, and said all sorts of regretful things. They had forgotten all about the enemy; they thought only of this one forlorn unit of the foe. Once my imagination persuaded me that the dying man gave me a reproachful look out of his shadowy eyes, and it seemed to me that I could rather he had stabbed me than done that. He muttered and mumbled like a dreamer in his sleep about his wife and his child; and I thought with a new despair, "This thing that I have done does not end with him; it falls upon *them* too, and they never did me any harm, any more than he."

In a little while the man was dead. He was killed in war; killed in fair and legitimate war; killed in battle, as you may say; and yet he was as sincerely mourned by the opposing force as if he had been their brother. The boys stood there a half-hour sorrowing over him, and recalling the details of the tragedy, and wondering who he might be, and if he were a spy, and saying that if it were to do over again they would not hurt him unless he attacked them first. It soon came out that mine was not the only shot fired; there were five others—a division of the guilt which was a great relief to me, since it in some degree lightened and diminished the burden I was carrying. There were six shots fired at once; but I was not in my right mind at the time, and my heated imagination had magnified my one shot into a volley.

The man was not in uniform, and was not armed. He was a stranger in the country; that was all we ever found out about him. The thought of him got to preying upon me every night; I could not get rid of it. I could not drive it away, the taking of that unoffending life seemed such a wanton thing. And it seemed an epitome of war; that all war must be just that—the killing of strangers against whom you feel no personal animosity; strangers whom, in other circumstances, you would help if you found them in trouble, and who would help you if you needed it. My campaign was spoiled. It seemed to me that I was not rightly equipped for this awful business; that war was intended for men, and I for a child's nurse. I resolved to retire from this avocation of sham soldiership while I could save some remnant of my self-respect. These morbid thoughts clung to me against reason; for at bottom I did not believe I had touched that man. The law of probabilities decreed me guiltless of his blood; for in all my small experience with guns I had never hit anything I had tried to hit, and I knew I had done my best to hit him. Yet there was no solace in the thought. Against a diseased imagination demonstration goes for nothing.

The rest of my war experience was of a piece with what I have already told of it. We kept monotonously falling back upon one camp or another, and eating up the farmers and their families. They ought to have shot us; on the contrary, they were as hospitably kind and courteous to us as if we had deserved it. In one of these camps we found Ab Grimes, an Upper Mississippi pilot, who afterward became famous as a dare-devil rebel spy, whose career bristled with desperate adventures. The look and style of his comrades suggested that they had not come into the war to play, and their deeds made good the conjecture later. They were fine horsemen and good revolver shots; but their favorite arm was the lasso. Each had one at his pommel, and could snatch a man out of the saddle with it every time, on a full gallop, at any reasonable distance.

In another camp the chief was a fierce and profane old blacksmith of sixty, and he had furnished his twenty recruits with gigantic home-made bowie-knives, to be swung with two hands, like the *machetes* of the Isthmus. It was a grisly spectacle to see that earnest band practising their murderous cuts and slashes under the eye of that remorseless old fanatic.

The last camp which we fell back upon was in a hollow near the village of Florida, where I was born—in Monroe County. Here we were warned one day that a Union colonel was sweeping down on us with a whole regiment at his heel. This looked decidedly serious. Our boys went apart and consulted; then we went back and told the other companies present that the war was a disappointment to us, and we were going to disband. They were getting ready themselves to fall back on some place or other, and we were only waiting for General Tom Harris, who was expected to arrive at any moment; so they tried to persuade us to wait a little while, but the majority of us said no, we were accustomed to falling back, and didn't need any of Tom Harris's help; we could get along perfectly well without him—and save time, too. So about half of our fifteen, including myself, mounted and left on the instant; the others yielded to persuasion and stayed—stayed through the war.

An hour later we met General Harris on the road, with two or three people in his company—his staff, probably, but we could not tell; none of them were in uniform; uniforms had not come into vogue among us yet. Harris ordered us back; but we told him there was a Union colonel coming with a whole regiment in his wake, and it looked as if there was going to be a disturbance; so we had concluded to go home. He raged a little, but it was of no use; our minds were made up. We had done our share; had killed one man, exterminated one army, such as it was; let him go and kill the rest, and that would end the war. I did not see that brisk young general again until last year; then he was wearing white hair and whiskers.

In time I came to know that Union colonel whose coming frightened me out of the war and crippled the Southern cause to that extent—General Grant. I came within a few hours of seeing him when he was as unknown as I was myself; at a time when anybody could have said, "Grant?—Ulysses S. Grant? I do not remember hearing the name before." It seems difficult to realize that there was once a time when such a remark could be rationally made; but there *was,* and I was within a few miles of the place and the occasion, too, though proceeding in the other direction.

The thoughtful will not throw this war paper of mine lightly aside as being valueless. It has this value: it is a not unfair picture of what went on in many and many a militia camp in the first months of the rebellion, when the green recruits were without discipline, without the steadying, and heartening influence of trained leaders; when all their circumstances were new and strange, and charged with exaggerated terrors, and before the invaluable experience of actual collision in the field had turned them from rabbits into soldiers. If this side of the picture of that early day has not before been put into history, then history has been to that degree incomplete, for it had and has its rightful place there. There was more Bull Run material scattered through the early camps of this country than exhibited itself at Bull Run. And yet it learned its trade presently, and helped to fight the great battles later. I could have become a soldier myself if I had waited. I had got part of it learned; I knew more about retreating than the man that invented retreating.

"How Men Feel in Battle"

S. H. M. Byers (1838–1933)

As a young Iowan traveling to Memphis, Tennessee, Samuel Hawkins Marshal Byers, known as "Marsh," was greatly distressed at the sight of slaves being whipped and beaten. When war began, he almost immediately joined the Fifth Iowa Volunteer Infantry Regiment. He saw action at Vicksburg and Chattanooga, where he was captured. Major Byers spent some of his captivity in Libby Prison in Virginia.

After transfer to another prison, he wrote the poem "Sherman's March to the Sea," which was set to music by another inmate, smuggled out during a prisoner exchange, and became an instant hit and Union rallying cry. When Byers escaped, he met Sherman and served for a time as a member of his staff.

Following the War, Byers wrote extensively, movingly, and with great immediacy about how soldiers deal with the physical and psychological horrors of going into battle. The photograph of soldiers tightly packed into a trench at Petersburg, Virginia, conveys a mixture of relaxation and uneasiness preceding the battle.

Sumter was fired on. I was twenty-two. I longed for the excitement of battle, the adventure of war; and so I enlisted in a regiment that was to be wiped out of existence before the war was over. More than a year passed. It was noon now, of the 19th of September, 1862. Possibly the fiercest battle of the civil war was about to begin—a battle in which our small brigade of three half-regiments was to lose six hundred and eight killed and wounded. My own regiment had but four hundred and eighty-two engaged, but two hundred and seventeen of them, with fifteen officers, were stretched dead or wounded in an hour. It was appalling.

B-157

That was war. That afternoon put a star on the shoulder of General Rosecrans. My regiment had been hoping for a great fight. We were tired of chasing "Pap" Price's battalions and guerrillas from the Missouri River to the Ozark Mountains, tired of being killed off in running fights, skirmishes, and ambuscades, where there was no honor. We wanted real war. At last, at Iuka, down in Mississippi, and close to the Tennessee River, they said they would stand up and fight. And they did! Not a soldier in the Fifth Iowa was more anxious to participate in a red-hot battle than myself. I was among those who had volunteered not more for patriotism than for hope of tremendous adventure. My chance had come. We marched from our camps at Jacinto as light-footed and as light-hearted that September morning as if we were going to a wedding. The sky was blue, the birds sang, the autumn leaves were red and beautiful. We seemed perfectly gay with anticipation of being killed. It seems astounding now.

The fact is, no one thought himself in severe danger. Some of us would be killed, we knew, of course, but each thought it would be the "other fellow." We sang jovial songs as we marched along; one, a song of my own composing. That gorgeous forenoon, hurrying through the woods for twenty miles, towards the enemy, we saw the poetry of war. Sundown saw five of my messmates and forty-two of my regiment dead in a ditch by the battle-field. Another one hundred and seventy-five were wounded. And we had all been so happy in the morning! An hour before the fight commenced we soldiers feared the enemy might run and get away. At last a shot was heard in the woods in front of us. Our advance-guard had run on to some Confederates in gray. "Form your regiment instantly, right and left across this road," cried a staff-officer, galloping up to our loved commander, Colonel Matthies. "Stand your ground here and fight them," added the officer. "Dat is just exactly vot I calculate to do," answered our colonel in his Teutonic accent. In three minutes the line was across the road and every eye peering into the thin woods in front. Just then, to my amazement, the colonel galloped up to me and said: "You have got your musket, but you must not fight. Something has happened to the quartermaster. Go back to the teams and hurry them ten miles to the rear." I was the most disappointed man in Grant's army. Protests did no good. "I trust you," he said. "You must go; another time you shall have your chance." Orders were orders. I hurried away, with the oncoming battle sounding in my ears, and in my heart a fixed resolve never to obey orders again, if that meant taking me from the side of my comrades. When we got the news back at the wagon-train that my regiment had been gloriously cut to pieces, I almost cried, that I had lost the chance to fall in battle. The fighting had been something terrible. The combatants nearly exterminated each other. They fought so close that if a man were hit, he was powder-burnt. One regiment of the enemy had every officer killed or wounded. Yet we wanted more of this. Time passed. My colonel kept his word. In a little time that same enemy, reinforced, rushed on to our works at Corinth. We were 25,000 inside the town, and they were 40,000 outside. All the moonlight night of October 5 my regiment, what was left of it, lay in a wagon road in the woods outside the works of Corinth and listened to the rumbling of the Confederate artillery as it was moving into place to attack us on the morrow. This time no orders hindered. A comrade who escaped being killed at Iuka lay under a blanket with me in the wagon road and in the moonlight.

The terrible experience at Iuka had sobered Jimmy King a little. He talked of what might happen at daylight. He said, too, he was "glad he had always led a good life." As for me, I was hopeful of a big time. I might of course get wounded—I almost hoped for this little honor,—but it was the "other fellow" who would certainly get killed. At daybreak of the 4th, Fort Robinette was picked out by the enemy as one of the points for their great final assault, and it proved one of the awfulest and bloodiest assaults of the civil war. There had been hard fighting all day of the 3d, and all our outer works were in the enemy's hands. On the morning of the 4th, my regiment with its division was placed some distance to the right of Robinette. We were in a field of high weeds. The orders were to lie down, as the enemy in overpowering numbers were about to assault us directly in front.

We lay there in the weeds for an hour without speaking. What a chance for strange thoughts! And the men, thinking of their comrades dead in the ditches of Iuka, did meditate. The suspense, lying there in the weeds, every moment expecting a crash of musketry in our faces, was something intense. The sun was red hot. Poor Billy Bodley, grieving for his only brother, just killed, crept over to me and whispered, "I am not afraid, but I am too sick to fight—you are the captain's friend; ask him to let me go back." He went, only to be killed on another field. He was just creeping back through the weeds, when some one cried out to us to "rise and fire." I was burning up with excitement, too excited to be scared. Instantly we were on our feet. I was in the rear rank. I could see the enemy perfectly. Some of them were in their shirt-sleeves, running from tree to tree and firing at us. I raised my musket and blazed away at nobody in particular. A comrade in front of me afterward said I "nearly shot his ear off." He glanced back once, he said, and I was only laughing. That was my first shot in an open, stand-up battle. We went on firing, biting our cartridges and loading with iron ramrods as fast as we could. I was constantly afraid lest the enemy would be on me before I could get that fool gun loaded. The destiny of the country was in my hands at that moment; only I wasn't thinking of the country, or anything else save that miserable old ramrod and that line of fellows a hundred yards in front. I must have swallowed whole spoonfuls of gunpowder in my haste biting the cartridges. I had thirst beyond description. My canteen was full of water, too, but who could stop then to take a drink! The fighting went on some minutes, yet not many men were dropping near me right or left. It must have been a ruse of the enemy, for suddenly he massed a heavy column to our left, and almost passing us, made that dreadful and historic assault on bloody Robinette. My regiment made a quick wheel half-way round, and there we stood and witnessed as brave deeds as were ever seen in any war. No soldiers could have stormed that fort and held it, yet now, suddenly, a great black column of Confederates debouched from the woods, spread out fanlike, and with a yell started to capture Fort Robinette. In front of them and about them lay fallen trees, making a strong abattis; in front of these, a deep, wide ditch; and in front of that, the fort, filled with cannon and soldiers. Every gun was loaded to the muzzle, and as the Confederates approached, a horrible whirlwind of bullets, grapeshot, and canister poured into their faces. They never halted. General Rogers, with a flag in one hand and a revolver in the other, led them straight into one of the awful death-traps of the war. Hundreds of them crossed the ditch, climbed into the fort, and with their muskets clubbed the men at the guns. Others lay dead on the fort's escarpment, their muskets folded in their arms. Useless courage, vain glory. In a moment, new Federal lines rose up behind the fort, and all was lost. The Confederates fled back among their dead, trampling them as they ran. Twice they had passed in front of my regiment, once as victors and once in horrible defeat. Standing there, looking at the horrible scene, and in the midst of the awful thunder of battle, I felt as if the world were coming to an end. It seemed the destruction of humanity, not a battle. If the ground had opened and swallowed us all up, it wouldn't have seemed strange. At that moment I was thinking neither of victory nor defeat. It was the tremendous spectacle, the awful noise, that overwhelmed me. Had that charge succeeded, my regiment would have been lost. We were speechless, breathless, as we watched the storming of the fort. Soon I went down to the grass before it. Six thousand dead and wounded Confederates lay in front of Corinth. I saw the body of Rogers, the brave of the brave, lying there. He was in his white-stocking feet. Some vandal had robbed him of his boots. He lay on his back, his face to the foe.

That night in the moonlight I stood on guard on the battle-field. I was under an oak-tree. The dead lay there unburied, among them two of my chums and classmates in a Western school. I had time to meditate on the awfulness of war, that night. But I did not. I was only thinking of the words of General Rosecrans, as he rode down the lines at Iuka, crying out, "Glorious Fifth Iowa." I, too, in the moonlight on the battle-field was saying, "Glorious Fifth Iowa." It was my regiment. How a soldier loves glory! I forgot my dead comrades and classmates in my pride in the regiment.

Forty years have passed. As I write this, I do not know that twenty of my regiment are alive. It was one of the commands that perished almost before the war was over. Later, when I was mustered out of the army as an escaped prisoner, the Secretary of War said to me, "You have no regiment. They are all gone. They fell gloriously.—You are the last man of the regiment." Is it any wonder that there, on the battle-field, alone in the moonlight, I was thinking only of the deeds of the regiment? I skip a few months. Again the chance is mine. I had not yet been killed or hurt. I had volunteered that something might happen. I wanted more adventure, and more and more; and it was all coming, but I did not know it. A last great attempt was to be made on Vicksburg. We had made so many attempts and failed. In all, ten thousand lives had been lost and Vicksburg was still standing there, a defiance to the Union army. A European war-office would have courtmartialled Grant for leaving his base as he did now, putting a mighty river behind him and starting into an enemy's country, almost without food for man or beast. We got used to strange warfare in the civil conflict, after a while. Anyway, there we now were, marching behind Vicksburg—here, there, anywhere—walking through dust shoe-mouth deep, roasting in the sun, sleeping in the road, fighting everywhere—Port Gibson, Raymond, Jackson, Champion Hills—victories, every one. We hardly waited to bury the dead. Day and night we kept going. We just marched and fought. At Jackson, an awful thunder-storm accompanied the battle. Forty years after I still laugh to think how a hundred times we soldiers dropped flat on our faces at every mighty clap of thunder, thinking it an exploding shell from the guns of the enemy. Suddenly Pemberton, with all his army, came boldly out of Vicksburg, to give us one great battle. He chose his ground among the magnolia woods of Champion Hills. My chance for adventure had come again. On the night of May 15th, my regiment got hold of a little flour. At dawn of the 16th we were mixing it with water, making dough balls to bake on the end of our ramrods over our little bivouac fires in the woods. It was all we had to eat. Once we heard faint sounds of cannon far away. Some horsemen were passing the bivouac. It was just daylight. I went out to the roadside, and there I saw General Grant galloping past, followed by aides who were jumping their horses over logs and stumps, trying to keep up with the commander. There were more sounds of cannon. "Fall in," sounded down the regiment. In five minutes we were making a forced march for Champion Hills. The fight had commenced and we were a dozen miles away. How we travelled! The cavalry did not more than keep up with us. We were nearly dying with thirst. The day was terrifically hot. As we neared the battle-field, we passed a dirty pond of water. We left the ranks and filled canteens and stomachs with a fluid fit only for swine to wallow in. One can't be too fastidious with a battle coming on. Already hundreds of wounded men were rushing to the rear. In a little time my regiment was stretched in line of battle, at the side of an open field. Beyond that field, in the wood and hills, the enemy was firing random shots into our silent unresisting line. What we were doing there, Heaven only knows. How little a subordinate soldier ever knows as to what he is about! His business is to march, keep still, be shot to pieces, and say nothing! The suspense of standing in that line was something awful. We were being shot down, and not firing a shot in return. There was again a chance to think, and I was thinking if I had not had enough of fool adventure! I was quartermaster sergeant, anyway. My post was at a safe place with the train, at the rear. Yet, here I was, just as in every fight of the Vicksburg campaign, volunteering to get myself shot.

The colonel had allowed a convalescent to perform my duties, while I went forth in search of fame. I hadn't long to think, for shortly General Grant rode up behind my regiment and dismounted, almost where I was standing in the line. It was something to see him in battle, and so close I could almost hear his talk. He had the inevitable cigar as he leaned against his horse, listening to the reports of aides as they galloped to him. An occasional man in the regiment threw up his arms, dropped his musket and fell dead. It created no remark. We just stood on, wondering what next. There was some mysterious nodding of heads between our colonel and General Grant, and then suddenly came an order,—"Fix bayonets—forward—double-quick—charge." We started on the run. Grant, I noticed, mounted his horse and rode away. As we were about to move, the colonel made me acting sergeant-major of the regiment. To be promoted right then, in such a place! General Grant, commanding the army, was not so proud as I was. Fear or no fear, I could do nothing now but pitch in and fight. Honor was at stake! We charged up and into the woods, under a heavy fire—till, suddenly, we were stopped by a blazing line of Confederate musketry. Then the two lines, the blue and the gray, stood two mortal hours (though it did not seem but a few minutes to me) and poured hot musketry into each other's face. I was struck twice, but slightly hurt. Comrades near me I saw covered with blood, their faces black with powder, fighting on. The dead lay everywhere unnoticed. Again I was biting cartridges and hurrying with that awful ramrod. A Confederate shot his ramrod through my hand. I was too busy, too excited, too hot, too thirsty, to think of it—to think of anything but loading and firing and standing my ground. We were winning Vicksburg right there, making Grant President that afternoon. Every torn face was a step toward the city, every dead man a ballot for the White House, yet neither White House nor ballot nor Vicksburg was in our thoughts. Would that awful line in front of us ever give way? That was all. The terrific fighting continued. I emptied my musket forty times, at men in front of me. Some took cartridges from the dead and fired fifty, sixty times. Once we were being flanked. A boy ran up to me crying: "My regiment has run. What will I do?" "Stay right here!" I shouted. "Load and fire." He did, until both his legs were shot off by a cannon-ball. That was war! I was getting adventure, too—lots of it! Before sundown the battle was over. Leaving our dead unburied, our wounded in the woods, we hurried on. We had taken Vicksburg, out there under the magnolia-trees of Champion Hills. The awful fighting for the city forts, later, would have been in vain had Grant's army been defeated that afternoon in May. We went on to the Black River and fought again. Not knowing of our victories, the government ordered Grant to abandon the campaign; let Vicksburg go. Think of it! The messenger came to him as he sat on his horse watching some brave regiments storm the breastworks defending Black River bridge. "It is too late," he said to the messenger. "Look yonder. Forty cannon are in our hands." And then, sitting there in his saddle on the battle-field, he wrote General Sherman a letter in pencil, telling of the victory. . . . Soon we approached the mighty forts and lines surrounding Vicksburg. The soldiers had had so many victories, they believed that they could storm the works. Grant let them try. That 22d of May saw the Union army hurled back into its own breastworks. The charge had been made by 35,000 men. My own brigade and regiment advanced at the centre. Three hundred cannon and all the mortar-boats bombarded the city before the charge. The Fifth Iowa crept up through the gullies and ravines very close to the fort. The cannonading and the hot sun made the warring terrible. I was ordered to carry some ammunition to the boys at the very front. The regiment lay to the boys at the very front. The regiment lay against the hillside under a galling fire. One hardly dared lift his head above the ground, fearing to be killed. I got my bundles of cartridges to the men and sat down in a depression in the hillside. I was safe as long as I did not move. Once more I had a chance to think, there, with the bullets whizzing within three feet of me. We could go neither forward nor back.

We were just sitting around and being killed. Still the attack had not been given up. Sitting in that protected spot, a dozen soldiers, with heads bowed low, crept past me. Each carried a musket and a little ladder. They were to make the desperate attempt to try and place these ladders across the ditch, when the regiment would climb over them and cross into the works. These laddermen passed so close I could look into their eyes. For once, at least, I felt death to be hovering very near. These men had surely volunteered to die. Few, or none of them, ever were seen again. Our assault failed. Our whole brigade crept down the gullies and ravines as best we could, and got away. Again we tried it at another point, and there our leader, Colonel Boomer, calling to the Iowa men to follow him, was shot dead. It was sundown and the storming of the city was abandoned. The siege commenced. Like beavers, we dug and dug till all the hills in front of the forts were honeycombed with rifle-pits. Every soldier at the front fired his hundred rounds a day, whether an enemy was seen or not. The men inside the forts did the same with us, and at intervals a hundred cannon poured exploding shells into the city.

One morning when I was out at the front rifle-pits I saw General Matthies creeping along the galleries to the pit where I was firing. He had a package in his hand wrapped in brown paper. To my astonishment he unfolded the paper and gave me an officer's sash. No wonder it hangs above my table as I write. "You are to be the adjutant of the regiment," he said. I do not know if the roar of the musketry then going on drowned my voice as I tried to thank him, or if in the circumstance of war he witnessed my delight. At a later battle, in the storming of Missionary Ridge, I saw him sitting under a tree, bleeding, a wound in his head that later led him to his grave. It was in a pause of the battle of Chattanooga. I was lying on the grass between two lines of the enemy. All around me were dead and wounded. Again I was having adventure. Again I had a chance to think. And before the doors of a Southern prison closed on me, as I lay there on the grass for just one moment, my mind went back to that village green where I had volunteered to go out and fight and, maybe, win adventure. I had had it all—and the worst, a thousand times, was yet to come. In a few minutes the Confederate lines closed in on me, and eighty of my regiment, of whom a handful only, dead or alive, were ever to return, marched away to Libby Prison. Many times I escaped, only to be retaken. Once, foot-free in the Confederacy, I entered a Southern regiment and, inside Atlanta, saw what great battles were from the standpoint of the Southern side. At last I got away, was placed on the staff of the great Sherman in the Carolines, and was the first to carry the news of his victories to the government at Washington. I had, as a boy, often wondered how men feel in war-times. After four years of war, adventure, and prison, I found it out. In all the civil war I slept but eight nights in a bed at home. I had longed for adventure. The memory of the past is now enough.

CONTRABANDS OF WAR

As the Northern army invaded the South, escaped slaves attached themselves to Union military camps for protection. They were sometimes referred to as "contrabands," the term applied to goods smuggled during wartime. Their numbers quickly became too large to accommodate within the camps, so the slaves set up camps just outside, sometimes called "slabtowns." Various strategies were considered to deal with these newly freed slaves. Large numbers joined black regiments after the Emancipation Proclamation made that possible. But even larger numbers succumbed to illness and death owing to the crowded and unsanitary conditions to which they were subjected during their indeterminate situation. Eventually, in 1865, the Freedman's Bureau was set up to provide assistance.

FROM *HOSPITAL SKETCHES*

Louisa May Alcott (1832–1888)

The book from which this excerpt comes was based on a series of newspaper stories that Alcott wrote for *The Commonwealth*, an abolitionist newspaper, in 1863; the articles themselves were based on letters Alcott wrote in 1862 while serving as a volunteer nurse in a Georgetown army hospital. (She was forced to return home after six weeks when she contracted typhoid fever, which permanently damaged her health.) Alcott herself did not regard the sketches very highly, considering that they had been written during odd moments during her service. However, perhaps because they brought the War home so immediately and vividly, they were an instant success and the founder of the newspaper recommended they be published in book form.

An advertising statement from the publisher of *Hospital Sketches* is noteworthy:

> A considerable portion of this volume was published in successive numbers of *The Commonwealth*, newspaper, of Boston. The sudden popularity the Sketches won from the general public, and the praise they received from literary men of distinguished ability, are sufficient reasons,—were any needed,—for their re-publication, thus revised and enlarged, in this more convenient and permanent form. As, besides paying the Author the usual copyright, the publisher has resolved to donate at least five cents for every copy sold to the support of orphans made fatherless or homeless by the war, no reproduction of any part of the contents now first printed

in these pages, will be permitted in any journal. Should the sale of the little book be large, the orphan's percentage will be doubled.

BOSTON, August, 1863

A Night

Being fond of the night side of nature, I was soon promoted to the post of night nurse, with every facility for indulging in my favorite pastime of "owling." My colleague, a black-eyed widow, relieved me at dawn, we two taking care of the ward, between us, like the immortal Sairy and Betsey, "turn and turn about." I usually found my boys in the jolliest state of mind their condition allowed; for it was a known fact that Nurse Periwinkle objected to blue devils, and entertained a belief that he who laughed most was surest of recovery. At the beginning of my reign, dumps and dismals prevailed; the nurses looked anxious and tired, the men gloomy or sad; and a general "Hark!-from-the-tombs-a-doleful-sound" style of conversation seemed to be the fashion: a state of things which caused one coming from a merry, social New England town, to feel as if she had got into an exhausted receiver; and the instinct of self-preservation, to say nothing of a philanthropic desire to serve the race, caused a speedy change in Ward No. 1.

More flattering than the most gracefully turned compliment, more grateful than the most admiring glance, was the sight of those rows of faces, all strange to me a little while ago, now lighting up, with smiles of welcome, as I came among them, enjoying that moment heartily, with a womanly pride in their regard, a motherly affection for them all. The evenings were spent in reading aloud, writing letters, waiting on and amusing the men, going the rounds with Dr. P., as he made his second daily survey, dressing my dozen wounds afresh, giving last doses, and making them cozy for the long hours to come, till the nine o'clock bell rang, the gas was turned down, the day nurses went off duty, the night watch came on, and my nocturnal adventure began.

My ward was now divided into three rooms; and, under favor of the matron, I had managed to sort out the patients in such a way that I had what I called, "my duty room," my "pleasure room," and my "pathetic room," and worked for each in a different way. One, I visited, armed with a dressing tray, full of rollers, plasters, and pins; another, with books, flowers, games, and gossip; a third, with teapots, lullabies, consolation, and sometimes, a shroud.

Wherever the sickest or most helpless man chanced to be, there I held my watch, often visiting the other rooms, to see that the general watchman of the ward did his duty by the fires and the wounds, the latter needing constant wetting. Not only on this account did I meander, but also to get fresher air than the close rooms afforded; for, owing to the stupidity of that mysterious "somebody" who does all the damage in the world, the windows had been carefully nailed down above, and the lower sashes could only be raised in the mildest weather, for the men lay just below. I had suggested a summary smashing of a few panes here and there, when frequent appeals to headquarters had proved unavailing, and daily orders to lazy attendants had come to nothing. No one seconded the motion, however, and the nails were far beyond my reach; for, though belonging to the sisterhood of "ministering angels," I had no wings, and might as well have asked for Jacob's ladder, as a pair of steps, in that charitable chaos.

One of the harmless ghosts who bore me company during the haunted hours, was Dan, the watchman, whom I regarded with a certain awe; for, though so much together, I never fairly saw his face, and, but for his legs, should never have recognized him, as we seldom met by day. These legs were remarkable, as was his whole figure, for his body was short, rotund, and done up in a big jacket, and muffler; his beard hid the lower part of his face, his hat-brim the upper; and all I ever discovered was a pair of sleepy eyes, and a very mild voice. But the legs!—very long, very thin, very crooked and feeble, looking like grey sausages in their tight coverings, without a ray of pegtopishness about them, and finished off with a pair of expansive, green cloth shoes, very like Chinese junks, with the sails down. This figure, gliding noiselessly about the dimly lighted rooms, was strongly suggestive of the spirit of a beer barrel mounted on cork-screws, haunting the old hotel in search of its lost mates, emptied and staved in long ago.

Another goblin who frequently appeared to me, was the attendant of the pathetic room, who, being a faithful soul, was often up to tend two or three men, weak and wandering as babies, after the fever had gone. The amiable creature beguiled the watches of the night by brewing jorums of a fearful beverage, which he called coffee, and insisted on sharing with me; coming in with a great bowl of something like mud soup, scalding hot, guiltless of cream, rich in an all-pervading flavor of molasses, scorch and tin pot. Such an amount of good will and neighborly kindness also went into the mess, that I never could find the heart to refuse, but always received it with thanks, sipped it with hypocritical relish while he remained, and whipped it into the slop-jar the instant he departed, thereby gratifying him, securing one rousing laugh in the doziest hour of the night, and no one was the worse for the transaction but the pigs. Whether they were "cut off untimely in their sins," or not, I carefully abstained from inquiring.

It was a strange life—asleep half the day, exploring Washington the other half, and all night hovering, like a massive cherubim, in a red rigolette, over the slumbering sons of man. I liked it, and found many things to amuse, instruct, and interest me. The snores alone were quite a study, varying from the mild sniff to the stentorian snort, which startled the echoes and hoisted the performer erect to accuse his neighbor of the deed, magnanimously forgive him, and wrapping the drapery of his couch about him, lie down to vocal slumber. After listening for a week to this band of wind instruments, I indulged in the belief that I could recognize each by the snore alone, and was tempted to join the chorus by breaking out with John Brown's favorite hymn:

"Blow ye the trumpet, blow!"

I would have given much to have possessed the art of sketching, for many of the faces became wonderfully interesting when unconscious. Some grew stern and grim, the men evidently dreaming of war, as they gave orders, groaned over their wounds, or damned the rebels vigorously; some grew sad and infinitely pathetic, as if the pain borne silently all day, revenged itself by now betraying what the man's pride had concealed so well. Often the roughest grew young and pleasant when sleep smoothed the hard lines away, letting the real nature assert itself; many almost seemed to speak, and I learned to know these men better by night than through any intercourse by day. Sometimes they disappointed me, for faces that looked merry and good in the light, grew bad and sly when the shadows came; and though they made no confidences in words, I read their lives, leaving them to wonder at the change of manner this midnight magic wrought in their nurse. A few talked busily; one drummer boy sang sweetly, though no persuasions could win a note from him by day; and several depended on being told what they had talked of in the morning. Even my constitutionals in the chilly halls, possessed a certain charm, for the house was never still. Sentinels tramped round it all night long, their muskets glittering in the wintry moonlight as they walked, or stood before the doors, straight and silent, as figures of stone, causing one to conjure up romantic visions of guarded forts, sudden surprises, and daring deeds; for in these war times the hum drum life of Yankeedom had vanished, and the most prosaic feel some thrill of that excitement which stirs the nation's heart, and makes its capital a camp of hospitals. Wandering up and down these lower halls, I often heard cries from above, steps hurrying to and fro, saw surgeons passing up, or men coming down carrying a stretcher, where lay a long white figure, whose face was shrouded and whose fight was done. Sometimes I stopped to watch the passers in the street, the moonlight shining on the spire opposite, or the gleam of some vessel floating, like a white-winged seagull, down the broad Potomac, whose fullest flow can never wash away the red stain of the land.

The night whose events I have a fancy to record, opened with a little comedy, and closed with a great tragedy; for a virtuous and useful life untimely ended is always tragical to those who see not as God sees. My headquarters were beside the bed of a New Jersey boy, crazed by the horrors of that dreadful Saturday. A slight wound in the knee brought him there; but his mind had suffered more than his body; some string of that delicate machine was over strained, and, for days, he had been reliving in imagination, the scenes he could not forget, till his distress broke out in incoherent ravings, pitiful to hear. As I sat by him, endeavoring to soothe his poor distracted brain by the constant touch of wet hands over his hot forehead, he lay cheering his comrades on, hurrying them back, then counting them as they fell around him, often clutching my arm, to drag me from the vicinity of a bursting shell, or covering up his head to screen himself from a shower of shot; his face brilliant with fever; his eyes restless; his head never still; every muscle strained and rigid; while an incessant stream of defiant shouts, whispered warnings, and broken laments, poured from his lips with that forceful bewilderment which makes such wanderings so hard to overhear.

It was past eleven, and my patient was slowly wearying himself into fitful intervals of quietude, when, in one of these pauses, a curious sound arrested my attention. Looking over my shoulder, I saw a one-legged phantom hopping nimbly down the room; and, going to meet it, recognized a certain Pennsylvania gentleman, whose wound-fever had taken a turn for the worse, and, depriving him of the few wits a drunken campaign had left him, set him literally tripping on the light, fantastic toe "toward home," as he blandly informed me, touching the military cap which formed a striking contrast to the severe simplicity of the rest of his decidedly undress uniform. When sane, the least movement produced a roar of pain or a volley of oaths; but the departure of reason seemed to have wrought an agreeable change, both in the man and his manners; for, balancing himself on one leg, like a meditative stork, he plunged into an animated discussion of the war, the President, lager beer, and Enfield rifles, regardless of any suggestions of mine as to the propriety of returning to bed, lest he be court-martialed for desertion.

Anything more supremely ridiculous can hardly be imagined than this figure, scantily draped in white, its one foot covered with a big blue sock, a dingy cap set rakingly askew on its shaven head, and placid satisfaction beaming in its broad red face, as it nourished a mug in one hand, an old boot in the other, calling them canteen and knapsack, while it skipped and fluttered in the most unearthly fashion. What to do with the creature I didn't know; Dan was absent, and if I went to find him, the perambulator might festoon himself out of the window, set his toga on fire, or do some of his neighbors a mischief. The attendant of the room was sleeping like a near relative of the celebrated Seven, and nothing short of pins would rouse him; for he had been out that day, and whiskey asserted its supremacy in balmy whiffs. Still declaiming, in a fine flow of eloquence, the demented gentleman hopped on, blind and deaf to my graspings and entreaties; and I was about to slam the door in his face, and run for help, when a second and saner phantom, "all in white," came to the rescue, in the likeness of a big Prussian, who spoke no English, but divined the crisis, and put an end to it, by bundling the lively monoped into his bed, like a baby, with an authoritative command to "stay put," which received added weight from being delivered in an odd conglomeration of French and German, accompanied by warning wags of a head decorated with a yellow cotton night cap, rendered most imposing by a tassel like a bell-pull. Rather exhausted by his excursion, the member from Pennsylvania subsided; and, after an irrepressible laugh together, my Prussian ally and myself were returning to our places, when the echo of a sob caused us to glance along the beds. It came from one in the corner—such a little bed!—and such a tearful little face looked up at us, as we stopped beside it! The twelve years old drummer boy was not singing now, but sobbing, with a manly effort all the while to stifle the distressful sounds that would break out.

"What is it, Teddy?" I asked, as he rubbed the tears away, and checked himself in the middle of a great sob to answer plaintively:

"I've got a chill, ma'am, but I ain't cryin' for that, 'cause I'm used to it. I dreamed Kit was here, and when I waked up he wasn't, and I couldn't help it, then."

The boy came in with the rest, and the man who was taken dead from the ambulance was the Kit he mourned. Well he might; for, when the wounded were brought from Fredericksburg, the child lay in one of the camps thereabout, and this good friend, though sorely hurt himself, would not leave him to the exposure and neglect of such a time and place; but, wrapping him in his own blanket, carried him in his arms to the transport, tended him during the passage, and only yielded up his charge when Death met him at the door of the hospital which promised care and comfort for the boy. For ten days, Teddy had shivered or burned with fever and ague, pining the while for Kit, and refusing to be comforted, because he had not been able to thank him for the generous protection, which, perhaps, had cost the giver's life. The vivid dream had wrung the childish heart with a fresh pang, and when I tried the solace fitted for his years, the remorseful fear that haunted him found vent in a fresh burst of tears, as he looked at the wasted hands I was endeavoring to warm:

"Oh! if I'd only been as thin when Kit carried me as I am now, maybe he wouldn't have died; but I was heavy, he was hurt worser than we knew, and so it killed him; and I didn't see him, to say good bye." This thought had troubled him in secret; and my assurances that his friend would probably have died at all events, hardly assuaged the bitterness of his regretful grief.

At this juncture, the delirious man began to shout; the one-legged rose up in his bed, as if preparing for another dart, Teddy bewailed himself more piteously than before: and if ever a woman was at her wit's end, that distracted female was Nurse Periwinkle, during the space of two or three minutes, as she vibrated between the three beds, like an agitated pendulum. Like a most opportune reinforcement, Dan, the bandy, appeared, and devoted himself to the lively party, leaving me free to return to my post; for the Prussian, with a nod and a smile, took the lad away to his own bed, and lulled him to sleep with a soothing murmur, like a mammoth bumble bee. I liked that in Fritz, and if he ever wondered afterward at the dainties which sometimes found their way into his rations, or the extra comforts of his bed, he might have found a solution of the mystery in sundry persons' knowledge of the fatherly action of that night.

Hardly was I settled again, when the inevitable bowl appeared, and its bearer delivered a message I had expected, yet dreaded to receive:

"John is going, ma'am, and wants to see you, if you can come."

"The moment this boy is asleep; tell him so, and let me know if I am in danger of being too late."

My Ganymede departed, and while I quieted poor Shaw, I thought of John. He came in a day or two after the others; and, one evening, when I entered my "pathetic room," I found a lately emptied bed occupied by a large, fair man, with a fine face, and the serenest eyes I ever met. One of the earlier comers had often spoken of a friend, who had remained behind, that those apparently worse wounded than himself might reach a shelter first. It seemed a David and Jonathan sort of friendship. The man fretted for his mate, and was never tired of praising John—his courage, sobriety, self-denial, and unfailing kindliness of heart; always winding up with: "He's an out an' out fine feller, ma'am; you see if he aint."

I had some curiosity to behold this piece of excellence, and when he came, watched him for a night or two, before I made friends with him; for, to tell the truth, I was a little afraid of the stately looking man, whose bed had to be lengthened to accommodate his commanding stature; who seldom spoke, uttered no complaint, asked no sympathy, but tranquilly observed what went on about him; and, as he lay high upon his pillows, no picture of dying statesman or warrior was ever fuller of real dignity than this Virginia blacksmith. A most attractive face he had, framed in brown hair and beard, comely featured and full of vigor, as yet unsubdued by pain; thoughtful and often beautifully mild while watching the afflictions of others, as if entirely forgetful of his own. His mouth was grave and firm, with plenty of will and courage in its lines, but a smile could make it as sweet as any woman's; and his eyes were child's eyes, looking one fairly in the face, with a clear, straightforward glance, which promised well for such as placed their faith in him. He seemed to cling to life, as if it were rich in duties and delights, and he had learned the secret of content. The only time I saw his composure disturbed, was when my surgeon brought another to examine John, who scrutinized their faces with an anxious look, asking of the elder: "Do you think I shall pull through, sir?" "I hope so, my man." And, as the two passed on, John's eye still followed them, with an intentness which would have won a clearer answer from them, had they seen it. A momentary shadow flitted over his face; then came the usual serenity, as if, in that brief eclipse, he had acknowledged the existence of some hard possibility, and, asking nothing yet hoping all things, left the issue in God's hands, with that submission which is true piety.

The next night, as I went my rounds with Dr. P., I happened to ask which man in the room probably suffered most; and, to my great surprise, he glanced at John:

"Every breath he draws is like a stab; for the ball pierced the left lung, broke a rib, and did no end of damage here and there; so the poor lad can find neither forgetfulness nor ease, because he must lie on his wounded back or suffocate. It will be a hard struggle, and a long one, for he possesses great vitality; but even his temperate life can't save him; I wish it could."

"You don't mean he must die, Doctor?"

"Bless you there's not the slightest hope for him; and you'd better tell him so before long; women have a way of doing such things comfortably, so I leave it to you. He won't last more than a day or two, at furthest."

I could have sat down on the spot and cried heartily, if I had not learned the wisdom of bottling up one's tears for leisure moments. Such an end seemed very hard for such a man, when half a dozen worn out, worthless bodies round him, were gathering up the remnants of wasted lives, to linger on for years perhaps, burdens to others, daily reproaches to themselves. The army needed men like John, earnest, brave, and faithful; fighting for liberty and justice with both heart and hand, true soldiers of the Lord. I could not give him up so soon, or think with any patience of so excellent a nature robbed of its fulfillment, and blundered into eternity by the rashness or stupidity of those at whose hands so many lives may be required. It was an easy thing for Dr. P. to say: "Tell him he must die," but a cruelly hard thing to do, and by no means as "comfortable" as he politely suggested. I had not the heart to do it then, and privately indulged the hope that some change for the better might take place, in spite of gloomy prophesies; so, rendering my task unnecessary. A few minutes later, as I came in again, with fresh rollers, I saw John sitting erect, with no one to support him, while the surgeon dressed his back. I had never hitherto seen it done; for, having simpler wounds to attend to, and knowing the fidelity of the attendant, I had left John to him, thinking it might be more agreeable and safe; for both strength and experience were needed in his case. I had forgotten that the strong man might long for the gentle tendance of a woman's hands, the sympathetic magnetism of a woman's presence, as well as the feebler souls about him. The Doctor's words caused me to reproach myself with neglect, not of any real duty perhaps, but of those little cares and kindnesses that solace homesick spirits, and make the heavy hours pass easier. John looked lonely and forsaken just then, as he sat with bent head, hands folded on his knee, and no outward sign of suffering, till, looking nearer, I saw great tears roll down and drop upon the floor. It was a new sight there; for, though I had seen many suffer, some swore, some groaned, most endured silently, but none wept. Yet it did not seem weak, only very touching, and straightway my fear vanished, my heart opened wide and took him in, as, gathering the bent head in my arms, as freely as if he had been a little child, I said, "Let me help you bear it, John."

Never, on any human countenance, have I seen so swift and beautiful a look of gratitude, surprise and comfort, as that which answered me more eloquently than the whispered—

"Thank you, ma'am, this is right good! this is what I wanted!"

"Then why not ask for it before?"

"I didn't like to be a trouble; you seemed so busy, and I could manage to get on alone."

"You shall not want it any more, John."

Nor did he; for now I understood the wistful look that sometimes followed me, as I went out, after a brief pause beside his bed, or merely a passing nod, while busied with those who seemed to need me more than he, because more urgent in their demands; now I knew that to him, as to so many, I was the poor substitute for mother, wife, or sister, and in his eyes no stranger, but a friend who hitherto had seemed neglectful; for, in his modesty, he had never guessed the truth. This was changed now; and, through the tedious operation of probing, bathing, and dressing his wounds, he leaned against me, holding my hand fast, and, if pain wrung further tears from him, no one saw them fall but me. When he was laid down again, I hovered about him, in a remorseful state of mind that would not let me rest, till I had bathed his face, brushed his "bonny brown hair," set all things smooth about him, and laid a knot of heath and heliotrope on his clean pillow. While doing this, he watched me with the satisfied expression I so liked to see; and when I offered the little nosegay, held it carefully in his great hand, smoothed a ruffled leaf or two, surveyed and smelt it with an air of genuine delight, and lay contentedly regarding the glimmer of the sunshine on the green. Although the manliest man among my forty, he said, "Yes, ma'am," like a little boy; received suggestions for his comfort with the quick smile that brightened his whole face; and now and then, as I stood tidying the table by his bed, I felt him softly touch my gown, as if to assure himself that I was there. Anything more natural and frank I never saw, and found this brave John as bashful as brave, yet full of excellencies and fine aspirations, which, having no power to express themselves in words, seemed to have bloomed into his character and made him what he was.

After that night, an hour of each evening that remained to him was devoted to his ease or pleasure. He could not talk much, for breath was precious, and he spoke in whispers; but from occasional conversations, I gleaned scraps of private history which only added to the affection and respect I felt for him. Once he asked me to write a letter, and as I settled pen and paper, I said, with an irrepressible glimmer of feminine curiosity, "Shall it be addressed to wife, or mother, John?"

"Neither, ma'am; I've got no wife, and will write to mother myself when I get better. Did you think I was married because of this?" he asked, touching a plain ring he wore, and often turned thoughtfully on his finger when he lay alone.

"Partly that, but more from a settled sort of look you have; a look which young men seldom get until they marry."

"I didn't know that; but I'm not so very young, ma'am, thirty in May, and have been what you might call settled this ten years; for mother's a widow, I'm the oldest child she has, and it wouldn't do for me to marry until Lizzy has a home of her own, and Laurie's learned his trade; for we're not rich, and I must be father to the children and husband to the dear old woman, if I can."

"No doubt but you are both, John; yet how came you to go to war, if you felt so? Wasn't enlisting as bad as marrying?"

"No, ma'am, not as I see it, for one is helping my neighbor, the other pleasing myself. I went because I couldn't help it. I didn't want the glory or the pay; I wanted the right thing done, and people kept saying the men who were in earnest ought to fight. I was in earnest, the Lord knows! but I held off as long as I could, not knowing which was my duty; mother saw the case, gave me her ring to keep me steady, and said 'Go': so I went."

A short story and a simple one, but the man and the mother were portrayed better than pages of fine writing could have done it.

"Do you ever regret that you came, when you lie here suffering so much?"

"Never, ma'am; I haven't helped a great deal, but I've shown I was willing to give my life, and perhaps I've got to; but I don't blame anybody, and if it was to do over again, I'd do it. I'm a little sorry I wasn't wounded in front; it looks cowardly to be hit in the back, but I obeyed orders, and it don't matter in the end, I know."

Poor John! it did not matter now, except that a shot in the front might have spared the long agony in store for him. He seemed to read the thought that troubled me, as he spoke so hopefully when there was no hope, for he suddenly added:

"This is my first battle; do they think it's going to be my last?"

"I'm afraid they do, John."

It was the hardest question I had ever been called upon to

answer; doubly hard with those clear eyes fixed on mine, forcing a truthful answer by their own truth. He seemed a little startled at first, pondered over the fateful fact a moment, then shook his head, with a glance at the broad chest and muscular limbs stretched out before him:

"I'm not afraid, but it's difficult to believe all at once. I'm so strong it don't seem possible for such a little wound to kill me."

Merry Mercutio's dying words glanced through my memory as he spoke: "'Tis not so deep as a well, nor so wide as a church door, but 'tis enough." And John would have said the same could he have seen the ominous black holes between his shoulders; he never had; and, seeing the ghastly sights about him, could not believe his own wound more fatal than these, for all the suffering it caused him.

"Shall I write to your mother, now?" I asked, thinking that these sudden tidings might change all plans and purposes; but they did not; for the man received the order of the Divine Commander to march with the same unquestioning obedience with which the soldier had received that of the human one; doubtless remembering that the first led him to life, and the last to death.

"No, ma'am; to Laurie just the same; he'll break it to her best, and I'll add a line to her myself when you get done."

So I wrote the letter which he dictated, finding it better than any I had sent; for, though here and there a little ungrammatical or inelegant, each sentence came to me briefly worded, but most expressive; full of excellent counsel to the boy, tenderly bequeathing "mother and Lizzie" to his care, and bidding him good bye in words the sadder for their simplicity. He added a few lines, with steady hand, and, as I sealed it, said, with a patient sort of sigh, "I hope the answer will come in time for me to see it"; then, turning away his face, laid the flowers against his lips, as if to hide some quiver of emotion at the thought of such a sudden sundering of all the dear home ties.

These things had happened two days before; now John was dying, and the letter had not come. I had been summoned to many death beds in my life, but to none that made my heart ache as it did then, since my mother called me to watch the departure of a spirit akin to this in its gentleness and patient strength. As I went in, John stretched out both hands:

"I know you'd come! I guess I'm moving on, ma'am."

He was; and so rapidly that, even while he spoke, over his

face I saw the grey veil falling that no human hand can lift. I sat down by him, wiped the drops from his forehead, stirred the air about him with the slow wave of a fan, and waited to help him die. He stood in sore need of help—and I could do so little; for, as the doctor had foretold, the strong body rebelled against death, and fought every inch of the way, forcing him to draw each breath with a spasm, and clench his hands with an imploring look, as if he asked, "How long must I endure this, and be still!" For hours he suffered dumbly, without a moment's respite, or a moment's murmuring; his limbs grew cold, his face damp, his lips white, and, again and again, he tore the covering off his breast, as if the lightest weight added to his agony; yet through it all, his eyes never lost their perfect serenity, and the man's soul seemed to sit therein, undaunted by the ills that vexed his flesh.

One by one, the men woke, and round the room appeared a circle of pale faces and watchful eyes, full of awe and pity; for, though a stranger, John was beloved by all. Each man there had wondered at his patience, respected his piety, admired his fortitude, and now lamented his hard death; for the influence of an upright nature had made itself deeply felt, even in one little week. Presently, the Jonathan who so loved this comely David, came creeping from his bed for a last look and word. The kind soul was full of trouble, as the choke in his voice, the grasp of his hand, betrayed; but there were no tears, and the farewell of the friends was the more touching for its brevity.

"Old boy, how are you?" faltered the one.

"Most through, thank heaven!" whispered the other.

"Can I say or do anything for you anywheres?"

"Take my things home, and tell them that I did my best."

"I will! I will!"

"Good bye, Ned."

"Good bye, John, good bye!"

They kissed each other, tenderly as women, and so parted, for poor Ned could not stay to see his comrade die. For a little while, there was no sound in the room but the drip of water, from a stump or two, and John's distressful gasps, as he slowly breathed his life away. I thought him nearly gone, and had just laid down the fan, believing its help to be no longer needed, when suddenly he rose up in his bed, and cried out with a bitter cry that broke the silence, sharply startling every one with its agonized appeal:

"For God's sake, give me air!"

It was the only cry pain or death had wrung from him, the only boon he had asked; and none of us could grant it, for all the airs that blew were useless now. Dan flung up the window. The first red streak of dawn was warming the grey east, a herald of the coming sun; John saw it, and with the love of light which lingers in us to the end, seemed to read in it a sign of hope of help, for, over his whole face there broke that mysterious expression, brighter than any smile, which often comes to eyes that look their last. He laid himself gently down; and, stretching out his strong right arm, as if to grasp and bring the blessed air to his lips in a fuller flow, lapsed into a merciful unconsciousness, which assured us that for him suffering was forever past. He died then; for, though the heavy breaths still tore their way up for a little longer, they were but the waves of an ebbing tide that beat unfelt against the wreck, which an immortal voyager had deserted with a smile. He never spoke again, but to the end held my hand close, so close that when he was asleep at last, I could not draw it away. Dan helped me, warning me as he did so that it was unsafe for dead and living flesh to lie so long together; but though my hand was strangely cold and stiff, and four white marks remained across its back, even when warmth and color had returned elsewhere, I could not but be glad that, through its touch, the presence of human sympathy, perhaps, had lightened that hard hour.

When they had made him ready for the grave, John lay in state for half an hour, a thing which seldom happened in that busy place; but a universal sentiment of reverence and affection seemed to fill the hearts of all who had known or heard of him; and when the rumor of his death went through the house, always astir, many came to see him, and I felt a tender sort of pride in my lost patient; for he looked a most heroic figure, lying there stately and still as the statue of some young knight asleep upon his tomb. The lovely expression which so often beautifies dead faces, soon replaced the marks of pain, and I longed for those who loved him best to see him when half an hour's acquaintance with Death had made them friends. As we stood looking at him, the ward master handed me a letter, saying it had been forgotten the night before. It was John's letter, come just an hour too late to gladden the eyes that had longed and looked for it so eagerly! yet he had it; for, after I had cut some brown locks for his mother, and taken off the ring to send her, telling how well the talisman had done its work, I kissed this good son for her sake, and laid the letter in his hand, still folded as when I drew my own away, feeling that its place was there, and making myself happy with the thought, that, even in his solitary place in the "Government Lot," he would not be without some token of the love which makes life beautiful and outlives death. Then I left him, glad to have known so genuine a man, and carrying with me an enduring memory of the brave Virginia blacksmith, as he lay serenely waiting for the dawn of that long day which knows no night.

WHITMAN AND THE WOUNDED

Walt Whitman (1819–1892)

In 1862, Whitman, responding to a newspaper report that his brother George might have been wounded, headed south in hopes of finding him. Though George's injuries were only superficial, Whitman was deeply moved by the suffering of the wounded soldiers and in December 1862 left New York for Washington to volunteer as a delegate of the Christian Coalition to nurse in the military hospitals. George was later captured by the Confederates, but furloughed almost immediately because of illness.

Specimen Days, which was published in 1882, is composed of diary entries written over the course of Whitman's life: reflections on his ancestry, childhood, the Civil War period, and his later years in Camden, New Jersey. The section on the Civil War is particularly affecting for the picture it paints in lucid, unadorned prose of Whitman's developing compassion for the suffering he witnessed.

"The Wound Dresser," published at the end of the War, is written in Whitman's characteristic free verse and describes the pain that he witnessed and worked to alleviate. The poem uses the device of the old veteran being interrogated by young people whose view is shaped by the soft glow of the romanticized past.

EXCERPT FROM *SPECIMEN DAYS*

DOWN AT THE FRONT.

FALMOUTH, VA., *opposite Fredericksburgh, December 21, 1862.*—Begin my visits among the camp hospitals in the army of the Potomac. Spend a good part of the day in a large brick mansion on the banks of the Rappahannock, used as a hospital since the battle—seems to have receiv'd only the worst cases. Out doors, at the foot of a tree, within ten yards of the front of the house, I notice a heap of amputated feet, legs, arms, hands, &c., a full load for a one-horse cart. Several dead bodies lie near, each cover'd with its brown woolen blanket. In the door-yard, towards the river, are fresh graves, mostly of officers, their names on pieces of barrel-staves or broken boards, stuck in the dirt. (Most of these bodies are subsequently taken up and transported north to their friends.) The large mansion is quite crowded upstairs and down, everything impromptu, no system, all bad enough, but I have no doubt the best that can be done; all the wounds pretty bad, some frightful, the men in their old clothes, unclean and bloody. Some of the wounded are rebel soldiers and officers, prisoners. One, a Mississippian, a captain, hit badly in the leg, I talk'd with some time; he ask'd me for papers, which I gave him. (I saw him three months afterward in Washington, with his leg amputated, doing well.) I went through the rooms, downstairs and up. Some of the men were dying. I had nothing to give at that visit, but wrote a few letters to folks home, mothers, &c. Also talk'd to three or four, who seem'd most susceptible to it, and needing it.

AFTER FIRST FREDERICKSBURG.

December 23 to 31.—The results of the late battle are exhibited everywhere about here in thousands of cases, (hundreds die every day,) in the camp, brigade, and division hospitals. These are merely tents, and sometimes very poor ones, the wounded lying on the ground, lucky if their blankets are spread on layers of pine or hemlock twigs, or small leaves. No cots; seldom even a mattress. It is pretty cold. The ground is frozen hard, and there is occasional snow. I go around from one case to another. I do not see that I do much good to these wounded and dying; but I cannot leave them. Once in a while some youngster holds on to me convulsively, and I do what I can for him; at any rate, stop with him and sit near him for hours, if he wishes it.

Besides the hospitals, I also go occasionally on long tours through the campus, talking with the men, &c. Sometimes at night among the groups around the fires, in their shebang enclosures of bushes. These are curious shows, full of characters and groups. I soon get acquainted anywhere in camp, with officers or men, and am always well used. Sometimes I go down on picket with the regiments I know best. As to rations, the army here at present seems to be tolerably well supplied, and the men have enough, such as it is, mainly salt pork and hard tack. Most of the regiments lodge in the flimsy little shelter-tents. A few have built themselves huts of logs and mud, with fire-places.

BACK TO WASHINGTON.

January, '63.—Left camp at Falmouth, with some wounded, a few days since, and came here by Aquia creek railroad, and so on government steamer up the Potomac. Many wounded were with us on the cars and boat. The cars were just common platform ones. The railroad journey of ten or twelve miles was made mostly before sunrise. The soldiers guarding the road came out from their tents or shebangs of bushes with rumpled hair and half-awake look. Those on duty were walking their posts, some on banks over us, others down far below the level of the track. I saw large cavalry camps off the road. At Aquia creek landing were numbers of wounded going north. While I waited some three hours, I went around among them. Several wanted word sent home to parents, brothers, wives, &c., which I did for them, (by mail the next day from Washington.) On the boat I had my hands full. One poor fellow died going up.

I am now remaining in and around Washington, daily visiting the hospitals. Am much in Patent-office, Eighth street, H street, Armory-square, and others. Am now able to do a little good, having money, (as almoner of others home,) and getting experience. To-day, Sunday afternoon and till nine in the evening, visited Campbell hospital; attended specially to one case in ward 1, very sick with pleurisy and typhoid fever, young man, farmer's son, D. F. Russell, company E, 60th New York, downhearted and feeble; a long time before he would take any interest; wrote a letter home to his mother, in Malone, Franklin county, N. Y., at his request; gave him some fruit and one or two other gifts; envelop'd and directed his letter, &c. Then went thoroughly through ward 6, observ'd every case in the ward, without, I think, missing one; gave perhaps from twenty to thirty persons, each one some little gift, such as oranges, apples, sweet crackers, figs, &c.

Thursday, Jan. 21.—Devoted the main part of the day to

Armory-square hospital; went pretty thoroughly through wards F, G, H, and I; some fifty cases in each ward. In ward F supplied the men throughout with writing paper and stamp'd envelope each; distributed in small portions, to proper subjects, a large jar of first-rate preserv'd berries, which had been donated to me by a lady—her own cooking. Found several cases I thought good subjects for small sums of money, which I furnish'd. (The wounded men often come up broke, and it helps their spirits to have even the small sum I give them.) My paper and envelopes all gone, but distributed a good lot of amusing reading matter; also, as I thought judicious, tobacco, oranges, apples, &c. Interesting cases in ward I; Charles Miller, bed 19, company D, 53d Pennsylvania, is only sixteen years of age, very bright, courageous boy, left leg amputated below the knee; next bed to him, another young lad very sick; gave each appropriate gifts. In the bed above, also, amputation of the left leg; gave him a little jar of raspberries; bed 1, this ward, gave a small sum; also to a soldier on crutches, sitting on his bed near. . . . (I am more and more surprised at the very great proportion of youngsters from fifteen to twenty-one in the army. I afterwards found a still greater proportion among the southerners.)

Evening, same day, went to see D. F. R., before alluded to; found him remarkably changed for the better; up and dress'd—quite a triumph; he afterwards got well, and went back to his regiment. Distributed in the wards a quantity of note-paper, and forty or fifty stamp'd envelopes, of which I had recruited my stock, and the men were much in need.

FIFTY HOURS LEFT WOUNDED ON THE FIELD.

Here is a case of a soldier I found among the crowded cots in the Patent-office. He likes to have some one to talk to, and we will listen to him. He got badly hit in his leg and side at Fredericksburgh that eventful Saturday, 13th of December. He lay the succeeding two days and nights helpless on the field, between the city and those grim terraces of batteries; his company and regiment had been compell'd to leave him to his fate. To make matters worse, it happen'd he lay with his head slightly down hill, and could not help himself. At the end of some fifty hours he was brought off, with other wounded, under a flag of truce. I ask him how the rebels treated him as he lay during those two days and nights within reach of them—whether they came to him—

whether they abused him? He answers that several of the rebels, soldiers and others, came to him at one time and another. A couple of them, who were together, spoke roughly and sarcastically, but nothing worse. One middle-aged man, however, who seem'd to be moving around the field, among the dead and wounded, for benevolent purposes, came to him in a way he will never forget; treated our soldier kindly, bound up his wounds, cheer'd him, gave him a couple of biscuits and a drink of whiskey and water; asked him if he could eat some beef. This good secesh, however, did not change our soldier's position, for it might have caused the blood to burst from the wounds, clotted and stagnated. Our soldier is from Pennsylvania; has had a pretty severe time; the wounds proved to be bad ones. But he retains a good heart, and is at present on the gain. (It is not uncommon for the men to remain on the field this way, one, two, or even four or five days.)

HOSPITAL SCENES AND PERSONS.

Letter Writing.—When eligible, I encourage the men to write, and myself, when called upon, write all sorts of letters for them, (including love letters, very tender ones.) Almost as I reel off these memoranda, I write for a new patient to his wife. M. de F., of the 17th Connecticut, company H, has just come up (February 17th) from Windmill point, and is received in ward H, Armory-square. He is an intelligent looking man, has a foreign accent, black-eyed and hair'd, a Hebraic appearance. Wants a telegraphic message sent to his wife, New Canaan, Conn. I agree to send the message—but to make things sure I also sit down and write the wife a letter, and dispatch it to the post-office immediately, as he fears she will come on, and he does not wish her to, as he will surely get well.

Saturday, January 30th.—Afternoon, visited Campbell hospital. Scene of cleaning up the ward, and giving the men all clean clothes—through the ward (6) the patients dressing or being dress'd—the naked upper half of the bodies—the good-humor and fun—the shirts, drawers, sheets of beds, & c., and the general fixing up for Sunday. Gave J. L. 50 cents.

Wednesday, February 4th.—Visited Armory-square hospital, went pretty thoroughly through wards E and D. Supplied paper and envelopes to all who wish'd—as usual, found plenty of men who needed those articles. Wrote letters. Saw and talk'd with two or three members of the Brooklyn 14th regt. A poor fellow in ward D, with a fearful wound in a fearful condition, was having some loose splinters of bone taken from the neighborhood of the wound. The operation was long, and one of great pain—yet, after it was well commenced, the soldier bore it in silence. He sat up, propp'd—was much wasted—had lain a long time quiet in one position (not for days only but weeks,) a bloodless, brown-skinn'd face, with eyes full of determination—belong'd to a New York regiment. There was an unusual cluster of surgeons, medical cadets, nurses, &c., around his bed—I thought the whole thing was done with tenderness, and done well. In one case, the wife sat by the side of her husband, his sickness typhoid fever, pretty bad. In another, by the side of her son, a mother—she told me she had seven children, and this was the youngest. (A fine, kind, healthy, gentle mother, good-looking, not very old, with a cap on her head, and dress'd like home—what a charm it gave to the whole ward.) I liked the woman nurse in ward E—I noticed how she sat a long time by a poor fellow who just had, that morning, in addition to his other sickness, bad hemorrhage—she gently assisted him, reliev'd him of the blood, holding a cloth to his mouth, as he coughed it up—he was so weak he could only just turn his head over on the pillow.

One young New York man, with a bright, handsome face, had been lying several months from a most disagreeable wound, receiv'd at Bull Run. A bullet had shot him right through the bladder, hitting him front, low in the belly, and coming out back. He had suffer'd much—the water came out of the wound, by slow but steady quantities, for many weeks—so that he lay almost constantly in a sort of puddle—and there were other disagreeable circumstances. He was of good heart, however. At present comparatively comfortable, had a bad throat, was delighted with a stick of horehound candy I gave him, with one or two other trifles.

PATENT-OFFICE HOSPITAL.

February 23.—I must not let the great hospital at the Patent-office pass away without some mention. A few weeks ago the vast area of the second story of that noblest of Washington buildings was crowded close with rows of sick, badly wounded and dying soldiers. They were placed in three very large apartments. I went there many times. It was a strange, solemn, and, with all its features of suffering and death, a sort of fascinating sight. I go sometimes at night to soothe and relieve particular cases.

Two of the immense apartments are fill'd with high and ponderous glass cases, crowded with models in miniature of every kind of utensil, machine or invention, it ever enter'd into the mind of man to conceive; and with curiosities and foreign presents. Between these cases are lateral openings, perhaps eight feet wide and quite deep, and in these were placed the sick, besides a great long double row of them up and down through the middle of the hall. Many of them were very bad cases, wounds and amputations. Then there was a gallery running above the hall in which there were beds also. It was, indeed, a curious scene, especially at night when lit up. The glass cases, the beds, the forms lying there, the gallery above, and the marble pavement under foot—the suffering, and the fortitude to bear it in various degrees—occasionally, from some, the groan that could not be repress'd—sometimes a poor fellow dying, with emaciated face and glassy eye, the nurse by his side, the doctor also there, but no friend, no relative—such were the sights but lately in the Patent-office. (The wounded have since been removed from there, and it is now vacant again.)

THE WOUND-DRESSER

1

An old man bending I come among new faces,
Years looking backward resuming in answer to children,
Come tell us old man, as from young men and maidens that
love me,
(Arous'd and angry, I'd thought to beat the alarum, and urge
relentless war,
But soon my fingers fail'd me, my face droop'd and I resign'd
myself,
To sit by the wounded and soothe them, or silently watch the
dead;)
Years hence of these scenes, of these furious passions, these
chances,
Of unsurpass'd heroes, (was one side so brave? the other was
equally brave;)
Now be witness again, paint the mightiest armies of earth,
Of those armies so rapid so wondrous what saw you to tell us?

What stays with you latest and deepest? of curious panics,
Of hard-fought engagements or sieges tremendous what
deepest remains?

2

O maidens and young men I love and that love me,
What you ask of my days those the strangest and sudden your
talking recalls,
Soldier alert I arrive after a long march cover'd with sweat and
dust,
In the nick of time I come, plunge in the fight, loudly shout in
the rush of successful charge,
Enter the captur'd works—yet lo, like a swift running river
they fade,
Pass and are gone they fade—I dwell not on soldiers' perils or
soldiers' joys,
(Both I remember well—many of the hardships, few the joys,
yet I was content.)

But in silence, in dreams' projections,
While the world of gain and appearance and mirth goes on,
So soon what is over forgotten, and waves wash the imprints
off the sand,
With hinged knees returning I enter the doors, (while for you
up there,
Whoever you are, follow without noise and be of strong
heart.)

Bearing the bandages, water and sponge,
Straight and swift to my wounded I go,
Where they lie on the ground after the battle brought in,
Where their priceless blood reddens the grass, the ground,
Or to the rows of the hospital tent, or under the roof'd
hospital,
To the long rows of cots up and down each side I return,
To each and all one after another I draw near, not one do I
miss,
An attendant follows holding a tray, he carries a refuse pail,
Soon to be fill'd with clotted rags and blood, emptied, and
fill'd again.

I onward go, I stop,
With hinged knees and steady hand to dress wounds,
I am firm with each, the pangs are sharp yet unavoidable,
One turns to me his appealing eyes—poor boy! I never knew
you,
Yet I think I could not refuse this moment to die for you, if that
would save you.

3

On, on I go, (open doors of time! open hospital doors!)
The crush'd head I dress, (poor crazed hand tear not the
bandage away,)
The neck of the cavalry-man with the bullet through and
through I examine,
Hard the breathing rattles, quite glazed already the eye, yet life
struggles hard,
(Come sweet death! be persuaded O beautiful death!
In mercy come quickly.)

From the stump of the arm, the amputated hand,
I undo the clotted lint, remove the slough, wash off the matter
and blood,
Back on his pillow the soldier bends with curv'd neck and side
falling head,
His eyes are closed, his face is pale, he dares not look on the
bloody stump,
And has not yet look'd on it.

I dress a wound in the side, deep, deep,
But a day or two more, for see the frame all wasted and
sinking,
And the yellow-blue countenance see.

I dress the perforated shoulder, the foot with the bullet-wound,
Cleanse the one with a gnawing and putrid gangrene, so sickening, so offensive,
While the attendant stands behind aside me holding the tray
and pail.

I am faithful, I do not give out,
The fractur'd thigh, the knee, the wound in the abdomen,
These and more I dress with impassive hand, (yet deep in my
breast a fire, a burning flame.)

4

Thus in silence in dreams' projections,
Returning, resuming, I thread my way through the hospitals,
The hurt and wounded I pacify with soothing hand,
I sit by the restless all the dark night, some are so young,
Some suffer so much, I recall the experience sweet and sad,
(Many a soldier's loving arms around this neck have cross'd and rested,
Many a soldier's kiss dwells on these bearded lips.)

1863

On January 1, 1863, President Lincoln issued the Emancipation Proclamation, freeing the slaves in all the states still in rebellion. His decision again balanced the political necessity of placating the border states and responding to the growing abolitionist pressure. Lincoln justified his action as a war measure and not as an act of political or social revolution. Whatever temporizing instincts shaped his decision, the proclamation redefined the War in new and radical ways. As the word of Jubilee Day, as it was called, spread across the South, Confederates faced a new and dangerous threat—war from within. The proclamation broke the bonds of servitude, the social glue of the Confederacy, and transformed every slave into an immediate threat to the social order and a potential combatant. Southerners judged the act provocative and pernicious, confirming that this was a war about slavery, targeting the social arrangements that had governed their lives for generations. The stakes were higher than ever, and Southerners now had to imagine what the consequences of defeat might be.

Northern Democrats, with their Southern sympathies and their increasingly popular argument for a negotiated peace based on the antebellum status quo, gave voice to fears that the Civil War was now a race war. With new conscription laws in the North and the South allowing the hiring of a substitute to serve in one's place, the draft and for some the War itself was tainted by issues of race, class, and ethnicity. Who was to do the fighting and for what purposes?

This volatile mixture exploded in New York City in three days of rioting that took one hundred twenty lives and included the lynching of eleven black men. A raw nerve of Northern racism was exposed, giving the Confederacy a moment of ironic celebration.

Frederick Douglass, a persistent critic of Lincoln and what he judged to be the president's gradual and cautious approach, seized the invitation of the proclamation to urge African-Americans to serve in the military. He wrote, "Who would be free themselves must strike the blow. . . . I urge you to fly to arms and smite to death the power that would bury the Government and your liberty in the same hopeless grave. This is your golden opportunity." His call to arms and the enthusiastic response of more than one hundred eighty thousand freedmen and slaves in forming their own Union regiments, of course under the command of white officers, was heartening. Their entrance into the War was met with contempt and rage by Confederate soldiers and deep suspicion by their Union counterparts.

Douglass believed that they would demonstrate the courage and strength necessary on the battlefield and in so doing establish the legitimacy of their claim to full citizenship. And distinguish themselves they did, with heroism and determination, reaffirming and deepening the persistent willingness of African-Americans to give blood in their quest for racial justice.

This was a new war, the awful war of "remorseless revenge" that many had feared. A longer and bloodier conflict was upon the nation. More lives, more men, more money, and more destruction would be the hallmarks of this intensifying conflict.

Grant laid siege to the city Vicksburg, the key to the Mississippi, in May, and after six weeks of bombardment that drove civilians into caves with little food, the city surrendered on July 4. Grant moved quickly to seize Port Hudson and secure the Mississippi, hopelessly splitting the Confederacy.

The Union successes in the west were offset by Lee's bold division of his army at Chancellorsville and the defeat of General Hooker, who withdrew. But the cost in Confederate lives was high and especially the devastating death of Stonewall Jackson, Lee's most able field general.

Attrition was beginning to exact a heavy price on the Confederacy with its limited economic and population base. It would be difficult to sustain the level of losses, and near impossible to find leadership replacement for generals like Stonewall Jackson. In April, a bread riot in the capital city of Richmond exposed the depths of the problem. The fabric of Confederate society was beginning to unravel, and efforts by Jefferson Davis to take necessary concerted actions to sustain the war effort were opposed by politicians and citizens who championed the inviolate character of states' rights against their own government.

Lee sought to build on the victory at Chancellorsville and take the fight to the enemy. A strike at Pennsylvania would alleviate pressure on Virginia, whose landscape and farms were depleted, and provide new sources of food for his men, threaten Washington, win international recognition, and strengthen the peace Democrats. For three days both armies engaged unprecedented numbers of troops, using them as human battering rams. Pickett's Charge marched fifteen thousand men into an open field where they were mowed down at six hundred yards by a thunderstorm of rifle volleys, a lethal demonstration of the weapon's accuracy and firepower. In fifty minutes, almost ten thousand men had been killed. Time was exhausting the South, sapping its resources and its will to continue the War. Now the only question was how much longer.

The Emancipation Proclamation and the Gettysburg Address were the bookends of freedom in this the third and most transformative year of the War. On November 19, speaking at the dedication of the memorial cemetery at Gettysburg, President Lincoln sanctified the shattered ground by cloaking the Civil War in the language, history, and significance of the American Revolution, thereby ennobling its objectives and justifying its sacrifices. The year 1863 redefined the War and claimed freedom and liberty its central issues.

The Emancipation Proclamation

On September 22, 1862, President Lincoln had declared his intention to issue a formal emancipation of all slaves in any state of the Confederacy that did not return to Union control by January 1, 1863. No state returned, and the executive order, signed and issued on January 1, 1863, freed the slaves in the ten states in rebellion, amounting to about 3.1 million of the 4 million slaves in the country as a whole. Slavery was not abolished in the border states that had remained loyal to the Union, and the order also expressly exempted those parts of the Confederacy that had already come under Union control. The proclamation in itself did not outlaw slavery nor did it make the former slaves citizens. But it did fundamentally change the nature of the War. After January 1, 1863, every Union victory extended the emancipation of slaves. In addition, the proclamation specifically announced the acceptance of black men into the Union military. By the end of the War, approximately two hundred thousand black soldiers and sailors had fought for the Union.

Whereas, on the twenty-second day of September, in the year of our Lord one thousand eight hundred and sixty-two, a proclamation was issued by the President of the United States, containing, among other things, the following, to wit:

"That on the first day of January, in the year of our Lord one thousand eight hundred and sixty-three, all persons held as slaves within any State or designated part of a State, the people whereof shall then be in rebellion against the United States, shall be then, thenceforward, and forever free; and the Executive Government of the United States, including the military and naval authority thereof, will recognize and maintain the freedom of such persons, and will do no act or acts to repress such persons, or any of them, in any efforts they may make for their actual freedom.

"That the Executive will, on the first day of January aforesaid, by proclamation, designate the States and parts of States, if any, in which the people thereof, respectively, shall then be in rebellion against the United States; and the fact that any State, or the people thereof, shall on that day be, in good faith, represented in the Congress of the United States by members chosen thereto at elections wherein a majority of the qualified voters of such State shall have participated, shall, in the absence of strong countervailing testimony, be deemed conclusive evidence that such State, and the people thereof, are not then in rebellion against the United States."

Now, therefore I, Abraham Lincoln, President of the United States, by virtue of the power in me vested as Commander-in-Chief, of the Army and Navy of the United States in time of actual armed rebellion against the authority and government of the United States, and as a fit and necessary war measure for suppressing said rebellion, do, on this first day of January, in the year of our Lord one thousand eight hundred and sixty-three, and in accordance with my purpose so to do publicly proclaimed for the full period of one hundred days, from the day first above mentioned, order and designate as the States and parts of States wherein the people thereof respectively, are this day in rebellion against the United States, the following, to wit:

Arkansas, Texas, Louisiana (except the Parishes of St. Bernard, Plaquemines, Jefferson, St. John, St. Charles, St. James Ascension, Assumption, Terrebonne, Lafourche, St. Mary, St. Martin, and Orleans, including the City of New Orleans), Mississippi, Alabama, Florida, Georgia, South Carolina, North Carolina, and Virginia, (except the forty-eight counties designated as West Virginia, and also the counties of Berkley, Accomac, Northampton, Elizabeth City, York, Princess Ann, and Norfolk, including the cities of Norfolk and Portsmouth), and which excepted parts, are for the present, left precisely as if this proclamation were not issued.

And by virtue of the power, and for the purpose aforesaid, I do order and declare that all persons held as slaves within said designated States, and parts of States, are, and henceforward shall be free; and that the Executive government of the United

States, including the military and naval authorities thereof, will recognize and maintain the freedom of said persons.

And I hereby enjoin upon the people so declared to be free to abstain from all violence, unless in necessary self-defence; and I recommend to them that, in all cases when allowed, they labor faithfully for reasonable wages.

And I further declare and make known, that such persons of suitable condition, will be received into the armed service of the United States to garrison forts, positions, stations, and other places, and to man vessels of all sorts in said service.

And upon this act, sincerely believed to be an act of justice, warranted by the Constitution, upon military necessity, I invoke the considerate judgment of mankind, and the gracious favor of Almighty God.

In witness whereof, I have hereunto set my hand and caused the seal of the United States to be affixed.

Done at the City of Washington, this first day of January, in the year of our Lord one thousand eight hundred and sixty three, and of the Independence of the United States of America the eighty-seventh.

By the President: ABRAHAM LINCOLN

On the Emancipation Proclamation

Frederick Douglass (1817–1895)

Douglass escaped from slavery on the eastern shore of Maryland at the age of eighteen. Mentored by the abolitionist William Lloyd Garrison, he vehemently disagreed with Garrison over the secession question; Douglass felt that secession would leave Southern slaves isolated and without hope. During the War, Douglass enjoyed great prominence as an orator and journalist, devoting himself to obtaining justice for African-Americans and advocating for their right to serve in the Union Army. He described the Emancipation Proclamation as the "dawn of a new day." Though he had a strong relationship with Lincoln and was called to the White House for consultation, because of Lincoln's failure to publicly advocate voting rights for freed blacks, Douglass did not support the president's bid for reelection in 1864, endorsing instead John C. Fremont.

In an oration at the unveiling of the Freeman's Monument on April 14, 1876, Douglass frankly acknowledged the limitation of Lincoln's racial attitudes as well as his undisputed leadership in the cause of emancipation.

The formal portrait that follows is of an unidentified African-American soldier in a Union uniform with his wife and daughters. It was discovered in Maryland.

The first of January, 1863, was a memorable day in the progress of American liberty and civilization. It was the turning-point in the conflict between freedom and slavery. A death-blow was given to the slaveholding rebellion. Until then the federal arm had been more than tolerant to that relic of barbarism. It had

defended it inside the slave States; it had countermanded the emancipation policy of John C. Fremont in Missouri, it had returned slaves to their so-called owners; it had threatened that any attempt on the part of the slaves to gain their freedom by insurrection, or otherwise, should be put down with an iron hand, it had even refused to allow the Hutchinson family to sing their anti-slavery songs in the camps of the Army of the Potomac; it had surrounded the houses of slaveholders with bayonets for their protection, and through its secretary of war, William H. Seward, had given notice to the world that, "however the war for the Union might terminate, no change would be made in the relation of master and slave." Upon this pro-slavery platform the war against the rebellion had been waged during more than two years. It had not been a war of conquest, but rather a war of conciliation. McClellan, in command of the army, had been trying, apparently, to put down the rebellion without hurting the rebels, certainly without hurting slavery and the government had seemed to coöperate with him in both respects. Charles Sumner, William Lloyd Garrison, Wendell Phillips, Gerrit Smith and the whole anti-slavery phalanx at the North, had denounced this policy, and had besought Mr. Lincoln to adopt an opposite one, but in vain. Generals in the field, and councils in the Cabinet, had persisted in advancing this policy through defeats and disasters, even to the verge of ruin. We fought the rebellion, but not its cause. The key to the situation was the four millions of slaves; yet the slave who loved us, was hated, and the slaveholder who hated us, was loved. We kissed the hand that smote us, and spurned the hand that helped us. When the means of victory were before us,—within our grasp—we went in search of the means of defeat. And now, on this day of January 1st, 1863, the formal and solemn announcement was made that thereafter the government would be found on the side of emancipation. This proclamation changed everything. It gave a new direction to the councils of the Cabinet, and to the conduct of the national arms. I shall leave to the statesman, the philosopher and the historian, the more comprehensive discussion of this document, and only tell how it touched me, and those in like condition with me at the time. I was in Boston, and its reception there may indicate the importance attached to it elsewhere. An immense assembly convened in Tremont Temple to await the first flash of the electric wires announcing the "new departure." Two years of war, prosecuted in the interests of slavery, had made free speech possible in Boston, and we were now met together to receive and celebrate the first utterance of the long-hoped-for proclamation, if it came, and, if it did not come, to speak our minds freely; for, in view of the past, it was by no means certain that it would come. The occasion, therefore, was one of both hope and fear. Our ship was on the open sea, tossed by a terrible storm; wave after wave was passing over us, and every hour was fraught with increasing peril. Whether we should survive or perish depended in large measure upon the coming of this proclamation. At least so we felt. Although the conditions on which Mr. Lincoln had promised to withhold it had not been complied with, yet, from many considerations, there was room to doubt and fear. Mr. Lincoln was known to be a man of tender heart, and boundless patience: no man could tell to what length he might go, or might refrain from going, in the direction of peace and reconciliation. Hitherto, he had not shown himself a man of heroic measures, and, properly enough, this step belonged to that class. It must be the end of all compromises with slavery—

a declaration that thereafter the war was to be conducted on a new principle, with a new aim. It would be a full and fair assertion that the government would neither trifle, or be trifled with, any longer. But would it come? On the side of doubt, it was said that Mr. Lincoln's kindly nature might cause him to relent at the last moment; that Mrs. Lincoln, coming from an old slaveholding family, would influence him to delay, and to give the slaveholders one other chance. Every moment of waiting chilled our hopes, and strengthened our fears. A line of messengers was established between the telegraph office and the platform of Tremont Temple, and the time was occupied with brief speeches from Hon. Thomas Russell of Plymouth, Miss Anna E. Dickinson (a lady of marvelous eloquence), Rev. Mr. Grimes, J. Sella Martin, William Wells Brown, and myself. But speaking or listening to speeches was not the thing for which the people had come together. The time for argument was passed. It was not logic, but the trump of jubilee, which everybody wanted to hear. We were waiting and listening as for a bolt from the sky, which should rend the fetters of four millions of slaves; we were watching, as it were, by the dim light of the stars, for the dawn of a new day; we were longing for the answer to the agonizing prayers of centuries. Remembering those in bonds as bound with them, we wanted to join in the shout for freedom, and in the anthem of the redeemed.

Eight, nine, ten o'clock came and went, and still no word. A visible shadow seemed falling on the expecting throng, which the confident utterances of the speakers sought in vain to dispel. At last, when patience was well-nigh exhausted, and suspense was becoming agony, a man (I think it was Judge Russell) with hasty step advanced through the crowd, and with a face fairly illumined with the news he bore, exclaimed in tones that thrilled all hearts, "It is coming!" "It is on the wires!!" The effect of this announcement was startling beyond description, and the scene was wild and grand. Joy and gladness exhausted all forms of expression, from shouts of praise to sobs and tears. My old friend Rue, a colored preacher, a man of wonderful vocal power, expressed the heartfelt emotion of the hour, when he led all voices in the anthem, "Sound the loud timbrel o'er Egypt's dark sea, Jehovah hath triumphed, his people are free." About twelve o'clock, seeing there was no disposition to retire from the hall, which must be vacated, my friend Grimes (of blessed memory), rose and moved that the meeting adjourn to the Twelfth Baptist church, of which he was pastor, and soon that church was packed from doors to pulpit, and this meeting did not break up till near the dawn of day. It was one of the most affecting and thrilling occasions I ever witnessed, and a worthy celebration of the first step on the part of the nation in its departure from the thraldom of ages.

There was evidently no disposition on the part of this meeting to criticise the proclamation; nor was there with any one at first. At the moment we saw only its antislavery side. But further and more critical examination showed it to be extremely defective. It was not a proclamation of "liberty throughout all the land, unto all the inhabitants thereof," such as we had hoped it would be, but was one marked by discriminations and reservations. Its operation was confined within certain geographical and military lines. It only abolished slavery where it did not exist, and left it intact where it did exist. It was a measure apparently inspired by the low motive of military necessity, and by so far as it was so, it would become inoperative and useless when military necessity should cease. There was much said in this line, and much that was narrow and erroneous. For my own part, I took the proclamation, first and last, for a little more than it purported, and saw in its spirit a life and power far beyond its letter. Its meaning to me was the entire abolition of slavery, wherever the evil could be reached by the Federal arm, and I saw that its moral power would extend much further. It was, in my estimation, an immense gain to have the war for the Union committed to the extinction of slavery, even from a military necessity. It is not a bad thing to have individuals or nations do right, though they do so from selfish motives. I approved the one-spur-wisdom of "Paddy," who thought if he could get one side of his horse to go, he could trust the speed of the other side.

The effect of the proclamation abroad was highly beneficial to the loyal cause. Disinterested parties could now see in it a benevolent character. It was no longer a mere strife for territory and dominion, but a contest of civilization against barbarism.

The proclamation itself was throughout like Mr. Lincoln. It was framed with a view to the least harm and the most good possible in the circumstances, and with especial consideration of the latter. It was thoughtful, cautious, and well guarded at all points. While he hated slavery, and really desired its destruction, he always proceeded against it in a manner the least likely to shock or drive from him any who were truly in sympathy with the preservation of the Union, but who were not friendly to emancipation. For this he kept up the distinction between loyal and disloyal slaveholders, and discriminated in favor of the one, as against the other. In a word, in all that he did, or attempted, he made it manifest that the one great and all-commanding object with him was the peace and preservation of the Union, and that this was the motive and main-spring of all his measures. His wisdom and moderation at this point were for a season useful to the loyal cause in the border States, but it may be fairly questioned whether it did not chill the union ardor of the loyal people of the North in some degree, and diminish rather than increase the sum of our power against the rebellion; for moderate, cautious, and guarded as was this proclamation, it created a howl of indignation and wrath amongst the rebels and their allies. The old cry was raised by the copperhead organs of "an abolition war," and a pretext was thus found for an excuse for refusing to enlist, and for marshaling all the negro prejudice of the North on the rebel side. Men could say they were willing to fight for the Union, but that they were not willing to fight for the freedom of the negroes; and thus it was made difficult to procure enlistments or to enforce the draft. This was especially true of New York, where there was a large Irish population. The attempt to enforce the draft in that city was met by mobs, riot, and bloodshed. There is perhaps no darker chapter in the whole history of the war than this cowardly and bloody uprising in July, 1863. For three days and nights New York was in the hands of a ferocious mob, and there was not sufficient power in the government of the country or of the city itself to stay the hand of violence and the effusion of blood. Though this mob was nominally against the draft which had been ordered, it poured out its fiercest wrath upon the colored people and their friends. It spared neither age nor sex; it hanged negroes simply because they were negroes; it murdered women in their homes, and burnt their homes over their heads; it dashed out the brains of young children against the lamp-posts; it burned the colored orphan asylum, a noble charity on the corner of Fifth avenue, and, scarce allowing time for the helpless two hundred children to make good their escape, plundered the building of every valuable piece of furniture; and forced colored men, women and children to seek concealment in cellars or garrets or wheresoever else it could be found, until this high carnival of crime and reign of terror should pass away.

New York City Draft Riots

David M. Barnes, the Metropolitan Police Services (July 13–17, 1863)

In March of 1863, the federal government passed the National Conscription Act, making all single men aged twenty to forty-five and married men up to thirty-five subject to a draft lottery. However, the act allowed drafted men to avoid conscription by supplying someone to take their place or to pay the government a three-hundred-dollar exemption fee, a buyout only the wealthy could afford. This created resentment among poor whites, many of them immigrants, who were also facing competition for jobs with free blacks. The Draft Riots were some of the most serious instances of urban social upheaval in American history, with widespread destruction of property, beatings, and lynchings of African-Americans. The "official" death toll was listed at 119, though many contemporary observers insisted that the number was much higher. Despite the horrific violence, Lincoln never declared martial law in New York City, but federal troops were sent to quell the rioting. While blacks fled the city in large numbers, the Twentieth Regiment U.S. Colored Troops, New York City's first black volunteer force in the Union Army, was formed in the aftermath.

MURDER OF COL. O'BRIEN.

The murder of Col. H. J. O'Brien, by the mob, on the afternoon of Tuesday of Riot Week, was characterized by appalling barbarities. After the battle between the police under Inspector Carpenter, in the Second Avenue, and after the police had left, Col. O'Brien, in command of two companies, 11th Regiment, N. Y. Vols., arrived at Thirty-fourth Street and Second Avenue. The rioters had reassembled, a collision ensued, and the military opened fire. The mob dispersed, and Col. O'BRIEN, leaving his command, walked up the avenue a short distance, entering a drug store. Returning to the street in a few moments, he was instantly surrounded by a vengeful and relentless crowd, which had re-collected, at once knocked down, beaten and mutilated shockingly till insensible. He thus lay for upwards of an hour, breathing heavily, and on any movement receiving kicks and stones. He was then taken by the heels, dragged around the street, and again left lying in it. For some four hours did he thus lay, subjected to infamous outrages, among them the occasional thrusting of a stick down his throat when gasping for breath. No one who did not seek to feed his brutality upon him was allowed to approach him. One man who sought to give him a drop of water was instantly set upon and barely escaped with his life. While still breathing, he was taken into the yard of his own house, near the scene, and there the most revolting atrocities were perpetrated, underneath which the life, that had so tenaciously clung to him, fled. No one could have recognized his remains. The murderers, satiated with their excess of fiendishness, left, and the body was allowed to be removed to Bellevue Hospital.

COLORED VICTIMS OF THE RIOT.

WM. HENRY NICHOLS (colored). Nichols resided at No. 147 East Twenty-eighth St. Mrs. STAAT, his mother, was visiting him. On Wednesday, July 15th, at 3 o'clock, the house was attacked by a mob with showers of bricks and stones. In one of the rooms was a woman with a child but three days old. The rioters broke open the door with axes and rushed in. NICHOLS and his mother fled to the basement; in a few moments the babe referred to was dashed by the rioters from the upper window into the yard, and instantly killed. The mob cut the water pipes above, and the basement was being deluged; ten persons, mostly women and children, were there, and they fled to the yard; in attempting to climb the fence Mrs. STAATS fell back from exhaustion; the rioters were instantly upon her; her son sprang to her rescue, exclaiming, "Save my mother, if you kill me." Two ruffians instantly seized him, each taking hold of an arm, while a third, armed with a crow-bar, calling upon them to hold his arms apart, deliberately struck him a savage blow on the head, felling him like a bullock. He died in the N. Y. Hospital two days after.

JAMES COSTELLO (col'd).—JAMES COSTELLO, No. 97 West Thirty-third Street, killed on Tuesday morning, July 14th. COSTELLO was a shoemaker, an active man in his business, industrious and sober. He went out early in the morning upon an errand, was accosted, and finally was pursued by a powerful man. He ran down the street; endeavored to make his escape; was nearly overtaken by his pursuer; in self-defence he turned and shot the rioter with a revolver. The shot proved to be mortal; he died two days after. COSTELLO was immediately set upon by the mob. They first mangled his body, then hanged it. They then cut down his body and dragged it through the gutters, smashing it with stones, and finally burnt it. The mob then attempted to kill Mrs. COSTELLO and her children, but she escaped by climbing fences and taking refuge in a police station-house.

ABRAHAM FRANKLIN (colored).—This young man, who was murdered by the mob on the corner of Twenty-seventh Street and Seventh Avenue, was a quiet, inoffensive man, of unexceptional character. He was a cripple, but supported himself and his mother, being employed as a coachman. A short time previous to the assault, he called upon his mother to see if anything could be done by him for her safety. The old lady said she considered herself perfectly safe; but if her time to die had come, she was ready to die. Her son then knelt down by her side, and implored the protection of Heaven in behalf of his mother. The old lady said that it seemed to her that good angels were present in the room. Scarcely had the supplicant risen from his knees, when the mob broke down the door, seized him, beat him in over the head and face with fists and clubs, and then hanged him in the presence of his parent. While they were thus engaged the military came and drove them away, cutting down the body of FRANKLIN, who raised his arm once slightly and gave a few signs of life. The military then moved on to quell other riots, when the mob returned and again suspended the now probably lifeless body of FRANKLIN, cutting out pieces of flesh, and otherwise shockingly mutilating it.

AUGUSTUS STUART (colored).—Died at Hospital, Blackwell's Island, July 22, from the effects of a blow received at the hands of the mob, on Wednesday evening of Riot Week. He had been badly beaten previously by a band of rioters, and was frightened and insane from the effects of the blows which he had received. He was running toward the Arsenal (State), Seventh Avenue and Thirty-seventh Street, for safety, when he was overtaken by the mob, from whom he received his death blow.

PETER HEUSTON.—PETER HEUSTON, sixty-three years of age, a Mohawk Indian, dark complexion, but straight hair, and for several years a resident of New York, proved a victim to the riots. HEUSTON served with the New York Volunteers in the Mexican war. He was brutally attacked and shockingly beaten, on the 13th of July, by a gang of ruffians, who thought him to be of the African race because of his dark complexion. He died within four days, at Bellevue Hospital, from his injuries.

JEREMIAH ROBINSON (colored).—He was killed in Madison near Catharine Street. His widow stated that her husband, in order to escape, dressed himself in some of her clothes, and, in company with herself and one other woman, left their residence and went toward one of the Brooklyn ferries. ROBINSON wore a hood, which failed to hide his beard. Some boys, seeing his beard, lifted up the skirts of his dress, which exposed his heavy boots. Immediately the mob set upon him, and the atrocities they perpetrated are so revolting that they are unfit for publication. They finally killed him, and threw his body into the river. His wife and her companion ran up Madison street, and escaped across the Grand Street Ferry to Brooklyn.

WILLIAM JONES (colored).—A crowd of rioters in Clarkson Street, in pursuit of a negro, who in self-defence had fired on some rowdies, met an inoffensive colored man returning from a bakery with a load of bread under his arm. They instantly set upon and beat him and, after nearly killing him, hung him to a lamp-post. His body was left suspended for several hours. A fire was made underneath him, and he was literally roasted as he hung, the mob reveling in their demoniac act. Recognition of the remains, on their being recovered, was impossible; and two women mourned for upwards of two weeks, in the case of this man, for the loss of their husbands. At the end of that time, the husband of one of the mourners, to her great joy, returned like one recovered from the grave. The principal evidence which the widow, Mary Jones, had to identify the murdered man as her husband, was the fact of his having a loaf of bread under his arm, he having left the house to get a loaf of bread a few minutes before the attack.

JOSEPH REED (colored).—This was a lad of seven years of age, residing at No. 147 East Twenty-eighth Street, with an aged grandmother and widowed mother. On Wednesday morning of the fearful week, a crowd of ruffians gathered in the neighborhood, determined on a work of plunder and death. They attacked the house, stole everything they could carry with them, and, after threatening the inmates, set fire to it. The colored people, who had the sole occupancy of the building, fled in confusion into the midst of the gathering crowd. And then the child was separated from his guardians. His youth and evident illness, even from the devils around him, it would be thought, should have insured his safety. But no sooner did they see his unprotected, defenceless condition, than a gang of fiendish men seized him, beat him with sticks, and bruised him with heavy cobblestones. But one, ten-fold more the servant of Satan than the rest, rushed at the child, and with the stock of a pistol struck him on the temple and felled him to the ground. A noble young fireman, by the name of JOHN F. GOVERN, of No. 39 Hose Company, instantly came to the rescue, and, single-handed, held the crowd at bay. Taking the wounded and unconscious boy in his arms, he carried him to a place of safety. The terrible beating and the great fright the poor lad had undergone was too much for his feeble frame; he died on the following Tuesday.

JOSEPH JACKSON (colored), aged 19 years, living in West Fifty-third Street, near Sixth Avenue, was in the industrious pursuit of his humble occupation of gathering provender for a herd of cattle, and when near the foot of Thirty-fourth Street, East River, July 15, was set upon by the mob, killed, and his body thrown into the river.

SAMUEL JOHNSON (colored).—On Tuesday night JOHNSON was attacked near Fulton Ferry by a gang who mercilessly beat and left him for dead. A proposition was made to throw him into the river, but for some reason the murderers took fright and fled. He was taken by some citizens to his home, and died the next day.

——WILLIAMS (colored).—He was attacked on the corner of Le Roy and Washington Streets, on Tuesday morning, July 14th, knocked down, a number of men jumped upon, kicked, and stamped upon him until insensible. One of the murderers knelt on the body and drove a knife into it; the blade being too small he threw it away and resorted to his fists. Another seized a huge stone, weighing near twenty pounds, and deliberately crushed it again and again on to the victim. A force of police, under Captain DICKSON, arrived and rescued the man, who was conveyed to the New York Hospital. He was only able to articulate "WILLIAMS" in response to a question as to his name, and remained insensible thereafter, dying in a few days.

ANN DERRICKSON.—This was a white woman, the wife of a colored man, and lived at No. 11 York Street. On Wednesday, July 15th, the rioters seized a son of deceased, a lad of about twelve years, saturated his clothes and hair with camphene, and then procuring a rope, fastened one end to a lamp-post, the other around his neck, and were about to set him on fire, and hang him; they were interfered with by some citizens and by the police of the First Ward, and their diabolical attempt at murder frustrated. While Mrs. DERRICKSON was attempting to save the life of her son she was horribly bruised and beaten with a cart rung. The victim, after lingering three or four weeks, died from the effects of her injuries.

BURNING OF THE COLORED ORPHAN ASYLUM. About 4 o'clock on the afternoon of Monday, July 13th, a mob of some three thousand attacked the Asylum for Colored Orphans on Fifth Avenue. The main building was four stories, with wings of three stories, and was capable of accommodating five hundred children. With the grounds, it extended from Forty-third to Forty-fourth Street. At the time the mob came upon it, there were, besides the officers and matrons, over two hundred children in it, from infancy to twelve years of age. Superintendent WM. E. DAVIS hurriedly fastened the doors, and while the mob were breaking them in the children were collected, and then escaped by the rear just as the ruffians had effected their entrance in front. Those entering at once proceeded to ransack and pillage every room in the building. Everything that could be was stolen, even to the dresses and trinkets of the orphans. What could not be carried off was destroyed. Meantime Chief Engineer DECKER reached the scene, and forced his way to the building. In attempting to address the mob, he was twice knocked down and finally forced into Fifth Avenue. Here some ten firemen joined him, and it was resolved to save the Asylum if possible. They boldly forced their way to and into the building. Here they were joined by Assistant Engineers LAMB and LEWIS. The chairs, desks, &c., had been broken up, piled in different parts of the building, and fires had been kindled on the first and second floors. The firemen scattered and extinguished all of them, and intimidated the rioters. Meanwhile some of the latter had succeeded in effectually firing the loft in every part; and the demonstration against the chief and his small band of associates had become too formidable; to save the building was impossible, and they reluctantly yielded it to the mob, who, with exulting yells, soon saw the Asylum wrapped in flames. In an hour and a half only a small portion of the walls remained.

The firemen who acted so gallantly with the Chief and his Assistants were members of Hook and Ladder Company No. 2, Hose Company No. 31, Engine Companies Nos. 7, 9, and 10.

After their escape from the building, the Orphans were hurried in mournful procession to the Twentieth Precinct, Captain WALLING, where they were sheltered and provided for until their removal to Blackwell's Island. Except the clothes they wore, not an article was saved for them. The loss to the Society in building, furniture, and clothing was estimated at $80,000.

EDWARD S. SANFORD, U. S. MILITARY TELEGRAPH SERVICE

NEW YORK, July 13, 1863.
(Received 12.10 p.m.)

Hon. E. M. STANTON.

SIR: What is represented as a serious riot is now taking place on Third avenue, at the provost-marshal's office. The office is said to have been burned, and the adjoining block to be on fire. Our wires in that direction have all been torn down. A report just in says the regulars from Governor's Island have been ordered to the vicinity.

Respectfully,
E. S. SANFORD.

NEW YORK, July 13, 1863.
(Received 2.30 p.m.)

Hon. E. M. STANTON,
Secretary of War.

SIR: The riot has assumed serious proportions, and is entirely beyond the control of the police. Superintendent Kennedy is badly injured. So far the rioters have everything their own way. They are estimated at from 30,000 to 40,000. I am inclined to think from 2,000 to 3,000 are actually engaged. Appearances indicate an organized attempt to take advantage of the absence of military force.

Respectfully,
E. S. SANFORD.

NEW YORK, July 13, 1863—9.30 p.m.
(Received 11.45 p.m.)

Hon. E. M. STANTON,
Secretary of War.

SIR: The situation is not improved since dark. The programme is diversified by small mobs chasing isolated negroes as hounds would chase a fox. I mention this to indicate to you that the spirit of mob is loose, and all parts of the city pervaded. The Tribune office has been attacked by a reconnoitering party, and partially sacked. A strong body of police repulsed the assailants, but another attack in force is threatened. The telegraph is especially sought for destruction. One office has been burned by the rioters, and several others compelled to close. The main office is shut, and the business transferred to Jersey City.

In brief, the city of New York is to-night at the mercy of a mob, whether organized or improvised, I am unable to say. As far as I can learn, the firemen and military companies sympathize too closely with the draft resistance movement to be relied upon for the extinguishment of fires or the restoration of order. It is to be hoped that to-morrow will open upon a brighter prospect than is promised to-night.

Respectfully,
E. S. SANFORD.

WAR DEPARTMENT,
Washington, July 14, 1863—1 a.m.

EDWARD S. SANFORD,
New York:

SIR: Your telegram of 9.30 just received. Please report to me immediately—1st. Whether any and what military force has been called out or employed by the city authorities or the drafting officers. 2d. What amount of injury has been done, so far as you know, to persons and to property. 3d. What measures, if any, have been taken by military or police authority to quell the riot.

EDWIN M. STANTON,
Secretary of War.

NEW YORK, July 14, 1863.

Hon. E. M. STANTON,
Secretary of War.

SIR: It was impossible to answer your questions fully. I gave you such information as I could get at headquarters. Several conflicts have taken place to-day, with more serious results from those of yesterday, which were principally confined on the side of the police to severe injuries. Three arsenals were attacked to-day by the rioters. At two points they were repulsed. At the third they were successful, and obtained possession of the arms, which were recaptured by the marines and regulars.

This morning nearly all the manufactories were visited by delegations from the rioters, who compelled the men to stop work. This adds to the number and somewhat to the strength of the mob. The mayor has turned over his power and forces to Governor Seymour, who is about issuing a proclamation. Have sent to headquarters for statement of facts, as far as known, and will forward immediately on reception. An immense crowd has gathered around the Evening Post office since I commenced this message. As yet they are undemonstrative. General Wool's message has arrived, but gives no further information. Will try my own resources. My opinion is that one good regiment of native-born troops, well commanded, arriving here by 12 o'clock to-night, would save the assay office, sub-treasury, and other Government property.

Respectfully,
E. S. SANFORD.

NEW YORK CITY, July 14, 1863.
(Received 12.30 p.m.)

Hon. E. M. STANTON,
Secretary of War.

SIR: Have seen General Wool. All the military which he can reach has been called for, but it now numbers only about 800 troops. These are aided by nearly 2,000 police. Governor Seymour has arrived, and General Wool reports him as co-operating heartily. He has called out several regiments, and General Wool has sent to New Jersey for two regiments; but, as far as I can see, the means of defense are entirely inadequate to control the present force of rioters.

The military had a collision with the mob in Thirty-fourth street an hour ago, and used ball-cartridge. Result not reported. The rioters are now (12 o'clock) in possession of Mayor Opdyke's house, and destroying it.

The chances appear to me to be against the immediate restoration of order in the city of New York. Will keep you advised of situation.

E. S. SANFORD.

NEW YORK, July 14, 1863—2.40 p.m.
(Received 4.30 p.m.)

Hon. E. M. STANTON,
Secretary of War.

SIR: You may judge of the capacity at headquarters here when every effort cannot extract any more information than I have forwarded. Excuse me for saying that this mob is testing the Government nearly as strongly as the Southern rebellion. If you cannot enforce the draft here, it will not be enforced elsewhere. The example will prove contagious, and similar events transpire in every large city. If you send sufficient force here to demonstrate the power of the Government, its effect will reach every part of the country, and one settlement answer for the whole.

Immediate action is necessary, or the Government and country will be disgraced.

Respectfully,
E. S. SANFORD.

NEW YORK, July 14, 1863.
(Received 5.10 p.m.)

Hon. E. M. STANTON.

SIR: It is reported from Boston that at 3 o'clock this afternoon a large body of armed men had assembled in North street to resist the draft. No details of the situation were received. I find it impossible to get any definite information from newspaper offices, police stations, or headquarters, of affairs here.

E. S. SANFORD.

WAR DEPARTMENT,
Washington, July 14, 1863—6.20 p.m.

Maj. E. S. SANFORD,
New York:

SIR: The Government will be able to stand the test, even if there should be a riot and mob in every ward of every city. The retreat of Lee's army, now in a rout and utterly broken, will leave an ample force at the disposal of the Government.

EDWIN M. STANTON,
Secretary of War.

NEW YORK, July 14, 1863.
(Received 8.40 p.m.)

Hon. E. M. STANTON,
Secretary of War.

SIR: We are expecting momentarily that our Southern wires will be cut, as the rioters are at work in their immediate neighborhood. It seems very important for the United States Government to define its position immediately in this city, and, if not done immediately, the opportunity will be lost. Governor Seymour has been sent for to come here immediately, and he is on his way. The police so far report themselves as having been successful in every fight, of which they have had many, but they say they are exhausted, and cannot much longer sustain the unequal contest. Not less than 10,000 good native soldiers ought to be here this moment to restore and enforce order.

E. S. SANFORD.

NEW YORK, July 15, 1863.
(Received 3 p.m.)

Hon. E. M. STANTON,
Secretary of War.

SIR: Have just returned from headquarters. Saw General Wool and Governor Seymour. The latter informed me that he had heard of organizations at Newark and Jersey City to prevent the passage of troops, and requested me to inform the Seventh Regiment. I learn from Philadelphia that this regiment will not reach there till 4 o'clock, which will make it due here about to-morrow morning. There does not seem to be any one here who is attending to these matters. Some one should superintend the transportation. If troops are to come in any numbers, all the equipments of the roads should be put on the Amboy line, which can be easily guarded, and boats enough sent from here to Amboy. The troops can land from on board boats at any desired point, and under cover of gunboats, if necessary.

The situation does not appear to me to improve. There are indications of riotous organizations at all points from which we hear. The settling place is New York, and, once determined here, all is fixed.

Respectfully,
E. S. SANFORD.

NEW YORK, July 15, 1863.
(Received 6.20 p.m.)

Hon. E. M. STANTON,
Secretary of War.

SIR: The following message just received from the manager of our Boston office. It came from New Rochelle by horse-power, our lines up to that point being destroyed. There was a considerable riot last night at Staten Island, and there are indications of outbreaks at Brooklyn and Williamsburg:

BOSTON, July 15, 1863—6.20 p.m.

Col. E. S. SANFORD:

SIR: Considerable excitement and gathering of people at North End yesterday; some fighting. Two police injured. Two companies regulars ordered up from Fort Independence; also two companies artillery from Readville. About 8 p.m. crowd made an attack on armory in Cooper street. All window glass demolished by brickbats. Troops fired a round of blank cartridges, and made a bayonet charge on mob, which retreated toward Charlestown street. Troops returned to armory, crowd following. A disturbance more intense. Large breach made in door of armory, which was then thrown open, and 6-pounder brass field pieces, loaded with canister shot, discharged full in the crowd. One man killed and several wounded. The crowd still refusing to leave, infantry marched out by platoons, and fired. One man and one woman killed by this discharge, and several wounded. Cooper street was then cleared.

Later in evening a battalion of dragoons formed line in Cooper street. Part of the crowd assembled at Dock Square, and a hardware store was broken into. Police fired fifteen or twenty shots.

At 8.40 p.m. alarm bells were rung, and another squad of police sent to Dock Square, which succeeded in keeping it clear until arrival of dragoons and company of infantry.

At 10 p.m. dragoons returned to Cooper street, the disturbance in Dock Square being quelled.

At 12.30 armory discovered to be on fire, but was saved from destruction by military. The Forty-fourth Massachusetts Regiment notified to assemble at their armory at 6 this morning.

G. F. MILLIKEN.

Respectfully,
E. S. SANFORD.

NEW YORK, July 15, 1863.
(Received 9.15 p.m.)

Hon. E. M. STANTON,
Secretary of War.

SIR: The situation of affairs here is quite as critical this morning as at any former time. As far as I can learn, there has not yet been much serious fighting, but the rioters are gathered in large crowds at various points, and for the first time making their appearance down town in the back streets. Whatever assistance is to come here, should have precedence over all other railroad arrangements.

E. S. SANFORD.

NEW YORK,
July 16, 1863.

Hon. E. M. STANTON,
Secretary of War.

SIR: The situation is evidently improved. Cars and omnibuses are running. The Hudson River Railroad has been relaid, and trains have come in and gone out without molestation. Laborers have resumed work at various points, and the lower part of the city presents its usual appearance.

The fighting last night was quite severe. At one time the mob had the best of it, and possession of our dead and wounded, including 2 officers of the Duryea Zouaves, killed, and Colonel [Edward] Jardine, severely wounded. General Brown sent all the force at his disposal. He retook the position, and brought off the dead and wounded. There were killed in this contest about 15 of our men and about 25 of the rioters. The mob were armed, organized, and fired at the word of command.

General Brown has now, including the Seventh Regiment, about 1,400 men under his command. He thinks the force for his special purposes should be increased to 3,000. It is impossible to ascertain how many troops there are here, owing to the conflict of authority under which each officer will report those belonging to himself and all the others. Yesterday one officer received, at nearly the same time, five conflicting orders from as many commanders-in-chief. There is no danger of getting too many troops here of the right kind. The indications, to my mind, are that the rioters are resting and organizing. They have got arms to a considerable extent, and use them pretty well. The agrarian mania has taken a strong hold of a certain class, and the cry of contrast between rich and poor is loudly raised. Every city and town that we hear from is effervescing. Philadelphia seems the most quiet, but, if once started, will be the most dangerous.

I have taken care that all press dispatches which went out this morning conveyed the right impression. The strong hand tightly grasped here will be felt all over the Union. When you have given us a leader, and he has 10,000 men at his command, the country will be safe.

Respectfully,
E. S. SANFORD.

NEW YORK, July 16, 1863.
(Received 7.10 p.m.)

Hon. E. M. STANTON,
Secretary of War.

SIR: There has been no fighting to-day of any consequence. The gatherings of excited people are confined at present to a small section of the upper part of the city.

I anticipate a renewal of trouble to-night, both here and in Brooklyn.

Advices from all quarters indicate that resistance to the draft will be made the pretext for rioting in nearly every large town in the country.

Respectfully,
E. S. SANFORD.

NEW YORK, July 17, 1863.
(Received 10.50 a.m.)

Hon. E. M. STANTON,
Secretary of War.

SIR: The situation this morning is similar to yesterday. Business is going forward in most parts of the city. No further attack has been made on our telegraph wires, and we are in connection with Boston.

The rioters made a harder fight last night than at any previous time, but were thoroughly whipped.

I will endeavor to obtain and transmit more detailed information.

Respectfully,
E. S. SANFORD.

NEW YORK, July 17, 1863.
(Received 2.07 p.m.)

Hon. E. M. STANTON,
Secretary of War.

SIR: Police Commissioner [Thomas C.] Acton reports that in a fight last night near Gramercy Park, the soldiers got the worst of it, and were driven back, leaving one of their number killed. Captain Putnam, of the regulars, started with two companies, and thoroughly routed the rioters, killing from 15 to 25, taking 16 prisoners, and bringing off the body of the sergeant, which was left at the first fight.

Police Commissioner Acton desires to make a special request for the promotion of Captain Putnam, Company F, Twelfth U. S. Infantry, this being the second time that he has encountered and overcome the rioters after they had gotten the better of our troops under other officers.

No disturbance has occurred this morning in any part of the city.

Respectfully,
E. S. SANFORD.

WASHINGTON, D.C.,
July 17, 1863—3.40 p.m.

Police Commissioner ACTON,
New York City:

SIR: The courage and gallantry of Captain Putnam, of the Twelfth Infantry, and of the soldiers of his command, against the rebel rioters in New York, has been unofficially communicated to this Department. Suitable acknowledgment will be made as soon as an official report is received. In the meantime, please do communicate to him, and the officers and soldiers who have acted under him, the thanks of this Department.

Your board will also please report all cases of gallantry and courage that may come to your knowledge, by officers or privates, in order that the Department may make proper acknowledgment.

EDWIN M. STANTON,
Secretary of War.

NEW YORK, July 17, 1863—3.45 p.m.
(Received 3.50 p.m.)

Hon. E. M. STANTON,
Secretary of War.

SIR: Up to this hour the city continues very quiet. The following is a synopsis of the remarks by Archbishop Hughes up to 2.45 p.m.:

I do not address you as the President, nor as a military commander, nor as the mayor, but as your father. You know that for years back I have been your friend: I have stood by you with my voice and with my pen. Now, as to the causes of this unhappy excitement. Some of your grievances I know are imaginary ones, though, unfortunately, many are real. Yet know of no country under the sun that has not more cause for a just complaint than we have in this.

The archbishop, who is in excellent voice, has entire control of the sympathies of the crowd of three or four thousand people.

Respectfully,
E. S. SANFORD.

NEW YORK CITY, July 18, 1863—1.30 p.m.
(Received 1.45 p.m.)

Hon. E. M. STANTON,
Secretary of War.

SIR: The plunder rioting is suppressed for the present, but there are strong indications of a formidable and widespread organization to resist the taking away of conscripts under the draft. This organization assumes a party aspect, and extends to the military of the city who are subject to draft. The party supposed to be most interested in sustaining the Government and draft, and the property-holders, show no intention to prepare for the emergency or to fight when it comes.

I give you this information, obtained by personal observation, to enable you to appreciate the position, and trust you will not consider it officious.

E. S. SANFORD.

"At Gettysburg: or What a Girl Saw and Heard of the Battle"

Matilda "Tillie" Pierce Alleman (1848–1914)

Tillie Pierce was fifteen when, on June 26, 1863, she witnessed a ragged band of Confederate soldiers enter the town of Gettysburg in search of any supplies they could forage: food, horses, and shoes, among other things. She and her classmates at the Young Ladies' Seminary located in the town were ordered to go home as quickly as possible. The following day the Union soldiers arrived, and the scene was set for the three-day battle. After hiding her clothes in the basement of her house, she left her parents and traveled with neighbors under the protection of Union soldiers to a farm six miles out of town. During her stay at Weikert Farm, close to the battle site at Little Round Top, she assisted in feeding and nursing the wounded. She movingly describes the distress and terror that this invasion of her peaceful world brought about. She published this account in 1888 when she was a married woman and mother, a rare and vivid description of civilian experience during a devastating battle on home turf.

We awoke early. It was impossible to become drowsy with the events of the previous day uppermost in our minds. We were prompt enough at breakfast that morning.

As more soldiers were expected, and in order to show how welcome they would be, my sister and I had, on the previous evening, prepared a tableful of bouquets which we intended to hand or throw to them as they passed our house.

We had no sooner finished our breakfast when it was

announced that troops were coming. We hastened up what we called the side street, (Breckenridge,) and on reaching Washington Street, again saw some of our army passing.

First came a long line of cavalry, then wagon after wagon passed by for quite awhile. Again we sang patriotic songs as they moved along. Some of these wagons were filled with stretchers and other articles; in others we noticed soldiers reclining, who were doubtless in some way disabled.

It was between nine and ten o'clock when we first noticed firing in the direction of Seminary Ridge. At first the sound was faint, then it grew louder. Soon the booming of cannon was heard, then great clouds of smoke were seen rising beyond the ridge. The sound became louder and louder, and was now incessant. The troops passing us moved faster, the men had now become excited and urged on their horses. The battle was waging. This was my first terrible experience.

I remember hearing some of the soldiers remarking that there was no telling how soon some of them would be brought back in those ambulances, or carried on the stretchers. I hardly knew what it meant, but I learned afterward, even before the day had passed.

It was almost noon when the last of the train had passed and I began to think of dinner and the folks at home.

I hurried back, and the first thing that met my gaze as I passed the parlor was the table full of flowers. The soldiers had passed and we had not given them the bouquets. They did not come by our house and in our haste to see them, we had forgotten all about the intended welcome.

Entering the dining-room I found dinner waiting, but I was too excited to eat, and so, soon finished my meal. After I had eaten what that day I called dinner, our neighbor, Mrs. Schriver, called at the house and said she would leave the town and go to her father's (Jacob Weikert), who lived on the Taneytown road at the eastern slope of the Round Top.

Mr. Schriver, her husband, was then serving in the Union Army, so that under all the circumstances at this time surrounding her, Mrs. Schriver did not feel safe in the house.

As the battle had commenced and was still progressing at the west of the town, and was not very far off, she thought it safer for herself and two children to go to her parents, who lived about three miles to the south. She requested that I be permitted to accompany her, and as it was regarded a safer place for me than to remain in town, my parents readily consented that I should go.

The only preparation I made for the departure, was to carry my best clothes down to the cellar, so that they might be safe when I returned; never thinking of taking any along, nor how long I would stay.

FLEEING FROM DANGER.

About one o'clock we started on foot; the battle still going on. We proceeded out Baltimore Street and entered the Evergreen Cemetery. This was our easiest and most direct route, as it would bring us to the Taneytown road a little further on.

As we were passing along the Cemetery hill, our men were already planting cannon.

They told us to hurry as fast as possible; that we were in great danger of being shot by the Rebels, whom they expected would shell toward us at any moment. We fairly ran to get out of this new danger.

As I looked toward the Seminary Ridge I could see and hear the confusion of the battle. Troops moving hither and thither; the smoke of the conflict arising from the fields; shells bursting in the air, together with the din, rising and falling in mighty undulations.

These things, beheld for the first time, filled my soul with the greatest apprehensions. We soon reached the Taneytown road, and while traveling along, were overtaken by an ambulance wagon in which was the body of a dead soldier. Some of the men told us that it was the body of General Reynolds, and that he had been killed during the forenoon in the battle.

We continued on our way, and had gotten to a little one and a half story house, standing on the west side of the road, when, on account of the muddy condition of the road, we were compelled to stop. This place on the following day became General Meade's headquarters.

While we were standing at the gate, not knowing what to do or where to go, a soldier came out and kindly told us he would try to get some way to help us further on, as it was very dangerous to remain there.

It began to look as though we were getting into new dangers at every step, instead of getting away from them.

We went into the house and after waiting a short time, this same soldier came to us saying:

"Now I have a chance for you. There is a wagon coming down the road and I will try to get them to make room for you."

The wagon was already quite full, but the soldier insisted and prevailed. We fully appreciated his kindness, and as he helped us on the wagon we thanked him very much.

But what a ride! I shall never forget it. The mud was almost up to the hubs of the wheels, and underneath the mud were rocks. The wagon had no springs, and as the driver was anxious to put the greatest distance between himself and the battle in the least time possible, the jolting and bumping were brought out to perfection.

At last we reached Mr. Weikert's and were gladly welcomed to their home.

It was not long after our arrival, until Union artillery came hurrying by. It was indeed a thrilling sight. How the men impelled their horses! How the officers urged the men as they all flew past toward the sound of the battle! Now the road is getting all cut up; they take to the fields, and all is an anxious, eager hurry! Shouting, lashing the horses, cheering the men, they all rush madly on.

Suddenly we behold an explosion; it is that of a caisson. We see a man thrown high in the air and come down in a wheat field close by. He is picked up and carried into the house. As they pass by I see his eyes are blown out and his whole person seems to be one black mass. The first words I hear him say is:

"Oh dear! I forgot to read my Bible to-day! What will my poor wife and children say?"

I saw the soldiers carry him up stairs; they laid him upon a bed and wrapped him in cotton. How I pitied that poor man! How terribly the scenes of war were being irresistibly portrayed before my vision.

After the artillery had passed, infantry began coming. I soon saw that these men were very thirsty and would go to the spring which is on the north side of the house.

I was not long in learning what I could do. Obtaining a bucket, I hastened to the spring, and there, with others, carried water to the moving column until the spring was empty. We then went to the pump standing on the south side of the house, and supplied water from it. Thus we continued giving water to our tired soldiers until night came on, when we sought rest indoors.

It was toward the close of the afternoon of this day that some of the wounded from the field of battle began to arrive where I was staying. They reported hard fighting, many wounded and killed, and were afraid our troops would be defeated and perhaps routed.

The first wounded soldier whom I met had his thumb tied up. This I thought was dreadful, and told him so.

"Oh," said he, "this is nothing; you'll see worse than this before long."

"Oh! I hope not," I innocently replied.

Soon two officers carrying their arms in slings made their appearance, and I more fully began to realize that something terrible had taken place.

Now the wounded began to come in greater numbers. Some limping, some with their heads and arms in bandages, some crawling, others carried on stretchers or brought in ambulances. Suffering, cast down and dejected, it was a truly pitiable gathering. Before night the barn was filled with the shattered and dying heroes of this day's struggle.

That evening Beckie Weikert, the daughter at home, and I went out to the barn to see what was transpiring there. Nothing before in my experience had ever paralleled the sight we then and there beheld. There were the groaning and crying, the struggling and dying, crowded side by side, while attendants sought to aid and relieve them as best they could.

We were so overcome by the sad and awful spectacle that we hastened back to the house weeping bitterly.

As we entered the basement or cellar-kitchen of the house, we found many nurses making beef tea for the wounded. Seeing that we were crying they inquired as to the cause. We told them where we had been and what we had seen. They no doubt appreciated our feelings for they at once endeavored to cheer us by telling funny stories, and ridiculing our tears. They soon dispelled our terror and caused us to laugh so much that many times when we should have been sober minded we were not; the reaction having been too sudden for our overstrung nerves.

I remember that at this time a chaplain who was present in

the kitchen stepped up to me while I was attending to some duty and said:

"Little girl, do all you can for the poor soldiers and the Lord will reward you."

I looked up in his face and laughed, but at once felt ashamed of my conduct and begged his pardon. After telling him what Beckie and I had seen, how the nurses had derided us for crying and that I now laughed when I should not, being unable to help myself, he remarked:

"Well it is much better for you and the soldiers to be in a cheerful mood."

The first day had passed, and with the rest of the family, I retired, surrounded with strange and appalling events, and many new visions passing rapidly through my mind.

LEE'S LETTER OF RESIGNATION AFTER THE DEFEAT AT GETTYSBURG

(1807–1870)

Stung by what he regarded as unfair criticism that he allowed Lee's army to escape across the Potomac after Gettysburg, General George Gordon Meade tendered his resignation to the President. Lincoln, in a letter addressed but never sent to Meade, was keenly displeased with the outcome of the battle:

> . . . my dear general, I do not believe you appreciate the magnitude of the misfortune involved in Lee's escape— He was within your easy grasp, and to have closed upon him would, in connection with our late successes, have ended the war— As it is, the war will be prolonged indefinitely. . . . Your golden opportunity is gone, and I am distressed immeasurably because of it. . . .

However, Meade's resignation was ultimately not accepted.

After the same battle, Confederate General Robert E. Lee also offered to resign as the head of his army. Overwhelmed by the tremendous loss of life and the defeat at Gettysburg, he wrote to President Jefferson Davis the letter that follows. Davis's refusal to accept his friend Lee's resignation was both respectful and conciliatory. He responded to Lee, ". . . where am I to find that new commander who is to possess the greater ability which you believe to be required?"

Scribner's Monthly for February contains the following, written by Gen. Robert E. Lee, tendering his resignation as commander of the Confederate Armies after the battle of Gettysburg:

CAMP ORANGE, Aug. 8,1863.

MR. PRESIDENT: Your letters of 28th July and 2d August have been received, and I have waited for a leisure hour to reply, but I fear that will never come. I am extremely obliged to you for the attention given to the wants of this Army, and the efforts made to supply them. Our absentees are returning, and I hope the earnest and beautiful appeal made to the country in your proclamation may stir up the whole people, and that they may see their duty, and perform it. Nothing is wanted but that their fortitude should equal their bravery, to insure the success of our cause. We must expect reverses, even defeats. They are sent to teach us wisdom and prudence, to call forth greater energies, and to prevent our falling into great disasters. Our people have only to be true and united, to bear manfully the misfortunes incident to war, and all will come right in the end.

I know how prone we are to censure, and how ready to blame others for the nonfulfillment of our expectations. This is unbecoming in a generous people, and I grieve to see its expression. The general remedy for the want of success in a military commander is his removal. This is natural, and in many instances proper. For, no matter what may be the ability of the officer, if he loses the confidence of his troops disaster must sooner or later ensue.

I have been prompted by these reflections, more than once since my return from Pennsylvania, to propose to your Excellency the propriety of selecting another commander for this Army. I have seen and heard of expressions of discontent in the public journals at the result of the expedition. I do not know how far this feeling extends in the Army. My brother-officers have been too kind to report it, and, so far, the troops have been too generous to exhibit it. It is fair, however, to suppose that it does exist, and success is so necessary to us that nothing should be risked to secure it. I therefore, in all sincerity, request your Excellency to take measures to supply my place. I do this with the more earnestness because no one is more aware than myself of my inability for the duties of my position. I cannot even accomplish what I myself desire. In addition, I sensibly feel the growing failure of my bodily strength. I have not yet recovered from the attack I experienced the past Spring. I am becoming more and more incapable of exertion, and am thus prevented from making the personal examinations and giving the personal supervision to the operations in the field which I feel to be necessary. I am so dull that in making use of the eyes of others I am frequently misled. Everything, therefore, points to the advantages to be derived from a new commander, and I the more anxiously urge the matter upon your Excellency from my belief that a younger and abler man than myself can readily be obtained. I know that he will have as gallant and brave an army as ever existed to second his efforts, and it would be the happiest day of my life to see at its head a worthy leader: one that would accomplish more than I could perform, and all that I have wished. I hope your Excellency will attribute my request to the true reason, my desire to serve my country and to do all in my power to insure the success of her righteous cause.

I have no complaints to make of any one but myself. I have received nothing but kindness from those above me, and the most considerate attention from my comrades and companions in arms. To your Excellency I am specially indebted for uniform kindness and consideration. You have done everything in your power to aid me in the work committed to my charge, without omitting anything to promote the general welfare. I pray that your efforts may at length be crowned with success, and that you may long live to enjoy the thanks of a grateful people. With sentiments of great esteem I am very respectfully and truly yours,

R.E. LEE, General.

THE DEATH OF STONEWALL JACKSON

(1824–1863)

Like other Virginians, Lt. General Thomas Jonathan Jackson was not immediately in favor of secession. Nonetheless, a West Point graduate, he rapidly rose to prominence in Lee's army. At the first battle of Manassas, after General Barnard Bee said of him, "There is Jackson standing like a stone wall," he became, on the instant, a legendary figure. Extremely religious, to the point, some thought, of fanaticism, he was always concerned about the spiritual welfare of his men.

In the lull after the Confederate victory at Fredericksburg, Jackson was visited in camp by his wife and five-month-old daughter. Learning that the Union Army was assembling nearby, he sent them to safety, but that nine-day interlude of domestic bliss appears to have been among the happiest periods of his life.

On May 2, 1863, during the battle of Chancellorsville, Jackson was hit at point-blank range by friendly fire from pickets who mistook him and his men for Union cavalry. Several other Confederate soldiers were killed or wounded. Jackson suffered two flesh wounds and a third that shattered the bone in his left arm above the elbow. The arm was amputated by surgeon Dr. Hunter McGuire, whose account follows. Hearing of Jackson's injury, Lee told his cook, "He has lost his left arm, but I my right." Jackson died of pneumonia eight days later, a bitter blow to Southern morale, despite the nominal Confederate victory.

Supported upon either side by his aides—Captain James P. Smith and Joseph Morrison—the General moved slowly and painfully towards the rear. Occasionally resting for a moment to shake off the exhaustion which pain and the loss of blood produced, he at last reached the line of battle, where most of the men were lying down to escape the shell and canister with which the Federals raked the road. General Pender rode up here to the little party and asked who was wounded, and Captain Smith, who had been instructed by General Jackson to tell no one of his injury, simply answered, "A Confederate officer"; but Pender recognized the General, and, springing from his horse, hurriedly expressed his regret, and added that his lines were so much broken he feared it would be necessary to fall back. At this moment the scene was a fearful one. The air seemed to be alive with the shrieks of shells and the whistling of bullets; horses, riderless and mad with fright, dashed in every direction; hundreds left the ranks and fled to the rear, and the groans of the wounded and dying mingled with the wild shouts of others to be led again to the assault. Almost fainting as he was, from loss of blood, fearfully wounded, and as he thought dying, Jackson was undismayed by this terrible scene. The words of Pender seemed to rouse him to life. Pushing aside the men who supported him, he stretched himself to his full height and answered feebly, but distinctly enough to be heard above the din of the battle: "General Pender, you must hold on to the field; you must hold out to the last."

It was Jackson's last order upon the field of battle. Still more exhausted by this effort, he asked to be permitted to lie down for a few moments, but the danger from the fire, and capture by the Federal advance, was too imminent, and his aids hurried him on. A litter having been obtained, he was placed upon it, and the bearers passed on as rapidly as the thick woods and rough ground permitted. Unfortunately, another one of the bearers was struck down, and the litter having been supported at each of the four corners by a man, fell and threw the General to the ground. The fall was a serious one, and as he touched the earth he gave, for the first time, expression to his suffering, and groaned piteously.

Captain Smith sprang to his side, and as he raised his head a bright beam of moonlight made its way through the thick foliage and rested upon the pale face of the sufferer. The captain was startled by its great pallor and stillness, and cried out: "Oh! General, are you seriously hurt?" "No," he answered, "don't trouble yourself, my friend, about me"; and presently added something about winning the battle first and attending to the wounded afterwards. He was placed upon the litter again, and carried a few hundred yards, when I met him with an ambulance. I knelt down by him and said, "I hope you are not badly hurt, General." He replied very calmly but feebly, "I am badly injured, Doctor; I fear I am dying." After a pause he continued, "I am glad you have come. I think the wound in my shoulder is still bleeding." His clothes were saturated with blood, and hemorrhage was still going on from the wound. Compression of the artery with the finger arrested it until, lights being procured from the ambulance, the handkerchief, which had slipped a little, was readjusted.

His calmness amid the dangers which surrounded him and at the supposed presence of death, and his uniform politeness, which did not forsake him, even under these, the most trying circumstances, were remarkable. His complete control, too, over his mind, enfeebled as it was by loss of blood, pain, &c., was wonderful. His suffering at this time was intense; his hands were cold, his skin clammy, his face pale, and his lips compressed and bloodless; not a groan escaped him—not a sign of suffering except the slight corrugation of his brow, the fixed, rigid face, and the thin lips so lightly compressed that the impression of the teeth could be seen through them. Except these, he controlled by his iron will all evidence of emotion, and more difficult than this even, he controlled that disposition to restlessness, which many of us have observed upon the field of battle, attending great loss of blood. Some whiskey and morphia were procured from Dr. Straith and administered to him, and placing him in the ambulance it was started for the corps field infirmary at the Wilderness tavern. Colonel Crutchfield, his chief of artillery, was also in the ambulance wagon. He had been wounded very seriously in the leg, and was suffering intensely.

The General expressed, very feelingly, his sympathy for Crutchfield, and once, when the latter groaned aloud, he directed the ambulance to stop, and requested me to see if something could not be done for his relief. Torches had been provided, and every means taken to carry them to the hospital as safely and easily as possible. I sat in the front part of the ambulance, with my finger resting upon the artery above the wound, to arrest bleeding if it should occur. When I was recognized by acquaintances and asked who was wounded, the General would tell me to say, "A Confederate officer." At one time he put his right hand upon my head, and pulling me down to him, asked if Crutchfield was dangerously injured. When answered "No, only painfully hurt," he replied, "I am glad it is no worse." In a few moments after Crutchfield did the same thing, and when he was told that the General was very seriously wounded, he groaned and cried out, "Oh, my God!" It was for this that the General directed the ambulance to be halted, and requested that something should be done for Crutchfield's relief.

After reaching the hospital he was placed in bed, covered with blankets, and another drink of whiskey and water given him. Two hours and a half elapsed before sufficient reaction took place to warrant an examination. At 2 o'clock, Sunday morning, Surgeons Black, Walls and Coleman being present, I informed him that chloroform would be given him, and his wounds examined. I told him that amputation would probably be required, and asked if it was found necessary whether it should be done at once. He replied promptly: "Yes, certainly. Dr. McGuire, do for me whatever you think best." Chloroform was then administered, and as he began to feel its effects, and its relief to the pain he was suffering, he exclaimed: "What an infinite blessing," and continued to repeat the word "blessing," until he became insensible. The round ball (such as is used for the smooth-bore Springfield musket), which had lodged under the skin upon the back of his right hand, was extracted first. It had entered the palm about the middle of the hand, and had fractured two of the bones. The left arm was then amputated about two inches below the shoulder, very rapidly and with slight loss of blood, the ordinary circular operation having been made. There were two wounds in his arm. The first and most serious was about three inches below the shoulder-joint, the ball dividing the main artery and fracturing the bone. The second was several inches in length; a ball having entered the outside of the forearm, an inch below the elbow, came out upon the opposite side just above the wrist. Throughout the whole of the operation, and until all the dressings were applied, he continued insensible. Two or three slight wounds of the skin of his face, received from the branches of trees when his horse dashed through the woods, were dressed simply with isinglass plaster.

About half-past 3 o'clock, Colonel (then Major) Pendleton,

the assistant adjutant-general, arrived at the hospital and asked to see the General. He stated that General Hill had been wounded, and that the troops were in great disorder. General Stuart was in command, and had sent him to see the General. At first I declined to permit an interview, but the colonel urged that the safety of the army and success of the cause depended upon his seeing him. When he entered the tent the General said: "Well, major, I am glad to see you. I thought you were killed." Pendleton briefly explained the condition of affairs, gave Stuart's message, and asked what should be done. General Jackson was at once interested, and asked in his quick, rapid way several questions. When they were answered, he remained silent for a moment, evidently trying to think; he contracted his brow, set his mouth, and for some moments was obviously endeavoring to concentrate his thoughts. For a moment it was believed he had succeeded, for his nostril dilated, and his eye flashed its old fire, but it was only for a moment; his face relaxed again, and presently he answered very feebly and sadly, "I don't know, I can't tell; say to General Stuart he must do what he thinks best." Soon after this he slept for several hours, and seemed to be doing well. The next morning he was free from pain, and expressed himself sanguine of recovery. He sent his aide-de-camp, Morrison, to inform his wife of his injuries, and to bring her at once to see him. The following note from General Lee was read to him that morning by Captain Smith: "I have just received your note, informing me that you were wounded. I cannot express my regret at the occurrence. Could I have directed events, I should have chosen, for the good of the country, to have been disabled in your stead. I congratulate you upon the victory, which is due to your skill and energy." He replied: "General Lee should give the praise to God."

About 10 o'clock his right side began to pain him so much that he asked me to examine it. He said he had injured it in falling from the litter the night before, and believed that he had struck it against a stone or the stump of a sapling. No evidence of injury could be discovered by examination. The skin was not broken or bruised, and the lung performed, as far as I could tell, its proper functions. Some simple application was recommended, in the belief that the pain would soon disappear.

At this time the battle was raging fearfully, and the sound of the cannon and musketry could be distinctly heard at the hospital. The General's attention was attracted to it from the first, and when the noise was at its height, and indicated how fiercely the conflict was being carried on, he directed all of his attendants, except Captain Smith, to return to the battlefield and attend to their different duties. By 8 o'clock Sunday night the pain in his side had disappeared, and in all respects he seemed to be doing well. He inquired minutely about the battle and the different troops engaged, and his face would light up with enthusiasm and interest when told how this brigade acted, or that officer displayed conspicuous courage, and his head gave the peculiar shake from side to side, and he uttered his usual "Good, good," with unwonted energy when the gallant behavior of the "Stonewall brigade" was alluded to. He said "the men of that brigade will be some day proud to say to their children, 'I was one of the Stonewall brigade.' " He disclaimed any right of his own to the name Stonewall. "It belongs to the brigade, and not to me." This night he slept well, and was free from pain.

A message was received from General Lee the next morning directing me to remove the General to Guinea's station as soon as his condition would justify it, as there was some danger of capture by the Federals, who were threatening to cross at Ely's Ford. In the meantime, to protect the hospital, some troops were sent to this point. The General objected to being moved, if, in my opinion, it would do him any injury. He said he had no objection to staying in a tent, and would prefer it if his wife, when she came, could find lodging in a neighboring house; "and if the enemy does come," he added, "I am not afraid of them; I have always been kind to their wounded, and I am sure they will be kind to me." General Lee sent word again late that evening that he must be moved if possible, and preparations were made to leave the next morning. I was directed to accompany and remain with him, and my duties with the corps as medical director were turned over to the surgeon next in rank. General Jackson had previously declined to permit me to go with him to Guinea's, because complaints had been so frequently made of general officers, when wounded, carrying off with them the surgeons belonging to their commands. When informed of this order of the commanding-general he said, "General Lee has always been very kind to me, and I thank him." Very early Tuesday morning he was placed in an ambulance and started for Guinea's station, and about 8 o'clock that evening he arrived at the Chandler house, where he remained till he died. Captain Hotchkiss, with a party of engineers, was sent in front to clear the road of wood, stone, etc., and to order the wagons out of the track to let the ambulance pass.

The rough teamsters sometimes refused to move their loaded wagons out of the way for an ambulance until told that it contained Jackson, and then, with all possible speed, they gave the way and stood with hats off and weeping as he went by. At Spotsylvania Courthouse and along the whole route men and women rushed to the ambulance, bringing all the poor delicacies they had, and with tearful eyes they blessed him and prayed for his recovery. He bore the journey well, and was cheerful throughout the day. He talked freely about the late battle, and among other things said that he had intended to endeavor to cut the Federals off from United States ford, and taking a position between them and the river, oblige them to attack him; and he added, with a smile: "My men sometimes fail to drive the enemy from a position, but they always fail to drive us away." He spoke of Rodes, and alluded in high terms to his magnificent behavior on the field Saturday evening. He hoped he would be promoted. He thought promotion for gallantry should be made at once, upon the field and not delayed. Made very early, or upon the field, they would be the greatest incentives to gallantry in others. He spoke of Colonel Willis (subsequently killed in battle), who commanded the skirmishers of Rodes's division, and praised him very highly, and referred to the deaths of Paxton and Boswell very feelingly. He alluded to them as officers of great merit and promise. The day was quite warm, and at one time he suffered from slight nausea. At his suggestion, I placed over his stomach a wet towel, and he expressed great relief from it. After he arrived at Chandler's house he ate some bread and tea with evident relish, and slept well throughout the entire night. Wednesday he was thought to be doing remarkably well. He ate heartily for one in his condition, and was uniformly cheerful.

I found his wounds to be very well to-day. Union by the first intention had taken place to some extent in the stump, and the rest of the surface of the wound exposed was covered with healthy granulations. The wound in his hand gave him little pain, and the discharge was healthy. Simple lint and water dressings were used, both for the stump and hand, and upon the palm of the latter a light, short splint was applied to assist in keeping at rest the fragments of the second and third metacarpal bones. He expressed great satisfaction when told that his wounds were healing, and asked if I could tell from their appearance how long he would probably be kept from the field. Conversing with Captain Smith a few moments afterwards, he alluded to his injuries, and said, "Many would regard them as a great misfortune; I regard them as one of the blessings of my life."

Captain Smith replied: "All things work together for good to those that love God."

"Yes," he answered, "that's it, that's it."

At my request Dr. Morrison came to-day and remained with him. About 1 o'clock Thursday morning, while I was asleep upon a lounge in his room, he directed his servant (Jim) to apply a wet towel to his stomach to relieve an attack of nausea, with which he was again troubled. The servant asked permission to first consult me, but the General knowing that I had slept none for nearly three nights, refused to allow the servant to disturb me, and demanded the towel. About daylight I was aroused, and found him suffering great pain. An examination disclosed pleuro-pneumonia of the right side. I believed, and the consulting physicians concurred in the opinion, that it was attributable to the fall from the litter the night he was wounded. The General himself referred it to this accident. I think the disease came on too soon after the application of the wet cloths to admit of the supposition, once believed, that it was induced by them. The nausea, for which the cloths were applied that night, may have been the result of inflammation already begun. Contusion of the lung, with extravasation of blood in his chest, was probably produced by the fall referred to, and shock and loss of blood prevented any ill effects until reaction had been well established, and then inflammation ensued. Cups were applied, and mercury, with antimony and opium, administered.

Towards the evening he became better, and hopes were again entertained of his recovery. Mrs. Jackson arrived to-day and nursed him faithfully to the end. She was a devoted wife and earnest Christian, and endeared us all to her by her great kindness and gentleness. The General's joy at the presence of his wife and child was very great, and for him unusually demonstrative. Noticing the sadness of his wife, he said to her tenderly: "I know you would gladly give your life for me, but I am perfectly resigned. Do not be sad. I hope I may yet recover. Pray for me, but always remember in your prayers to use the petition, 'Thy will be done.' "

Friday his wounds were again dressed, and although the quantity of the discharge from them had diminished, the process of healing was still going on. The pain in his side had disappeared, but he breathed with difficulty, and complained of a feeling of great exhaustion. When Dr. Breckenridge (who, with Dr. Smith, had been sent for in consultation) said he hoped that a blister which had been applied would afford him great relief, he expressed his own confidence in it, and in his final recovery.

Dr. Tucker, from Richmond, arrived on Saturday, and all that human skill could devise was done to stay the hand of death. He suffered no pain to-day, and his breathing was less difficult, but he was evidently hourly growing weaker.

When his child was brought to him to-day he played with it for some time, frequently caressing it and calling it his "little comforter." At one time he raised his wounded hand above his head and closing his eyes, was for some moments silently engaged in prayer. He said to me: "I see from the number of physicians that you think my condition dangerous, but I thank God, if it is His will, that I am ready to go."

About daylight on Sunday morning Mrs. Jackson informed him that his recovery was very doubtful, and that it was better that he should be prepared for the worst. He was silent for a moment, and then said: "It will be infinite gain to be translated to Heaven." He advised his wife, in the event of his death, to return to her father's house, and added: "You have a kind and good father, but there is no one so kind and good as your Heavenly Father." He still expressed a hope of his recovery, but requested her, if he should die, to have him buried in Lexington, in the Valley of Virginia. His exhaustion increased so rapidly that at 11 o'clock Mrs. Jackson knelt by his bed and told him that before the sun went down he would be with his Saviour. He replied: "Oh, no; you are frightened, my child; death is not so near; I may yet get well." She fell over upon the bed, weeping bitterly, and told him again that the physicians said there was no hope. After a moment's pause he asked her to call me. "Doctor, Anna informs me that you have told her that I am to die to-day; is it so?" When he was answered, he turned his eyes toward the ceiling and gazed for a moment or two as if in intense thought, then replied: "Very good, very good, it is all right." He then tried to comfort his almost heart-broken wife, and told her that he had a great deal to say to her, but he was too weak.

Colonel Pendleton came into the room about 1 o'clock, and he asked him, "Who was preaching at headquarters to-day?" When told that the whole army was praying for him, he replied: "Thank God, they are very kind." He said: "It is the Lord's Day; my wish is fulfilled. I have always desired to die on Sunday."

His mind now began to fail and wander, and he frequently talked as if in command upon the field, giving orders in his old way; then the scene shifted and he was at the mess-table, in conversation with members of his staff; now with his wife and child; now at prayers with his military family. Occasional intervals of return of his mind would appear, and during one of them I offered him some brandy and water, but he declined it, saying, "It will only delay my departure, and do no good; I want to preserve my mind, if possible, to the last." About half-past one he was told that he had but two hours to live, and he answered again, feebly, but firmly, "Very good, it is all right."

A few moments before he died he cried out in his delirium, "Order A. P. Hill to prepare for action! Pass the infantry to the front rapidly! Tell Major Hawks," then stopped, leaving the sentence unfinished. Presently a smile of ineffable sweetness spread itself over his pale face, and he cried quietly and with an expression as if of relief, "Let us cross over the river and rest under the shade of the trees"; and then, without pain or the least struggle, his spirit passed from earth to the God who gave it.

GRANT'S ACCOUNT OF THE SIEGE OF VICKSBURG

(May–July 1863)

After a series of victories in the surrounding area, on May 22, 1863, Major General Ulysses S. Grant and the Army of the Tennessee began a siege of Vicksburg, the fortified city on the Mississippi that was, in President Jefferson Davis's words, the "nail head that holds the two halves of the South together." Six weeks of relentless bombardment followed. On July 4, one day after Lee's loss at Gettysburg, Lieutenant General John C. Pemberton was forced to surrender the city and some thirty thousand troops. On July 9, learning of the capture of Vicksburg, the garrison at Fort Hudson, the last Confederate stronghold on the river, surrendered, giving the Union control of the entire Mississippi. Scott's Anaconda Plan was succeeding; the Confederacy was effectively cut in two.

I now determined upon a regular siege—to "out-camp the enemy," as it were, and to incur no more losses. The experience of the 22d convinced officers and men that this was best, and they went to work on the defences and approaches with a will. With the navy holding the river, the investment of Vicksburg was complete. As long as we could hold our position the enemy was limited in supplies of food, men and munitions of war to what they had on hand. These could not last always.

The crossing of troops at Bruinsburg commenced April 30th. On the 18th of May the army was in rear of Vicksburg. On the 19th, just twenty days after the crossing, the city was completely invested and an assault had been made: five distinct battles (besides continuous skirmishing) had been fought and won by the Union forces; the capital of the State had fallen and its arsenals, military manufactories and everything useful for military purposes had been destroyed; an average of about one hundred and eighty miles had been marched by the troops engaged; but five days' rations had been issued, and no forage; over six thousand prisoners had been captured, and as many more of the enemy had been killed or wounded; twenty-seven heavy cannon and sixty-one field-pieces had fallen into our hands; and four hundred miles of the river, from Vicksburg to Port Hudson, had become ours. The Union force that had crossed the Mississippi River up to this time was less than forty-three thousand men. One division of these, Blair's, only arrived in time to take part in the battle of Champion's Hill, but was not engaged there; and one brigade, Ransom's of McPherson's corps, reached the field after the battle. The enemy had at Vicksburg, Grand Gulf, Jackson, and on the roads between these places, over sixty thousand men. They were in their own country, where no rear guards were necessary. The country is admirable for defence, but difficult for the conduct of an offensive campaign. All their troops had to be met. We were fortunate, to say the least, in meeting them in detail: at Port Gibson seven or eight thousand; at Raymond, five thousand; at Jackson, from eight to eleven thousand; at Champion's Hill, twenty-five thousand; at the Big Black, four thousand. A part of those met at Jackson were all that was left of those encountered at Raymond. They were beaten in detail by a force smaller than their own, upon their own ground. Our loss up to this time was:

	KILLED	WOUNDED	MISSING
Port Gibson	131	719	25
South Fork Bayou Pierre	..	1	..
Skirmishes, May 3	1	9	..
Fourteen Mile Creek	6	24	..
Raymond	66	339	39
Jackson	42	251	7
Champion's Hill	410	1,844	187
Big Black	39	237	3
Bridgeport	..	1	..
Total	695	3,425	259

Of the wounded many were but slightly so, and continued on duty. Not half of them were disabled for any length of time.

After the unsuccessful assault of the 22d the work of the regular siege began. Sherman occupied the right starting from the river above Vicksburg, McPherson the centre (McArthur's division now with him) and McClernand the left, holding the road south to Warrenton. Lauman's division arrived at this time and was placed on the extreme left of the line.

In the interval between the assaults of the 19th and 22d, roads had been completed from the Yazoo River and Chickasaw Bayou, around the rear of the army, to enable us to bring up supplies of food and ammunition; ground had been selected and cleared on which the troops were to be encamped, and tents and cooking utensils were brought up. The troops had been without these from the time of crossing the Mississippi up to this time. All was now ready for the pick and spade. Prentiss and Hurlbut were ordered to send forward every man that could be spared. Cavalry especially was wanted to watch the fords along the Big Black, and to observe Johnston. I knew that Johnston was receiving reinforcements from Bragg, who was confronting Rosecrans in Tennessee. Vicksburg was so important to the enemy that I believed he would make the most strenuous efforts to raise the siege, even at the risk of losing ground elsewhere.

My line was more than fifteen miles long, extending from Haines' Bluff to Vicksburg, thence to Warrenton. The line of the enemy was about seven. In addition to this, having an enemy at Canton and Jackson, in our rear, who was being constantly reinforced, we required a second line of defence facing the other way. I had not troops enough under my command to man these. General Halleck appreciated the situation and, without being asked, forwarded reinforcements with all possible dispatch.

The ground about Vicksburg is admirable for defence. On the north it is about two hundred feet above the Mississippi River at the highest point and very much cut up by the washing rains; the ravines were grown up with cane and underbrush, while the sides and tops were covered with a dense forest. Farther south the ground flattens out somewhat, and was in cultivation. But here, too, it was cut up by ravines and small streams. The enemy's line of defence followed the crest of a ridge from the river north of the city eastward, then southerly around to the Jackson road, full three miles back of the city; thence in a southwesterly direction to the river. Deep ravines of the description given lay in front of these defences. As there is a succession of gullies, cut out by rains along the side of the ridge, the line was necessarily very irregular. To follow each of these spurs with intrenchments, so as to command the slopes on either side, would have lengthened their line very much. Generally therefore, or in many places, their line would run from near the head of one gully nearly straight to the head of another, and an outer work triangular in shape, generally open in the rear, was thrown up on the point; with a few men in this outer work they commanded the approaches to the main line completely.

The work to be done, to make our position as strong against the enemy as his was against us, was very great. The problem was also complicated by our wanting our line as near that of the enemy as possible. We had but four engineer officers with us. Captain Prime, of the Engineer Corps, was the chief, and the work at the beginning was mainly directed by him. His health soon gave out, when he was succeeded by Captain Comstock, also of the Engineer Corps. To provide assistants on such a long line I directed that all officers who had graduated at West Point, where they had necessarily to study military engineering, should in addition to their other duties assist in the work.

The chief quartermaster and the chief commissary were graduates. The chief commissary, now the Commissary-General of the Army, begged off, however, saying that there was nothing in engineering that he was good for unless he would do for a sap-roller. As soldiers require rations while working in the ditches as well as when marching and fighting, and as we would be sure to lose him if he was used as a sap-roller, I let him off. The general is a large man; weighs two hundred and twenty pounds, and is not tall.

We had no siege guns except six thirty-two pounders, and there were none at the West to draw from. Admiral Porter, however, supplied us with a battery of navy-guns of large calibre, and with these, and the field artillery used in the campaign, the siege began. The first thing to do was to get the artillery in batteries where they would occupy commanding positions; then establish the camps, under cover from the fire of the enemy but as near up as possible; and then construct rifle-pits and covered ways, to connect the entire command by the shortest route. The enemy did not harass us much while we were constructing our batteries. Probably their artillery ammunition was short; and their infantry was kept down by our sharpshooters, who were always on the alert and ready to fire at a head whenever it showed itself above the rebel works.

In no place were our lines more than six hundred yards from the enemy. It was necessary, therefore, to cover our men by something more than the ordinary parapet. To give additional protection sand bags, bullet-proof, were placed along the tops of the parapets far enough apart to make loop-holes for musketry. On top of these, logs were put. By these means the men were enabled to walk about erect when off duty, without fear of annoyance from sharpshooters. The enemy used in their defence explosive musket-balls, no doubt thinking that, bursting over our men in the trenches, they would do some execution; but I do not remember a single case where a man was injured by a piece of one of these shells. When they were hit and the ball exploded, the wound was terrible. In these cases a solid ball would have hit as well. Their use is barbarous, because they produce increased suffering without any corresponding advantage to those using them.

The enemy could not resort to our method to protect their men, because we had an inexhaustible supply of ammunition to draw upon and used it freely. Splinters from the timber would have made havoc among the men behind.

There were no mortars with the besiegers, except what the navy had in front of the city; but wooden ones were made by taking logs of the toughest wood that could be found, boring them out for six or twelve pound shells and binding them with strong iron bands. These answered as cochorns, and shells were successfully thrown from them into the trenches of the enemy.

The labor of building the batteries and intrenching was largely done by the pioneers, assisted by negroes who came within our lines and who were paid for their work; but details from the troops had often to be made. The work was pushed forward as rapidly as possible, and when an advanced position was secured and covered from the fire of the enemy the batteries were advanced. By the 30th of June there were two hundred and twenty guns in position, mostly light field-pieces, besides a battery of heavy guns belonging to, manned and commanded by the navy. We were now as strong for defence against the garrison of Vicksburg as they were against us; but I knew that Johnston was in our rear, and was receiving constant reinforcements from the east. He had at this time a larger force than I had had at any time prior to the battle of Champion's Hill.

As soon as the news of the arrival of the Union army behind Vicksburg reached the North, floods of visitors began to pour in. Some came to gratify curiosity; some to see sons or brothers who had passed through the terrible ordeal; members of the Christian and Sanitary Associations came to minister to the wants of the sick and the wounded. Often those coming to see a son or brother would bring a dozen or two of poultry. They did not know how little the gift would be appreciated. Many of the soldiers had lived so much on chickens, ducks and turkeys without bread during the march, that the sight of poultry, if they could get bacon, almost took away their appetite. But the intention was good.

Among the earliest arrivals was the Governor of Illinois, with most of the State officers. I naturally wanted to show them what there was of most interest. In Sherman's front the ground was the most broken and most wooded, and more was to be seen without exposure. I therefore took them to Sherman's headquarters and presented them. Before starting out to look at the lines—possibly while Sherman's horse was being saddled—there were many questions asked about the late campaign, about which the North had been so imperfectly informed. There was a little knot around Sherman and another around me, and I heard Sherman repeating, in the most animated manner, what he had said to me when we first looked down from Walnut Hills upon the land below on the 18th of May, adding: "Grant is entitled to every bit of the credit for the campaign; I opposed it. I wrote him a letter about it." But for this speech it is not likely that Sherman's opposition would have ever been heard of. His untiring energy and great efficiency during the campaign entitle him to a full share of all the credit due for its success. He could not have done more if the plan had been his own.

On the 26th of May I sent Blair's division up the Yazoo to drive out a force of the enemy supposed to be between the Big Black and the Yazoo. The country was rich and full of supplies of both food and forage. Blair was instructed to take all of it. The cattle were to be driven in for the use of our army, and the food and forage to be consumed by our troops or destroyed by fire; all bridges were to be destroyed, and the roads rendered as nearly impassable as possible. Blair went forty-five miles and was gone almost a week. His work was effectually done. I requested Porter at this time to send the marine brigade, a floating nondescript force which had been assigned to his command and which proved very useful, up to Haines' Bluff to hold it until reinforcements could be sent.

On the 26th I also received a letter from Banks, asking me to reinforce him with ten thousand men at Port Hudson. Of course I could not comply with his request, nor did I think he needed them. He was in no danger of an attack by the garrison in his front, and there was no army organizing in his rear to raise the siege.

On the 3d of June a brigade from Hurlbut's command arrived, General Kimball commanding. It was sent to Mechanicsburg, some miles north-east of Haines' Bluff and about midway between the Big Black and the Yazoo. A brigade of Blair's division and twelve hundred cavalry had already, on Blair's return from the Yazoo, been sent to the same place with instructions to watch the crossings of the Big Black River, to destroy the roads in his (Blair's) front, and to gather or destroy all supplies.

On the 7th of June our little force of colored and white troops across the Mississippi, at Milliken's Bend, were attacked by about 3,000 men from Richard Taylor's trans-Mississippi command. With the aid of the gunboats they were speedily repelled. I sent Mower's brigade over with instructions to drive the enemy beyond the Tensas Bayou; and we had no further trouble in that quarter during the siege. This was the first important engagement of the war in which colored troops were under fire. These men were very raw, having all been enlisted since the beginning of the siege, but they behaved well.

On the 8th of June a full division arrived from Hurlbut's command, under General Sooy Smith. It was sent immediately to Haines' Bluff, and General C. C. Washburn was assigned to the general command at that point.

On the 11th a strong division arrived from the Department of the Missouri under General Herron, which was placed on our left. This cut off the last possible chance of communication between Pemberton and Johnston, as it enabled Lauman to close up on McClernand's left while Herron intrenched from Lauman to the water's edge. At this point the water recedes a few hundred yards from the high land. Through this opening no doubt the Confederate commanders had been able to get messengers under cover of night.

On the 14th General Parke arrived with two divisions of

Burnside's corps, and was immediately dispatched to Haines' Bluff. These latter troops—Herron's and Parke's—were the reinforcements already spoken of sent by Halleck in anticipation of their being needed. They arrived none too soon.

I now had about seventy-one thousand men. More than half were disposed across the peninsula, between the Yazoo at Haines' Bluff and the Big Black, with the division of Osterhaus watching the crossings of the latter river farther south and west from the crossing of the Jackson road to Baldwin's ferry and below.

There were eight roads leading into Vicksburg, along which and their immediate sides, our work was specially pushed and batteries advanced; but no commanding point within range of the enemy was neglected.

On the 17th I received a letter from General Sherman and one on the 18th from General McPherson, saying that their respective commands had complained to them of a fulsome, congratulatory order published by General McClernand to the 13th corps, which did great injustice to the other troops engaged in the campaign. This order had been sent North and published, and now papers containing it had reached our camps. The order had not been heard of by me, and certainly not by troops outside of McClernand's command until brought in this way. I at once wrote to McClernand, directing him to send me a copy of this order. He did so, and I at once relieved him from the command of the 13th army corps and ordered him back to Springfield, Illinois. The publication of his order in the press was in violation of War Department orders and also of mine. . . .

On the 22d of June positive information was received that Johnston had crossed the Big Black River for the purpose of attacking our rear, to raise the siege and release Pemberton. The correspondence between Johnston and Pemberton shows that all expectation of holding Vicksburg had by this time passed from Johnston's mind. I immediately ordered Sherman to the command of all the forces from Haines' Bluff to the Big Black River. This amounted now to quite half the troops about Vicksburg. Besides these, Herron and A. J. Smith's divisions were ordered to hold themselves in readiness to reinforce Sherman. Haines' Bluff had been strongly fortified on the land side, and on all commanding points from there to the Big Black at the railroad crossing batteries had been constructed. The work of connecting by rifle-pits where this was not already done, was an easy task for the troops that were to defend them.

We were now looking west, besieging Pemberton, while we were also looking east to defend ourselves against an expected siege by Johnston. But as against the garrison of Vicksburg we were as substantially protected as they were against us. Where we were looking east and north we were strongly fortified, and on the defensive. Johnston evidently took in the situation and wisely, I think, abstained from making an assault on us because it would simply have inflicted loss on both sides without accomplishing any result. We were strong enough to have taken the offensive against him; but I did not feel disposed to take any risk of losing our hold upon Pemberton's army, while I would have rejoiced at the opportunity of defending ourselves against an attack by Johnston.

From the 23d of May the work of fortifying and pushing forward our position nearer to the enemy had been steadily progressing. At three points on the Jackson road, in front of Leggett's brigade, a sap was run up to the enemy's parapet, and by the 25th of June we had it undermined and the mine charged. The enemy had countermined, but did not succeed in reaching our mine. At this particular point the hill on which the rebel work stands rises abruptly. Our sap ran close up to the outside of the enemy's parapet. In fact this parapet was also our protection. The soldiers of the two sides occasionally conversed pleasantly across this barrier; sometimes they exchanged the hard bread of the Union soldiers for the tobacco of the Confederates; at other times the enemy threw over hand-grenades, and often our men, catching them in their hands, returned them.

Our mine had been started some distance back down the hill; consequently when it had extended as far as the parapet it was many feet below it. This caused the failure of the enemy in his search to find and destroy it. On the 25th of June at three o'clock, all being ready, the mine was exploded. A heavy artillery fire all along the line had been ordered to open with the explosion. The effect was to blow the top of the hill off and make a crater where it stood. The breach was not sufficient to enable us to pass a column of attack through. In fact, the enemy having failed to reach our mine had thrown up a line farther back, where most of the men guarding that point were placed. There were a few men, however, left at the advance line, and others working in the countermine, which was still being pushed to find ours. All that were there were thrown into the air, some of them coming down on our side, still alive. I remember one colored man, who had been under ground at work when the explosion took place, who was thrown to our side. He was not much hurt, but terribly frightened. Some one asked him how high he had gone up. "Dun no, massa, but t'ink 'bout t'ree mile," was his reply. General Logan commanded at this point and took this colored man to his quarters, where he did service to the end of the siege.

As soon as the explosion took place the crater was seized by two regiments of our troops who were near by, under cover, where they had been placed for the express purpose. The enemy made a desperate effort to expel them, but failed, and soon retired behind the new line. From here, however, they threw hand-grenades, which did some execution. The compliment was returned by our men, but not with so much effect. The enemy could lay their grenades on the parapet, which alone divided the contestants, and roll them down upon us; while from our side they had to be thrown over the parapet, which was at considerable elevation. During the night we made efforts to secure our position in the crater against the missiles of the enemy, so as to run trenches along the outer base of their parapet, right and left; but the enemy continued throwing their grenades, and brought boxes of field ammunition (shells), the fuses of which they would light with portfires, and throw them by hand into our ranks. We found it impossible to continue this work. Another mine was consequently started which was exploded on the 1st of July, destroying an entire rebel redan, killing and wounding a considerable number of its occupants and leaving an immense chasm where it stood. No attempt to charge was made this time, the experience of the 25th admonishing us. Our loss in the first affair was about thirty killed and wounded. The enemy must have lost more in the two explosions than we did in the first. We lost none in the second.

From this time forward the work of mining and pushing our position nearer to the enemy was prosecuted with vigor, and I determined to explode no more mines until we were ready to explode a number at different points and assault immediately after. We were up now at three different points, one in front of each corps, to where only the parapet of the enemy divided us.

At this time an intercepted dispatch from Johnston to Pemberton informed me that Johnston intended to make a determined attack upon us in order to relieve the garrison at Vicksburg. I knew the garrison would make no formidable effort to relieve itself. The picket lines were so close to each other—where there was space enough between the lines to post pickets—that the men could converse. On the 21st of June I was informed, through this means, that Pemberton was preparing to escape, by crossing to the Louisiana side under cover of night; that he had employed workmen in making boats for that purpose; that the men had been canvassed to ascertain if they would make an assault on the "Yankees" to cut their way out; that they had refused, and almost mutinied, because their commander would not surrender and relieve their sufferings, and had only been pacified by the assurance that boats enough would be finished in a week to carry them all over. The rebel pickets also said that houses in the city had been pulled down to get material to build these boats with. Afterwards this story was verified: on entering the city we found a large number of very rudely constructed boats.

All necessary steps were at once taken to render such an attempt abortive. Our pickets were doubled; Admiral Porter was notified, so that the river might be more closely watched; material was collected on the west bank of the river to be set on fire and light up the river if the attempt was made; and batteries were established along the levee crossing the peninsula on the Louisiana side. Had the attempt been made the garrison of Vicksburg would have been drowned, or made prisoners on the Louisiana side. General Richard Taylor was expected on the west bank to co-operate in this movement, I believe, but he did not come, nor could he have done so with a force sufficient to be of service. The Mississippi was now in our possession from its source to its mouth, except in the immediate front of Vicksburg and of Port Hudson. We had nearly exhausted the country, along a line drawn from Lake Providence to opposite Bruinsburg. The roads west were not of a character to draw supplies over for any considerable force.

By the 1st of July our approaches had reached the enemy's ditch at a number of places. At ten points we could move under cover to within from five to one hundred yards of the enemy. Orders were given to make all preparations for assault on the 6th of July. The debouches were ordered widened to afford easy egress, while the approaches were also to be widened to admit the troops to pass through four abreast. Plank, and bags filled with cotton packed in tightly, were ordered prepared, to enable the troops to cross the ditches.

On the night of the 1st of July Johnston was between Brownsville and the Big Black, and wrote Pemberton from there that about the 7th of the month an attempt would be made to create a diversion to enable him to cut his way out. Pemberton was a prisoner before this message reached him.

On July 1st Pemberton, seeing no hope of outside relief, addressed the following letter to each of his four division commanders:

> Unless the siege of Vicksburg is raised, or supplies are thrown in, it will become necessary very shortly to evacuate the place. I see no prospect of the former, and there are many great, if not insuperable obstacles in the way of the latter. You are, therefore, requested to inform me with as little delay as possible, as to the condition of your troops and their ability to make the marches and undergo the fatigues necessary to accomplish a successful evacuation.

Two of his generals suggested surrender, and the other two practically did the same. They expressed the opinion that an attempt to evacuate would fail. Pemberton had previously got a message to Johnston suggesting that he should try to negotiate with me for a release of the garrison with their arms. Johnston replied that it would be a confession of weakness for him to do so; but he authorized Pemberton to use his name in making such an arrangement.

On the 3d about ten o'clock A.M. white flags appeared on a portion of the rebel works. Hostilities along that part of the line ceased at once. Soon two persons were seen coming towards our lines bearing a white flag. They proved to be General Bowen, a division commander, and Colonel Montgomery, aide-de-camp to Pemberton, bearing the following letter to me:

> I have the honor to propose an armistice for unknown hours, with the view to arranging terms for the capitulation of Vicksburg. To this end, if agreeable to you, I will appoint three commissioners, to meet a like number to be

> named by yourself at such place and hour to-day as you may find convenient. I make this proposition to save the further effusion of blood, which must otherwise be shed to a frightful extent, feeling myself fully able to maintain my position for a yet indefinite period. This communication will be handed you under a flag of truce, by Major-General John S. Bowen.

It was a glorious sight to officers and soldiers on the line where these white flags were visible, and the news soon spread to all parts of the command. The troops felt that their long and weary marches, hard fighting, ceaseless watching by night and day, in a hot climate, exposure to all sorts of weather, to diseases and, worst of all, to the gibes of many Northern papers that came to them saying all their suffering was in vain, that Vicksburg would never be taken, were at last at an end and the Union sure to be saved.

Bowen was received by General A. J. Smith, and asked to see me. I had been a neighbor of Bowen's in Missouri, and knew him well and favorably before the war; but his request was refused. He then suggested that I should meet Pemberton. To this I sent a verbal message saying that, if Pemberton desired it, I would meet him in front of McPherson's corps at three o'clock that afternoon. I also sent the following written reply to Pemberton's letter:

"Your note of this date is just received, proposing an armistice for several hours, for the purpose of arranging terms of capitulation through commissioners, to be appointed, etc. The useless effusion of blood you propose stopping by this course can be ended at any time you may choose, by the unconditional surrender of the city and garrison. Men who have shown so much endurance and courage as those now in Vicksburg, will always challenge the respect of an adversary, and I can assure you will be treated with all the respect due to prisoners of war. I do not favor the proposition of appointing commissioners to arrange the terms of capitulation, because I have no terms other than those indicated above."

At three o'clock Pemberton appeared at the point suggested in my verbal message, accompanied by the same officers who had borne his letter of the morning. Generals Ord, McPherson, Logan and A. J. Smith, and several officers of my staff, accompanied me. Our place of meeting was on a hillside within a few hundred feet of the rebel lines. Near by stood a stunted oak-tree, which was made historical by the event. It was but a short time before the last vestige of its body, root and limb had disappeared, the fragments taken as trophies. Since then the same tree has furnished as many cords of wood, in the shape of trophies, as "The True Cross."

Pemberton and I had served in the same division during part of the Mexican War. I knew him very well therefore, and greeted him as an old acquaintance. He soon asked what terms I proposed to give his army if it surrendered. My answer was the same as proposed in my reply to his letter. Pemberton then said, rather snappishly, "The conference might as well end," and turned abruptly as if to leave. I said, "Very well." General Bowen, I saw, was very anxious that the surrender should be consummated. His manner and remarks while Pemberton and I were talking, showed this. He now proposed that he and one of our generals should have a conference. I had no objection to this, as nothing could be made binding upon me that they might propose. Smith and Bowen accordingly had a conference, during which Pemberton and I, moving a short distance away towards the enemy's lines, were in conversation. After a while Bowen suggested that the Confederate army should be allowed to march out with the honors of war, carrying their small arms and field artillery. This was promptly and unceremoniously rejected. The interview here ended, I agreeing, however, to send a letter giving final terms by ten o'clock that night.

Word was sent to Admiral Porter soon after the correspondence with Pemberton commenced, so that hostilities might be stopped on the part of both army and navy. It was agreed on my paging with Pemberton that they should not be renewed until our correspondence ceased.

When I returned to my headquarters I sent for all the corps and division commanders with the army immediately confronting Vicksburg. Half the army was from eight to twelve miles off, waiting for Johnston. I informed them of the contents of Pemberton's letters, of my reply and the substance of the interview, and that I was ready to hear any suggestion; but would hold the power of deciding entirely in my own hands. This was the nearest approach to a "council of war" I ever held. Against the general, and almost unanimous judgment of the council I sent the following letter:

"In conformity with agreement of this afternoon, I will submit the following proposition for the surrender of the City of Vicksburg, public stores, etc. On your accepting the terms proposed, I will march in one division as a guard, and take possession at eight A.M. to-morrow. As soon as rolls can be made out, and paroles be signed by officers and men, you will be allowed to march out of our lines, the officers taking with them their side-arms and clothing, and the field, staff and cavalry officers one horse each. The rank and file will be allowed all their clothing, but no other property. If these conditions are accepted, any amount of rations you may deem necessary can be taken from the stores you now have, and also the necessary cooking utensils for preparing them. Thirty wagons also, counting two two-horse or mule teams as one, will be allowed to transport such articles as cannot be carried along. The same conditions will be allowed to all sick and wounded officers and soldiers as fast as they become able to travel. The paroles for these latter must be signed, however, whilst officers present are authorized to sign the roll of prisoners."

By the terms of the cartel then in force, prisoners captured by either army were required to be forwarded as soon as possible to either Aiken's landing below Dutch Gap on the James River, or to Vicksburg, there to be exchanged, or paroled until they could be exchanged. There was a Confederate commissioner at Vicksburg, authorized to make the exchange. I did not propose to take him a prisoner, but to leave him free to perform the functions of his office. Had I insisted upon an unconditional surrender there would have been over thirty thousand men to transport to Cairo, very much to the inconvenience of the army on the Mississippi. Thence the prisoners would have had to be transported by rail to Washington or Baltimore; thence again by steamer to Aiken's—all at very great expense. At Aiken's they would have had to be paroled, because the Confederates did not have Union prisoners to give in exchange. Then again Pemberton's army was largely composed of men whose homes were in the South-west; I knew many of them were tired of the war and would get home just as soon as they could. A large number of them had voluntarily come into our lines during the siege, and requested to be sent north where they could get employment until the war was over and they could go to their homes.

Late at night I received the following reply to my last letter:

"I have the honor to acknowledge the receipt of your communication of this date, proposing terms of capitulation for this garrison and post. In the main your terms are accepted; but, in justice both to the honor and spirit of my troops manifested in the defence of Vicksburg, I have to submit the following amendments, which, if acceded to by you, will perfect the agreement between us. At ten o'clock A.M. to-morrow, I propose to evacuate the works in and around Vicksburg, and to surrender the city and garrison under my command, by marching out with my colors and arms, stacking them in front of my present lines. After which you will take possession. Officers to retain their side-arms and personal property, and the rights and property of citizens to be respected."

This was received after midnight. My reply was as follows:

"I have the honor to acknowledge the receipt of your communication of 3d July. The amendment proposed by you cannot be acceded to in full. It will be necessary to furnish every officer and man with a parole signed by himself, which, with the completion of the roll of prisoners, will necessarily take some time. Again, I can make no stipulations with regard to the treatment of citizens and their private property. While I do not propose to cause them any undue annoyance or loss, I cannot consent to leave myself under any restraint by stipulations. The property which officers will be allowed to take with them will be as stated in my proposition of last evening; that is, officers will be allowed their private baggage and side-arms, and mounted officers one horse each. If you mean by your proposition for each brigade to march to the front of the lines now occupied by it, and stack arms at ten o'clock A.M., and then return to the inside and there remain as prisoners until properly paroled, I will make no objection to it. Should no notification be received of your acceptance of my terms by nine o'clock A.M. I shall regard them as having been rejected, and shall act accordingly. Should these terms be accepted, white flags should be displayed along your lines to prevent such of my troops as may not have been notified, from firing upon your men."

Pemberton promptly accepted these terms.

During the siege there had been a good deal of friendly sparring between the soldiers of the two armies, on picket and where the lines were close together. All rebels were known as "Johnnies," all Union troops as "Yanks." Often "Johnny" would call:

"Well, Yank, when are you coming into town?" The reply was sometimes: "We propose to celebrate the 4th of July there." Sometimes it would be: "We always treat our prisoners with kindness and do not want to hurt them;" or, "We are holding you as prisoners of war while you are feeding yourselves." The garrison, from the commanding general down, undoubtedly expected an assault on the fourth. They knew from the temper of their men it would be successful when made; and that would be a greater humiliation than to surrender. Besides it would be attended with severe loss to them.

The Vicksburg paper, which we received regularly through the courtesy of the rebel pickets, said prior to the fourth, in speaking of the "Yankee" boast that they would take dinner in Vicksburg that day, that the best receipt for cooking a rabbit was "First ketch your rabbit." The paper at this time and for some time previous was printed on the plain side of wall paper. The last number was issued on the fourth and announced that we had "caught our rabbit."

I have no doubt that Pemberton commenced his correspondence on the third with a two-fold purpose: first, to avoid an assault, which he knew would be successful, and second, to prevent the capture taking place on the great national holiday, the anniversary of the Declaration of American Independence. Holding out for better terms as he did he defeated his aim in the latter particular.

At the appointed hour the garrison of Vicksburg marched out of their works and formed line in front, stacked arms and marched back in good order. Our whole army present witnessed this scene without cheering. Logan's division, which had approached nearest the rebel works, was the first to march in; and the flag of one of the regiments of his division was soon floating over the courthouse. Our soldiers were no sooner inside the lines than the two armies began to fraternize. Our men had had full rations from the time the siege commenced, to the close. The enemy had been suffering, particularly towards the last. I myself saw our men taking bread from their haversacks and giving it to the enemy they had so recently been engaged in starving out. It was accepted with avidity and with thanks.

Pemberton says in his report:

"If it should be asked why the 4th of July was selected as the day for surrender, the answer is obvious. I believed that upon that day I should obtain better terms. Well aware of the vanity of our foe, I knew they would attach vast importance to the entrance on the 4th of July into the stronghold of the great river, and that, to gratify their national vanity, they would yield then what could not be extorted from them at any other time."

This does not support my view of his reasons for selecting the day he did for surrendering. But it must be recollected that his first letter asking terms was received about 10 o'clock A.M., July 3d. It then could hardly be expected that it would take twenty-four hours to effect a surrender. He knew that Johnston was in our rear for the purpose of raising the siege, and he naturally would want to hold out as long as he could. He knew his men would not resist an assault, and one was expected on the fourth. In our interview he told me he had rations enough to hold out for some time—my recollection is two weeks. It was this statement that induced me to insert in the terms that he was to draw rations for his men from his own supplies.

On the 4th of July General Holmes, with an army of eight or nine thousand men belonging to the trans-Mississippi department, made an attack upon Helena, Arkansas. He was totally defeated by General Prentiss, who was holding Helena with less than forty-two hundred soldiers. Holmes reported his loss at 1,636, of which 173 were killed; but as Prentiss buried 400, Holmes evidently understated his losses. The Union loss was 57 killed, 127 wounded, and between 30 and 40 missing. This was the last effort on the part of the Confederacy to raise the siege of Vicksburg.

On the third, as soon as negotiations were commenced, I notified Sherman and directed him to be ready to take the offensive against Johnston, drive him out of the State and destroy his army if he could. Steele and Ord were directed at the same time to be in readiness to join Sherman as soon as the surrender took place. Of this Sherman was notified.

I rode into Vicksburg with the troops, and went to the river to exchange congratulations with the navy upon our joint victory. At that time I found that many of the citizens had been living under ground. The ridges upon which Vicksburg is built, and those back to the Big Black, are composed of a deep yellow clay of great tenacity. Where roads and streets are cut through, perpendicular banks are left and stand as well as if composed of stone. The magazines of the enemy were made by running passage-ways into this clay at places where there were deep cuts. Many citizens secured places of safety for their families by carving out rooms in these embankments. A door-way in these cases would be cut in a high bank, starting from the level of the road or street, and after running in a few feet a room of the size required was carved out of the clay, the dirt being removed by the door-way. In some instances I saw where two rooms were cut out, for a single family, with a door-way in the clay wall separating them. Some of these were carpeted and furnished with considerable elaboration. In these the occupants were fully secure from the shells of the navy, which were dropped into the city night and day without intermission.

I returned to my old headquarters outside in the afternoon, and did not move into the town until the sixth. On the afternoon of the fourth I sent Captain Wm. M. Dunn of my staff to Cairo, the nearest point where the telegraph could be reached, with a dispatch to the general-in-chief. It was as follows:

"The enemy surrendered this morning. The only terms allowed is their parole as prisoners of war. This I regard as a great advantage to us at this moment. It saves, probably, several days in the capture, and leaves troops and transports ready for immediate service. Sherman, with a large force, moves immediately on Johnston, to drive him from the State. I will send troops to the relief of Banks, and return the 9th army corps to Burnside."

This news, with the victory at Gettysburg won the same day, lifted a great load of anxiety from the minds of the President, his Cabinet and the loyal people all over the North. The fate of the Confederacy was sealed when Vicksburg fell. Much hard fighting was to be done afterwards and many precious lives were to be sacrificed; but the MORALE was with the supporters of the Union ever after.

I at the same time wrote to General Banks informing him of the fall and sending him a copy of the terms; also saying I would send him all the troops he wanted to insure the capture of the only foothold the enemy now had on the Mississippi River. General Banks had a number of copies of this letter printed, or at least a synopsis of it, and very soon a copy fell into the hands of General Gardner, who was then in command of Port Hudson. Gardner at once sent a letter to the commander of the National forces saying that he had been informed of the surrender of

Vicksburg and telling how the information reached him. He added that if this was true, it was useless for him to hold out longer. General Banks gave him assurances that Vicksburg had been surrendered, and General Gardner surrendered unconditionally on the 9th of July. Port Hudson with nearly 6,000 prisoners, 51 guns, 5,000 small-arms and other stores fell into the hands of the Union forces: from that day to the close of the rebellion the Mississippi River, from its source to its mouth, remained in the control of the National troops.

Pemberton and his army were kept in Vicksburg until the whole could be paroled. The paroles were in duplicate, by organization (one copy for each, Federals and Confederates), and signed by the commanding officers of the companies or regiments. Duplicates were also made for each soldier and signed by each individually, one to be retained by the soldier signing and one to be retained by us. Several hundred refused to sign their paroles, preferring to be sent to the North as prisoners to being sent back to fight again. Others again kept out of the way, hoping to escape either alternative.

Pemberton appealed to me in person to compel these men to sign their paroles, but I declined. It also leaked out that many of the men who had signed their paroles, intended to desert and go to their homes as soon as they got out of our lines. Pemberton hearing this, again appealed to me to assist him. He wanted arms for a battalion, to act as guards in keeping his men together while being marched to a camp of instruction, where he expected to keep them until exchanged. This request was also declined. It was precisely what I expected and hoped that they would do. I told him, however, that I would see that they marched beyond our lines in good order. By the eleventh, just one week after the surrender, the paroles were completed and the Confederate garrison marched out. Many deserted, and fewer of them were ever returned to the ranks to fight again than would have been the case had the surrender been unconditional and the prisoners sent to the James River to be paroled.

As soon as our troops took possession of the city guards were established along the whole line of parapet, from the river above to the river below. The prisoners were allowed to occupy their old camps behind the intrenchments. No restraint was put upon them, except by their own commanders. They were rationed about as our own men, and from our supplies. The men of the two armies fraternized as if they had been fighting for the same cause. When they passed out of the works they had so long and so gallantly defended, between lines of their late antagonists, not a cheer went up, not a remark was made that would give pain. Really, I believe there was a feeling of sadness just then in the breasts of most of the Union soldiers at seeing the dejection of their late antagonists.

The day before the departure the following order was issued:

"Paroled prisoners will be sent out of here to-morrow. They will be authorized to cross at the railroad bridge, and move from there to Edward's Ferry, and on by way of Raymond. Instruct the commands to be orderly and quiet as these prisoners pass, to make no offensive remarks, and not to harbor any who fall out of ranks after they have passed."

"My Cave Life in Vicksburg"

Mary Webster Loughborough (1836–1887)

Mary Webster Loughborough was the wife of a Confederate soldier, and like a number of women married to officers, she wanted to be as close to him as safely possible during the long siege of Vicksburg. But in the spring and early summer of 1863, during intense bombardment of the area by federal boats on the Mississippi and ground troops surrounding the city, she and her two-year-old daughter together with other civilians sought refuge in the shallow makeshift caves carved out of the hills surrounding Vicksburg. She writes of her fear of exploding shells and the increasing privation that ensued as the sultry summer weather came on. Mary emerged from the caves for the first time when a truce was called on July 3, 1863, to discuss terms of surrender, which occurred the following day. She recorded her experiences in a journal, first published in 1864.

I was sitting near the entrance, about five o'clock, thinking of the pleasant change—oh, bless me!—that to-morrow would bring, when the bombardment commenced more furiously than usual, the shells falling thickly around us, causing vast columns of earth to fly upward, mingled with smoke. As usual, I was uncertain whether to remain within or run out. As the rocking and trembling of the earth was very distinctly felt, and the explosions alarmingly near, I stood within the mouth of the cave ready to make my escape, should one chance to fall above our domicile. In my anxiety I was startled by the shouts of the servants and a most fearful jar and rocking of the earth, followed by a deafening explosion, such as I had never heard before. The cave filled instantly with powder smoke and dust. I stood with a tingling, prickling sensation in my head, hands, and feet, and with a confused brain. Yet alive!—was the first glad thought that came to me;—child, servants, all here, and saved!—from some great danger, I felt. I stepped out, to find a group of persons before my cave, looking anxiously for me; and lying all around, freshly torn, rose bushes, arbor-vitæ trees, large clods of earth, splinters, pieces of plank, wood, &c. A mortar shell had struck the corner of the cave, fortunately so near the brow of the hill, that it had gone obliquely into the earth, exploding as it went, breaking large masses from the side of the hill—tearing away the fence, the shrubbery and flowers—sweeping all, like an avalanche, down near the entrance of my good refuge.

I stood dismayed, and surveyed the havoc that had been made around me, while our little family under it all had been mercifully preserved. Though many of the neighboring servants had been standing near at the time, not one had been injured in the slightest degree; yet, pieces of plank, fragments of earth, and splinters had fallen in all directions. A portion of earth from the roof of my cave had been dislodged and fallen. Saving this, it remained intact.

That evening some friends sat with me: one took up my guitar and played some pretty little airs for us; yet, the noise of the shells threw a discord among the harmonies. To me it seemed like the crushing and bitter spirit of hate near the light and grace of happiness. How could we sing and laugh amid our suffering fellow beings—amid the shriek of death itself?

This, only breaking the daily monotony of our lives!—this thrilling knowledge of sudden and horrible death occurring near us, told to-night and forgotten in to-morrow's renewal!—this sad news of a Vicksburg day! A little negro child, playing in the yard, had found a shell; in rolling and turning it, had innocently pounded the fuse; the terrible explosion followed, showing, as the white cloud of smoke floated away, the mangled remains of a life that to the mother's heart had possessed all of beauty and joy.

A young girl, becoming weary in the confinement of the cave, hastily ran to the house in the interval that elapsed between the slowly falling shells. On returning, an explosion sounded near her—one wild scream, and she ran into her mother's presence, sinking like a wounded dove, the life blood flowing over the light summer dress in crimson ripples from a death-wound in her side, caused by the shell fragment.

A fragment had also struck and broken the arm of a little boy playing near the mouth of his mother's cave. This was one day's account.

I told of my little girl's great distress when the shells fell thickly near us—how she ran to me breathless, hiding her head in my dress without a word; then cautiously looking out, with her anxious face questioning, would say: "Oh! mamma, was it a mortar tell?" Poor children, that their little hearts should suffer and quail amid these daily horrors of war!

The next evening, about four o'clock, M——'s dear face appeared. He told us that he had heard of all the danger through which we had passed, and was extremely anxious to have us out of reach of the mortar shells, and near him; he also thought we would find our new home on the battle field far superior to this; he wished us to go out as soon as possible. As at this hour in the evening, for the last week, the Federal guns had been quiet until almost sundown, he urged me to be ready in the shortest time possible; so I hastened our arrangements, and we soon were in the ambulance, driving with great speed toward the rifle pits.

O the beautiful sunlight and the fresh evening air! How glowing and delightful it all seemed after my incarceration under the earth! I turned to look again and again at the setting sun and the brilliant crimson glow that suffused the atmosphere. All seemed glad and radiant: the sky—the flowers and trees along our drive—the cool and fragrant breeze—all, save now and then the sullen boom of the mortar, as it slowly cast its death-dealing shell over the life we were leaving behind us.

Were it not for the poor souls still within, I could have clapped my hands in a glad, defiant jubilee as I heard the reports, for I thought I was leaving my greatest fear of our old enemy in the desolate cave of which I had taken my last contemptuous glance; yet, the fear returned forcibly to me afterward.

FROM *THE DIARY OF KATE STONE*

(1842–1907)

In 1861, Kate Stone was a twenty-year-old expecting to enjoy an immediate future of parties and social gatherings, courtship and eventually marriage. She lived with her widowed mother, six brothers, and younger sister at Brokenburn, a prosperous plantation with about one hundred fifty slaves in Madison Parish, Louisiana. But, by 1862, the area had become the focus of the Union campaign to take control of the Mississippi. The population of two thousand whites (as against some seven thousand slaves) had lost most of its eligible males to the Confederate Army, leaving an unprotected civilian population to face the demands of the Union Army and a black population shaking off the shackles of slavery. Formerly subdued and trusted slaves were exercising their long pent-up resentment. Distancing herself from the general "shock" at their behavior, Kate frankly acknowledged, "If I were in their place, I'd do the same."

The Stone family escaped the volatile situation and after a harrowing and humiliating journey became refugees in Tyler, Texas, which Kate described as a "dark corner of the Confederacy" and where Kate bitterly received the news of the fall of Vicksburg and finally Lee's surrender. In 1865, she returned to Brokenburn to find the former plantation empty and defaced; three of her brothers and numerous relatives and friends had lost their lives during the War.

March 20: We have wakened three mornings to the booming of cannon and have gone to sleep to the same music, but we have not heard what they are doing. Sometimes we hear the beating of drums, supposedly at Omega. We are too near "the pomp and circumstance of glorious war" to find it pleasant. No Yankees in this section since Saturday. Perhaps the troops have been concentrated at Vicksburg. The Yankees who passed through the place discussed stopping to raid the house, but the captain with them said, as there were only ladies and children here, they would let us alone. We did not know a Yankee could have so much chivalry. Hope it will develop in the other raiding bands.

The two Mrs. Richardsons and Mrs. Spain went out to camp to get letters of protection. The general gave a letter to Mrs. Spain, as she was a widow, but refused letters to the others unless their husbands or brothers would come out and take the oath. Mr. A. Richardson started the next day to swear allegiance but was dissuaded by a friend. Miss W. Richardson went to the boat with her mother and came back boasting that she had caught a Yankee beau. Imagine any girl falling so low. No other girl in the country would acknowledge having even a Yankee acquaintance. Mrs. Graves' papers did not prove a perfect safeguard as a squad took all their good horses.

Mamma, Mr. Hardison, Mr. Valentine, and Mr. Jeffries seem to be the only people left in the country who have not applied for protection. We hope we shall never be so pressed as to be forced to ask a favor of a Yankee.

March 22: We have had an exciting time since the last date. Two Yankees came out Friday guided by John Graves and carried off my horse Wonka in spite of all we could do.

Wonka was racing around the yard, glad to be at liberty after being tied out so long, when two most villainous-looking Yankees rode up to the gallery where we three ladies and the two children were standing. They had pistols in their hands and proposed a "swap," but we all refused of course and begged them not to take the horse. Mamma even offered to pay the price for him, but the greatest villain of the two refused bluntly and worked himself into a towering rage while the other, the smooth villain, galloped off to catch the horse. I called to one of the Negroes to open the gate, thinking it would give Wonka a chance to escape, but as they seemed afraid I ran to do it myself. When the wretch called to me impudently to stop, I did not notice him but threw the gate open. He then dashed up with the pistol pointed at my head (I thought I had never seen such bright caps) and demanded in the most insolent tone how I dared to open a gate when he ordered it shut. I looked at him and ran on to open the other gate. Just then Mamma called to me that they had caught the horse, and as I turned to go in the house the man cursed and said, "I had just as soon kill you as a hoppergrass." I was not frightened but I was furiously angry and would have been glad to have seen him lying dead. And I never saw Mamma so angry. Aunt Laura took it more calmly, and the little girls were frightened. Johnny was sick with fever. In five minutes the man had changed saddles and was riding my prancing, beautiful pet gaily off, leaving in his place a pack of animated bones, covered with sorrel skin. Some one said it was an old horse taken from Mr. Noland.

I cried the rest of the day and half of the night. We had had the horse tied out in the cane for days, and not ten minutes before the men came, Webster brought him up and said that he would die if he was kept tied up where the mosquitoes could get to him any longer. So I told Webster to turn him in the yard and went out to see, and I never saw him look finer. At that moment the Negroes called from the kitchen that the Yankees were coming, and in a minute they were dashing up to the gallery and in ten minutes more were racing away on my horse.

I think I will never see lilac blooms again without recalling this sad incident. We had all just come in from the garden and had great sprays of the purple flowers in our hands and stuck in the children's hats, and when the Yankees rode away and the excitement subsided we were still holding the tossing, fragrant plumes. This is the third time these same two wretches have been plundering out here. They were of the party that took Mr. Valentine and robbed Mr. Hardison and Mr. McPherson. Friday is the day they come. That must be their furlough time.

The Negroes all behaved very well while the men were here. Most of them hid, and the others did not show the slightest disposition to go with them, though the Yankees asked them to go. They made William help catch the horse by cursing and holding a pistol to his head, and then invited him to go along with them to camp. He refused most positively, and they rode off without doing any further damage. These two returned by way of Mrs. Hardison's, stopping to have a long talk with her Negroes, and took one of her mules, crossing just below the house. The effect of their talk with Mr. Hardison's Negroes came out today when six of the men with their children and clothes walked off in broad daylight after a terrible row, using the most abusive language to Mrs. Hardison. Mr. Hardison expected to get home today and move them all to Monroe, but he has waited too long. The other Negroes declare they are free and will leave as soon as they get ready. Mrs. Hardison sent for Johnny and Mr. McPherson early this morning. Johnny went at once but they could do nothing. None of them have even a gun. A Negro has stolen Mr. Hardison's. But guns are of no use to people in our dilemma. To use one would only be to invite complete destruction from the soldiers.

The river is rising rapidly, and the levee at Lake Providence has been cut. It looks like we are going to be overflowed, a misfortune that we will welcome if it drives the Yankees away. No effort is made to hold the levees; in fact, they spoke of cutting the one at Pecan Grove before the Yankees came up, and it is a pity they did not. A few feet more of water would be a protection as the Yankees would not be able to come out in boats.

This country is in a deplorable state. The outrages of the Yankees and Negroes are enough to frighten one to death. The sword of Damocles in a hundred forms is suspended over us, and there is no escape. The water hems us in. The Negroes on Mrs. Stevens', Mr. Conley's, Mr. Catlin's, and Mr. Evans' places ran off to camp and returned with squads of soldiers and wagons and moved off every portable thing—furniture, provisions, etc., etc. A great many of the Negroes camped at Lake Providence have been armed by the officers, and they are a dreadful menace to the few remaining citizens. The country seems possessed by demons, black and white.

March 24: Storms and rain for two days. There has been almost constant rain since Christmas. The oldest inhabitants say they never saw such persistent rains. It might be the rainy season of the tropics. Some think the cannonading at Vicksburg brings on the rains. It is seldom we hear the cannon that it is not succeeded by showers or a downpour, and often it is difficult to distinguish between the burst of thunder and the roar of the guns.

The firing has been kept up, now fast then slow, for several days until today there is quiet. The sound comes over the water with such distinctness as to rattle the windows, and when the river is low we scarcely hear the guns.

Johnny brought us news Sunday. (Sunday does not seem like

Sunday nowadays. It's always the time of the greatest excitement.) He said that Mrs. Graves was going Monday to see the Yankee general and would try to get my horse returned. That we know is a hopeless job, but we wrote asking her to report the behavior of the two men, giving the names they gave us and telling of their frequent raids out this way. Mrs. Hardison also wrote asking her to represent to the commanding general that there are only women and children in these homes, and, if he will allow marauding parties to continue to harass us, at least to send an officer in charge. Mrs. Graves says that the pickets are very strict now and that it is hard to get through the lines. The Graves have lost twenty of their Negroes. The letters of protection do them no good. Mrs. Hardison's servants have behaved worse than anyone's. They have done everything but strike her and have used very abusive language. The leader is a boy or man, Charles, who ran to the Yankees among the first and soon returned to stay at home. He said he had enough of Yankees.

The life we are leading now is a miserable, frightened one—living in constant dread of great danger, not knowing what form it may take, and utterly helpless to protect ourselves. It is a painful present and a dark future with the wearing anxiety and suspense about our loved ones. We long for news from the outside world, and yet we shudder to think what evil tidings it may bring us. Could we hear that all our soldiers are well, the troubles here at home would seem but light ones.

We beguile the time sewing and reading well-thumbed books, starting at every sound, and in the evening play backgammon or chess. Aunt Laura has just learned backgammon and enjoys playing a game. Little Sister has third-day chills and looks thin and pale. It seems impossible to break them without quinine, and we can get none. Johnny is at last almost well. Beverly's hair has been cut short and she looks like a pretty little boy and is delighted with her appearance.

So my and My Brother's old friend, Joe Wicks, is dead. And he died, as a Southern boy should, leading his men in action. He was adjutant of a Tennessee regiment and was killed in a skirmish near Oxford months ago. What a host of pleasant memories his name awakens—of the happy Clinton days when I was a little girl of twelve off at school for the first time, with My Brother as protector and comforter, and Joe my first little lover. What a gay, guileless time we all had together, boarding there with his sister, Mrs. Rhodes. "Green be the grass above thee, friend of my early years."

[Anchorage, La.] *April 10:* Brother Walter died February 15, 1863, at Cotton Gin, Miss. Again has God smitten us, and this last trouble is almost more than we can bear. I can hardly believe that our bright, merry little Brother Walter has been dead for seven weeks. And we cannot realize that he is gone forevermore. Even peace will not restore him to us all. It is hard, hard that he should have to go, so full of life and happiness and with such promise of a noble manhood. We were always so proud of our six stalwart boys, and again one is snatched away and we cannot think of them without tears. O Father, "Thou has promised Thou wilt not always chide, neither wilt Thou keep Thine anger forever. Have Mercy upon us, O Father, and spare Thou those who are left."

For seven long weeks my dear little brother has been sleeping in his lonely grave, far from all who loved him, and we knew it not until a few days ago. Even as I write, I feel his tears on my cheek and see him as I saw him last when I bade him good-bye in Vicksburg, reining his horse on the summit of the hill and turning with flushed cheeks and tearful eyes to wave me a last farewell. And by the side of this picture is another that has haunted me ever since reading that fatal letter: I see him lying cold and still, dressed in black, in his plain black coffin. His slender hands are worn and brown with the toil of the last four months and are crossed on his quiet breast. His handsome clear-cut features are glaring cold and white, and the white lids are drawn down over the splendid grey eyes, so easy to fill with tears or brighten with laughter. The smile we knew so well is resting on his lips. Happy boy, free from the toil and turmoil of life, safe in the morning of life in a glorious immortality.

It breaks our hearts to think of him sick and dying among strangers, a Negro's face the only familiar one near him. I can hear him asking so eagerly, "Has Brother Coley come?" They say he longed so to see him, and he had been dead two weeks before Brother Coley knew it. All we know of his death is from a letter of Brother Coley's written on the sixteenth of March, the day Van Dorn's cavalry left Arkalona for the raid into Tennessee. Brother Walter had fever but he rode all day. The next morning he still suffered with fever, and he and two other soldiers of his company were left at the house of Mrs. Owens near Cotton Gin, a little town in north Mississippi. Pompey, Joe Carson's boy, was left to wait on him. The next morning the other two soldiers were well enough to follow on, and they carried a note from Mrs. Owens telling Brother Coley that his brother was very sick and that he had better return. He did not get the note for two weeks. Brother Walter had developed a severe case of pneumonia, and on the fifth evening, February 15 at 3 o'clock, he passed away with no friend but Pompey near him. It wrings my heart to think of him suffering and alone. I hope he did not realize that Death was so near and all he loved so far away. Poor little fellow, he was not used to strangers. He has been surrounded by loved and familiar faces all his short life. He was eighteen in December and died in February. He was but a boy and could not stand the hardships of a soldier's life. Four months of it killed him. We have no likeness of him. He has left only a memory and a name.

> He will come not back though all be won,
> Whose young heart beat so high.

[Anchorage, La.] *April 15:* Tomorrow at daybreak we leave here on our way to Monroe [La.]. This has been but a resting place on our journey to the unknown. At Mr. Templeton's on Bayou Macon, we will take a flat for Delhi where we will take the cars for Monroe. We hope to reach there sometime during the night. Jimmy has secured two rooms for us at a Mr. Deane's in the hills four miles from Monroe, across the Ouachita. These are Mamma's plans if she can carry them through, but everything is uncertain from the getting of the flat to the rent of the rooms. No plans are fixed in these troublesome times. First come, first served is the motto. Engagements stand for nothing.

But we must certainly leave here, as we have trespassed on these kind friends for two weeks. Now, they are preparing to move on themselves, and we would surely be in the way. They have been exceedingly kind. No relatives could have been kinder, and Dr. Carson even wants to send us down to Delhi in one of his skiffs, a trip of two days. He is in all the hurry and bustle of moving not only his own family but several hundred Negroes, his own and those belonging to the large Bailey estate, for which he is executor. The more I see of Dr. Carson the more I am impressed with the beauty and nobility of his character. He has a tremendous undertaking before him, so many women and children to be moved and sheltered, and he feels deeply the responsibility. Mamma will not take advantage of his kindness about the skiff. We will get down the Macon from Col. Templeton's someway. Mrs. Carson has given Sister a complete suit of Katie's clothes, as Sister, in our escape from home, got off with only the clothes she had on. She and Katie are the same size, and the clothes fit nicely. She has also given me a pair of nice gaiters such as it would be impossible to buy in the Confederacy. As I have only a pair of old half-worn shoes and can get no more, they are most acceptable. Mamma will get mourning for Sister in Monroe, if possible. We feel that black should be our only wear.

Mrs. Carson and the children will follow us to Monroe in a few days, and we have all planned to go out to Texas together, camping out. "Times change and men change with them"—trite but true. A year ago would we have thought of receiving, or of a friend offering, clothes as a present? Now we are as pleased to receive a half-worn garment from a friend as the veriest beggar that goes from door to door. How else shall we cover our nakedness? We have lost all and as yet can buy nothing. A year ago would we have thought of going even to the house of a friend to spend some time without an invitation? And tomorrow we are all going—seven of us with bag and baggage (very little of that, though)—to stay an indefinite time with a lady we have seen only once, and without any invitation, trusting only that, as she is a lady, she will be kind to us in our distress.

Richmond Bread Riots

(April 2, 1863)

The War had a devastating effect on the Confederate economy. In the Richmond area, farms were stripped by foraging troops, from both North and South. Moreover, the population of the city had doubled since the beginning of the War, resulting in dire shortages of food and goods and a spiraling increase in the cost of what was available.

On April 2, several women marched to Capitol Square and confronted the governor about the situation, but he offered no assurance of assistance. Shouting, "Bread, bread, bread," the women began smashing windows and looting stores. Eventually, their number exceeded one thousand mostly women and children—those left behind by the War.

An alternate account of the riot, more confrontational than the one cited below, describes an encounter with President Davis in which he flings money from his pockets at the women and threatens to have them fired upon if they do not disperse in five minutes. In that account, those who initiated the riot are captured, and some are jailed.

A Richmond woman described the scene in a letter written to a friend on April 2, 1863:

"Something very sad has just happened in Richmond—something that makes me ashamed of all my jeremiads over the loss of the petty comforts and conveniences of life—hats, bonnets, gowns, stationery, books, magazines, dainty food.

"Since the weather has been so pleasant, I have been in the habit of walking in the Capitol Square before breakfast every morning . . . Yesterday, upon arriving, I found within the gates a crowd of women and boys—several hundreds of them, standing quietly together.

BAKERY

"I sat on a bench near, and one of the number left the rest and took the seat beside me. She was a pale, emaciated girl, not more than eighteen . . . As she raised her hand to remove her sunbonnet and use it for a fan, her loose calico sleeve slipped up and revealed the mere skeleton of an arm. She perceived my expression as I looked at it, and hastily pulled down her sleeve with a short laugh. 'This is all that's left of me!' she said. 'It seems real funny, don't it? . . . We are starving. As soon as enough of us get together, we are going to the bakeries and each of us will take a loaf of bread. That is little enough for the government to give us after it has taken all our men.'

". . . The crowd now rapidly increased, and numbered, I am sure, more than a thousand women and children. It grew and grew until it reached the dignity of a mob—a bread riot. They impressed all the light carts they met, and marched along silently and in order. They marched through Cary Street and Main, visiting the stores of the speculators and emptying them of their contents. Governor Letcher sent the mayor to read the Riot Act, and as this had no effect on the crowd, the city battalion came up. The women fell back with frightened eyes, but did not obey the order to disperse.

"The President [Jefferson Davis] then appeared, ascended a dray, and addressed them. It is said he was received at first with hisses from the boys, but after he had spoken some little time with great kindness and sympathy, the women moved quietly on, taking their food with them. General Elze and General Winder wished to call troops from the camps to 'suppress the women,' but [Secretary of War James] Seddon, a wise man, declined to issue the order. While I write women and children are still standing in the streets, demanding food, and the government is issuing to them rations of rice."

The Gettysburg Address

(November 19, 1863)

After the battle of Gettysburg (July 1–3, 1863), many of the dead were hastily laid to rest in shallow graves on the battlefield. Within a few months, seventeen acres of land at the site were purchased to serve as a proper burial place for the Union dead. The cemetery was designed by the landscape architect William Saunders. At the dedication, the process of reburial was far from complete. The highly regarded orator Edward Everett was the principal speaker, and the president was invited to make "a few appropriate remarks." Everett spoke for two hours, Lincoln for under five minutes.

Arguably the most famous speech in American history, the Gettysburg Address was, contrary to popular legend, carefully worked on by Lincoln, though the words "under God" may have been a spur of the moment addition, since they do not appear in the manuscript from which he spoke. (There are in fact five signed manuscripts, each named for the person to whom it was presented, all containing slight variations.) In this speech Lincoln chose to focus not on the specifics of the battle but on the larger issue of the War's significance to the nation and the world. When commended for the speech, Lincoln was said to have expressed relief that it was not a total failure.

Four score and seven years ago our fathers brought forth on this continent a new nation, conceived in liberty, and dedicated to the proposition that all men are created equal.

Now we are engaged in a great civil war, testing whether that nation, or any nation so conceived and so dedicated, can long endure. We are met on a great battle-field of that war. We have come to dedicate a portion of that field, as a final resting place for those who here gave their lives that that nation might live. It is altogether fitting and proper that we should do this.

But, in a larger sense, we can not dedicate, we can not consecrate, we can not hallow this ground. The brave men, living and dead, who struggled here, have consecrated it, far above our poor power to add or detract. The world will little note, nor long remember what we say here, but it can never forget what they did here. It is for us the living, rather, to be dedicated here to the unfinished work which they who fought here have thus far so nobly advanced. It is rather for us to be here dedicated to the great task remaining before us—that from these honored dead we take increased devotion to that cause for which they gave the last full measure of devotion—that we here highly resolve that these dead shall not have died in vain—that this nation, under God, shall have a new birth of freedom—and that government of the people, by the people, for the people, shall not perish from the earth.

Four score and seven years ago our fathers brought forth, upon this continent, a new nation, conceived in Liberty, and dedicated to the proposition that all men are created equal.

Now we are engaged in a great civil war, testing whether that nation, or any nation, so conceived, and so dedicated, can long endure. We are met here on a great battle-field of that war. We have come to dedicate a portion of it as a final resting place for those who here gave their lives, that that nation might live. It is altogether fitting and proper that we should do this.

But in a larger sense we can not dedicate—we can not consecrate—we can not hallow this ground. The brave men, living and dead, who struggled here, have consecrated it far above our poor power to add or detract. The world will little note, nor long remember, what we say here, but can never forget what they did here. It is for us, the living, rather to be dedicated here to the unfinished work which they have, thus far, so nobly carried on. It is rather

1864

In March of 1864 Lincoln finally found his man: Ulysses S. Grant was appointed general in chief. Grant was the single-minded commander, the fearless and relentless soldier, who would satisfy Lincoln's desire to pursue Lee and bring the War home to the South. Grant's appointment was intended to counter the mythic tactical power of Lee, who came to embody the endurance of the Confederacy in the face of overwhelming economic and organizational problems. Grant understood that Lee had to be engaged and defeated at any price. He appreciated the necessity of waging war on the Confederate homeland and destroying its ability and will to continue the fight. Uncontrollable inflation, falling agriculture production (especially in staples), vanishing labor force, transportation breakdowns, and a ravaged landscape were continuing to exhaust the South. Tougher conscription laws in the Confederacy could not replace increasing desertions and mounting battle casualties. Now Grant needed to accelerate that process.

President Lincoln suspended the prisoner exchanges that Grant believed had only served to replenish the Confederate ranks, but the consequences for Union prisoners were especially dire. Andersonville prison in Georgia opened in February and was immediately overcrowded, housing upward of thirty thousand prisoners with little food, poor shelter, and no medical care. These conditions were not surprising, given the scarcity of resources in the South and the priority needs of soldiers in the field. This living death house and others in the North and South imprisoned more than four hundred thousand men, of whom fifty thousand died during the course of the War.

Grant devised a three-pronged assault, with Sherman cutting through the South, Sheridan in the Shenandoah, and Butler moving against Richmond with Grant's admonition that "where Lee goes there you will go also."

Forty days of relentless battles from the Rapidan to the James rivers in May and June began in the densely forested wilderness. Confederate general James Longstreet was seriously wounded, further decimating Lee's leadership corps.

Undaunted by his own high losses, Grant moved against Lee at Spotsylvania and battled for five days. Fighting was especially brutal at "Bloody Angle," where hand-to-hand warfare filled the trenches with bodies. With an increasing disregard for winning and losing or his own casualties, Grant attacked the fortified positions of Lee at Cold Harbor and sustained seven thousand losses in twenty minutes. Even though Lee's casualties were fewer and he won Cold Harbor, in the new calculus, death and attrition weakened his armies' resiliency and recovery. In Grant's endgame, breaking Lee was both a battle plan and a psychological strategy. By midyear Lee recognized that winning had been turned on its head and costly victories like Cold Spring could translate victory into defeat.

A Confederate described the battle at Cold Spring as "a perfect picture of gloom, destruction, and death—a very Golgotha of horrors." Some soldiers pinned their names on their uniforms in hopes of being identified after a battle whose only certain outcome seemed death itself. What sustained them? How did they go on day after day? Religious faith in a redemptive God, commitment to the cause, loyalty to one's state, attachment to charismatic officers and generals, affection for comrades in arms, and a growing sense of resignation—a mix of these sustained warriors on both sides in the last awful year of this the bloodiest of wars.

In a prescient letter, Confederate colonel Edward H. Armstrong asked,

> How will we meet them? They have immense numbers of men, and certainly numbers two to one in our last fight. . . .We must be successful in the end but when will the end be? The South will be as I believe a desert: from one end to the other, all property will be destroyed, and the whole country a wilderness, before this thing ceases. The Yankees have settled heads on our destruction and are resolved to subdue us, though they perish themselves in the attempt. . . .We can hold on for several years. . . .Time

> will show. I am not at all discouraged, though you might think so from reading the above. I would not accept a discharge from the army now if it was given to me. I shall share in its victories and defeats; until I am called to go with many better men who preceded me. I am as firmly resolved now as at first; to go forward in the path of my duty regardless of the consequences.

News of the stalemate in Virginia and the durability of Lee's Army of Northern Virginia gave heart to the Democrats, who nominated former General McClellan to run for president on a peace platform. In spite of some internal pushing and shoving within the party, the Republicans again nominated Lincoln, reaffirmed the policy of unconditional surrender and endorsed a constitutional amendment to end slavery. The outcome now hinged on news from the battlefield. Lincoln felt pessimistic and worried about the soldier vote and made plans for a transition to a new government.

The somber mood in Washington deepened in July, after Confederate general Jubal Early's raid got within five miles of the capital.

In August the tide began to turn with news of Admiral Farragut's naval victory in closing the port at Mobile Bay and further tightening the blockade. In the same month, Sherman moved against Atlanta and defeated General Hood, who had replaced the skilled Joseph Johnston. Sherman promised in a telegram to Halleck, to "make the inside of Atlanta too hot to be endured." On September 1, Atlanta fell. This proved to be a double victory; not only was the gateway to the South in Union hands but Lincoln's reelection was now secured.

The war of attrition shifted from battlefield to civil society. The new targets were the railroads, the factories, the farms, and the homes that supplied the Confederacy. Sherman planned a three-hundred-mile march to the sea. He wrote to General Grant on October 9, 1864, boasting that he would "make Georgia howl." He gave new meaning to living off the land; his men ate well and left a trail of burning barns and sacked homes. The harshness of his action shocked the South and buried any notion of a chivalrous war or respect for civil boundaries. Sherman believed that a "people who will persevere in war beyond a certain limit ought to know the consequences. Many, many peoples with less pertinacity have been wiped out of national existence."

Georgia howled and the Confederacy was now gasping for breath.

"A Reminiscence of Robert E. Lee"

General John Daniel Imboden (1823–1895)

In 1861, Robert E. Lee set aside his personal desire to avoid secession and followed Virginia into the Confederacy. Offered a command in the United States Army by President Lincoln, he was unwilling to consider taking up arms against fellow Virginians.

After an inauspicious start to his Confederate military career, during which time he became known as "Granny Lee" for his presumed timidity at the Battle of Cheat Mountain, Lee, as commander of the Army of Northern Virginia, won major victories at the Second Battle of Manassas, Fredericksburg, and Chancellorsville. Following the failure of his effort to take the fight into the North at Gettysburg, Lee blamed himself and offered to resign. President Davis refused his offer. Lee became commander-in-chief of the Confederate forces only late in the War, in January 1865.

At the end of the War, Lee urged and exemplified a return to full loyalty to the United States government, though politically he sided with those who would keep freed blacks from obtaining voting rights. Lee served for five years as president of Washington College (now Washington and Lee University) and died of pneumonia in 1870. On January 30, 1975, full citizenship was restored to Lee by President Gerald Ford effective June 13, 1865.

One of his staff said of him at the victorious battle of Chancellorsville as he rode at the head of his battalions ". . . as I looked upon him in the complete fruition of the success which his genius, courage, and confidence in his army had won, I thought that it must have been from such a scene that men in ancient days rose to the dignity of gods." That apotheosis, perhaps begun at West Point, where as an undergraduate he failed to receive a single demerit, continues.

General John D. Imboden, a fellow Virginian, had no military training, but acquitted himself with distinction during the Civil War. An interesting aspect of Imboden's prewar political career is that he advocated for the secession of Virginia as an independent state that could serve as a mediator between the North and South to enact a new union with more clearly defined states' rights.

Long before the close of the war General Lee was almost universally regarded by us as the ablest and best of all our generals, and by many as a statesman superior in forecast and judgment to any in the Confederate councils. He was the only man in the South, so far as my knowledge extends, who at the commencement of hostilities, fully appreciated the character and magnitude of the struggle we had engaged in. And I know that even then, while he was hopeful of success, he had serious forebodings of failure.

Virginia seceded on the 17th of April, 1861, and on the 19th we occupied Harper's Ferry with about one thousand volunteer militia under the command of General Kenton Harper of my own county, Augusta. I commanded the artillery of the expedition. The excitement throughout the State was at fever heat, and was intensified in our little army at the "Ferry" by daily rumors that a large force was preparing to move against us from Washington. We had no line of telegraph that we could use to Richmond, and it took two days to send a letter and as long to get a reply. Under these circumstances General Harper, who was urgent for reinforcements, selected me, his county man, to go to Richmond and lay before the military authorities a statement of our condition and necessities. I arrived in the city, I think, on the 2d of May about 12 o'clock, and immediately saw Governor Letcher. From him I learned for the first time that the Convention had conferred the command-in-chief of the Virginia troops on General Lee, and that he had accepted it and established his headquarters in the city. The Governor sent me to him. It was Sunday, and I found the General entirely alone in a small room on Bank street near the Capitol. It was the first time I had met him, and I am sure he was then the handsomest man I had ever seen. His hair and moustache—he wore no beard—were only slightly silvered with gray, just enough to harmonize fully with his rich ruddy complexion, a little bronzed, and to give perfect dignity to the expression of his grand and massive features. His manner was grave, but frank and cordial. He wore a simple undress military suit, without badge or ornament of any kind, and there was nothing in his surroundings to indicate high military rank.

He received my despatches quietly, ran his eye over them hastily, and as General Harper referred to me for additional general information in regard to the situation at the "Ferry," General Lee, by a series of questions directly to the point, soon obtained from me every fact I possessed, and informed me that by 12 o'clock the next day he would have his despatches ready for me.

I rose to take my leave, when he asked me to resume my seat, remarking that he wished to talk with me about the condition of the country, and the terrible storm which was so soon to burst upon it in all its fury. Alluding to the fact that I had represented Augusta, the most populous and wealthy county in the State, for several years in the Legislature, he said he desired to impress me as he should endeavor to impress every other Virginian he met, whose position might be assumed to give him some influence over the people of his acquaintance, with the gravity and danger of our situation, and the imperative necessity for immediate and thorough preparation for defence. Growing warm and earnest, he said: "I fear our people do not yet realize the magnitude of the struggle they have entered upon, nor its probable duration and the sacrifices it will impose upon them. The United States Government," he said, "is one of the most powerful upon earth. I know the people and the Government we have to contend with. In a little while they will be even more united than we are. Their resources are almost without limit. They have a thoroughly organized government, commanding the respect and, to some extent, the fears of the world. Their army is complete in all its details and appointments, and it will be commanded by the foremost soldier of the country, General Scott, whose devotion to the

Union cause is attested by his drawing his sword against his native State. They have also a navy that in a little while will blockade our ports and cut us off from all the world. They have nearly all the workshops and skilled artisans of the country, and will draw upon the resources of other nations to supply any deficiency they may feel. And above all, we shall have to fight the prejudices of the world, because of the existence of slavery in our country. Our enemies will have the ear of other powers, while we cannot be heard, and they will be shrewd enough to make the war appear to be merely a struggle on our part for the maintenance of slavery; and we shall thus be without sympathy, and most certainly without material aid from other powers. To meet all this we have a government to form, an army to raise, organize, and equip, as best we may. We are without a treasury and without credit. We have no ships, few arms, and few manufactures. Our people are brave and enthusiastic, and will be united in defence of a just cause. I believe we can succeed in establishing our independence, if the people can be made to comprehend at the outset that to do so they must endure a longer war and far greater privations than our fathers did in the Revolution of 1776. We will not succeed until the financial power of the North is completely broken, and this can occur only at the end of a long and bloody war. Many of our people think it will soon be over, that perhaps a single campaign and one great battle will end it. This is a fatal error, and must be corrected or we are doomed. Above all, Virginians must prepare for the worst. Our country is of wide extent and great natural resources, but the conflict will be mainly in Virginia. She will become the Flanders of America before this war is over, and her people must be prepared for this. If they resolve at once to dedicate their lives and all they possess to the cause of constitutional government and Southern independence, and to suffer without yielding as no other people have been called upon to suffer in modern times, we shall with the blessing of God succeed in the end; but when it will all end no man can foretell. I wish I could talk to every man, woman, and child in the State now, and impress them with these views."

This is almost literally his language, though many of the positions taken by him were elaborated and enforced with the greatest earnestness. His views made a most profound impression on me at the time, and, as he designed, were afterwards repeated whenever the opportunity occurred. He talked in this way to many others. One corroborative anecdote I recall. Colonel T. S. Flournoy, once a leading Whig member of Congress from Virginia, and the opponent of Henry A. Wise in 1855 for Governor, had been a Union member of the Secession Convention; but when the State went out he was one of the first to raise a regiment of cavalry for the field, which was mustered into service early in 1861. A gallant son of Colonel F., who was afterwards killed in battle, was captain of a splendid company of young fellows well mounted; but the Governor, having only called for infantry, did not accept them, much to their disappointment. Thereupon they prevailed on Colonel Flournoy, who was in the Convention, to see General Lee and appeal to him to use his influence with Governor Letcher to accept the company as cavalry, or they would dismount and go in as infantry. General Lee listened attentively, and when he had heard all the facts he replied: "Colonel Flournoy, tell your son to go home and drill his men thoroughly, and not to become impatient. They will have the opportunity to see service to their hearts' content, and the time will come when they will be far more anxious to get out of the army than they now are to get in." His prediction proved to be literally true.

The prophetic forecast of General Lee became widely known, and as subsequent events verified his judgment, it aided materially in giving him that control over the public mind of the South that enabled him often by a simple expression of his wishes to procure larger supplies and aid for his army than the most stringent acts of Congress and merciless impressment orders could obtain. The people came to regard him as the only man who could possibly carry us through the struggle successfully. The love of his troops for him knew no bounds, because they had implicit faith in his ability, and knew he was a sympathizing friend in all their trials. I witnessed an incident that showed his tenderness of heart and sympathy for his men.

About a week after the seven days' battles around Richmond, which ended in McClellan's retreat to the James at Harrison's Landing, I had business at headquarters, then established about three miles out of Richmond. On my arrival I learned he had been called to town by President Davis, but would return about noon. By the time he came half a dozen generals were waiting for him. He saw them one at a time and despatched their business, and they departed. My business required me to wait till a written order could be prepared for me. During this delay a fine-looking, tall, and stalwart soldier came in, dressed in dirty shirt and trousers, and with an old slouch hat in his hand. The General accosted him: "Well, my man, what can I do for you?"

"General, I have come straight to headquarters to get a furlough for a few days."

The General said: "Don't you know I have issued a general order that no furloughs can be granted at this time?"

"Yes; that order was read at dress-parade last night, and that's the reason I have come to you, for I knew it was no use for me to apply through my captain and colonel."

"Then do you expect me to be the first to disregard my own orders?"

"Yes, General; and if you will listen to me, I think you will do it."

"Well, let me hear what you have to say."

"You see, General, I am from the Eastern Shore of Maryland. I left my wife and children there last summer on my farm with plenty of 'niggers' to support them well, and came over and volunteered for the war. I have been in all the fights, and have never been absent a day from duty. I get letters from home now and then, and everything has been going on well till lately. Here is a letter from my wife, brought over lately by some scouts, and she says since the Yankees have got to scouting about there the 'niggers' are doing badly, and she thinks they will all run away. Now, General, I am.in for the war, and my wife backs me in it, but you see if I lose them 'niggers' it will leave my wife and little children in a mighty bad fix. I want a furlough for about a week. I know where I can get a boat and some help, and I'll go over there some dark night and bring the 'nigger' men over here and hire them out to support my family. My mind will then be easy, and I'll never ask for another furlough. Now, General, take the thing home to yourself and you can't refuse me, I know."

The General directed him to wait on the porch outside and he would think about it. The man retired, and the General walked the room several times and remarked to those present, "That is a hard case. That man is evidently honest and truthful, and I am sure is a good soldier, and the poor fellow is in great trouble. But I can't violate my own orders and give him a furlough." After some reflection he remarked, "I have it," and called to one of his staff and said, "Ascertain that man's name, company, and regiment, and make an order detailing him for secret service across the Potomac for ten days." He then informed the soldier what he had done, and directed him to cross the river and procure all the information he could, and before his return he might make his own arrangements about his negroes, and when he came back to report any information he obtained about the enemy to headquarters.

It was this sort of interest in his men that endeared him so much to them. At the time of this incident his mind was occupied with the great events of the preceding two weeks, and, with his generals and the Cabinet at Richmond, he was doubtless absorbed with the gravest public questions; and yet he took time to hear a soldier's story of family troubles, and actually to invent a way to relieve him without impairing his discipline.

The great simplicity of his habits was another ground of popularity. He fared no better than his troops. Their rough, scant rations were his as well. There were times when for weeks our army had nothing but bread and meat to live on, and not enough of that. On one occasion some molasses was obtained and sent to the field. One of General Lee's staff who was caterer that week—that is, he drew the rations for the headquarters mess—set a small pitcher of molasses before the General at dinner, who was delighted to eat it with his hot corn-bread. Seeing his satisfaction, the catering colonel remarked, "General, I secured five gallons for headquarters." "Was there so much for every mess the size of ours?" said the General. "Oh, no. The supply won't last a week." "Then I direct, Colonel, that you immediately return every drop you have, and send an order that no molasses shall be issued to officers or men except the sick in hospital." The Colonel was dumfounded, and never afterward boasted of his superior providence as caterer for the mess.

When the two armies were on the opposite banks of the Rappahannock in the winter of '63–'64, meat was sometimes very scarce in ours. Even the usual half-pound per diem ration could not always be issued. During one of these periods of scarcity, on a very stormy day, several corps and division generals were at headquarters, and were waiting for the rain to abate before riding to their camps, when General Lee's negro cook announced dinner. The General invited his visitors to dine with him. On repairing to the table a tray of hot corn-bread, a boiled head of cabbage seasoned with a very small piece of bacon, and a bucket of water constituted the repast. The piece of meat was so small that all politely declined taking any, expressing themselves as "very fond of boiled cabbage and corn-bread," on which they dined. Of course the General was too polite to eat meat in the presence of guests who had declined it. But later in the afternoon, when they had all gone, feeling very hungry, he called his servant and asked him to bring him a piece of bread and meat. The darkey looked perplexed and embarrassed, and after scratching his head some time said in a deprecating tone, "Lord, Mas Robert, dat meat what I sot before you at dinner warn't ours. I had jest burrowed dat piece of middlin' from one of de couriers to season de cabbage in de pot, and seein' as you was gwine to have company at dinner I put on de dish wid de cabbage for looks. But when I seed you an' none of de genelmen toche it I 'cluded you all knowed it was borrowed, and so after dinner I saunt it back to de boy whar it belonged to. I's mighty sorry, Mas Robert, I didn't know yon wanted some, for den I would a trick a piece off'n it any how 'fore I saunt it home."

So the General got no meat that day. Anecdotes like these, founded on actual fact, would spread through the army, and often reconciled a hungry, ragged Confederate to his hardships.

General Lee never indulged himself in any of the formal pomps of high military rank. All was simplicity around him, and he was as accessible to the private soldier as to the corps commander. But there was a grandeur and dignity of character about the man that was a perfect barrier to all levity of deportment and unbecoming familiarity in his presence. He was possessed, too, of the loftiest courage, and his men knew it. On one occasion in battle a portion of his line gave way under a terrible fire, and when rallied showed some hesitation in resuming their lost ground. He rode to the front and ordered them to follow him. Not a man moved. Some one cried out:

"General! that's no place for you, and we will not move an inch until you go to our rear, and then we will charge the enemy."

He had to yield, and as he rode slowly back a wild yell went up, and at a run the line rushed forward, regained their position, and drove the enemy back.

Can the world wonder that when this leader laid down his

sword and ordered his handful of ragged and famishing veterans to stack arms as prisoners of war, and bade them a long and last farewell, they crowded round his horse in weeping groups, and in the excess of their sorrowing embraces almost pulled him to the ground?

"BURIED ALIVE"

Dan Tyler (Harper's Weekly, May 6, 1864)

"Buried Alive" is based on a firsthand account of one of the ugliest racial incidents in the Civil War. On April 12, 1864, General Nathan Bedford Forrest and a Confederate cavalry division captured the Union garrison at Fort Pillow, Tennessee, and proceeded, after the surrender, to kill almost all of the black troops, some of whom were burned or buried alive. White Union soldiers were also massacred. The atrocity foregrounded the question of how captured black soldiers were to be treated—as rebellious slaves or prisoners of war.

A congressional commission on the conduct of the war investigated the incident, and Daniel Tyler, a private in Company B, 6th United States Heavy Artillery, recovering from injuries received at Fort Pillow, gave sworn testimony. The commission concluded that a massacre had occurred. There was general outrage in the North and even a call from within Lincoln's cabinet for the killing of an equal number of Confederate prisoners in retaliation. While condemning the massacre, Lincoln rejected the idea of retaliation in kind, insisting instead that it was the army's responsibility to make the enemy feel that black soldiers were indeed Union troops.

General Forrest was never prosecuted and after the War became the first Imperial Wizard of the Ku Klux Klan.

My name is Daniel Tyler, and my skin is dark, as my mother's was before me. I have heard that my father had a white face, but I think his heart and life were blacker than my mother's skin. I was born a slave, and remained a slave until last April, when I found deliverance and shelter under the flag that

my master was fighting to dishonor. I shall never forget the day when freedom came to me. I was working in the fields down in Alabama, my heart full of bitterness and unutterable longings. I had dreamed for two long years of escape from my bondage; the thought sung to me through the dark nights, and filled all the days with a weird sort of nervous expectation. But my dreams had proved nothing more than dreams; the opportunity I yearned for did not come. But that day, working in the fields, suddenly along the dusty road there flashed a long column of loyal cavalry, the old flag flying at its head. How my heart leaped at the sight; how, like revelation, came the thought: "This, Daniel Tyler, is your opportunity!" Need I tell you how I acted upon that thought; how, in one second of time, I leaped out of slavery into freedom, and from a slave became a man?

Well, joining the flashing column, I rode with them for days, coming at last into Baton Rouge, and thence, having joined a regiment of my own people, came to Memphis. Thence four hundred of us came to Fort Pillow. But there are not four hundred of us today, for three hundred and odd were murdered in cold blood only a week ago by Forrest's rough-riders.

It was a day of horrors—that 12th of March. There were seven hundred of us in all in the fort—three hundred whites of the Thirteenth Tennessee Cavalry, and four hundred blacks, as I have said, all under command of brave Major Booth. The fort consisted simply of earth-works, on which we had mounted half a dozen guns. We knew that Forrest had been pillaging the country all about us, and imagined that perhaps he would pay us a visit; but the thought did not alarm us, though we knew, those of us who were black, that we had little to expect at the hands of the rebels. At last, about sunrise on the morning of the 12th, Forrest, with some 6,000 men, appeared and at once commenced an attack. We met the assault bravely, and for two hours the fight went on briskly. Then a flag of truce came in from Forrest, asking an unconditional surrender, but Major Bradford—Major Booth having been wounded—declined to surrender unless the enemy would treat those of us who were black as prisoners of war, which, of course, they refused to do, and the fight went on. The enemy, in the next few hours, made several desperate charges, but were each time repulsed. At last, about four o'clock in the afternoon, they sent in another flag. We ceased firing out of respect to the flag; but Forrest's men had no such notions of honor and good faith. The moment we stopped firing they swarmed all about the fort, and while the flag was yet withdrawing, made a desperate charge from all sides. Up to that time only about thirty of our men had been hurt. But in this charge, the enemy got within the earth-works, and forthwith there ensued a scene which no pen can describe. Seeing that all resistance was useless, most of us threw down our arms, expecting, and many begging for, quarter. But it was in vain. Murder was in every rebel heart; flamed in every rebel eye. Indiscriminate massacre followed instantly upon our surrender. Some of us, seeking shelter, ran to the river and tried to conceal ourselves in the bushes, but for the most part in vain. The savages, pursuing, shot down the fugitives in their tracks. There was Manuel Nichols, as brave a soldier as ever carried a musket. He had been a free negro in Michigan, but volunteered a year ago to fight for the Union. He, with others, had sought a shelter under the bank of the river, but a cold-blooded monster found him, and putting a pistol close to his head, fired, failing however to kill the brave fellow. He was then hacked on the arm, and only a day after died, delirious, in the hospital. Then there was Robert Hall, another colored soldier, who was lying sick in the hospital when the massacre commenced. The devils gashed his head horribly with their sabres, and then cut off part of his right hand, which he had lifted in a mute appeal for mercy. Then there was Harrison, of the Thirteenth Tennessee, who was shot four times after surrender, and then robbed of all his effects. Before I was shot, running along the river bank, I counted fifty dead Union soldiers lying in their blood. One had crawled into a hollow log and was killed in it, another had got over the bank in the river, and on to a board that run out into the water, and when I saw him was already stark and stiff. Several had tried to hide in crevices made by the falling bank, and could not be seen without difficulty, but they were singled out and killed. One negro corporal, Jacob Wilson, who was down on the river bank, seeing that no quarter was shown, stepped into the water so that he lay partly under it. A rebel coming along asked him what was the matter: he said he was badly wounded, and the rebel, after taking from his pocket all the money he had, left him. It happened to be near by a flat-boat tied to the bank. When all was quiet Wilson crawled into it, and got three more wounded comrades also into it, and cut loose. The boat floated out into the channel and was found ashore some miles below. There were, alas, few such fortunate escapes.

I was shot near the river just about dark. Running for my life, a burly rebel struck me with his carbine, putting out one eye, and then shot me in two places. I thought he would certainly leave me with that, but I was mistaken. With half a dozen others, I was at once picked up and carried to a ditch, into which we were tossed like so many brutes, white and black together. Then they covered us with loose dirt, and left us to die. Oh, how dark and desolate it was! Under me were several dead, and right across my breast lay a white soldier, still alive! How he clutched and strained! How, hurt and weak as I was, with only one hand free, I struggled for air and life, feeling my strength waning every moment! It was a strange thing to lie there buried, and yet be able to think and pray. Maybe, friend, you have known what agony was, but you never had such pains of soul as I had down there in that living grave. I thought I could feel the worms gnawing at my flesh; I am sure I had a taste of what death is, with the added pain of knowing that I was not dead, and yet unable to live in that dark, dismal tomb. So I clutched and strained and struggled on, digging upward as I could with my one puny hand. At last—oh joy!—a faint streak of light looked in; my hand had carved an avenue to the world of life! But would I dare to lift my head? Might not some rebel, standing by, strike me down again on the moment? But I could not die there in that grave; I must escape. Slowly, painfully, I rolled the burden from my breast—he was dead by that time—and then carefully crept out from that living death. It was dark, and no one was near. A moment I stood up on my feet; then?

The next thing I remember I was in the hospital where I am now. They had found me just where I fell, and brought me to a place of safety, where, after a while, consciousness returned. I have been here a week now; and I think I shall get well. I lie in the cot where poor Robert Hall lay when he was butchered by the rebels. They showed me, yesterday, a letter he had written the day before the massacre to his wife. He had learned to read and write at Memphis, after his enlistment, and used to send a message to his wife and children, who still remained there, every week or so. This was his letter which a surgeon had helped him put together:

"Dear Mammy"—it ran—"I am very sick here in the hospital, but am better than I was, and hope to get well soon. They have been very kind to me; and I find it very sweet to suffer for the dear flag that gives me shelter. You must not worry on my account. Tell Katy she must not forget to say her prayers and to study her lessons carefully now while she has an opportunity. And, mammy, take good care of the baby; I dreamed of her last night, and I think how sad it would be to die and never see her little face again. But then chaplain says it will be right in heaven, and he knows better than we do. And, mammy, don't forget we are free now; teach both the darlings to be worthy of their estate."

That was poor Hall's letter—it had not been sent, and we have no heart to send it now. He will never see the baby's face here; but then God may let him see it up yonder! I hope to recover and get away from here very soon; I want to be in my place again; for I have something to avenge now, and I can not bear to wait. Poor Hall's blood is crying to me from the ground; and I want to be able, sometime, to say to Manuel Nichols's wife, up there in Michigan, that his fall has had its compensation. And may God speed the day when this whole slaveholders' rebellion—what remains of it—shall be "Buried Alive!"

Black Soldiers' Petition for Equal Pay

The battle for emancipation notwithstanding, discriminatory practices infiltrated the Union military. Though black troops served with distinction, their use was curtailed by suspicion and prejudice. Black enlisted men were inevitably commanded by white officers. Black soldiers were paid $10 per month, from which $3 was automatically deducted for clothing, while white soldiers received $13 per month with no deduction. In early June of 1864, Private Sylvester Ray of the Second U.S. Colored Cavalry was recommended for trial because he refused to accept pay inferior to that of white soldiers. Later that same month, Congress passed a resolution requiring equal pay for the U.S. Colored Troops and made the action retroactive. Black soldiers were to receive the same rations and supplies and comparable medical care as well.

Your Excellency, Abraham Lincoln:

Your Excellency will pardon the presumption of an humble individual like myself, in addressing you, but the earnest Solicitation of my Comrades in Arms beside the genuine interest felt by myself in the matter is my excuse. . . . The main question is, Are we Soldiers, or are we Labourers? We are fully armed, and equipped, have done all the various Duties pertaining to a Soldier's life, have conducted ourselves to the complete satisfaction of General Officers, who were, if anything, prejudiced against us, but who now [after Fort Wagner] afford us all the encouragement and honor due us. . . .

Now, your Excellency, we have done a Soldier's Duty. Why Can't we have a Soldier's pay? You caution the Rebel Chieftain, that the United States knows

no distinction in her Soldiers. She insists on having all her Soldiers of whatever creed or Color, to be treated according to the usages of War. Now if the United States exacts uniformity of treatment of her soldiers from the Insurgents, would it not be well and consistent to set the example herself by paying all her Soldiers alike?

We of this Regt. were not enlisted under any "contraband" act. But we do not wish to be understood as rating our Service of more Value to the Government than the service of the ex-slave. Their Service is undoubtedly worth much to the Nation, but Congress made express provision touching their case, as slaves freed by military necessity, and assuming the Government to be their temporary Guardian. Not so with us. Freemen by birth and consequently having the advantage of thinking and acting for ourselves so far as the Laws would allow us, we do not consider ourselves fit subject for the Contraband act.

We appeal to you, Sir,   to have us justly Dealt with.   Our Patriotism, our enthusiasm will have a new impetus, to exert our energy more and more to aid our Country. Not that our hearts ever flagged in Devotion . . . but We feel as though our Country spurned us, now that we are sworn to serve her. Please give this a moment's attention.

—James Henry Gooding

The Battle of Mobile Bay (August 5, 1864)

Harrie Webster, Third Assistant Engineer, USS *Manhattan* (dates not known)

As the War progressed, especially after the capture of New Orleans and Galveston in 1862, Alabama's Mobile Bay became crucial to the Confederacy. As the Anaconda continued to squeeze the South, other ports along the Gulf of Mexico were neutralized by the Union blockade, and Mobile Bay was the only open port east of Texas; it became the principal site for blockade running. Ships filled with goods—some containing military supplies, others consumer products much in demand in the South—left Nassau, Havana, and Bermuda attempting to sneak by the Union Navy.

The naval war, led by rear Admiral David Farragut, ultimately became a battle of new technologies: Northern ironclad ships versus the Southern ironclad *Tennessee* and the Confederate torpedoes (sunken mines) in the harbor at Mobile.

About half past seven, while the action was at its height, our gun had just been revolved for a shot at Fort Morgan, a momentary view was had of the *Tecumseh,* and in that instant occurred the catastrophe whereby a good ship filled with men, with a brave captain, in the twinkling of an eye vanished from the field of battle.

A tiny white comber [a long curling wave] of froth curled around her bow, a tremendous shock ran through our ship as though we had struck a rock, and as rapidly as these words flow from my pen the *Tecumseh* reeled a little to starboard, her bows settled beneath the surface, and while we looked her stern lifted high in the air with the propeller still revolving, and the ship pitched out of sight like an arrow twanged from the bow. We

were steaming slowly ahead when this tragedy occurred and, being close aboard of the ill-fated craft, we were in imminent danger of running foul of her as she sank. "Back hard" was the order shouted below to the engine room, and, as the *Manhattan* felt the effects of the reversed propeller, the bubbling water round our bows, and the huge swirls on either hand, told us that we were passing directly over the struggling wretches fighting with death in the *Tecumseh.*

The effect on our men was in some cases terrible. One of the firemen was crazed by the incident. But the battle was not yet over. After coming to a standstill for a few minutes, during which the commotion of the water set up by the foundered ship passed away, the *Manhattan* steamed ahead into line and took the duty by now being performed by her lost consort. As the *Tecumseh* sank to the bottom, the crew of the *Hartford* sprang to her starboard rail and gave three ringing cheers in defiance of the enemy and in honor of the dying.

Perhaps some drowning wretch on the *Tecumseh* took that cheer in his ears as he sank to a hero's grave, and we may imagine the sound as it pierced the roar of battle, giving courage to some fainting heart as his face turned for the last time to the light of that sun whose rising and setting was at an end for him.

But Mobile Bay was yet before us. Immediately following the events just related, my tour of duty in the turret ended for the time being, and I once more returned to the engine room. The first effect of going from the cool air of the turret to the terrible heat of the engine room was that of a curious chilliness. This, in a minute or two, was succeeded by a most copious perspiration, so violent that one's clothing became soaking wet, and the perspiration coursing down the scantily clothed body and limbs, filled the shoes so that they "chuckled" as one walked.

At 150 F. the glass in a lantern will crackle and break, the lamps burn dimly, and it is impossible to handle any metal with the bare hands. Pieces of canvas, like flat-iron holders [flat irons were heated on a hot stove and then used to press or iron clothing; holders were similar to hot pads] alone enable one to grasp a handrail or valve handle. Of course frequent bulletins of the fight were brought to the poor devils sweating their lives out in the engine room, and we got some idea of what was going on through the signal which at frequent intervals came from the pilot house. . . . The sounds produced by a shot striking our turret were far different from what I had anticipated. The scream of the shot would arrive at about the same time with the projectile, with far from a severe thud, and then the air would be filled with that peculiar shrill singing sound of violently broken glass, or perhaps more like the noise made by flinging a nail violently through the air. The shock of discharge of our own guns was especially hard on the ears of those in the turret, and it seemed at times as though the tympanums must give way. . . . At about eight o'clock the fire on our port hand began to slacken, and the word was passed below that the wooden fleet had entered the bay and that the fight was over.

"In the Libby"

Except for Andersonville in southwest central Georgia, the Libby was the most notorious prison in the Confederacy. Located in Richmond, Virginia, the Libby (its name came from the sign left on the building by the previous owner) was a hastily converted former tobacco warehouse comprising three four-story attached buildings. Intended for no more than a thousand prisoners, the buildings held up to forty-two hundred men at one time. Prisoners were confined to the two top floors, where it was stiflingly hot in the summer and freezing in the winter. Living conditions were extremely bad; the food, sometimes lacking altogether, was poor; and sanitation was practically nonexistent. Illnesses such as scurvy, chronic diarrhea, dysentery, and typhoid pneumonia killed several men daily. Bodies were left in a cellar until a wagonload was accumulated and carted away. There is no verifiable death toll from the Libby; in 1864 the captured soldiers held there were removed to Georgia prisons. All records from the Libby were destroyed at the end of the War.

The following article was published in *Harper's Weekly* on February 20, 1864.

I could never think of Jem as dead, though I certainly had no definite grounds for my belief to stand on—in the very teeth, too, of the formidable fact that all effort to find him—and many and strenuous ones had been made—had thus far proved futile. He had enlisted as a private—Jem had always a dash of romance about him—and had thereby nothing to distinguish him in that awful mangled heap at Gettysburg; and yet I could never fancy his poor body lying under that mournful slab raised for "the unknown," though bankrupt of reason for my conviction.

So when I found myself at Richmond, with that curious aptness of the soul for winnowing out the few grains of good perdue in a whole harvest of evil, my heart gave a quick upward bound at the thought, "Perhaps I shall find Jem here"—Jem was my younger brother, and my pet from petticoats up—otherwise the outlook wasn't too bright.

The rebels had made a dash on our hospital, which was in about as good fighting condition as the general run of hospitals, took fifty of our boys out of their beds, among them one poor fellow, Simms I think, with his leg just off, and their surgeons; probably by way of padding for an article in the Examiner—I know of no other reason, as we were all non-combatants, and they had already mouths enough to feed—and there we were, huddled together in the street, Eugene Delacroix, a cool, resolute fellow, Robert Allan, and myself, with our poor men lying all about, some groaning and ghastly with pain, and the most merciless sun beating down upon us, scorching out our very lives as we stood there three mortal hours. Probably some red tape was to be unwound somewhere—but at last they brought carts into which they huddled our sick and wounded and dashed off, jolting and jostling them as they drove recklessly over the rough pavement very much after the manner of a butcher with a load of calves.

Allan said something about it and was immediately overhauled by the Chief of Police, the Provost Marshal, and Heaven knows what all; and then we were relieved by the Richmond authorities of whatever money we were so unfortunate as to have about us, and marched with lighter pockets, if not hearts, to Libey Prison. Then I began to look out for Jem and got my first sup of disappointment. They had placed us of course in the officers' room. Jem was a private, and might be one of the hundred and fifty tramping noisily over our heads, or in some of the rooms below, or in some other prison; and in either case he might almost as well have been in Soudan for all hope of meeting him; or, and it was my last hope, he might be in the hospitals, where it was possible that we should be allowed to do service. Delacroix suggested that. The room, our future prison, was in the third story and crowded, for there were already some two hundred officers confined there. The air was stifling, loaded with so many breaths; the hot glaring sun beat in pitilessly at the broken unshaded window, added to which, at that moment, were the fumes of the single stove allowed for the cooking of the rations. Ah! If the tender, white-handed mothers and wives, if the gay girls dancing in Northern ball-rooms could but have looked in this bare, cheerless, unceiled room, with unglazed panes at best, and frequently only bits of canvas and strips of boards nailed over the openings, unplastered walls, unevery thing belonging to common decency or comfort, I think their merriment would have grown half-terrible to them, and, through the sweet delirious waltz-music, would sound out something like a wail! Each day a certain number among us were detailed for cooking and scrubbing service, and in due course of time I had my turn at both, and fell into it, I think quite naturally; but I could never get over my secret wonder at Delacroix when similarly employed, he was so precisely the man that it was impossible to imagine in any such predicament—I had always an undefined notion that the laws of nature contained a special clause for his benefit, and that no dilemma would ever dare face him, much less offer him its horns.

As for poor Allan he succumbed at once, and went about in a very miserable way indeed, though men of more calibre might be pardoned for being a little down on their luck. There were put up bare wooden bunks for about half of us; the rest must sleep on the floor: pillow and mattresses there were none—a blanket you might have if you were fortunate enough to have brought one with you—otherwise none. The rations were scanty; but water, the muddy, brackish water of the James River, was even more sparingly dealt out. I thought of the old border-riders vowing candles as long as their whingers to St. Mary when in a scrape. I would have given one as long as the Bunker Hill monument to St. Croton could he have interfered in our behalf. Not specially heroic this, but still I maintain worth the chronicling; for to keep up good heart and firm courage, as the majority of our men did, unwashed, unrested, half-starved, as we soon were, and treated like dogs through long monotonous days of a dreary and cheerless captivity, needs more pluck—enduring pluck of the kind that will bear a strain on it, than ever was required for a forlorn hope. Meanwhile the days crawled on—dragged is too fast a word for prison time—and constantly I was on the sharp look-out for fun. As Delacroix had said, we soon obtained access to the hospitals for Union soldiers, visiting them daily. They were three in number, and from the first hour of our entrance I should have thought complaint a blasphemy. They used to bring there the poor wretches from the tobacco factories and

Belle Isle, worn almost to skeletons, sometimes with the skin literally dried on the bone, moving masses of filth and rags, snatching at any article of food as they passed, groveling and struggling weakly for it like dogs, many of them actually in the agonies of death, taken there that they might be said to have died in hospital. In one day the ambulance brought us eighteen, and eleven out of them died; in fact, we saw little but such sombre processions. We had little medicine to give them, and no food but a scanty measure of corn-bread and sweet potatoes; and this for men down with dysentery and typhoid pneumonia. These, too, were men in the last stages of disease; hundreds more, fit subjects for hospital treatment, were left on the island and in the prisons for lack of hospital accommodation. In the three Union hospitals the average of deaths was forty a day. We lived in an atmosphere of death; corpses were on every side of us. We did what we could; but after all it was little more than standing with our hands fast bound to witness sufferings that we could not alleviate. I had done looking for Jem. I hoped now that he was dead. Better that his handsome head lay low among a heap of unknown slain than to have been tortured all these months in a Richmond prison.

Our own condition was not improving. The weather was growing colder, and the wind whistled most unpromisingly through our broken windows. Stoves were put up, but no fuel was given to burn in them; and sleeping on bare planks, without mattress or covering, was getting to be a problem. There was a falling off also in the matter of rations—corn-bread and two ounces of rice now was our daily allowance; added to this, daily brutality and insolence on the part of the under-keepers, dead silence from home, and the long, hopeless winter setting in; but the edge of all this was blunted for me by the hospital horrors. My very sleep was dreadful with dying groans and pitiful voices calling on those who, thank God! will never know how they died.

One morning the ambulance had brought a load of fourteen from the island, and when I came to the hospital, a little later than usual, I found Delacroix standing by the side of one of them—a young man, judging from the skeleton-like but still powerful frame—an old one, from the pinched and ghastly face—a dying one, at all events. Used as we were to horrors, I saw that Delacroix was laboring under some unusual emotion. He was white to the very lips. I understood why when he muttered in my ear the word "Starving!" Low as it was uttered, the poor boy caught the word.

"Yes," he said, feebly. "It is quite useless, gentlemen—no," turning from the bread that Delacroix offered, "I loathe it now. For days and days I have been mad for it. I have had murder in my heart. I thought if one died the rest might live. Once we caught a dog and roasted him, and quarreled over the bits. We had no cover; we lay on the scorching sand, and when the terrible heats were over came the raw fogs and bitter wind."

He stopped, seemingly from exhaustion, and lay a few moments silent; then the pitiful voice commenced again.

"We were very brave for a while; we thought help was coming. We never dreamed they could go on at home eating, lying soft, and making merry while we were dying by inches. I think if my brother knew? If ever you get back I charge you, before God, find out Robert Bence, surgeon of the____ Maine. Tell him that his brother Jem starved to death on Belle Isle, and that thousands more are—Ah! just Heaven! the pain again! O Christ! help me! have?!

The words died away in inarticulate ravings. He tossed his arms wildly over his head; his whole frame racked with the most awful throes. And this was my poor boy; so wasted, so horribly transformed, that I had not known him. His glazing eyes had not recognized me. His few remaining hours were one long, raving agony. He never knew that his brother was by his side. I died over and over again, standing there in my utter helplessness. I had never so thanked God as when his moaning fell away into the merciful silence of death. Delacroix, who had remained with me, vented his grief and wrath in the bitterest curses; but I was stunned. My grief was so vast that I could not then fully comprehend it. There were in store for me days of future horror, hours of sickening remembrance of his agony, of maddening thought of that most awful and protracted torture; cold, hunger, disease, despair, all at once; but then I waited in silence till they had taken him away, with the nine others dead out of the fourteen brought there in the morning, and then went mechanically back with Delacroix. It was after sundown, but the first sight that saluted us in the prison was a row of pails and brushes, and the keepers detailing the officers for the duty of scrubbing. At that Delacroix burst out, angrily,

"How the devil do you think we are going to sleep on these

floors after they are scrubbed, and without fires to dry them? Is your Government trying to kill us with sleeplessness, since it can't starve us out? Already we have walked all one night this week, because lying down was impossible."

The keeper turned, with an ugly grin on his brutal face: "Since you are so delicate you can try the dungeons for a day or two. You won't be troubled with scrubbing there; and you find the company that is fit for a Yankee—in the vermin."

So Delacroix was marched off to the dungeons, as poor Davies had been the week before, though scarcely over the typhoid fever—as Major White and Colonel Straight have since been, and many another hapless officer, for a trivial offense or none at all. They kept him there three days in that noisome hole. He came out looking a little pale, but plucky as ever. The spite of a brutal man is a hound that never tires. The keeper watched his opportunity, swore that he saw Delacroix looking out a window (this high offense was punishable with death), and put him down again—for four days, this time. Then we got another turn of the hand-screw. We were no longer allowed to attend the hospitals. Delacroix's eyes flashed.

"There goes the last obstacle to escape. While I thought I could be of use to our poor fellows here I would not go; but now—I have had plenty of time to think down there, and I have thought to purpose. I have a plan. If you like you can try it with me; if not, I go alone."

To know how sounded that word "escape" one must first have realized a prison. The risk was enormous, and failure meant the damp dungeons of the Libey, of which Delacroix gave no alluring description. The plan, however, was feasible. By agreement each managed to secure a sleeping-place near the door, and when all was quiet stole out, shoes slung about our necks, to the upper story, where was a sky-light, through which we were soon out on the roof, and in present possession of our freedom, though it was to be regretted that it was so many stories high. We went straight to the end of our roof, Delacroix, in his walks, having noted that the second building above us was empty; but the adjoining house, unfortunately, was a two-story building, so that we were forced to descend by help of the lightning-rod, which Delacroix did well enough, going down hand over hand with the ease of a cat; while I, less agile, met with one or two slips, and came down with a final thump, which should have startled the guards below, but did not, luckily for us. Then we found ourselves on a level with the third-story window of the next house—the empty one. "But how if it shouldn't be empty?" I whispered. "It is empty," returned Delacroix, energetically, leaning across the little chasm of division to open the sash. "Now, will you go first?"

In I went—bare floor—empty rooms—open doors; that looked uninhabited, at any rate. Delacroix followed; and then we began to make our way down in the Egyptian darkness, getting several stumbles, and nearly breaking our necks on the last flight of stairs—a most villainous one. The lower door was bolted, but, being on the inside, it proved no such mighty matter to open it. Then there was a cold, damp rush of air, and we dimly made out that we were in a small back yard, over-looked by tall buildings, showing ghost-like against the sky. The gate was locked, and we did not stop to pry it open, but took the fence in gallant style, and away! Scarce any one was stirring, and walking leisurely through the dark and quiet streets, by morning light we were well out of Richmond; and now commenced the real perils of our journey; first the brightening light, which urged us to all possible speed in finding a cover. Delacroix had a pocket-compass, and by it we struck a north-easterly course, going on bravely till presently we came plump on a fort—peril number two. "Down!" whispered Delacroix, dropping on hands and knees in the grass. I followed his example in all haste, and so we wormed our way some hundred yards onward. Suddenly Delacroix clutched my wrist. Something was vibrating in the air—a dull, heavy, regular sound, caught all the more readily from our nearness to the ground, and with it a curious, faint tinkle, growing nearer, sounding out loudly now on the raw air. Both exclaimed, at the same instant, "Cavalry, by George!" It was an even chance whether they would ride us down or miss us; but there was nothing left save to crouch lower in the grass, and crouch we did. Doubtless some sweet saint at home was praying for us, for the chance proved in our favor. On they came, at an easy gallop, spurs and sabres jingling, and chatting carelessly; passed us, little dreaming who were their neighbors for that moment; died away into silence the echo of hoofs and tinkle of spurs. But now daylight was a very positive affair indeed, further travel too dangerous, and even Delacroix admitted, with a groan, that remaining where we were was our only safety.

"Remaining where we were" sounds like ease and rest—a peaceful phrase, in fact, conveying a notion of repose; but it was a marvelously hard thing to do. There was the probability of discovery; then, spite of peril, we were in a very desperation of sleepiness, and dropping off continually, to wake up in a panic, fancying that our foes were upon us. We were chilled to the heart; what with night-dews, and raw air, the dampness of the earth, and the enervation of our imprisonment; and as the day wore on we grew ravenous as wolves. Surely night was never before half so welcome, though words have not in them an expression of the difficulties of our way. The sacred soil stuck to our tired feet as if it had been in the Secession interest, and were all the briars sworn rebels they could not have caught and torn us more persistently. Once we floundered into a morass. "Courage," quoth Delacroix, "the Libey dungeons are worse." Twenty times over I should have lain down in a sullen despair, had it not been for his undaunted courage, pushing on spite of everything, himself included.

Daybreak found us in the "open," quite out of reach of any cover. A little ahead the road turned sharply, cutting off our view, but both heard a sound of singing, to which quick steps sounding out in the frosty air kept time, and the singing and walking grew every moment plainer. It was coming toward us. Delacroix laid a hand on his pistols, but I had already caught the words,

"Berry early in de mornin', when de Lor' pass by, when de Lor' pass by, and invite me to come," chanted to one of the barbaric refrains, so often heard on the plantations, and stayed his hand. The next moment the singer same in sight—a negro, as I had thought. He would have passed us without seeming to notice, but Delacroix stopped him, saying, briefly, "We are Union officers, runaways from Richmond; weary, starving, and in want of a hiding-place. Will you help us?"

A sudden gleam lighted up the man's dark face. "Sartain, mas'r. De Linkum men fight for poor nigga—nigga help when he kin. Dis chile hide mas'r safe as ef he be in Washington."

"And if he betrays us—"

"I'll blow his brains out," returned Delacroix, promptly.

"Small consolation that."

"It is our only chance, at any rate, and besides the sky won't fall. He is honest."

But for all that he watched him like a cat. At the first suspicious move our colored friend would have found short shrift. I had my hand on my knife, and Delacroix's revolver was in dangerous readiness. As yet, however, there was no need for action. We met not a soul, and guiding us to a fodder-house, he assured us that we might rest there at ease till dark. We were so dead tired that we scarcely waited for the end of his assurance before we threw ourselves on the floor and were off asleep. From a rest as deep and sweet as the peace of Heaven I was startled by a hand on my shoulder. My knife was out on the instant. "Cut de pone, mas'r, not me," cried our negro guide, retreating in some alarm. He had brought us some corn pones. We fell on them like starved wolves, and then off to sleep again, till the dark made it safe to recommence our journey. Our guide did not take the road, however, but struck across toward what we recognized as the colored quarters of a plantation. "Supper first," he observed, sententiously, ushering us into one of the low wooden buildings. We had expected solitude and silence, and got a shock. The room was crowded, and fresh comers pouring in every moment.

"It is a trap!" cried Delacroix. "We are betrayed."

"Mas'r too quick," answered our guide; "dis am a 'spression ob de feelin' in de cullud brest, dat all. Ebery one, big and little, come to bress de Lor'and de brave Linkum ossifers. Hercules, gib de gemmen seats; you, Cesar," to a little grinning twelve-year-old imp, "quit dat yer. Git de oder little chaps and deflect youselves as pickets. Sojer march roun'and roun', gun on he shoulder: hold he head so high. Can't eben see poor nigga, he sech great man. O Lor'! tink de nigga no 'count; neber tink we hab pickets too, and de Linkum men right under he nose, he! He! Sue, push dat yer chicken dis way. Lizy, gib us de pone and milk. Don' stan' nudgin' and winkin'. Step about gals, be spry."

It was plain that this was a man in authority, though how much was due to calibre, and how much to a ragged military coat, minus the buttons, and a hat, curiously jammed and broken, was too delicate an analysis for men in our condition. The room was crowded, for the news of our hiding had gone from mouth to mouth through the entire plantation, and every soul was there to welcome us. There was little or no noise; but the intense, thrilling excitement on every dusky face was a thing not soon to be forgotten. "Telled ye so!" cried one old woman; "allers said de good Lor' hear de groanin' and sighin' sometime.

Oh! chil'en, I pray night and day all dese yer years sence dey sell away my little Sue. 'O Lor', make dem like a wheel'; and ole Sam, he say dat a debil's prayer; but I hearn it in de Bible—hearn Mas'r Arnold read it he ownself; and now, sure enuf, de Lor' hab make 'em no 'count—jest like a wheel rollin', rollin', can't fin' no rest till dey roll straight down to eberlastin' ruin; and de jubilee's comin' and de Lor' bress dese men dat bring it. De Lor' ob glory keep 'em safe; and oh! mas'r, tell de good Linkum men strike hard—he's groanin' sech a weary time."

She was interrupted by our guide, who plainly thought his prerogative in danger.

"Dat's enuf, ole Susan. Curus how women's tongues kin run. Time to sperse, laides and gemmen, and, 'member now, no noise. Now ef mas'r's ready—"

The sentence was completed by a sudden dropping of his military coat and dignity together, placing him at once in his former light of an every day member of society. The remainder of our journey had in it little of adventure. Our guide led us around the pickets, moralizing all the way on, "He hold he head so high—tink nigga no 'count," and ferried us across the Mattapony. Here we were given into the keeping of another negro, passed a damp but monotonous day in the woods, were treated to another plantation supper; then another day hiding, another night in pushing through morass and forest, another guide. As good old Bunyan has it, "we were bemired to purpose"—were torn and foot-sore; but at last we reached the Rappahannock. There our guide left us, and there we passed a day watching men oystering in the river, and wishing for a few of them on shore. The programme was simple now. We had only to wait till midnight, take one of the gun-boats; but oh! those hours of chilled and aching waiting!

The friends who welcomed us with open arms gazed at us with a sort of terror, so wan, ragged, haggard, ghastly, was our appearance. Delacroix looked at least five years older; while I—but small marvel if I have changed—I have always in my ears that moaning voice, "Tell him that his brother Jem starved to death on Belle Isle!" I have the vision before me night and day of that writhing frame, that lone, raving agony; and there are thousands more to freeze and starve! God help them!

The Campaign of 1864

Lincoln was not popular during his first term in office. Particularly objectionable to many were the Emancipation Proclamation and the draft. In the extremely contentious election campaign of 1864, Lincoln, the Republican incumbent, was running against Democrat George McClellan, who had served as a major general in the War and, after being removed from command by Lincoln for his indecisiveness, left the military. The biggest issue in the campaign was how the increasingly unpopular and costly War was going to be ended. The "Copperheads," also called "Peace Democrats," supported a peace agreement between the Union and the Confederacy at all costs, even if this meant giving up on the Union or compromising with the Southern states.

The ballads on these song sheets, which doubled as election posters, spell out clearly the terms of the contest, as in this verse from the one opposite:

Kind folks if you will listen I'll sing to you a song
It's all about the people's nomination
Of the present Backwoods lawyer the Country's had enough
And we want a true statesman for that station
Who shall we nominate?
To save the ship of state
From wrecking in the sea of dissolution
The people shout McClellan he has proved himself a man
That will stand by the laws and Constitution.

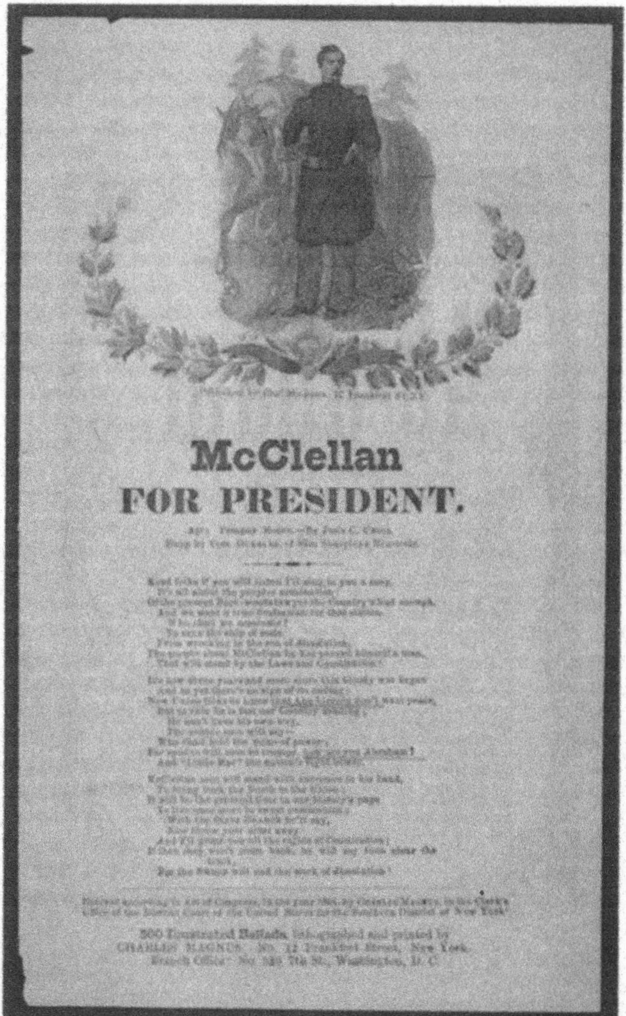
McClellan
FOR PRESIDENT.

No. 591.
Filed September 17. 1864
by H. Cann

SECOND COMING
OF
"Abraham."

The First Chapter of Cann's Prophecy.

Entered according to Act of Congress, in the year 1864, by H. Cann, in the Clerk's Office, of the District Court of the Eastern District of Pennsylvania.

And ABRAHAM shall come again unto us, and the people of the Earth will rejoice and clap their hands and shout for joy; and Abraham shall have power over the Ruler of the South, and many of them which are astray shall cling to him to be saved; and they shall cry with a loud voice begging to come back under the old flag, and then Abraham will say unto them, How often would I have gathered you together but you were joined to your Idol Davis so we cannot let you alone.

Oh ye Davisites! how can ye rebel against your Country, ye backsliding rebels. I now say unto you, that the people of this country will say on the second Tuesday of November, 1864, that I shall return again unto the White House on the fourth of March, 1865, the place which the people of the United States shall appoint unto me, that the people of the South may give up their wicked ways and live to the laws of their Country, and then the multitude of the people shall clap their hands with joy and the old Flag of our Country shall wave in triumph forever, and the rebels shall cry out, Oh Abraham! oh Abraham! Come and save us from destruction, poverty and dishonor, and we will come back and live in union again forever.

1233

Long Abraham Lincoln a Little Longer.

The Fall of Atlanta

(September 1–2, 1864)

Between May and August of 1864, Major General William Tecumseh Sherman's Union forces conducted a protracted campaign to capture Atlanta, considered a critical rail and manufacturing center. However, for the Confederacy, Atlanta was strategic in another way. Knowing that the North was rapidly tiring of the War, the South hoped to fend off the attack on Atlanta and so dampen Lincoln's chances of reelection. But Sherman's relentless bombardment devastated the city, which suffered additional destruction from extensive, unchecked fires. General Hood's Confederate troops were forced to evacuate, and, on September 1 and 2, the city fell, reviving Northern spirits, solidifying Lincoln's reelection chances in November, and giving Sherman a free hand to begin his march to the sea and consolidate the destruction of the heart of the South.

Sherman's March to the Sea

(November 15–December 21, 1864)

William Tecumseh Sherman (1820–1891)

The march to the sea traces a military maneuver from the capture of Atlanta to the fall of Savannah. Under General William Tecumseh Sherman, some sixty-two thousand Union soldiers marched in two columns cutting a sixty-mile swath of destruction over a distance of nearly three hundred miles. There were few civilian casualties and only sporadic military resistance.

Sherman's objective was the destruction of railroad lines, bridges, cotton gins, and other infrastructure and the confiscation of horses, cattle, wagons, food, and vegetables. He employed "bummers," foraging soldiers who plundered the land to keep the Union Army provisioned. Among the principles of engagement laid out by the general were to use aggression only with resisters, not to enter the homes of the inhabitants, and to leave some provision for those civilians who remained behind during the winter months. Of course the practice was hard to control once foraging began. This unopposed destruction of the heart of the South resulted in fairly complete demoralization. The Cause was truly lost.

The army reached Savannah in early December. On December 21, the mayor surrendered in exchange for the protection of lives and property of the citizens. Sherman sent a telegraphed message to President Lincoln: "I beg to present you as a Christmas gift the City of Savannah, with one hundred and fifty guns and plenty of ammunition, also about twenty-five thousand bales of cotton."

It is said that Sherman hated the song "Marching Through Georgia" (1865), which was routinely played whenever he appeared at public gatherings.

[SPECIAL FIELD ORDERS, NO. 119]

HEADQUARTERS MILITARY DIVISION OF THE MISSISSIPPI IN THE FIELD, KINGSTON, GEORGIA, November 8, 1864

The general commanding deems it proper at this time to inform the officers and men of the Fourteenth, Fifteenth, Seventeenth, and Twentieth Corps, that he has organized them into an army for a special purpose, well known to the War Department and to General Grant. It is sufficient for you to know that it involves a departure from our present base, and a long and difficult march to a new one. All the chances of war have been considered and provided for, as far as human sagacity can. All he asks of you is to maintain that discipline, patience, and courage, which have characterized you in the past; and he hopes, through you, to strike a blow at our enemy that will have a material effect in producing what we all so much desire, his complete overthrow. Of all things, the most important is, that the men, during marches and in camp, keep their places and do not scatter about as stragglers or foragers, to be picked up by a hostile people in detail. It is also of the utmost importance that our wagons should not be loaded with any thing but provisions and ammunition. All surplus servants, noncombatants, and refugees, should now go to the rear, and none should be encouraged to encumber us on the march. At some future time we will be able to provide for the poor whites and blacks who seek to escape the bondage under which they are now suffering. With these few simple cautions, he hopes to lead you to achievements equal in importance to those of the past.

By order of Major-General W. T. Sherman, L. M. DAYTON, Aide-de-Camp.

[SPECIAL FIELD ORDERS, NO. 120.]

HEADQUARTERS MILITARY DIVISION OF THE MISSISSIPPI IN THE FIELD, KINGSTON, GEORGIA, November 9, 1864

1. For the purpose of military operations, this army is divided into two wings viz.:

The right wing, Major-General O. O. Howard commanding, composed of the Fifteenth and Seventeenth Corps; the left wing, Major-General H. W. Slocum commanding, composed of the Fourteenth and Twentieth Corps.

2. The habitual order of march will be, wherever practicable, by four roads, as nearly parallel as possible, and converging at points hereafter to be indicated in orders. The cavalry, Brigadier-General Kilpatrick commanding, will receive special orders from the commander-in-chief.

3. There will be no general train of supplies, but each corps will have its ammunition-train and provision-train, distributed habitually as follows: Behind each regiment should follow one wagon and one ambulance; behind each brigade should follow a due proportion of ammunition-wagons, provision-wagons, and ambulances. In case of danger, each corps commander should change this order of march, by having his advance and rear brigades unencumbered by wheels. The separate columns will start habitually at 7 a.m., and make about fifteen miles per day, unless otherwise fixed in orders.

4. The army will forage liberally on the country during the march. To this end, each brigade commander will organize a good and sufficient foraging party, under the command of one or more discreet officers, who will gather, near the route traveled, corn or forage of any kind, meat of any kind, vegetables, corn-meal, or whatever is needed by the command, aiming at all times to keep in the wagons at least ten days' provisions for his command, and three days' forage. Soldiers must not enter the dwellings of the inhabitants, or commit any trespass; but, during a halt or camp, they may be permitted to gather turnips, potatoes, and other vegetables, and to drive in stock in sight of their camp. To regular foraging-parties must be intrusted the gathering of provisions and forage, at any distance from the road traveled.

5. To corps commanders alone is intrusted the power to destroy mills, houses, cotton-gins, etc.; and for them this general principle is laid down:

In districts and neighborhoods where the army is unmolested, no destruction of each property should be permitted; but should guerrillas or bushwhackers molest our march, or should the inhabitants burn bridges, obstruct roads, or otherwise manifest local hostility, then army commanders should order and enforce a devastation more or less relentless, according to the measure of such hostility.

6. As for horses, mules, wagons, etc., belonging to the inhabitants, the cavalry and artillery may appropriate freely and without limit; discriminating, however, between the rich, who are usually hostile, and the poor and industrious, usually neutral or friendly. Foraging-parties may also take mules or horses, to replace the jaded animals of their trains, or to serve as pack-mules for the regiments or brigades. In all foraging, of whatever kind, the parties engaged will refrain from abusive or threatening language, and may, where the officer in command thinks proper, give written certificates of the facts, but no receipts; and they will endeavor to leave with each family a reasonable portion for their maintenance.

7. Negroes who are able-bodied and can be of service to the several columns may be taken along; but each army commander will bear in mind that the question of supplies is a very important one, and that his first duty is to see to those who bear arms.

8. The organization, at once, of a good pioneer battalion for each army corps, composed if possible of negroes, should be attended to. This battalion should follow the advance-guard, repair roads and double them if possible, so that the columns will not be delayed after reaching bad places. Also, army commanders should practise the habit of giving the artillery and wagons the road, marching their troops on one side, and instruct their troops to assist wagons at steep hills or bad crossings of streams.

9. Captain O. M. Poe, chief-engineer, will assign to each wing of the army a pontoon-train, fully equipped and organized; and the commanders thereof will see to their being properly protected at all times.

By order of Major-General W. T. Sherman,

L. M. DAYTON, Aide-de-Camp.

FROM *THE MEMOIRS OF GENERAL WILLIAM T. SHERMAN* (1875)

The greatest possible attention had been given to the artillery and wagon trains. The number of guns had been reduced to sixty-five, or about one gun to each thousand men, and these were generally in batteries of four guns each.

Each gun, caisson, and forges was drawn by four teams of horses. We had in all about twenty-five hundred wagons, with teams of six mules to each, and six hundred ambulances, with two horses to each. The loads were made comparatively light, about twenty-five hundred pounds net; each wagon carrying in addition the forage needed by its own team: Each soldier carried on his person forty rounds of ammunition, and in the wagons were enough cartridges to make up about two hundred rounds per man, and in like manner two hundred rounds of assorted ammunition were carried for each gun.

The wagon-trains were divided equally between the four corps, so that each had about eight hundred wagons, and these usually on the march occupied five miles or more of road. Each corps commander managed his own train; and habitually the artillery and wagons had the road, while the men, with the exception of the advance and rear guards, pursued paths improvised by the aide of the wagons, unless they were forced to use a bridge or causeway in common.

I reached Atlanta during the afternoon of the 14th, and found that all preparations had been made—Colonel Beckwith, chief commissary, reporting one million two hundred thousand rations in possession of the troops, which was about twenty days' supply, and he had on hand a good supply of beef-cattle to be driven along on the hoof. Of forage, the supply was limited, being of oats and corn enough for five days, but I knew that within that time we would reach a country well stocked with corn, which had been gathered and stored in cribs, seemingly for our use, by Governor Brown's militia.

Colonel Poe, United States Engineers, of my staff, had been busy in his special task of destruction. He had a large force at work, had leveled the great depot, round house, and the machine-shops of the Georgia Railroad, and had applied fire to the wreck. One of these machine-shops had been used by the rebels as an arsenal, and in it were stored piles of shot and shell, some of which proved to be loaded, and that night was made hideous by the bursting of shells, whose fragments came uncomfortably near Judge Lyon's house, in which I was quartered. The fire also reached the block of stores near the depot, and the heart of the city was in flames all night, but the fire did not reach the parts of Atlanta where the court-house was, or the great mass of dwelling houses.

The march from Atlanta began on the morning of November 15th, the right wing and cavalry following the railroad southeast toward Jonesboro', and General Slocum with the Twentieth Corps leading off to the east by Decatur and Stone Mountain, toward Madison. These were divergent lines, designed to threaten both Mason and Augusta at the same time, so as to prevent a concentration at our intended destination, or "objective," Milledgeville, the capital of Georgia, distant southeast about one hundred miles. The time allowed each column for reaching Milledgeville was seven days. I remained in Atlanta during the 15th with the Fourteenth Corps, and the rear-guard of the right wing, to complete the loading of the trains, and the destruction of the buildings of Atlanta which could be converted to hostile uses, and on the morning of the 16th started with my personal staff, a company of Alabama cavalry, commanded by Lieutenant Snelling, and an infantry company, commanded by Lieutenant McCrory, which guarded our small train of wagons.

My staff was then composed of Major L. M. Dayton, aide-de-camp and acting adjutant-general, Major J. C. McCoy, and Major J. C. Audenried, aides. Major Ward Nichols had joined some weeks before at Gaylesville, Alabama, and was attached as an acting aide-de-camp. Also Major Henry Hitchcock had joined at the same time as judge-advocate. Colonel Charles Ewing was inspector-general, and Surgeon John Moore medical director. These constituted our mess. We had no tents, only the flies, with which we nightly made bivouacs with the assistance of the abundant pine-boughs, which made excellent shelter, as well as beds.

Colonel L. C. Easton was chief-quartermaster; Colonel Amos Beckwith, chief-commissary; Colonel O. M. Poe, chief-engineer; and Colonel T. G. Baylor, chief of ordnance. These invariably rode with us during the day, but they had a separate camp and mess at night.

General William F. Barry had been chief of artillery in the previous campaign, but at Kingston his face was so swollen with erysipelas that he was reluctantly compelled to leave us for the rear; and he could not, on recovering, rejoin us till we had reached Savannah.

About 7 a.m. of November 16th we rode out of Atlanta by the Decatur road, filled by the marching troops and wagons of the Fourteenth Corps; and reaching the hill, just outside of the old rebel works, we naturally paused to look back upon the scenes of our past battles. We stood upon the very ground whereon was fought the bloody battle of July 22d, and could see the copse of wood where McPherson fell. Behind us lay Atlanta, smouldering and in ruins, the black smoke rising high in the air, and hanging like a pall over the ruined city. Away off in the distance, on the McDonough road, was the rear of Howard's column, the gun-barrels glistening in the sun, the white-topped wagons stretching away to the south; and right before us the Fourteenth Corps, marching steadily and rapidly, with a cheery look and swinging pace, that made light of the thousand miles that lay between us and Richmond. Some band, by accident, struck up the anthem of "John Brown's soul goes marching on"; the men caught up the strain, and never before or since have I heard the chorus of "Glory, glory, hallelujah!" done with more spirit, or in better harmony of time and place.

Then we turned our horses' heads to the east; Atlanta was soon lost behind the screen of trees, and became a thing of the past. Around it clings many a thought of desperate battle, of hope and fear, that now seem like the memory of a dream; and I have never seen the place since. The day was extremely beautiful, clear sunlight, with bracing air, and an unusual feeling of exhilaration seemed to pervade all minds—a feeling of something to come, vague and undefined, still full of venture and intense interest. Even the common soldiers caught the inspiration, and many a group called out to me as I worked my way past them, "Uncle Billy, I guess Grant is waiting for us at Richmond!" Indeed, the general sentiment was that we were marching for Richmond, and that there we should end the war, but how and when they seemed to care not; nor did they measure the distance, or count the cost in life, or bother their brains about the great rivers to be crossed, and the food required for man and beast, that had to be gathered by the way. There was a "devil-may-care" feeling pervading officers and men, that made me feel the full load of responsibility, for success would be accepted as a matter of course, whereas, should we fail, this "march" would be adjudged the wild adventure of a crazy fool. I had no purpose to march direct for Richmond by way of Augusta and Charlotte, but always designed to reach the sea-coast first at Savannah or Port Royal, South Carolina, and even kept in mind the alternative of Pensacola.

The first night out we camped by the road-side near Lithonia. Stone Mountain, a mass of granite, was in plain view, cut out in clear outline against the blue sky; the whole horizon was lurid with the bonfires of rail-ties, and groups of men all night were carrying the heated rails to the nearest trees, and bending them around the trunks. Colonel Poe had provided tools for ripping up the rails and twisting them when hot; but the best and easiest way is the one I have described, of heating the middle of the iron-rails on bonfires made of the cross-ties, and then winding them around a telegraph-pole or the trunk of some convenient sapling. I attached much importance to this destruction of the railroad, gave it my own personal attention, and made reiterated orders to others on the subject.

The next day we passed through the handsome town of Covington, the soldiers closing up their ranks, the color-bearers unfurling their flags, and the bands striking up patriotic airs. The white people came out of their houses to behold the sight, spite of their deep hatred of the invaders, and the negroes were simply frantic with joy. Whenever they heard my name, they clustered about my horse, shouted and prayed in their peculiar style, which had a natural eloquence that would have moved a stone. I have witnessed hundreds, if not thousands, of such scenes; and can now see a poor girl, in the very ecstasy of the Methodist "shout," hugging the banner of one of the regiments, and jumping up to the "feet of Jesus."

I remember, when riding around by a by-street in Covington, to avoid the crowd that followed the marching column, that some one brought me an invitation to dine with a sister of Sam. Anderson, who was a cadet at West Point with me; but the messenger reached me after we had passed the main part of the town. I asked to be excused, and rode on to a place designated for camp, at the crossing of the Ulcofauhachee River, about four miles to the east of the town. Here we made our bivouac, and I walked up to a plantation-house close by, where were assembled many negroes, among them an old, gray-haired man, of as fine a head as I ever saw. I asked him if he understood about the war and its progress. He said he did; that he had been looking for the "angel of the Lord" ever since he was knee-high, and, though we professed to be fighting for the Union, he supposed that slavery was the cause, and that our success was to be his freedom. I asked him if all the negro slaves comprehended this fact, and he said they surely did. I then explained to him that we wanted the slaves to remain where they were, and not to load us down with useless mouths, which would eat up the food needed for our fighting men; that our success was their assured freedom; that we could receive a few of their young, hearty men as pioneers; but that, if they followed us in swarms of old and young, feeble and helpless, it would simply load us down and cripple us in our great task. I think Major Henry Hitchcock was with me on that occasion, and made a note of the conversation, and I believe that old man spread this message to the slaves, which was carried from mouth to mouth, to the very end of our journey, and that it in part saved us from the great danger we incurred of swelling our numbers so that famine would have attended our progress. It was at this very plantation that a soldier passed me with a ham on his musket, a jug of sorghum-molasses under his arm, and a big piece of honey in his hand, from which he was eating, and, catching my eye, he remarked sotto voce and carelessly to a comrade, "Forage liberally on the country," quoting from my general orders. On this occasion, as on many others that fell under my personal observation, I reproved the man, explained that foraging must be limited to the regular parties properly detailed, and that all provisions thus obtained must be delivered to the regular commissaries, to be fairly distributed to the men who kept their ranks.

From Covington the Fourteenth Corps (Davis's), with which I was traveling, turned to the right for Milledgeville, via Shady Dale. General Slocum was ahead at Madison, with the Twentieth Corps, having torn up the railroad as far as that place, and thence had sent Geary's division on to the Oconee, to burn the bridges across that stream, when this corps turned south by Eatonton, for Milledgeville, the common "objective" for the first stage of the "march." We found abundance of corn, molasses, meal, bacon, and sweet-potatoes. We also took a good many cows and oxen, and a large number of mules. In all these the country was quite rich, never before having been visited by a hostile army; the recent crop had been excellent, had been just gathered and laid by for the winter. As a rule, we destroyed none, but kept our wagons full, and fed our teams bountifully.

The skill and success of the men in collecting forage was one of the features of this march. Each brigade commander had authority to detail a company of foragers, usually about fifty men, with one or two commissioned officers selected for their boldness and enterprise. This party would be dispatched before daylight with a knowledge of the intended day's march and camp; would proceed on foot five or six miles from the route traveled by their brigade, and then visit every plantation and farm within range. They would usually procure a wagon or family carriage, load it with bacon, corn-meal, turkeys, chickens, ducks, and every thing that could be used as food or forage, and would then regain the main road, usually in advance of their train. When this came up, they would deliver to the brigade commissary the supplies thus gathered by the way. Often would I pass these foraging-parties at the roadside, waiting for their wagons to come up, and was amused at their strange collections—mules, horses, even cattle, packed with old saddles and loaded with hams, bacon, bags of cornmeal, and poultry of every character and description. Although this foraging was attended with great danger and hard work, there seemed to be a charm about it that attracted the soldiers, and it was a privilege to be detailed on such a party. Daily they returned mounted on all sorts of beasts, which were at once taken from them and appropriated to the general use; but the next day they would start out again on foot, only to repeat the experience of the day before. No doubt, many acts of pillage, robbery, and violence, were committed by these parties of foragers, usually called "bummers;" for I have since heard of jewelry taken from women, and the plunder of articles that never reached the commissary; but these acts were exceptional and incidental. I never heard of any cases of murder or rape; and no army could have carried along sufficient food and forage for a march of three hundred miles; so that foraging in some shape was necessary. The country was sparsely settled, with no magistrates or civil authorities who could respond to requisitions, as is done in all the wars of Europe; so that this system of foraging was simply indispensable to our success. By it our men were well supplied with all the essentials of life and health, while the wagons retained enough in case of unexpected delay, and our animals were well fed. Indeed, when we reached Savannah, the trains were pronounced by experts to be the finest in flesh and appearance ever seen with any army.

Habitually each corps followed some main road, and the foragers, being kept out on the exposed flank, served all the military uses of flankers. The main columns gathered, by the roads traveled, much forage and food, chiefly meat, corn, and sweet-potatoes, and it was the duty of each division and brigade quartermaster to fill his wagons as fast as the contents were issued to the troops. The wagon-trains had the right to the road always, but each wagon was required to keep closed up, so as to leave no gaps in the column. If for any purpose any wagon or group of wagons dropped out of place, they had to wait for the rear. And this was always dreaded, for each brigade commander wanted his train up at camp as soon after reaching it with his men as possible.

I have seen much skill and industry displayed by these quartermasters on the march, in trying to load their wagons with corn and fodder by the way without losing their place in column. They would, while marching, shift the loads of wagons, so as to have six or ten of them empty. Then, riding well ahead, they would secure possession of certain stacks of fodder near the road, or cribs of corn, leave some men in charge, then open fences and a road back for a couple of miles, return to their trains, divert the empty wagons out of column, and conduct them rapidly to their forage, load up and regain their place in column without losing distance. On one occasion I remember to have seen ten or a dozen wagons thus loaded with corn from two or three full cribs, almost without halting. These cribs were built of logs, and roofed. The train-guard, by a lever, had raised the whole side of the crib a foot or two; the wagons drove close alongside, and the men in the cribs, lying on their backs, kicked out a wagon-load of corn in the time I have taken to describe it.

In a well-ordered and well-disciplined army, these things might be deemed irregular, but I am convinced that the ingenuity of these younger officers accomplished many things far better than I could have ordered, and the marches were thus made, and the distances were accomplished, in the most admirable way. Habitually we started from camp at the earliest break of dawn, and usually reached camp soon after noon. The marches varied from ten to fifteen miles a day, though sometimes on extreme flanks it was necessary to make as much as twenty, but the rate of travel was regulated by the wagons; and, considering the nature of the roads, fifteen miles per day was deemed the limit.

The pontoon-trains were in like manner distributed in about equal proportions to the four corps, giving each a section of about nine hundred feet. The pontoons were of the skeleton pattern, with cotton-canvas covers, each boat, with its proportion of balks and cheeses, constituting a load for one wagon. By uniting two such sections together, we could make a bridge of eighteen hundred feet, enough for any river we had to traverse; but habitually the leading brigade would, out of the abundant timber, improvise a bridge before the pontoon-train could come up, unless in the cases of rivers of considerable magnitude, such as the Ocmulgee, Oconee, Ogeechee, Savannah, etc.

On the 20th of November I was still with the Fourteenth Corps, near Eatonton Factory, waiting to hear of the Twentieth Corps; and on the 21st we camped near the house of a man named Mann; the next day, about 4 p.m., General Davis had halted his head of column on a wooded ridge, overlooking an extensive slope of cultivated country, about ten miles short of Milledgeville, and was deploying his troops for camp when I got up. There was a high, raw wind blowing, and I asked him why he had chosen so cold and bleak a position. He explained that he had accomplished his full distance for the day, and had there an abundance of wood and water. He explained further that his advance-guard was a mile or so ahead; so I rode on, asking him to let his rear division, as it came up, move some distance ahead into the depression or valley beyond. Riding on some distance to the border of a plantation, I turned out of the main road into a cluster of wild-plum bushes, that broke the force of the cold November wind, dismounted, and instructed the staff to pick out the place for our camp.

The afternoon was unusually raw and cold. My orderly was at hand with his invariable saddlebags, which contained a change of under-clothing, my maps, a flask of whiskey, and bunch of cigars. Taking a drink and lighting a cigar, I walked to a row of negro-huts close by, entered one and found a soldier or two warming themselves by a wood-fire. I took their place by the fire, intending to wait there till our wagons had got up, and a camp made for the night. I was talking to the old negro woman, when some one came and explained to me that, if I would come farther down the road, I could find a better place. So I started on foot, and found on the main road a good double-hewed-log house, in one room of which Colonel Poe, Dr. Moore, and others, had started a fire. I sent back orders to the "plum-bushes" to bring our horses and saddles up to this house, and an orderly to conduct our headquarter wagons to the same place. In looking around the room, I saw a small box, like a candle-box, marked "Howell Cobb," and, on inquiring of a negro, found that we were at the plantation of General Howell Cobb, of Georgia, one of the leading rebels of the South, then a general in the Southern army, and who had been Secretary of the United States Treasury in Mr. Buchanan's time. Of course, we confiscated his property, and found it rich in corn, beans, pea-nuts, and sorghum-molasses. Extensive fields were all round the house; I sent word back to General Davis to explain whose plantation it was, and instructed him to spare nothing. That night huge bonfires consumed the fence-rails, kept our soldiers warm, and the teamsters and men, as well as the slaves, carried off an immense quantity of corn and provisions of all sorts.

In due season the headquarter wagons came up, and we got supper. After supper I sat on a chair astride, with my back to a good fire, musing, and became conscious that an old negro, with a tallow-candle in his hand, was scanning my face closely. I inquired, "What do you want, old man!" He answered, "Dey say you is Massa Sherman." I answered that such was the case, and inquired what he wanted. He only wanted to look at me, and kept muttering, "Dis nigger can't sleep dis night." I asked him why he trembled so, and he said that he wanted to be sure that we were in fact "Yankees," for on a former occasion some rebel cavalry had put on light-blue overcoats, personating Yankee troops, and many of the negroes were deceived thereby, himself among the number had shown them sympathy, and had in consequence been unmercifully beaten therefor. This time he wanted to be certain before committing himself; so I told him to go out on the porch, from which he could see the whole horizon lit up with camp-fires, and he could then judge whether he had ever seen any thing like it before. The old man became convinced that the "Yankees" had come at last, about whom he had been dreaming all his life; and some of the staff officers gave him a strong drink of whiskey, which set his tongue going. Lieutenant Spelling, who commanded my escort, was a Georgian, and recognized in this old negro a favorite slave of his uncle, who resided about six miles off; but the old slave did not at first recognize his young master in our uniform. One of my staff-officers asked him what had become of his young master, George. He did not know, only that he had gone off to the war, and he supposed him killed, as a matter of course. His attention was then drawn to Spelling's face, when he fell on his knees and thanked God that he had found his young master alive and along with the Yankees. Spelling inquired all about his uncle and the family, asked my permission to go and pay his uncle a visit, which I granted, of course, and the next morning he described to me his visit. The uncle was not cordial, by any means, to find his nephew in the ranks of the host that was desolating the land, and Spelling came back, having exchanged his tired horse for a fresher one out of his uncle's stables, explaining that surely some of the "bummers" would have got the horse had he not.

"Ethiopia Saluting the Colors"

Walt Whitman

In the mid-nineteenth century, "Ethiopian" was synonymous with "African." This poem, first published in 1871, imagines an old slave woman from the Georgia fields, marked by her root culture and her memories of capture as a child in Africa. (In fact, no slaves were imported to the West from Ethiopia; that country provided slaves for the Middle Eastern markets.) In this poem, the woman rises regally to salute the red, white, and blue of the American flag as General Sherman's troops file by on their way through Georgia. The colors in the old woman's turban are yellow, red, and green, the colors of the Ethiopian flag; the colors of one culture saluting those of another. The "I" of the poem is a Union soldier, a member of Sherman's army, who observes her with a series of questions, underscoring her mysteriousness—her powerful otherness.

The poem's formal rhyming structure is unusual for Whitman. It was later set to music by Harry Burleigh, in an arrangement invoking "Marching Through Georgia."

Who are you dusky woman, so ancient hardly human,
With your woolly-white and turban'd head, and bare bony feet?
Why rising by the roadside here, do you the colors greet?
('Tis while our army lines Carolina's sands and pines,
Forth from thy hovel door thou Ethiopia com'st to me,
As under doughty Sherman I march toward the sea.)
Me master years a hundred since from my parents sunder'd,
A little child, they caught me as the savage beast is caught,
Then hither me across the sea the cruel slaver brought.

No further does she say, but lingering all the day,
Her high-borne turban'd head she wags, and rolls her darkling eye,
And courtesies to the regiments, the guidons moving by.
What is it fateful woman, so blear, hardly human?
Why wag your head with turban bound, yellow, red and green?
Are the things so strange and marvelous you see or have seen?

1865

There is a long-standing search for ways to lay hands on the complicating and surprising turns of history. One favorite device of historians is chronology and the use of dates to frame or bracket events such as the American Civil War with the years 1861–1865. Commemorations like the sesquicentennial deepen our confidence that the War is bounded by these dates and, in a sense, knowable. We are comforted by the seemingly predictable sequence of events, which is so often repeated in our minds that we come to see them as inevitable. Familiarity with chronology and the deeply imbedded stories of the War confirm our intellectual confidence in the progress of history and the inevitability of what happened.

In reality, few had predicted the character and the length of the War or foresaw how it would end. If anything, one is impressed by the erratic turn of events of 1865, which did not so much end the War but simply stopped the fighting.

The year brought not a conclusion but a denouement—an unraveling of the plot as it spun out into the future. This year was as filled with uncertainty as a bracket for the end of the War as 1861 was for its beginnings. If the origins of the Civil War are rooted in colonial slavery and revolutionary equivocation, the struggles for civil rights and racial justice in our own time find their roots in the incomplete and unpredictable events of 1865.

In January the House of Representatives passed the Thirteenth Amendment, which outlawed slavery and involuntary servitude except as punishment for a crime, completing the unfinished work of the Emancipation Proclamation. Its ratification by year's end established the legal freedom of all African-Americans and initiated a revolution that would reorder social relations in radically new and unanticipated ways. This became a struggle that would extend the consequences of 1865 for over a century. One of the most profound long-term effects of the amendment was the license it gave to the criminalization and wholesale imprisonment of the freedman. The proviso that "Neither slavery nor involuntary servitude, *except as a punishment for crime whereof the party shall have been duly convicted*, shall exist within the United States, or any place subject to their jurisdiction" opened the door to a postwar neoslavery with dire consequences for African-Americans.

In February Sherman's March extended into the Carolinas, spreading destruction and mayhem while meeting with little sustained resistance. An effort to end the War failed when Southern negotiators meeting with Lincoln in February insisted on recognition of their independence. This failure highlights the uncertainty about the terms of surrender and the ad hoc nature of the endgame. Another example of the improvisatory efforts to cobble together a settlement is Sherman's Special Field Order No. 15, which confiscated four hundred thousand acres of land and sought to redistribute it to families of the freedmen, but was later reversed by President Andrew Johnson.

The shoeless and starving Confederate Army, reduced by increasing casualties and alarming desertions, reached such extremis that on March 13 the Congress authorized the enlistment of slaves into the army, an idea that even General Lee embraced. This was a change of such magnitude that many Southerners, among them President Davis, were chagrined and opposed the act. The South was now running on little more than hope and prayer. Increasing food shortages and hyperinflation pressured the home front and the ensuing pleas for help drew many soldiers away from the battlefield back to their distressed families.

Lincoln's Second Inaugural Address began, in the broadest terms, to turn the nation toward the task of "binding up the wounds . . . securing lasting peace." A war whose objectives had evolved over the preceding four years lacked a coherent peace plan and the nation would need all the political acumen of its skilled president to steer the ship of state into a safe harbor.

On March 25, Lee unsuccessfully attacked Grant at Petersburg; a second attempt, on April 1, also failed. These successive defeats forced Lee to abandon Richmond on April 2. If war were a chess match, as many imagined, this was checkmate—the end move.

The meeting at Appomattox on April 9 concretized the hopelessness of the situation, and Lee surrendered the Army of Northern Virginia. Grant provided generous terms—soldiers were paroled and allowed to retain their horses and officers permitted to keep their sidearms; rations were distributed to the hungry Confederates. Grant understood that the War was over.

But only in a limited sense had the surrender of Lee's army ended the War: skirmishing continued for a few weeks and the Confederate government had not surrendered. While this issue of surrender was complicated by the desire to deny the Confederacy standing as an independent state, it left the design of the peace an open question—the work of Reconstruction. Thus, in a real sense, the War did not end at Appomattox.

Five days later, Lincoln was assassinated, severing the bond of continuity between war and peace and depriving the country of the gift of his wartime experience and political sagacity. The shock of this event and the national outpouring of grief that engulfed the country deepened the sense of shattered ground.

Lincoln was quickly canonized as the Martyr President, enshrined in the popular imagination as a secular saint who was increasingly abstracted from the political world of his presidency and his tough, often brutal, decisions as commander in chief. In his apotheosis and sanctification we see the veil of mythology slowly being drawn over Lincoln and enabling equally mythical constructs of "the bloody shirt" (on the Northern side) and "the lost cause" (on the Southern side). The Civil War did not end in1865. The shape of postwar America and the condition of the freedman remained contentious and uncertain. Careful reading and reflection on the documents, the diaries, the letters, the images, and the poetry collected in *On Shattered Ground* will help us see the past and connect its words and feelings to the world we live in.

"THE TWO CHRISTMAS EVENINGS"

Lydia Maria Child (1802–1880)

"The Two Christmas Evenings" first appeared in *Our Young Folks* in 1866. One of a large number of magazines published for young people, it contained stories, poems, and articles by some of the leading writers of the era that modeled the ethical and selfless behavior that was expected of children, especially during the tumultuous War years. Like much of the writing published in *Our Young Folks*, Child's story is unabashedly didactic. She herself was a committed activist on behalf of women, Native Americans, and African-Americans, free and slave.

The story capitalizes on the tremendous excitement about the War that was stimulated on the domestic scene. Northern children not only read books and magazine stories written for young audiences, played war games, watched plays, and participated in pageants, but they also raised money and "picked lint" for the cause. And, of course, they listened to the stories of returning veterans and shared in mourning lost loved ones.

In the South, the experience of children, whether black or white, was more likely to include actual privation and the early assumption of adult responsibilities.

It was a beautiful Christmas Eve. A light snow had fallen just before night, and made the city streets look clean. Icicles hanging from the roofs glittered in the moonlight, and the trees on the Common looked as if they had put on white feathers for a festival.

Mrs. Rich's parlor was brighter than the moonlight splendor without. The folding-doors were open. A clear flame rose from the cannel-coal as it split and crackled in the grate; the gas burned brilliantly in the chandeliers; at the upper end of the room was an Evergreen Tree, with a sparkling crown of little lamps, and gay with festoons of ribbons and trinkets; the carpet was like a meadow enamelled with flowers; the crimson damask curtains glowed in the brilliant light; and the gilded paper on the walls gleamed here and there, like the bright edges of little sun-set clouds. Mrs. Rich was just putting some finishing touches to the Tree, when the great clock on the staircase struck seven, and the pattering of feet was heard. The door opened, and Papa entered with a group of children. There was Frank, in all the dignity of his fourteen years; earnest-looking Isabel, who was about twelve; Ellen, not much over nine, whose honest face had an expression of thoughtfulness beyond her years; and little Alice, whom they named Pet Poodle, because she had such a quantity of soft, light curls falling about her face. In her first stammering of this name she called herself Petty Poo, and they all adopted her infantile abbreviation.

The Evergreen Tree and the treasures with which it was covered produced but slight excitement in the minds of the older children. As they approached it, they said, "How tastefully you have arranged it, mamma!" and they quietly awaited the distribution of the gifts, like well-trained young ladies and gentlemen. But little Alice, who opened her blue eyes on the world only four years before, had not done wondering yet. She capered up to the tree, and, pointing to one thing after another, said, "Isn't dat pooty?" A large doll had been sent to her last Christmas, and when she spied one seated among the green boughs, she gave a little shout, and cried out, "Dare is nudder dolly for Petty Poo!" She was told Aunt Jane had sent it to her, and she received it with unalloyed satisfaction. "Tank Aunt Jane," said she. "Dis dolly's eyes is b'oo, and tudder dolly's is b'ack." Well pleased with this variety in her family, she hugged it up, and seated herself on the carpet to examine the little blue rosettes on the shoes.

When Mr. Rich handed his son a handsomely illustrated copy of "The Arabian Nights," he received it with a bow, and, turning over the leaves carelessly, said, "I wonder what Uncle Joe sent me this for! I have one edition, and I don't want another." Isabel took a gold bracelet that was offered her, and, slipping it on her wrist, remarked to her brother, "I don't think this bracelet

Cousin Emma has sent me cost so much as the one I sent her last Christmas." "And see this gutta-percha watch-chain that Cousin Joe has sent me," rejoined Frank. "You know I sent him a gold one last year." "If you read what is written on the card," said his father, "you will see that it was made in the Hospital, by his brave brother, Captain George." Frank glanced over the writing, and replied, "Yes, sir; but I should rather have had the gold one." Mary received a handsome French work-box, filled with elegant implements for sewing. She said, "I am much obliged to Aunt Jane"; but she set it aside after a slight examination, and returned to the tree again. Many more presents were distributed,—beaded nets for the hair, books, photographs, bronze dogs, Parian images, and all sorts of things. But Petty Poo was the only one who seemed to take a very lively interest. She stood by the table hugging her doll, expressing her admiration of everything by little shouts, and holding out her hand now and then to receive a paper of sugared almonds, a china lamb, or a little horse on rollers. The last thing that was taken from the tree was a small basket, containing a doll's nightgown and nightcap. This furnished her with delightful employment. She seated herself on the carpet and undressed her doll, and when she had made her ready for the night, she said, "Now Petty Poo will go to bed, and take all her tings wid her; and dolly wid de b'ack eyes may s'eep in de drawer." When she had been kissed all round, she was carried upstairs, and mamma followed, to have another kiss from the little darling before her blue eyes closed for the night.

When Mrs. Rich returned to the parlor, Isabel said archly, "Are you *sure,* mamma, that you took everything from the Christmas Tree?" and mamma, who knew she was about to be surprised, replied, "I believe so; but I will go and look, dear." Among the boughs she found a rustic watch-case, an embroidered ottoman-cover, and a pretty worsted shawl, on which Frank and Isabel and Ellen had each written their names, and added, "For my dear mother." Mrs. Rich smiled lovingly, as she wrapped the shawl about her, and put her watch in the case, and spread the cover on the ottoman, and said the colors were beautifully arranged.

"We made them entirely ourselves," said the young folks; "and we had *such* a job to keep you from finding out what we were doing!"

"Thank you, my dear children," replied the happy mother.

She kissed them all, and they clung about her, and asked again and again if she really thought the things were pretty.

"Perhaps you have not found *all* yet," said Ellen. "Please look again."

After a diligent search, which was purposely prolonged a little, a box was found hidden away under the boughs. It contained a set of chessmen, a crocheted purse, and a worsted comforter for the neck, on which Frank and Isabel and Ellen had written, "For my dear father," with the names of each appended; and again they said, exultingly, "We made them all ourselves, papa."

"Thank you, my children," replied Mr. Rich. "So, Frank, these chessmen are what you have so long been busy about at Uncle John's turning lathe." He smiled as he added, "I will not say I had rather have gold ones; for such neat workmanship done by my son is more valuable to me than gold could be. And Isabel, dear, I don't know whether this handsome purse cost so much as the skates I gave you for a Christmas present, but I certainly like it better than any purse I could buy." The brother and sister blushed a little, for they understood the rebuke conveyed in his words. But he patted their heads and kissed them, and as they nestled close up to him, he folded them all in his arms. "So my little Ellen has made me a red, white, and blue comforter," said he. "How grand I shall feel walking down State Street with this round my neck!"

"Then you *will* wear it, papa?" said Ellen, with a glad little jump.

"Wear it? Indeed I will," replied her father; "and proud I shall be of the loyal colors, and of my little daughter's work."

"Ellen is very patriotic," said her mother. "I think papa would like to hear her play 'The Star-Spangled Banner.' "

The little girl ran eagerly to the music-stool; for she had been practising the tune very diligently, in hopes she should be invited to play. Frank and Isabel kept their fingers moving to the music, and when it ceased, papa exclaimed, "Bravo!" He was really pleased with his little daughter's improvement, and that made her as light-hearted as a bird. . . .

The next evening, when little Alice went away with her nurse, after kissing them all "Good night," she peeped into the door again to say, "Dolly wid de b'oo eyes is going to s'eep in de drawer, and dolly wid de b'ack eyes is going to s'eep wid

Petty Poo." They smiled upon her, and threw her kisses, and when the door closed after her, Mr. Rich remarked, "Even with Petty Poo the novelty of Christmas gifts don't last long. What part of your Christmas evening did you enjoy most, my children?"

"When I was playing to you, and you liked it," replied Ellen.

"When you and mamma seemed so pleased with the things we made for you," said Isabel.

"And you, my son?" inquired Mr. Rich.

Frank replied, that was the only part of the evening he cared much about.

"I thought so," rejoined his father. "Have any of you thought what might be the reason?"

The young folks were silent, each one trying to think what their father expected them to say.

"I will tell you how I explain it," continued Mr. Rich. "I learned long ago that it is not the *having* things, but the *doing* things, which makes people happy. You enjoyed the presents you gave us, because you had expended ingenuity and industry upon them. Nothing you could have bought for us would have given either you or us half the pleasure."

"And they were working for *others,* not for *themselves,*" added their mother. "That greatly increased the charm."

Her husband smiled approvingly, as he rejoined, "You have said the best word, my dear."

The children looked in the fire thoughtfully. At last, Isabel broke the silence by saying, "When we went to bed last night, Ellen and I said we didn't know what was the reason we felt so little pleasure, when so many had tried to please us."

Their father rejoined, "The trouble is, you have so many handsome things that the charm of novelty is lost. A poor child would feel as rich as Croesus with one of the many things you think so little of."

Isabel looked up eagerly and exclaimed, "Papa, that makes me think of something. We will agree with our uncles and aunts and cousins, not to exchange Christmas gifts next year. We will do something else."

"What can we do?" asked Ellen. "I should admire to do something different."

"We'll give dolls and picture-books and tops to the children in the Orphan Asylum," replied her sister.

"That is a very good thought," said their mother.

"And, papa, you said it made folks happy to do things themselves," remarked Ellen. "So we'll make up the dolls and dress them ourselves; and we'll knit comforters and mittens and hoods for the poor children; and we'll make balls for the boys; and ever so many things. Won't we, Issy?"

"Where are you going to get money enough to buy the dolls' heads, and stuff to make the hoods and comforters of?" inquired Frank.

His sisters looked puzzled. Mr. and Mrs. Rich said nothing; for they wanted the children to work out their own plan and depend on their own resources. After a little reflection, Isabel said, "We could have a Fair. Not a public fair, mamma; but a sort of pleasant party for our uncles and aunts and cousins and particular friends. We've got ever so many things laid up in our drawers, that we might sell as well as not."

"O, but that would never do," rejoined Ellen; "for they were given to us, and we couldn't sell people their own things. But if they will agree not to give us any presents next Christmas, we can buy worsted and dolls' heads with our money, instead of buying bracelets and vases for them; and they have so many they don't want them."

"That's true," answered Isabel; "and we could do without many of the things that we are buying every week."

Their father looked highly pleased, and said, "That will be another good thing, to have a generous motive for practising economy. I will buy ten dollars' worth of whatever things you make yourselves."

"And so will I," said their mother.

"You might lend us the twenty dollars beforehand, and take your pay in the things we make," said Frank. "I will make some cups and balls for the girls, and some bats for the boys."

His father looked at him with a significant smile, and said, "One thing you may be sure of, my son. The poor boys will be too glad of their wooden bats to complain because they are not gold ones."

"Please, father, don't remind me of that again," replied Frank, coloring. . . .

It was a pleasure to the parents to see how the planning of things and the doing of things waked up the energies of their young folks. Almost every morning Isabel and Ellen would bound into the breakfast-room, with eager faces, saying, "Good morning, papa and mamma. We've got a new idea." The phrase became a family joke.

"Bless me!" exclaimed Mr. Rich, when they came jumping in as usual one morning. "What's coming on the carpet next? Some new idea I suppose. What a privilege it is to have a family so full of ideas!"

"Why, papa," replied Ellen, "you know Issy acts charades beautifully. Frank has written one, and she's going to act it at the Fair, and charge the visitors five cents apiece. Perhaps we shall get as much as five dollars; and that would buy a good many dolls' heads or picture-books for the orphans."

Another morning, Isabel was in great ecstasy over a plan Ellen had suggested. "O papa, it is such a bright idea!" exclaimed she. "We are going to have a Tableau of Europe, Asia, Africa, and America. Petty Poo is going to be Europe, with some pearl beads on her neck and arms, and Frank's miniature ship beside her. We are going to paint little Cousin Joe yellowish brown, and dress him up like a Chinese Mandarin, and seat him on a tea-chest. That's for Asia, you know. We are going to paint little John reddish brown, with a coronet of feathers on his head; and Frank is going to make a bow and arrow for him. That's for America. You remember that bright-looking little black girl, Kitty Jones? We're going to ask her mother to lend her to us, and we'll dress her up for Africa. Frank says she ought to be leaning on an elephant's tusk, but I don't know where we could get one."

"What's the child thinking of!" exclaimed Mr. Rich. "Why, you might as well give me a meeting-house steeple for a cane. What could such a little creature do with an elephant's tusk, five or six feet long; taller than I am?"

"Perhaps we can find a baby elephant's tusk," replied Isabel. "We shall have to charge ten cents apiece for the Tableau, it will be so much trouble."

The weeks passed on, bringing with them a succession of new projects. Many of them were nipped in the bud by adverse circumstances; but whether they ripened or not, they occupied the young brains of the children and gave their bodies healthy exercise. They were impatient for spring to come, that they might remove to their country-house in Dorchester. There they could pick up hen's feathers, and color them pink with cochineal, and blue with indigo, for ornamenting the dolls' hats.

Sometimes the cockerel dropped a gaudy feather that needed no coloring, and great was their joy over the prize. Then they wanted autumn to come, that they might find moss-acorns; for mamma had given them some pieces of her brown silk dress, and promised to show them how to make little emery-balls, that would look like real acorns when they were fastened in the mossy cups. An unthought-of value was imparted to every scrap of pretty ribbon or calico, and to broken strings of beads that had long been rolling about. Even little Alice caught the prevailing spirit, and was every day bringing a doll's sash, or some other of her little treasures, saying, "Dis is for de orfins." The children of this wealthy family had never before experienced the great pleasure of turning everything to some good use; and the novelty was very delightful to them.

When relatives and friends heard the proposal not to exchange Christmas presents, they were very much surprised, and some were half disposed to be offended. The children soon reconciled them, however, by saying, "It is not because we are ungrateful for your presents, or unwilling to send presents to you. But we have thought of a new plan, and when you come to know something about it, we hope you will like it." They of course perceived that something uncommonly engrossing was going forward, but could not find out exacdy what; and this little air of mystery added a new charm to the enterprise.

What with lessons in English and French, and music and dancing, and all their plans for the Fair, December came round again without the children's ever having occasion to say, "I wish I knew what to do." The large drawing-room was arranged for their accommodation on the eventful evening. At one extremity, English ivy was trained round a large hoop to form a framework for the Tableau. When the screen was removed, and pearl-white Alice, and yellowish-brown Joe, and reddish-brown John, and brown-black Kitty were seen grouped behind the ivy, they really made a very pretty picture.

Little Joe looked very funny in his Chinese cap, with a peacock's feather in it, a little round button atop, and a long braid of hair tied on behind. Alice was charming in white muslin, with some small blue flowers and strings of pearl beads hanging among her flaxen curls. John had a coronet of turkey's feathers, and a short beaver-skin skirt, fastened round the waist with a gaudy belt of many colored wampum. Bead-embroidered moccasins covered his feet. In one hand he carried a bow and arrow, trimmed with red and yellow ribbon, and in the other a stuffed squirrel, to represent the fur trade. Kitty Jones wore a short skirt of yellow merino. Her arms and feet were bare, with the exception of strips of gilt paper on wrists and ankles. On her head was a crown of gilt paper surmounted by an ostrich-feather. Frank had fashioned a piece of wood into the resemblance of a small tusk, and painted it suitably, that she might represent the trade of Africa in gold and ivory and ostrich-feathers.

The little ones behaved very properly, till Alice spied out her white poodle sniffing round the room in search of her. Then she forgot all the instructions she had received, and called out, "Poody! Poody!" That was a very improper proceeding for Europe, with a ship by her side to represent the commerce of the world. And it made Asia laugh out loud; which was an unheard of want of dignity in a Mandarin upon a state occasion. America grinned rather too broadly for a sedate Indian chief. Africa was perfectly motionless in every muscle; and looked a little bit afraid; which Frank said was very natural, considering Europe was so near with her ship, and still carrying on the slave-trade; a remark which his sisters and cousins thought quite witty.

After the little ones were dismissed with kisses and candy, Frank came tottering in, bent half double, with a white wig on his head, an hour-glass in one hand and a scythe in the other. He was followed by Isabel, handsomely dressed in the newest mode. Afterward Ellen and her mother appeared, dressed just as women and little girls dressed forty years ago. "O how funny they look! Did you ever see such frights?" shouted the young folks. They all agreed that it was very easy to guess the first, and the second, and the whole of the charade had been acted. When they had taken off their disguises, friends and relatives began to compliment them. Ellen, who was always ready to praise her sister, because she really thought her something uncommon, replied, "Isabel acted her part beautifully; flirting her fan, courtesying, and swinging her crinoline; but I didn't do anything only walk round with an old bonnet on my head. I never *could* act charades well."

"There is one thing she can do well," said Isabel. "She preaches beautifully."

"O Isabel! How *can* you say so?" exclaimed Ellen, blushing scarlet.

"It's nothing more than the truth," persisted Isabel. "I heard you preach a beautiful sermon at Carry Rice's party."

The company, amused at her confusion, began to say, "Ellen, you must let us hear you preach. We will give you ten cents apiece for a sermon."

This offer tempted her; she thought of the dolls and tops the money would buy. She allowed them to place her on a stool, but when she found herself there, with all of them looking at her, she felt very much heated, and said, bashfully, "Ladies and gentlemen, I don't know what to preach about. When I was at Carry Rice's, some of the girls and boys got into a quarrel, and I preached to them from the text, 'Return good for evil.' But you are not quarrelling. Besides, everybody preaches about the war now, and I do want the Rebels to be beaten; so that text won't do; and I don't know what text to take."

"Proclaim Liberty throughout all the land, to all the inhabitants thereof," said her father, in a loud, clear voice.

"That's a good text," said Ellen, brightening up. "Liberty ought to be proclaimed to all, because it ought to be. They say they used to whip the slaves down in Dixie for trying to learn to read and write. That was very wrong. There's little Kitty Jones, that was Africa to-night; she's as bright as a steel button. She learns her letters a great deal faster than our Alice; and it would be a sin and a shame to whip her for it. The slaveholders wouldn't like to have their children whipped for learning, and they ought to do to others as they would be done by. Besides, it would be better for the white folks down there if liberty was proclaimed to all. They wouldn't be so violent-tempered, and go round stabbing folks with bowie-knives, if they hadn't been used to beating and banging slaves about when they were boys. And if they hadn't slaves to wait upon 'em, they would find out what a great pleasure it is to learn how to do things, and to help themselves. So you see, if we beat the Rebels, and proclaim liberty to all, we *shall* return good for evil; and that text would have done for my sermon, if I had thought about it. But then I think the greatest reason why we ought to proclaim liberty to all is because we ought to. And I don't know as I have anything more to say to-night."

As she descended from her eminence, all in a flutter, her friends came up to offer their money; and Uncle Joe patted her on the head as he said, "I've heard some sermons that were not so well worth ten cents."

There was a short recess, and Isabel played lively tunes while the guests walked about and ate ice-creams, which the girls had made, under their mother's directions. Over the refreshment-table Frank had printed, in large letters, "Home Manufacture." All the articles were sold before ten o'clock; for the secret was discovered, and everybody wanted to help on the good work. The children were impatient to have the guests go, that they might count their money. They were greatly surprised and delighted to find they had received more than two hundred dollars. They kissed papa and mamma, and kissed each other, and said, over and over again, "Didn't we have a good time?"

When they had sobered down a little, Isabel, looking up archly, said, "Papa and mamma, I've got a new idea."

"I dare say she has," said Ellen; "she's always having new ideas."

"And what is it now?" asked their mother.

"We have got so much more money than we expected," replied Isabel, "that I think we can do two things. You know that slave woman down South, who hid Cousin George when the Rebels were after him? He wrote to us that she had a very pretty, bright little girl. Seeing Kitty Jones tonight has made me think about her. I should like to spend half our money in picture-books and toys for the freed children."

"Good! good!" exclaimed Ellen, clapping her hands.

They all agreed with her, and when their articles were collected together, they were divided into two parcels, one of which was immediately sent off to the islands of South Carolina; the other half was reserved till the day before Christmas, when they were conveyed to the Orphan Asylum. Frank procured a pretty evergreen tree, and they all went to help the Superintendent arrange the articles upon it. The little inmates of the asylum were kept in the dark about the whole affair till evening, when they were marched into the room in procession, two and two. They were very shy in presence of the strangers. A few of them gazed with wonder on the lighted Christmas Tree, and some little laughs were heard; but most of them stood with fingers on their mouths, looking down. When hoods and mittens, and balls and bats, and tops and skates, and dolls and picture-books were distributed among them, a few jumped and laughed; but most of them made little formal bows and courtesies, and said, "Thank'ee, ma'am," "Thank'ee, sir," as they had been taught to do. When the articles were all distributed, the Superintendent conducted them to the play-room. She returned a few minutes afterward, and said to Mr. Rich and his family, "They were constrained before strangers; but I have left the door of the play-room ajar, and I should like you to have a peep in."

Such a merry scene! The orphans were jumping and skipping about, tossing up their balls and dancing their dolls. "See how high my ball goes!" shouted one. "See what a pretty dolly I've got!" said another.

"O mamma! this pays us for all our work," said Isabel.

"I thought you were paid in doing the work," rejoined her mother.

"So we were," said Ellen; "but this pays us over again."

While they were putting on their cloaks to return home, a chubby little orphan asked the Superintendent for a "fower." When asked what she wanted it for, she answered, "For de lady dat did give me de dolly." When she had received a geranium blossom, she went to Isabella and bashfully held up her flower. Isabella thanked her and kissed her, and she trotted off in a state of high satisfaction.

When the family returned to their elegant parlor, there were only ashes in the grate, the gas burned low, with a seething sound, and the gleams of the gilded paper were hidden by a veil of shadow. But the cheeks of the children glowed as they had not glowed under the brilliancy of the last year's Christmas Eve.

"O, what a pleasant world this is!" exclaimed Ellen.

Isabel took up a graceful Parian vase for one flower, and said. "Mamma, won't this geranium keep longer if I put salt in the water?"

Her mother smiled as she replied, "You are not apt to be so very careful of the flowers that are given you. But I see, my dear child, that you are learning by experience how much more blessed it is to give than to receive."

The water in the vase was changed every day; and when the blossom fell, the petals were pressed in a book, and under them was written, "The Little Orphan's Gift, on Christmas Eve. . . ."

In a few weeks they received a letter from Cousin George, in which he wrote: "Dear cousins, your box arrived safely, and the teachers distributed the things on New Year's Eve. I would have given fifty dollars if you could have looked upon the scene. Such uproarious joy I never witnessed. Such singing and shouting are never heard among white folks. I wrote to you that the slave woman, who saved me from the horrors of a Rebel prison by hiding me under some straw in her hut, was here at work for wages. Her little Chloe is not much older than Petty Poo, and is as pretty, in a different way. Such glorious brown eyes you never saw. When the doll with two babies was given her, she jumped and capered, and danced and sung, till my sides ached with laughing. All these people naturally express their feelings in music; and little Chloe, small as she is, has the gift. She sings whatever tune comes into her head, and makes words to suit it as she goes along. It would have done your hearts good to hear her sing:

How kind de Yankee ladies is!
So kind I nebber see!
How kind de Yankee ladies is,
To gib dese tings to me!

I made a sketch of her merry little face on a leaf of my pocket-book, while she was singing, and if I had colored crayons here I think I could make you a pretty picture. It is a pity you could not have had her for your Tableau; though I have no doubt she would have laughed when the white poodle appeared on the stage, and in all probability she would have jumped down to catch him."

Not long afterward Captain George came home on a fortnight's leave of absence. And, hurried as he was, he found time to make a picture of little Chloe in colored crayons. The yellow cheeks and the great brown eyes made it look like a coreopsis blossom in the sunshine; and the face had such a happy, merry expression, that everybody laughed who looked at it. Isabel printed under it: "From Cousin George. A Souvenir of our Useful Christmas." It was framed and hung in the breakfast-room; and one day they found that Frank had pasted on the back the following inscription: "This is a commentary on the 'booful preach' Ellen made at our Fair, from the text, 'Proclaim Liberty throughout the land, to all the inhabitants thereof.' "

The Sack and Destruction of Columbia, South Carolina

William Gilmore Simms (1806–1870)

Simms was a chronicler of the antebellum South, a poet, novelist, and historian with a large body of regional work. A South Carolinian, he was proslavery and an ardent secessionist. There is some feeling among contemporary critics that he was a neglected but potentially important American writer whose career was derailed by the Civil War. By the time South Carolina was able to take up an interest in regional literature after the War, Simms was dead. This account of the sacking, however influenced by his own partisan views, raises questions about Sherman's control over the infamous march.

A frequently cited introduction to the Simms text from a contemporary Confederate archive describes the event as a cultural hate crime:

> In late 1864 and early 1865, 62,000 battle-hardened Northern soldiers, under the command of William Tecumseh Sherman, marched through Georgia and South Carolina, destroying everything in their path. Sherman had promised that he would "make Georgia howl" and "punish South Carolina as she deserves" for her "sins" against the Union. In the name of "destroying slavery" and with the blessings of Abraham Lincoln, Sherman's troops destroyed civilian homes, desecrated graves, raped and murdered helpless women and children, and left thousands, both White and Black, in their wake to forage through the de-

struction for what food they could find. This book details the horrors experienced by the citizens of Columbia, South Carolina, at the hands of their Northern invaders.

SHERMAN'S ENTRANCE INTO SOUTH CAROLINA—DESTRUCTION OF PROPERTY IN THE LOW COUNTRY.

The march of the Federals into our State was characterized by such scenes of license, plunder and general conflagration, as very soon showed that the threats of the Northern press, and of their soldiery, were not to be regarded as mere *brutum fulmen.* Day by day brought to the people of Columbia tidings of atrocities committed, and more extended progress. Daily did long trains of fugitives line the roads, with wives and children, and horses and stock and cattle, seeking refuge from the pursuers. Long lines of wagons covered the highways. Half-naked people cowered from the winter under bush tents in the thickets, under the eaves of houses, under railroad sheds, and in old cars left them along the route. All these repeated the same story of suffering, violence, poverty and nakedness. Habitation after habitation, village after village—one sending up its signal flames to the other, presaging for it the same fate—lighted the winter and midnight sky with crimson horrors.

No language can describe nor can any catalogue furnish an adequate detail of the wide-spread destruction of homes and property. Granaries were emptied, and where the grain was not carried off, it was strewn to waste under the feet of the cavalry or consigned to the fire which consumed the dwelling. The negroes were robbed equally with the whites of food and clothing. The roads were covered with butchered cattle, hogs, mules and the costliest furniture. Valuable cabinets, rich pianos, were not only hewn to pieces, but bottles of ink, turpentine, oil, whatever could efface or destroy, was employed to defile and ruin. Horses were ridden into the houses. People were forced from their beds, to permit the search after hidden treasures.

The beautiful homesteads of the parish country, with their wonderful tropical gardens, were ruined; ancient dwellings of black cypress, one hundred years old, which had been reared by the fathers of the republic—men whose names were famous in Revolutionary history—were given to the torch as recklessly as were the rude hovels; choice pictures and works of art, from Europe, select and numerous libraries, objects of peace wholly, were all destroyed. The inhabitants, black no less than white, were left to starve, compelled to feed only upon the garbage to be found in the abandoned camps of the soldiers. The corn scraped up from the spots where the horses fed, has been the only means of life left to thousands but lately in affluence.

And thus plundering, and burning, the troops made their way through a portion of Beaufort into Barnwell District, where they pursued the same game. The villages of Buford's Bridge, of Barnwell, Blackville, Graham's, Bamberg, Midway, were more or less destroyed; the inhabitants everywhere left homeless and without food. The horses and mules, all cattle and hogs, whenever fit for service or for food, were carried off, and the rest shot. Every implement of the workman or the farmer, tools, plows, hoes, gins, looms, wagons, vehicles, was made to feed the flames.

From Barnwell to Orangeburg and Lexington was the next progress, marked everywhere by the same sweeping destruction. Both of these court towns were partially burned.

Outrages on Negro Women—A Lady in Child-Bed Frightened to Death—Fathers Protecting Their Daughters—A New Use for Parlors.

We have adverted to the outrages which were perpetrated within the households of the citizen, where, unrestrained by the rebuking eyes of their own comrades, and unresisted by their interposition, cupidity, malignity and lust, sought to glut their several appetites. The cupidity generally triumphed over the lust. The greed for gold and silver swallowed up the more animal passions, and drunkenness supervened in season for the safety of many.

We have heard of some few outrages, or attempts at outrage,

of the worst sort, but the instances, in the case of white females, must have been very few. There was, perhaps, a wholesome dread of goading to desperation the people whom they had despoiled of all but honor. They could see, in many watchful and guardian eyes, the lurking expression which threatened sharp vengeance, should their trespasses proceed to those extremes which they yet unquestionably contemplated.

The venerable Mr. H——stood ready, with his *couteau de chasse*, made bare in his bosom, hovering around the persons of his innocent daughters. Mr. O——, on beholding some too familiar approach to one of his daughters, bade the man stand off at the peril of his life; saying that while he submitted to be robbed of property, he would sacrifice life without reserve—his own and that of the assailant—before his child's honor should be abused.

Mr. James G. Gibbes with difficulty, pistol in hand, and only with the assistance of a Yankee officer, rescued two young women from the clutches of as many ruffians.

We have been told of successful outrages of this unmentionable character being practiced upon women dwelling in the suburbs. Many are understood to have taken place in remote country settlements, and two cases are described where young negresses were brutally forced by the wretches and afterwards murdered—one of them being thrust, when half dead, head down, into a mud puddle, and there held until she was suffocated. But this must suffice.

The shocking details should not now be made, but that we need, for the sake of truth and humanity, to put on record the horrid deeds. And yet, we should grossly err if, while showing the forbearance of the soldiers in respect to our *white* women, we should convey to any innocent reader the notion that they exhibited a like forbearance in the case of the *black*. The poor negroes were terribly victimized by their assailants, many of them, besides the instance mentioned, being left in a condition little short of death. Regiments, in successive *relays*, subjected scores of these poor women to the torture of their embraces, and—but we dare not further pursue the subject. There are some horrors which the historian dare not pursue—which the painter dare not delineate. They both drop the curtain over crimes which humanity bleeds to contemplate.

Some incidents of gross brutality, which show how well prepared were these men for every crime, however monstrous, may be given.

A lady, undergoing the pains of labor, had to be borne out on a mattress into the open air, to escape the fire. It was in vain that her situation was described as the soldiers applied the torch within and without the house, after they had penetrated every chamber and robbed them of all that was either valuable or portable. They beheld the situation of the sufferer, and laughed to scorn the prayer for her safety.

Another lady, Mrs. J——, was but recently confined. Her condition was very helpless. Her life hung upon a hair. The men were apprised of all the facts in the case. They burst into the chamber—took the rings from the lady's fingers—plucked the watch from beneath her pillow, and so overwhelmed her with terror, that she sunk under the treatment—surviving their departure but a day or two.

In several instances, parlors, articles of crockery, and even beds, were used by the soldiers as if they were water closets. In one case, a party used vessels in this way, then put them on the bed, fired at and smashed them to pieces, emptying the filthy contents over the bedding.

In several cases, newly made graves were opened, the coffins taken out, broken open, in search of buried treasure, and the corpses left exposed. Every spot in grave-yard or garden, which seemed to have been recently disturbed, was sounded with sword, or bayonet, or ramrod, in their desperate search after spoil.

Another Day of Horrors—When Will It End?—The Bugles—Blackened Walls—Sympathizing Soldiers.

The morning of Saturday, the 18th of February, opened still with its horrors and terrors, though somewhat diminished in their intensity. A lady said to an officer at her house, somewhere about 4 o'clock that morning:

"In the name of God, sir, when is this work of hell to be ended?"

He replied: "You will hear the bugles at sunrise, when a

guard will enter the town and withdraw these troops. It will then cease, and not before."

Sure enough, with the bugle's sound, and the entrance of fresh bodies of troops, there was an instantaneous arrest of incendiarism. You could see the rioters carried off in groups and squads, from the several precincts they had ravaged, and those which they still meditated to destroy.

The tap of the drum, the sound of the signal cannon, could not have been more decisive in its effect, more prompt and complete. But two fires were *set*, among private dwellings, after sunrise; and the flames only went up from a few places, where the fire had been last applied; and these were rapidly expiring.

The best and most beautiful portion of Columbia lay in ruins. Never was ruin more complete; and the sun rose with a wan countenance, peering dimly through the dense vapors which seemed wholly to overspread the firmament. Very miserable was the spectacle. On every side ruins, and smoking masses of blackened walls, and towers of grim, ghastly chimneys, and between, in desolate groups, reclining on mattress, or bed, or earth, were wretched women and children, gazing vacantly on the site of a once blessed abode of home and innocence.

Roving detachments of the soldiers passed around and among them. There were those who looked and lingered nigh, with taunt and sarcasm. Others there were, in whom humanity did not seem wholly extinguished; and others again, to their credit, be it said, who were truly sorrowful and sympathizing, who had labored for the safety of family and property, and who openly deplored the dreadful crime, which threatened the lives and honors of the one, and destroyed so completely the other.

A Slave's Memory of the War

Mittie Freeman

On August 27, 1937, eighty-six-year-old Mittie Freeman was interviewed at her granddaughter's home in North Little Rock, Arkansas, by Beulah Sherwood Hagg for the Federal Writers' Project of the WPA. The interview, excerpted here, is one of more than two thousand firsthand accounts by former slaves of their life in bondage. Mittie Freeman's story is included in *Slave Narratives: A Folk History of Slavery in the United States from Interviews with Former Slaves: Volume II, Arkansas Narratives, Part 2.* According to her reported age in 1937, she would have been ten years old at the beginning of the War.

Orange county, Mississippi was where I was borned at but I been right here in Arkansas before sech thing as war gonna be. In slavery, it was, when my white folks done come to Camden. You know where that is?—Camden on the Ouachita? That's the place where we come. Yes, ma'am, it was long before the war when the doctor—I means Dr. Williams what owned my pappy and all us younguns—say we going to Arkansas. Theys rode in the fine carriages. Us slaves rode in ox wagons. Lord only knows how long it tuck a-coming. Every night we camped. I was jest a little tike then but I has remembrance of everything. The biggest younguns had to walk till theys so tired theys couldn't hardly drag they feets; them what had been a-riding had to get out the ox wagon and walk a far piece; so it like this we go on.

Dr. Williams always wanted to keep his slaves together. He was sure good man. He didn't work his slaves hard like some. My pappy was a kind of a manager for Doctor. Doctor tended his business and pappy runned the plantation where we lived at. Our good master died before freedom. He willed us slaves to his chilrun. You know—passeled (parcelled) us out, some to this child, some to that. I went to his daughter, Miss Emma. Laws-a-Mercy, how I wishes I could see her face onct more afore I dies. I heerd she married rich. Unh-unh! I'd shore love to see her onct more.

After old master died, poor old pappy got sent to another plantation of the fam'ly. It had a overseer. He was a northerner man and the meantest devil ever put foot on a plantation. My father was a gentleman; yes, ma'am, he was jest that. He had been brung up that-a-way. Old master teached us to never answer back to no white folks. But one day that overseer had my pappy whipped for sompin he never done, and pappy hit him.

So after that, he sent pappy down to New Orleans to be sold. He said he would liked to kill pappy, but he didn't dare 'cause he didn't owned him. Pappy was old. Every auction sale, all the young niggers be sold; everybody pass old pappy by. After a long time—oh, maybe five years—one day they ax pappy—"Are you got some white folks back in Arkansas?" He telled them the Williams white folks in Camden on the Ouachita. Theys white. After while theys send pappy home. Miss, I tells you, nobody never seen sech a home coming. Old Miss and the young white folks gathered round and hugged my old black pappy when he come home; they cry on his shoulder, so glad to git him back. That's what them Williams folks thought of their slaves. Yes, ma'am.

Old Miss was name Miss 'liza. She skeered to stay by herself after old master died. I was took to be her companion. Every day she wanted me to bresh her long hair and bathe her feet in cool water; she said I was gentle and didn't never hurt her. One day I was a standing by the window and I seen smoke—blue smoke a rising over beyond a woods. I heerd cannons a-booming and axed her what was it. She say: "Run, Mittie, and hide yourself. It's the Yanks. Theys coming at last, Oh lordy!" I was all incited (excited) and told her I didn't want to hide, I wanted to see 'em. "No" she say, right firm. "Ain't I always told you Yankees has horns on their heads? They'll get you. Go on now, do like I tells you." So I runs out the room and went down by the big gate. A high wall was there and a tree put its branches right over the top. I clim up and hid under the leaves. They was coming, all a marching. The captain opened our big gate and marched them in. A soldier seen me and said, "Come on down here; I want to see you." I told him I would, if he would take off his hat and show me his horns.

The day freedom came, I was fishing with pappy. My remembrance is sure good. All a-suddent cannons commence a-booming, it seem like everywhere. You know what that was, Miss? It was the fall of Richmond. Cannons was to roar every place when Richmond fell. Pappy jumps up, throws his pole and everything, and grabs my hand, and starts flying towards the house. "It's victory," he keep on saying. "It's freedom. Now we'es gwine be free." I didn't know what it all meant.

It seem like it tuck a long time fer freedom to come. Everything jest kept on like it was. We heard that lots of slaves was getting land and some mules to set up fer theirselves; I never knowed any what got land or mules nor nothing.

We all stayed right on the place till the Yankees came through. They was looking for slaves what was staying on. Now we was free and had to git off the plantation. They packed us in their big amulance . . . you say it wasn't a amulance,—what was it? Well, then, their big covered army wagons, and tuck us to Little Rock. Did you ever know where the old penitentiary was? Well, right there is where the Yanks had a great big barracks. All chilluns and growd womens was put there in tents. Did you know that the fust real free school in Little Rock was opened by the govment for colored chullens? Yes, ma'am, and I went to it, right from the day we got there.

They took pappy and put him to work in the big commissary; it was on the corner of Second and Main Street. He got $12.00 a month and all the grub we could eat. Unh-unh! Didn't we live good? I sure got a good remembrance, honey. Can't you tell? Yes, ma'am. They was plenty of other refugees living in them barracks, and the govment taking keer of all of 'em.

The Surrender at Appomattox

Ulysses S. Grant

On April 7, 1865, four days after the fall of the Confederate capital at Richmond to the Army of the Potomac and with Lee's army in retreat, Grant initiated a correspondence with Lee; in it, both generals expressed the wish to avoid any further useless "effusion of blood." Lee, aware that his army was surrounded and his men weak and exhausted, acknowledged that there was little choice but the surrender of the Army of Northern Virginia and asked to be informed of the proposed terms of such a surrender. Grant and Lee met on April 9, 1865, in the parlor of Wilmer McLean's house in the village of Appomattox Courthouse. The difference in appearance between the two men has become the stuff of legend—Grant smaller and disheveled, Lee erect and impeccably uniformed. The meeting between the two lasted approximately two and a half hours; the terms of surrender were agreed upon, and, after receiving salutes of respect from Grant and his staff, a somber Lee departed to convey the news to his troops. Though scattered fighting continued for another month, the surrender marked the end of the War.

The Personal Memoirs of Ulysses S. Grant were written during the last years of his life, as he was dying of throat cancer, in an effort to secure a financial legacy for his family. The two-volume edition was published by his friend Mark Twain and became a bestseller, achieving, though he did not live to see it, the financial success he had hoped for. *The Memoirs* were and still are much admired for their plain, direct style in dealing with the extraordinary events in which he was a key participant and essential witness.

On the 8th I had followed the Army of the Potomac in rear of Lee. I was suffering very severely with a sick headache, and stopped at a farmhouse on the road some distance in rear of the main body of the army. I spent the night in bathing my feet in hot water and mustard, and putting mustard plasters on my wrists and the back part of my neck, hoping to be cured by morning. During the night I received Lee's answer to my letter of the 8th, inviting an interview between the lines on the following morning. But it was for a different purpose from that of surrendering his army, and I answered him as follows:

HEADQUARTERS ARMIES OF THE U.S., April 9, 1865.
GENERAL R. E. LEE, Commanding C. S. A.
Your note of yesterday is received. As I have no authority to treat on the subject of peace, the meeting proposed for ten A.M. to-day could lead to no good. I will state, however, General, that I am equally anxious for peace with yourself, and the whole North entertains the same feeling. The terms upon which peace can be had are well understood. By the South laying down their arms they will hasten that most desirable event, save thousands of human lives and hundreds of millions of property not yet destroyed. Sincerely hoping that all our difficulties may be settled without the loss of another life, I subscribe myself, etc.,
U. S. GRANT, Lieutenant-General.

I proceeded at an early hour in the morning, still suffering with the headache, to get to the head of the column. I was not more than two or three miles from Appomattox Court House at the time, but to go direct I would have to pass through Lee's army, or a portion of it. I had therefore to move south in order to get upon a road coming up from another direction.

When the white flag was put out by Lee, as already described, I was in this way moving towards Appomattox Court House, and consequently could not be communicated with immediately, and be informed of what Lee had done. Lee, therefore, sent a flag to the rear to advise Meade and one to the front to Sheridan, saying that he had sent a message to me for the purpose of having a meeting to consult about the surrender of his army, and asked for a suspension of hostilities until I could be communicated with. As they had heard nothing of this until the fighting had got to be severe and all going against Lee, both of these commanders hesitated very considerably about suspending hostilities at all. They were afraid it was not in good faith, and we had the Army of Northern Virginia where it could not escape except by some deception. They, however, finally consented to a suspension of hostilities for two hours to give an opportunity of communicating with me in that time, if possible. It was found that, from the route I had taken, they could probably not be able to communicate with me and get an answer back within the time fixed unless the messenger should pass through the rebel lines. Lee, therefore, sent an escort with the officer bearing this message through his lines to me.

April 9, 1865.
GENERAL: I received your note of this morning on the picket-line whither I had come to meet you and ascertain definitely what terms were embraced in your proposal of yesterday with reference to the surrender of this army.
I now request an interview in accordance with the offer contained in your letter of yesterday for that purpose.
R. E. LEE, General.
LIEUTENANT-GENERAL U. S. GRANT Commanding U. S. Armies.

When the officer reached me I was still suffering with the sick headache, but the instant I saw the contents of the note I was cured. I wrote the following note in reply and hastened on:

April 9, 1865.
GENERAL R. E. LEE, Commanding C. S. Armies.
Your note of this date is but this moment (11.50 A.M.) received, in consequence of my having passed from the Richmond and Lynchburg road to the Farmville and Lynchburg road. I am at this writing about four miles west of Walker's Church and will push forward to the front for the purpose of meeting you. Notice sent to me

on this road where you wish the interview to take place will meet me.
U.S. GRANT, Lieutenant-General.

I was conducted at once to where Sheridan was located with his troops drawn up in line of battle facing the Confederate army near by. They were very much excited, and expressed their view that this was all a ruse employed to enable the Confederates to get away. They said they believed that Johnston was marching up from North Carolina now, and Lee was moving to join him; and they would whip the rebels where they now were in five minutes if I would only let them go in. But I had no doubt about the good faith of Lee, and pretty soon was conducted to where he was. I found him at the house of Mr. McLean, at Appomattox Court House, with Colonel Marshall, one of his staff officers, awaiting my arrival. The head of his column was occupying a hill, on a portion of which was an apple orchard, beyond a little valley which separated it from that on the crest of which Sheridan's forces were drawn up in line of battle to the south.

Before stating what took place between General Lee and myself, I will give all there is of the story of the famous apple tree.

Wars produce many stories of fiction, some of which are told until they are believed to be true. The war of the rebellion was no exception to this rule, and the story of the apple tree is one of those fictions based on a slight foundation of fact. As I have said, there was an apple orchard on the side of the hill occupied by the Confederate forces. Running diagonally up the hill was a wagon road, which, at one point, ran very near one of the trees, so that the wheels of vehicles had, on that side, cut off the roots of this tree, leaving a little embankment. General Babcock, of my staff, reported to me that when he first met General Lee he was sitting upon this embankment with his feet in the road below and his back resting against the tree. The story had no other foundation than that. Like many other stories, it would be very good if it was only true.

I had known General Lee in the old army, and had served with him in the Mexican War; but did not suppose, owing to the difference in our age and rank, that he would remember me, while I would more naturally remember him distinctly, because he was the chief of staff of General Scott in the Mexican War.

When I had left camp that morning I had not expected so

soon the result that was then taking place, and consequently was in rough garb. I was without a sword, as I usually was when on horseback on the field, and wore a soldier's blouse for a coat, with the shoulder straps of my rank to indicate to the army who I was. When I went into the house I found General Lee. We greeted each other, and after shaking hands took our seats. I had my staff with me, a good portion of whom were in the room during the whole of the interview.

What General Lee's feelings were I do not know. As he was a man of much dignity, with an impassible face, it was impossible to say whether he felt inwardly glad that the end had finally come, or felt sad over the result, and was too manly to show it. Whatever his feelings, they were entirely concealed from my observation; but my own feelings, which had been quite jubilant on the receipt of his letter, were sad and depressed. I felt like anything rather than rejoicing at the downfall of a foe who had fought so long and valiantly, and had suffered so much for a cause, though that cause was, I believe, one of the worst for which a people ever fought, and one for which there was the least excuse. I do not question, however, the sincerity of the great mass of those who were opposed to us.

General Lee was dressed in a full uniform which was entirely new, and was wearing a sword of considerable value, very likely the sword which had been presented by the State of Virginia; at all events, it was an entirely different sword from the one that would ordinarily be worn in the field. In my rough traveling suit, the uniform of a private with the straps of a lieutenant-general, I must have contrasted very strangely with a man so handsomely dressed, six feet high and of faultless form. But this was not a matter that I thought of until afterwards.

We soon fell into a conversation about old army times. He remarked that he remembered me very well in the old army; and I told him that as a matter of course I remembered him perfectly, but from the difference in our rank and years (there being about sixteen years' difference in our ages), I had thought it very likely that I had not attracted his attention sufficiently to be remembered by him after such a long interval. Our conversation grew so pleasant that I almost forgot the object of our meeting. After the conversation had run on in this style for some time, General Lee called my attention to the object of our meeting, and said that he had asked for this interview for the purpose of getting from me the terms I proposed to give his army. I said that I meant merely that his army should lay down their arms, not to take them up again during the continuance of the war unless duly and properly exchanged. He said that he had so understood my letter.

Then we gradually fell off again into conversation about matters foreign to the subject which had brought us together. This continued for some little time, when General Lee again interrupted the course of the conversation by suggesting that the terms I proposed to give his army ought to be written out. I called to General Parker, secretary on my staff, for writing materials, and commenced writing out the following terms:

APPOMATTOX C. H., VA.,
Ap 19th, 1865.
GEN. R. E. LEE, Comd'g C. S. A.
GEN: In accordance with the substance of my letter to you of the 8th inst., I propose to receive the surrender of the Army of N. Va. on the following terms, to wit: Rolls of all the officers and men to be made in duplicate. One copy to be given to an officer designated by me, the other to be retained by such officer or officers as you may designate. The officers to give their individual paroles not to take up arms against the Government of the United States until properly exchanged, and each company or regimental commander sign a like parole for the men of their commands. The arms, artillery and public property to be parked and stacked, and turned over to the officer appointed by me to receive them. This will not embrace the side-arms of the officers, nor their private horses or baggage. This done, each officer and man will be allowed to return to their homes, not to be disturbed by United States authority so long as they observe their paroles and the laws in force where they may reside.
Very respectfully, U. S. GRANT, Lt. Gen.

When I put my pen to the paper I did not know the first word that I should make use of in writing the terms. I only knew what was in my mind, and I wished to express it clearly, so that there could be no mistaking it. As I wrote on, the thought occurred to me that the officers had their own private horses and effects, which were important to them, but of no value to us; also that it would be an unnecessary humiliation to call upon them to deliver their side arms.

No conversation, not one word, passed between General Lee and myself, either about private property, side arms, or kindred subjects. He appeared to have no objections to the terms first proposed; or if he had a point to make against them he wished to wait until they were in writing to make it. When he read over that part of the terms about side arms, horses and private property of the officers, he remarked, with some feeling, I thought, that this would have a happy effect upon his army.

Then, after a little further conversation, General Lee remarked to me again that their army was organized a little differently from the army of the United States (still maintaining by implication that we were two countries); that in their army the cavalrymen and artillerists owned their own horses; and he asked if he was to understand that the men who so owned their horses were to be permitted to retain them. I told him that as the terms were written they would not; that only the officers were permitted to take their private property. He then, after reading over the terms a second time, remarked that that was clear.

I then said to him that I thought this would be about the last battle of the war—I sincerely hoped so; and I said further I took it that most of the men in the ranks were small farmers. The whole country had been so raided by the two armies that it was doubtful whether they would be able to put in a crop to carry themselves and their families through the next winter without the aid of the horses they were then riding. The United States did not want them and I would, therefore, instruct the officers I left behind to receive the paroles of his troops to let every man of the Confederate army who claimed to own a horse or mule take the animal to his home. Lee remarked again that this would have a happy effect.

He then sat down and wrote out the following letter:

HEADQUARTERS ARMY OF NORTHERN VIRGINIA,
April 9, 1865.
GENERAL:—I received your letter of this date containing the terms of the surrender of the Army of Northern Virginia as proposed by you. As they are substantially the same as those expressed in your letter of the 8th

inst., they are accepted. I will proceed to designate the proper officers to carry the stipulations into effect.
R. E. LEE, General. LIEUT.-GENERAL U. S. GRANT.

While duplicates of the two letters were being made, the Union generals present were severally presented to General Lee.

The much talked of surrendering of Lee's sword and my handing it back, this and much more that has been said about it is the purest romance. The word sword or side arms was not mentioned by either of us until I wrote it in the terms. There was no premeditation, and it did not occur to me until the moment I wrote it down. If I had happened to omit it, and General Lee had called my attention to it, I should have put it in the terms precisely as I acceded to the provision about the soldiers retaining their horses.

General Lee, after all was completed and before taking his leave, remarked that his army was in a very bad condition for want of food, and that they were without forage; that his men had been living for some days on parched corn exclusively, and that he would have to ask me for rations and forage. I told him "certainly," and asked for how many men he wanted rations. His answer was "about twenty-five thousand"; and I authorized him to send his own commissary and quartermaster to Appomattox Station, two or three miles away, where he could have, out of the trains we had stopped, all the provisions wanted. As for forage, we had ourselves depended almost entirely upon the country for that.

Generals Gibbon, Griffin and Merritt were designated by me to carry into effect the paroling of Lee's troops before they should start for their homes—General Lee leaving Generals Longstreet, Gordon and Pendleton for them to confer with in order to facilitate this work. Lee and I then separated as cordially as we had met, he returning to his own lines, and all went into bivouac for the night at Appomattox.

Soon after Lee's departure I telegraphed to Washington as follows:

HEADQUARTERS APPOMATTOX C. H., VA., April 9th, 1865, 4.30 P.M.
HON. E. M. STANTON, Secretary of War, Washington.
General Lee surrendered the Army of Northern Virginia this afternoon on terms proposed by myself. The ac-

companying additional correspondence will show the conditions fully.
U. S. GRANT, Lieut.-General.

When news of the surrender first reached our lines our men commenced firing a salute of a hundred guns in honor of the victory. I at once sent word, however, to have it stopped. The Confederates were now our prisoners, and we did not want to exult over their downfall.

I determined to return to Washington at once, with a view to putting a stop to the purchase of supplies, and what I now deemed other useless outlay of money. Before leaving, however, I thought I would like to see General Lee again; so next morning I rode out beyond our lines towards his headquarters, preceded by a bugler and a staff-officer carrying a white flag.

Lee soon mounted his horse, seeing who it was, and met me. We had there between the lines, sitting on horseback, a very pleasant conversation of over half an hour, in the course of which Lee said to me that the South was a big country and that we might have to march over it three or four times before the war entirely ended, but that we would now be able to do it as they could no longer resist us. He expressed it as his earnest hope, however, that we would not be called upon to cause more loss and sacrifice of life; but he could not foretell the result. I then suggested to General Lee that there was not a man in the Confederacy whose influence with the soldiery and the whole people was as great as his, and that if he would now advise the surrender of all the armies I had no doubt his advice would be followed with alacrity. But Lee said, that he could not do that without consulting the President first. I knew there was no use to urge him to do anything against his ideas of what was right.

I was accompanied by my staff and other officers, some of whom seemed to have a great desire to go inside the Confederate lines. They finally asked permission of Lee to do so for the purpose of seeing some of their old army friends, and the permission was granted. They went over, had a very pleasant time with their old friends, and brought some of them back with them when they returned.

When Lee and I separated he went back to his lines and I returned to the house of Mr. McLean. Here the officers of both armies came in great numbers, and seemed to enjoy the meeting as much as though they had been friends separated for a long time while fighting battles under the same flag. For the time being it looked very much as if all thought of the war had escaped their minds. After an hour pleasantly passed in this way I set out on horseback, accompanied by my staff and a small escort, for Burkesville Junction, up to which point the railroad had by this time been repaired.

Anderson Returns to Fort Sumter

(April 14, 1865)

Fort Sumter was the object of sustained Union assault after 1863, but it was never actually surrendered by the Confederacy. It was, in fact, abandoned in 1864 after Sherman forced the evacuation of Charleston, South Carolina.

Robert Anderson, now General Anderson, who became a hero in the North after the fall of Fort Sumter in 1861, retired from the army in 1863. But, on April 14, 1865, exactly four years after the surrender, he returned to the ruins of the fort to reraise the thirty-three-star flag he had so unwillingly hauled down. That same evening, President Lincoln was assassinated.

THE DEATH OF ABRAHAM LINCOLN

Gideon Welles

Gideon Welles, Lincoln's Secretary of the Navy and staunch ally, was awakened on the night of April 14, 1865, with the news that the president had been shot while attending the play *Our American Cousin* at Ford's Theater in Washington. The distraught Welles rushed first to the theater, where he encountered agitated crowds. He was directed to the Petersen house across the street, to which the unconscious president had been taken. In this account from his diary, Welles especially notes the stunned and grieving African-Americans thronging the streets.

The President had been carried across the street from the theater to the house of a Mr. Peterson [*sic*]. We entered by ascending a flight of steps above the basement and passing through a long hall to the rear, where the President lay extended on a bed, breathing heavily. Several surgeons were present, at least six, I should think more. Among them I was glad to observe Doctor Hall, who, however, soon left. I inquired of Doctor Hall, as I entered, the true condition of the President. He replied the President was dead to all intents, although he might live three hours or perhaps longer.

The giant sufferer lay extended diagonally across the bed, which was not long enough for him. He had been stripped of his clothes. His large arms, which were occasionally exposed, were of a size which one would scarce have expected from his spare appearance. His slow, full respiration lifted the clothes with each breath that he took. His features were calm and striking. I had never seen them appear to better advantage than for the first hour, perhaps, that I was there. After that his right eye began to swell and that part of his face became discolored.

Senator Sumner was there, I think, when I entered. If not he came in soon after, as did Speaker Colfax, Mr. Secretary Mc-

Culloch, and the other members of the cabinet, with the exception of Mr. Seward. A double guard was stationed at the door and on the sidewalk to repress the crowd, which was of course highly excited and anxious. The room was small and overcrowded. The surgeons and members of the cabinet were as many as should have been in the room, but there were many more, and the hall and other rooms in the front or main house were full. One of these rooms was occupied by Mrs. Lincoln and her attendants, with Miss Harris. Mrs. Dixon and Mrs. Kinney came to her about twelve o'clock. About once an hour Mrs. Lincoln would repair to the bedside of her dying husband and with lamentation and tears remain until overcome by emotion.

A door which opened upon a porch or gallery, and also the windows, were kept open for fresh air. The night was dark, cloudy, and damp, and about six it began to rain. I remained in the room until then without sitting or leaving it, when, there being a vacant chair which some one left at the foot of the bed, I occupied it for nearly two hours, listening to the heavy groans and witnessing the wasting life of the good and great man who was expiring before me.

About 6 A.M. I experienced a feeling of faintness and for the first time after entering the room a little past eleven I left it and the house and took a short walk in the open air. It was a dark and gloomy morning, and rain set in before I returned to the house some fifteen minutes later. Large groups of people were gathered every few rods, all anxious and solicitous. Some one or more from each group stepped forward as I passed to inquire into the condition of the President and to ask if there was no hope. Intense grief was on every countenance when I replied that the President could survive but a short time. The colored people especially—and there were at this time more of them, perhaps, than of whites—were overwhelmed with grief.

A little before seven I went into the room where the dying President was rapidly drawing near the closing moments. His wife soon after made her last visit to him. The death struggle had begun. Robert, his son, stood with several others at the head of the bed. He bore himself well but on two occasions gave way to overpowering grief and sobbed aloud, turning his head and leaning on the shoulder of Senator Sumner. The respiration of the President became suspended at intervals and at last entirely ceased at twenty-two minutes past seven.

ABRAHAM LINCOLN'S FUNERAL

(April 21–May 3, 1865)

Lincoln's seventeen-hundred-mile funeral journey, almost an exact reverse of the inauguration journey five years earlier, began in Washington on April 21, 1865, following days of elaborate planning and ceremony in the capital. After considerable negotiation over the site, the journey ended at Oak Ridge Cemetery in Springfield, Illinois, on May 3. There were eleven separate services and several trackside events en route. Millions of people witnessed the passage of the train, day and night, in raw, rainy weather, and filed by the open coffin at the city viewing sites. The numbers occasionally resulted in near riots. Elaborate preparations and massive processions were conducted at the principal cities of Baltimore, Harrisburg, Philadelphia, New York, Albany, Buffalo, Cleveland, Columbus, Indianapolis, Chicago, and at the burial in Springfield. A variety of stately hearses with all the trappings of the Victorian funeral met the train to bear the body to ceremonies and viewing sites. A funeral director and embalmer traveled with the cortege to attend to the appearance of the corpse. By New York, Lincoln's face showed visible discoloration; thereafter deterioration increased rapidly, to the distress of those viewing the body.

Mary Lincoln did not accompany her husband's body to Springfield because she was so distraught, but the body of Willie Lincoln, buried in Georgetown, was exhumed and taken with the president's body for reburial together with that of three-year-old Eddie Lincoln, already buried in Illinois. Mrs. Lincoln first visited the grave a month later.

The description of the funeral that follows appeared in *Harpers Weekly* on May 6, 1865, and the engraving of the funeral procession in New York City was published on May 13.

Never, was King or Emperor honored with such obsequies as those with which our Republic has laid to rest its greatest hero. It was not the pomp of the procession, not the splendor of the funereal rites, that gave character to the touching ceremony, but the infinite tenderness and love of a great people. It was the sorrow in every heart that moved each outward expression of affection. It was the universal grief so heavily draped our streets. Not only the mansions of the rich, but the squalid hovels of the poor put on the habit of mourning. The reward which the Republic gives to its faithful servants is not alone that the people have raised them to the seat of honor, but that when they fall in their country's cause their principal monument is the people's love.

The funeral ceremony proper took place at Washington on the 19th of April, at the White House. The remains of the President lay in the Green Room, in a metallic coffin. On each side of the coffin were four silver handles, with stars between, a vein of silver winding around the whole cast in a serpentine form. This rested upon a canopied catafalque, and was decorated with wreaths of moss and evergreen, with white flowers and lilies intermingled. Around the catafalque, at noon, were gathered the family of the President, the officiating clergymen, the delegates from New York City, the heads of Bureaus, representatives of the Sanitary and Christian Commissions, the Governors of several States, the Assistant Secretaries, a large number of Congressmen, officers of the Supreme Court, and the Diplomatic Corps.

Reverend Dr. HALL opened the services by reading from the Episcopal service of the Dead. This was followed by an eloquent and affecting prayer by Bishop SIMPSON of the Methodist Episcopal Church. This portion of the service was most touching. At the close of his fervent appeal to the throne of Grace the Bishop repeated the Lord's Prayer, in which the whole audience joined as with one voice. The effect was sublime beyond any power of words to express, and the whole audience was melted to tears under its effect. Reverend Dr. Gunther, the pastor of the church which the President and his family were in the habit of attending, preached the funeral discourse. The service was

closed with prayer by Reverend Dr. GRAY, chaplain of the Senate.

The procession started from the White House at 2 P.M. and proceeded up Pennsylvania Avenue to the Capitol amidst the tolling of bells and the firing of minute-guns. The funeral car was carried up the steps of the Capitol, beneath the very spot where, six weeks before, the President had delivered his second Inaugural, and into the Rotunda, where the body was removed from the car to another catafalque, where a second service was read. Here the procession dispersed, leaving the remains of the President in the Rotunda, where they were open to view the next day.

A little before seven o'clock on the morning of the 21st the remains were escorted to the depot of the Baltimore and Ohio Railroad. Lieutenant-General GRANT followed immediately after the hearse. At ten o'clock the train arrived at Baltimore, and the coffin was laid in the Exchange for three or four hours, when the train started for Harrisburg, where it arrived in the evening. The next morning (the 22d) the cortege proceeded to Philadelphia, where the body was laid in Independence Hall and exposed to the view of thousands.

On the 24th New York city received the remains of the President. The scene upon the route from the ferry landing at the foot of Desbrosses Street, and at the City Hall, where the body was laid in state, was inexpressibly solemn and impressive. Early in the morning crowds of people gathered in the City Hall Park, and waited there for hours in order to obtain a view of the features of their departed hero. This scene was only exceeded in solemnity by the procession of the following day—the largest that ever thronged the streets of the great metropolis. It started at one o'clock P.M., proceeding up Broadway to Fourteenth Street, through Fourteenth Street to Fifth Avenue, and thence through Thirty-fourth Street to the Hudson River Railroad Depot on the way to Springfield, Illinois, where the President is to be buried.

Among the many tributes to President LINCOLN one of the best was that paid by HENRY WARD BEECHER in a discourse delivered on the 23d. The following extract we quote as appropriate to the funeral ceremony:

> And now the martyr is moving in triumphal march, mightier than when alive. The nation rises up at every stage of

his coming. Cities and States are his pall-bearers, and the cannon speaks the hours with solemn progression. Dead, dead, dead, he yet speaketh. Is WASHINGTON dead? Is HAMPDEN dead? Is DAVID dead? Is any man that was ever fit to live dead? Disenthralled of flesh, risen to the unobstructed sphere where passion never comes, he begins his illimitable work. His life is now grafted upon the infinite, and will be fruitful, as no earthly life can be. Pass on, thou that hast overcome! Your sorrows, oh people, are his paeans; your bells and bands and muffled drums sound triumph in his ears. Wail and weep here; God makes it echo joy and triumph there. Pass on! Four years ago, oh Illinois, we took from thy midst an untried man, and from among the people; we return him to you a mighty conqueror. Not thine any more, but the nation's; not ours, but the world's. Give him place, oh ye prairies! In the midst of this great continent his dust shall rest, sacred treasure to myriads who shall pilgrim to that shrine to kindle anew their zeal and patriotism. Ye winds that move over the mighty places of the West chant his requiem! Ye people, behold the martyr whose blood, as so many articulate words, pleads for fidelity, for law, for liberty!

Abraham Lincoln: His Great Funeral Cortege, from Washington City to Springfield, Illinois

John Carroll Power (1819–1894)

The ferry boat landed at the foot of Desbrosses street, New York city, at ten o'clock a.m., April 24, and the coffin was at once conveyed to a magnificent hearse or funeral car, prepared especially for the occasion. The platform of this car was fourteen feet long and eight feet wide. On the platform, which was five feet from the ground, there was a dais, on which the coffin rested. This gave it sufficient elevation to be readily seen by those at a distance, over the heads of the multitude. Above the dais there was a canopy fifteen feet high, supported by columns, and in part by a miniature temple of liberty. The platform was covered with black cloth, which fell at the sides nearly to the ground. It was edged with silver bullion fringe, which hung in graceful festoons. Black cloth hung from the sides, festooned with silver stars, and was also edged with silver fringe. The canopy was trimmed in like manner, with black cloth, festooned and spangled with silver bullion, the corners surmounted by rich plumes of black and white feathers. At the base of each column were three American flags, slightly inclined outward, festooned and covered with crape.

The temple of liberty was represented as being deserted, or rather despoiled, having no emblems of any kind, in or around it, except a small flag on the top, at half-mast. The inside of the car was lined with white satin, fluted. From the centre of the canopy, a large eagle was suspended, with outspread wings, and holding in its talons a laurel wreath. The platform around the coffin was strewn with flowers. The hearse or funeral car was drawn by sixteen white horses, covered with black cloth trimming, each led by a groom.

From the foot of Desbrosses street, the remains were escorted by the Seventh regiment New York National Guards, to Hudson street, thence to Canal street, up Canal street to Broadway, and down Broadway to the west gate of the City Hall Park.

The procession which followed the remains was in keeping with the funeral car, the whole being indescribably grand and imposing. As far as the eye could see, a dense mass of people, many of them wearing some insignia of mourning, filled the streets and crowded every window. The fronts of the houses were draped in mourning, and the national ensign displayed at half-mast from the top of almost every building. The procession was simply a dense mass of human beings. During the time it was moving, minute guns were fired at different points, and bells were tolled from nearly all the church steeples in the city. The chime on Trinity church wailed forth the tune of Old Hundred in a most solemn and impressive manner.

On arriving at the City Hall, the coffin was borne into the rotunda, amid the solemn chanting of eight hundred voices, and was placed on a magnificent catafalque, which had been prepared for its reception. The Hall was richly and tastefully decorated with the national colors and mourning drapery, and the coffin almost buried with rare and costly floral offerings. A large military guard, in addition to the Guard of Honor, kept watch over the sacred dust. All day and all night long, the living tide pressed into the Hall, to take a last look at the martyred remains. At the solemn hour of midnight, between the twenty-fourth and the twenty-fifth days of April, the German musical societies of New York, numbering about one thousand voices, performed a requiem in the rotunda of the City Hall, with the most thrilling effect. About ten o'clock, on the morning of April 25, while a galaxy of distinguished officers were assembled around the coffin, Captain Parker Snow, commander of the Arctic and Antarctic expedition, presented some very singular relics. They consisted of a leaf from the book of Common Prayer and a piece of paper, on which were glued some fringes. They were found in a boat, under the skull of a skeleton which had been identified as the remains of one of Sir John Franklin's men. The most singular thing about these relics was the fact that the only words that were preserved in a legible condition were "THE MARTYR," in capitals. General Dix deposited these relics in the coffin. At a few minutes past eleven o'clock, the coffin was closed, preparatory to resuming its westward journey. Notwithstanding such vast numbers had viewed the corpse, there were thousands who had waited for hours, in the long lines, to obtain a look at the well known face, who were obliged to turn away sadly disappointed. This disappointment was not confined to any class or condition of men. The coffin had just been closed, in the presence of the Sergeants of the Veteran Reserve Corps—who were in readiness to convey it to the hearse—and a number of distinguished army officers, whose commissions had been signed by the deceased; when the first to realize the disappointment were the representatives of Great Britain, Russia and France. They came in, glittering with scarlet, gold and silver lace, high coat collars, bearing embroidered cocked hats under their arms, with other costly trappings, and high birth and breeding in every gesture, desirous of seeing the corpse, but they were too late.

At about half past twelve o'clock, the magnificent hearse or funeral car, drawn by sixteen white horses, each led by a groom, as on the day before, appeared on Broadway, at the west gate of City Hall Park. The coffin was next conveyed to the car. Then commenced the farewell part of the funeral pageant given by the commercial metropolis of the nation to the memory of Abraham Lincoln. A military force of more than fifteen thousand men, with the staffs of several brigades and divisions, with their batteries, and the civic societies of every conceivable kind, in a great city, which joined in the demonstration, formed a double line about five miles long—equal to a single column of ten miles. In many parts of the procession, twenty men walked abreast. It was composed of eight grand divisions, each division having a marshal, with aids. It moved through the streets to the tolling of bells, the firing of minute guns and the music of a large number of bands. The animosities and division walls of parties, in politics, and sects and denominations, in religion, if not obliterated, were so far lowered, for the time being, that all parties could shake hands over them. Archbishop McClosky, the highest dignitary in the Roman Catholic church, in this country, walked side by side, in the procession, with Rev. Joseph P. Thompson, D. D., one of the most radical of the Congregational reformers of our land.

I have said that all party lines were, for the time, hidden from view, but it devolves upon me to notice one exception. Notwithstanding the blending of so many hearts in the great national sorrow, the city authorities of New York, true to their Tammany instincts, took measures to prevent the colored people from joining in the procession. They had deferred a procession of their own, on the Wednesday before, in order that five thousand of their number might be ready to show their love and respect for the emancipator of their race, by joining the procession to escort his remains on their way to the tomb. When it was known that the city authorities were trying to keep them out of the procession, Secretary Stanton interfered, and the order was set aside, but it was too late to give them such assurance of protection as to bring out their full numbers.

"THE DEATH OF ABRAHAM LINCOLN"

Walt Whitman

Whitman delivered this lecture on the anniversary of Lincoln's death on April 14, 1879, at Steck Hall in Manhattan to an audience of between sixty and eighty people. Thereafter, it became for him an annual event, given in Philadelphia in 1880, in Boston in 1881, and in a number of prestigious venues to audiences that included celebrities like Mark Twain and James Russell Lowell. Increasing ill health compelled Whitman to discontinue the lecture after 1890.

Unlike the lyric and symbolic tribute to Lincoln, "When Lilacs Last in the Dooryard Bloom'd," the lecture has the immediacy of an eyewitness account, which it is, though not Whitman's. The companion and friend of his post–Civil War years, Peter Doyle, a former Confederate artilleryman, whom Whitman met in a Washington hospital, had been attending *Our American Cousin* at Ford's Theater on the night of the assassination. He was so stunned by the event that he had to be ordered to leave afterward. Whitman made excellent use of Doyle's reminiscences, incorporating into the lecture vivid details of the unfolding event. He emphasized as well his own interpretation of Lincoln's death as integral to the rebirth of the nation.

How often since that dark and dripping Saturday—that chilly April day, now fifteen years bygone—my heart has entertain'd the dream, the wish, to give of Abraham Lincoln's death, its own special thought and memorial. Yet now the sought-for opportunity offers, I find my notes incompetent, (why, for truly profound themes, is statement so idle? why does the right phrase never offer?) and the fit tribute I dream'd of, waits unprepared as ever. My talk here indeed is less because of itself or anything in it, and nearly altogether because I feel a desire, apart from any talk, to specify the day, the martyrdom. It is for this, my friends. I have call'd you together. Oft as the rolling years bring back this hour, let it again, however briefly, be dwelt upon. For my own part, I hope and desire, till my own dying day, whenever the 14th or 15th of April comes, to annually gather a few friends, and hold its tragic reminiscence. No narrow or sectional reminiscence. It belongs to these States in their entirety—not the North only, but the South—perhaps belongs most tenderly and devoutly to the South, of all; for there, really, this man's birth-stock. There and thence his antecedent stamp. Why should I not say that thence his manliest traits—his universality—his canny, easy ways and words upon the surface—his inflexible determination and courage at heart? Have you never realized it, my friends, that Lincoln, though grafted on the West, is essentially, in personnel and character, a Southern contribution?

And though by no means proposing to resume the Secession war to-night, I would briefly remind you of the public conditions preceding that contest. For twenty years, and especially during the four or five before the war actually began, the aspect of affairs in the United States, though without the flash of military excitement, presents more than the survey of a battle, or any extended campaign, or series, even of Nature's convulsions. The hot passions of the South—the strange mixture at the North of inertia, incredulity, and conscious power—the incendiarism of the abolitionists—the rascality and grip of the politicians, unparalle'd in any land, any age. To these I must not omit adding the honesty of the essential bulk of the people everywhere—yet with all the seething fury and contradiction of their natures more arous'd than the Atlantic's waves in wildest equinox. In politics, what can be more ominous, (though generally unappreciated then)—what more significant than the Presidentiads of Fillmore and Buchanan? proving conclusively that the weakness and wickedness of elected rulers are just as likely to afflict us here, as in the countries of the Old World, under their monarchies, emperors, and aristocracies. In that Old World were everywhere heard underground rumblings, that died out, only to again surely return. While in America the volcano, though civic yet, continued to grow more and more convulsive—more and more stormy and threatening.

In the height of all this excitement and chaos, hovering on the edge at first, and then merged in its very midst, and destined to play a leading part, appears a strange and awkward figure. I shall not easily forget the first time I ever saw Abraham Lincoln. It must have been around the 18th or 19th of February, 1861. It was rather a pleasant afternoon, in New York city, as he arrived there from the West, to remain a few hours, and then pass on to Washington, to prepare for his inauguration. I saw him in Broadway, near the site of the present Post-office. He came down, I think from Canal street, to stop at the Astor House. The broad spaces, sidewalks, and street in the neighborhood, and for some distance, were crowded with solid masses of people, many thousands. The omnibuses and other vehicles had all been turn'd off, leaving an unusual hush in that busy part of the city. Presently two or three shabby hack barouches made their way with some difficulty through the crowd, and drew up at the Astor House entrance. A tall figure step'd out of the centre of these barouches, paus'd leisurely on the sidewalk, look'd up at the granite walls and looming architecture of the grand hotel—then, after a relieving stretch of arms and legs, turn'd round for over a minute to slowly and good-humoredly scan the appearance of the vast and silent crowds. There were no speeches—no compliments—no welcome—as far as I could hear, not a word said. Still much anxiety was conceal'd in that quiet. Cautious persons had fear'd some mark'd insult or indignity to the President-elect—for he possess'd no personal popularity at all in New York city, and very little political. But it was evidently tacitly agreed that if the few political supporters of Mr. Lincoln present would entirely abstain from any demonstration on their side, the immense majority, who were any thing but supporters, would abstain on their side also. The result was a sulky, unbroken silence, such as certainly never before characterized so great a New York crowd.

Almost in the same neighborhood I distinctly remember'd seeing Lafayette on his visit to America in 1825. I had also personally seen and heard, various years afterward, how Andrew Jackson, Clay, Webster, Hungarian Kossuth, Filibuster Walker, the Prince of Wales on his visit, and other celebres, native and foreign, had been welcom'd there—all that indescribable human roar and magnetism, unlike any other sound in the universe—the glad exulting thunder-shouts of countless unloos'd throats of men! But on this occasion, not a voice—not a sound. From the top of an omnibus, (driven up one side, close by, and block'd by the curbstone and the crowds,) I had, I say, a capital view of it all, and especially of Mr. Lincoln, his look and gait—his perfect composure and coolness—his unusual and uncouth height, his dress of complete black, stovepipe hat push'd back on the head, dark-brown complexion, seam'd and wrinkled yet canny-looking face, black, bushy head of hair, disproportionately long neck, and his hands held behind as he stood observing the people. He look'd with curiosity upon that immense sea of faces, and the sea of faces return'd the look with similar curiosity. In both there was a dash of comedy, almost farce, such as Shakespere puts in his blackest tragedies. The crowd that hemm'd around consisted I should think of thirty to forty thousand men, not a single one his personal friend—while I have no doubt, (so frenzied were the ferments of the time,) many an assassin's knife and pistol lurk'd in hip or breast-pocket there, ready, soon as break and riot came.

But no break or riot came. The tall figure gave another relieving stretch or two of arms and legs; then with moderate pace, and accompanied by a few unknown looking persons, ascended the portico-steps of the Astor House, disappear'd through its broad entrance—and the dumb-show ended.

I saw Abraham Lincoln often the four years following that date. He changed rapidly and much during his Presidency—but this scene, and him in it, are indelibly stamped upon my recollection. As I saw on the top of my omnibus, and had a good view of him, the thought, dim and inchoate then, has since come out clear enough, that four sorts of genius, four mighty and primal hands, will be needed to the complete limning of this man's future portrait—the eyes and brains and finger-touch of Plutarch and Eschylus and Michel Angelo, assisted by Rabelais.

And now—(Mr. Lincoln passing on from this scene to Washington, where he was inaugurated, amid armed cavalry, and sharpshooters at every point—the first instance of the kind in our history—and I hope it will be the last)—now the rapid succession of well-known events, (too well known—I believe, these days, we almost hate to hear them mention'd)—the national flag fired on at Sumter—the uprising of the North, in paroxysms of astonishment and rage—the chaos of divided councils—the call for troops—the first Bull Run—the stunning cast-down, shock, and dismay of the North—and so in full flood the Secession war. Four years of lurid, bleeding, murky, murderous war. Who paint those years, with all their scenes?—the hard-fought engagements—the defeats, plans, failures—the gloomy hours, days, when our Nationality seem'd hung in pall of doubt, perhaps death—the Mephistophelean sneers of foreign lands and attachés—the dreaded Scylla of European interference, and the Charybdis of the tremendously dangerous latent strata of secession sympathizers throughout the free States, (far more numerous than is supposed)—the long marches in summer—the hot sweat, and many a sunstroke, as on the rush to Gettysburg in '63—the night battles in the woods, as under Hooker at Chancellorsville—the camps in winter—the military prisons—the hospitals—(alas! alas! the hospitals.)

The Secession war? Nay, let me call it the Union war. Though whatever call'd, it is even yet too near us—too vast and too closely overshadowing—its branches unform'd yet, (but certain,) shooting too far into the future—and the most indicative and mightiest of them yet ungrown. A great literature will yet arise out of the era of those four years, those scenes—era compressing centuries of native passion, first-class pictures, tempests of life and death—an inexhaustible mine for the histories, drama, romance, and even philosophy, of peoples to come—indeed the verteber of poetry and art, (of personal character too,) for all future America—far more grand, in my opinion, to the hands capable of it, than Homer's siege of Troy, or the French wars to Shakspere.

But I must leave these speculations, and come to the theme I have assign'd and limited myself to. Of the actual murder of President Lincoln, though so much has been written, probably the facts are yet very indefinite in most persons' minds. I read from my memoranda, written at the time, and revised frequently and finally since.

The day, April 14, 1865, seems to have been a pleasant one throughout the whole land—the moral atmosphere pleasant too—the long storm, so dark, so fratricidal, full of blood and doubt and gloom, over and ended at last by the sun-rise of such an absolute National victory, and utter break-down of Secessionism—we almost doubted our own senses! Lee had capitulated beneath the apple-tree of Appomattox. The other armies, the flanges of the revolt, swiftly follow'd. And could it really be, then? Out of all the affairs of this world of woe and failure and disorder, was there really come the confirm'd, unerring sign of plan, like a shaft of pure light—of rightful rule—of God? So the day, as I say, was propitious. Early herbage, early flowers, were out. (I remember where I was stopping at the time, the season being advanced, there were many lilacs in full bloom. By one of those caprices that enter and give tinge to events without being at all a part of them, I find myself always reminded of the great tragedy of that day by the sight and odor of these blossoms. It never fails.)

But I must not dwell on accessories. The deed hastens. The popular afternoon paper of Washington, the little "Evening Star," had spatter'd all over its third page, divided among the advertisements in a sensational manner, in a hundred different places, The President and his Lady will be at the Theatre this evening. . . . (Lincoln was fond of the theatre. I have myself seen him there several times. I remember thinking how funny it was that he, in some respects the leading actor in the stormiest drama known to real history's stage through centuries, should sit there and be so completely interested and absorb'd in those human jack-straws, moving about with their silly little gestures, foreign spirit, and flatulent text.)

On this occasion the theatre was crowded, many ladies in rich and gay costumes, officers in their uniforms, many well-known citizens, young folks, the usual clusters of gas-lights, the usual magnetism of so many people, cheerful, with perfumes, music of violins and flutes—(and over all, and saturating all, that vast, vague wonder, Victory, the nation's victory, the triumph of the Union, filling the air, the thought, the sense, with exhilaration more than all music and perfumes.)

The President came betimes, and, with his wife, witness'd the play from the large stage-boxes of the second tier, two thrown into one, and profusely draped with the national flag. The acts and scenes of the pieces—one of those singularly writtten compositions which have at least the merit of giving entire relief to an audience engaged in mental action or business excitements and cares during the day, as it makes not the slightest call on either the moral, emotional, esthetic, or spiritual nature—a piece, ("Our American Cousin,") in which, among other characters, so call'd, a Yankee, certainly such a one as was never seen, or the least like it ever seen, in North America, is introduced in England, with a varied fol-de-rol of talk, plot, scenery, and such phantasmagoria as goes to make up a modern popular drama—had progress'd through perhaps a couple of its acts, when in the midst of this comedy, or non-such, or whatever it is to be call'd, and to offset it, or finish it out, as if in Nature's and the great Muse's mockery of those poor mimes, came interpolated that scene, not really or exactly to be described at all, (for on the many hundreds who were there it seems to this hour to have left a passing blur, a dream, a blotch)—and yet partially to be described as I now proceed to give it. There is a scene in the play representing a modern parlor, in which two unprecedented English ladies are inform'd by the impossible Yankee that he is not a man of fortune, and therefore undesirable for marriage-catching purposes; after which, the comments being finish'd, the dramatic trio make exit, leaving the stage clear for a moment. At this period came the murder of Abraham Lincoln. Great as all its manifold train, circling round it, and stretching into the future for many a century, in the politics, history, art, &c., of the New World, in point of fact the main thing, the actual murder, transpired with the quiet and simplicity of any commonest occurrence—the bursting of a bud or pod in the growth of vegetation, for instance. Through the general hum following the stage pause, with the change of positions, came the muffled sound of a pistol-shot, which not one-hundredth part of the audience heard at the time—and yet a moment's hush—somehow, surely, a vague startled thrill—and then, through the ornamented, draperied, starr'd and striped space-way of the President's box, a sudden figure, a man, raises himself with hands and feet, stands a moment on the railing, leaps below to the stage, (a distance of perhaps fourteen or fifteen feet,) falls on one knee, quickly recovers himself, rises as if nothing had happen'd, (he really sprains his ankle, but unfelt then)—and so the figure, Booth, the murderer, dress'd in plain black broadcloth, bare-headed, with full, glossy, raven hair, and his eyes like some mad animal's flashing with light and resolution, yet with a certain strange calmness, holds aloft in one hand a large knife—walks along not much back from the footlights—turns fully toward the audience his face of statuesque beauty, lit by those basilisk eyes, flashing with desperation, perhaps insanity—launches out in a firm and steady voice the words Sic semper tyrannis—and then walks with neither slow nor very rapid pace diagonally across the back of the stage, and disappears. (Had not all this terrible scene—making the mimic ones preposterous—had it not all been rehears'd, in blank, by Booth, beforehand?)

A moment's hush—a scream—the cry of murder—Mrs. Lincoln leaning out of the box, with ashy cheeks and lips, with involuntary cry, pointing to the retreating figure, He has kill'd the President. And still a moment's strange, incredulous suspense—and then the deluge!—then that mixture of horror, noises, uncertainty—(the sound, somewhere back, of a horse's hoofs clattering with speed)—the people burst through chairs and railings, and break them up—there is inextricable confusion and terror—women faint—quite feeble persons fall, and are trampled on—many cries of agony are heard—the broad stage suddenly fills to suffocation with a dense and motley crowd, like some horrible carnival—the audience rush generally upon it, at least the strong men do—the actors and actresses are all there in their play-costumes and painted faces, with mortal fright showing through the rouge—the screams and calls, confused talk—redoubled, trebled—two or three manage to pass up water from the stage to the President's box—others try to clamber up—&c., &c.

In the midst of all this, the soldiers of the President's guard, with others, suddenly drawn to the scene, burst in—(some two hundred altogether)—they storm the house, through all the tiers, especially the upper ones, inflamed with fury, literally charging the audience with fix'd bayonets, muskets and pistols, shouting Clear out! clear out! you sons of——. . . . Such the wild scene, or a suggestion of it rather, inside the play-house that night.

Outside, too, in the atmosphere of shock and craze, crowds of people, fill'd with frenzy, ready to seize any outlet for it, come near committing murder several times on innocent individuals. One such case was especially exciting. The infuriated crowd, through some chance, got started against one man, either for words he utter'd, or perhaps without any cause at all, and were proceeding at once to actually hang him on a neighboring lamp-post, when he was rescued by a few heroic policemen, who placed him in their midst, and fought their way slowly and amid great peril toward the station house. It was a fitting episode of the whole affair. The crowd rushing and eddying to and fro—the night, the yells, the pale faces, many frighten'd people trying in vain to extricate themselves—the attack'd man, not yet freed from the jaws of death, looking like a corpse—the silent, resolute, half-dozen policemen, with no weapons but their little clubs, yet stern and steady through all those eddying swarms—made a fitting side-scene to the grand tragedy of the murder. They gain'd the station house with the protected man, whom they placed in security for the night, and discharged him in the morning.

And in the midst of that pandemonium, infuriated soldiers, the audience and the crowd, the stage, and all its actors and actresses, its paint-pots, spangles, and gas-lights—the life blood from those veins, the best and sweetest of the land, drips slowly down, and death's ooze already begins its little bubbles on the lips.

Thus the visible incidents and surroundings of Abraham Lincoln's murder, as they really occur'd. Thus ended the attempted secession of these States; thus the four years' war. But the main things come subtly and invisibly afterward, perhaps long afterward—neither military, political, nor (great as those are,) historical. I say, certain secondary and indirect results, out of the tragedy of this death, are, in my opinion, greatest. Not the event of the murder itself. Not that Mr. Lincoln strings the principal points and personages of the period, like beads, upon the single string of his career. Not that his idiosyncrasy, in its sudden appearance and disappearance, stamps this Republic with a stamp more mark'd and enduring than any yet given by any one man—(more even than Washington's;)—but, join'd with these, the immeasurable value and meaning of that whole tragedy lies, to me, in senses finally dearest to a nation, (and here all our own)—the imaginative and artistic senses—the literary and dramatic ones. Not in any common or low meaning of those terms, but a meaning precious to the race, and to every age. A long and varied series of contradictory events arrives at last at its highest poetic, single, central, pictorial denouement. The whole involved, baffling, multiform whirl of the secession period comes to a head, and is gather'd in one brief flash of lightning-illumination—one simple, fierce deed. Its sharp culmination, and as it were solution, of so many bloody and angry problems, illustrates those climax-moments on the stage of universal Time, where the historic Muse at one entrance, and the tragic Muse at the other, suddenly ringing down the curtain, close an immense act in the long drama of creative thought, and give it radiation, tableau, stranger than fiction. Fit radiation—fit close! How the imagination—how the student loves these things! America, too, is to have them. For not in all great deaths, nor far or near—not Cæsar in the Roman senate-house, nor Napoleon passing away in the wild night-storm at St. Helena—not Paleologus, falling, desperately fighting, piled over dozens deep with Grecian corpses—not calm old Socrates, drinking the hemlock—outvies that terminus of the secession war, in one man's life, here in our midst, in our own time—that seal of the emancipation of three million slaves—that parturition and delivery of our at last really free Republic, born again, henceforth to commence its career of genuine homogeneous Union, compact, consistent with itself.

Nor will ever future American Patriots and Unionists, indifferently over the whole land, or North or South, find a better moral to their lesson. The final use of the greatest men of a Nation is, after all, not with reference to their deeds in themselves, or their direct bearing on their times or lands. The final use of a heroic-eminent life—especially of a heroic-eminent death—is its indirect filtering into the nation and the race, and to give, often at many removes, but unerringly, age after age, color and fibre to the personalism of the youth and maturity of that age, and of mankind. Then there is a cement to the whole people, subtler, more underlying, than any thing in written constitution, or courts or armies—namely, the cement of a death identified thoroughly with that people, at its head, and for its sake. Strange, (is it not?) that battles, martyrs, agonies, blood, even assassination, should so condense—perhaps only really, lasting condense—a Nationality.

I repeat it—the grand deaths of the race—the dramatic deaths of every nationality—are its most important inheritance-value—in some respects beyond its literature and art—(as the hero is beyond his finest portrait, and the battle itself beyond its choicest song or epic.) Is not here indeed the point underlying all tragedy? the famous pieces of the Grecian masters—and all masters? Why, if the old Greeks had had this man, what trilogies of plays—what epics—would have been made out of him! How the rhapsodes would have recited him! How quickly that quaint tall form would have enter'd into the region where men vitalize gods, and gods divinify men! But Lincoln, his times, his death—great as any, any age—belong altogether to our own, and are autochthonic. (Sometimes indeed I think our American days, our own stage—the actors we know and have shaken hands, or talk'd with—more fateful than any thing in Eschylus—more heroic than the fighters around Troy—afford kings of men for our Democracy prouder than Agamemnon—models of character cute and hardy as Ulysses—deaths more pitiful than Priam's.)

When, centuries hence, (as it must, in my opinion, be centuries hence before the life of these States, or of Democracy, can be really written and illustrated,) the leading historians and dramatists seek for some personage, some special event, incisive enough to mark with deepest cut, and mnemonize, this turbulent Nineteenth century of ours, (not only these States, but all over the political and social world)—something, perhaps, to close that gorgeous procession of European feudalism, with all its pomp and caste-prejudices, (of whose long train we in America are yet so inextricably the heirs)—something to identify with terrible identification, by far the greatest revolutionary step in the history of the United States, (perhaps the greatest of the world, our century)—the absolute extirpation an erasure of slavery from the States—those historians will seek in vain for any point to serve more thoroughly their purpose, than Abraham Lincoln's death.

Dear to the Muse—thrice dear to Nationality—to the whole human race—precious to this Union—precious to Democracy—unspeakably and forever precious—their first great Martyr Chief.